WEBSTER'S
New Explorer
Dictionary
of Quotations

WEBSTER'S
New Explorer
Dictionary
of Quotations

Created in Cooperation with
the Editors of
MERRIAM-WEBSTER

FEDERAL
STREET
PRESS

A Division of Merriam-Webster, Incorporated
Springfield, Massachusetts

This edition published by
Federal Street Press
A Division of Merriam-Webster, Incorporated
P.O. Box 281
Springfield, MA 01102

Federal Street Press books are available for bulk purchase
for sales promotion and premium use.
For details write the manager of special sales,
Federal Street Press, P.O. Box 281, Springfield, MA 01102

Library of Congress Catalog Card Number: 99-67808

ISBN 1-892859-13-0

Printed in the United States of America

10 9 8 7 6 5 4 3 2

Preface

WEBSTER'S NEW EXPLORER DICTIONARY OF QUOTATIONS is a collection of 4,000 quotations on a wide variety of topics that have traditionally engaged the human imagination, topics such as Anger, Beauty, Birth, Death, Life, Love, Money, Power, and Truth. In addition, the collection also includes quotations regarding some relatively modern concerns: America and Americans, Automobiles, Computers, Photography, Technology, and Television. Within all of these categories, we have sought to provide a mixture of the traditional and the modern, the well known and not so well known, the literary and the popular.

We are indebted to those who have gone before us in establishing the pattern and principles on which quotation books are founded. While we have endeavored to offer the reader a fresh selection of quotations, we could not omit many of the most familiar words of the world's greatest thinkers and writers. Thus, it is inevitable that many of the quotations here will also be found in other quotation books. A close observer may find differences in the way that a single passage is presented in different quotation books. Sometimes an error is involved, and we have been able to correct some of these from our research in the original sources. More often the difference is simply a matter of how words originally written in another language are translated into English, or of the fact that a work written in English may differ in wording from edition to edition.

In general, we have attempted to stay with the original styling used by an author. However, we have Americanized spelling in most cases, the poems of Robert Burns being a notable exception. We have also used English titles of foreign-language works where a standard translated version exists. Quotations from the Bible have been taken from the Authorized (King James) Version.

Quotations in this book are gathered together under approximately 400 subject categories, and the categories themselves are in alphabetical order. Within each category, quotations are given alphabetically by author. In addition, cross-references are given for words that are closely related to names of categories and for words that are a part of category names:

Behavior—see ACTION; MANNERS

Compliments—see PRAISE and FLATTERY

Computers—see also TECHNOLOGY

Defeat—see VICTORY and DEFEAT

For each quotation, we have attempted to identify both the author and the original source in which the quotation can be found. For quotations that first appeared in speeches or letters, we have designated the source simply as "speech" or "letter." For quotations whose author is known but whose original source cannot be determined, we have used the designation "attributed."

Following some quotations there are bracketed editorial notes that provide additional information about the wording, context, authorship, or source of the quotation or even about similar passages by other writers.

The chief business of the American people is business.—CALVIN COOLIDGE, speech {1925}
[Often quoted as: "The business of America is business."]

For years I thought what was good for our country was good for General Motors, and vice versa.—CHARLES E. WILSON, said in testimony before a U.S. Senate hearing
[Wilson, former president of General Motors, said this in his confirmation hearings for Secretary of Defense. It is often misquoted as: "What's good for General Motors is good for the country."]

A precedent embalms a principle.—BENJAMIN DISRAELI, speech {1848}
[This has also been attributed to William Scott (Lord Stowell).]

For unto whomsoever much is given, of him shall be much required.—BIBLE, *Luke 12:48*
[John F. Kennedy paraphrased this in a speech in 1961: "For of those to whom much is given, much is required."]

Early to bed and early to rise makes a man healthy, wealthy, and wise.—BENJAMIN FRANKLIN, *Poor Richard's Almanac*
[James Thurber's variant in *Fables for Our Time:* "Early to rise and early to bed makes a man healthy and wealthy and dead."]

Following the quotations section of the book, there is an Index of Authors Quoted. This is an alphabetical list of the authors quoted with references to the subject categories under which they are quoted. When an author is quoted in an editorial note following a quotation, the reader is directed to the category and author's name under which the quotation is listed. At an index entry for an author who is one of two or more joint authors, the reader is directed to the category and the name of the first-listed author. The index also contains entries for alternative names of people known by more than one name, especially in the case of authors using pen names. In the index, *Mc-* names are alphabetized as if spelled *Mac-*.

The quotations were selected, annotated, and assigned to categories by Sharon Goldstein, working in consultation with the Merriam-Webster Editorial Department. Fact-checking and proofreading were done by Eileen M. Haraty and Mary W. Cornog. Data entry was done by Karen J. Levister. Frederick C. Mish, Editorial Director, and John M. Morse, Executive Editor, helped to prepare the plan for the book. Copyediting and overall project design and coordination were provided by Robert D. Copeland, Senior Editor.

WEBSTER'S
New Explorer
Dictionary
of Quotations

Ability

Natural abilities are like natural plants, that need pruning by study. —FRANCIS BACON, *Essays*

In the last analysis, ability is commonly found to consist mainly in a high degree of solemnity. —AMBROSE BIERCE, *The Devil's Dictionary*

Natural ability without education has more often attained to glory and virtue than education without natural ability. —CICERO, *Pro Archia Poeta*

The superior man is distressed by his want of ability. —CONFUCIUS, *Analects*

The winds and waves are always on the side of the ablest navigators. —EDWARD GIBBON, *The Decline and Fall of the Roman Empire*

It is a great ability to be able to conceal one's ability. —LA ROCHEFOUCAULD, *Maxims*

Competence, like truth, beauty and contact lenses, is in the eye of the beholder. —LAURENCE J. PETER, *The Peter Principle*

Every man loves what he is good at. —THOMAS SHADWELL, *A True Widow*

Intelligence is quickness to apprehend as distinct from ability, which is capacity to act wisely on the thing apprehended. —ALFRED NORTH WHITEHEAD, *Dialogues*

Absence

Absence makes the heart grow fonder,
Isle of Beauty, fare thee well!
            —THOMAS HAYNES BAYLY, *Isle of Beauty*

1

[Bayly's wording is the wording now current, but the thought is ancient. Sextus Propertius wrote in his *Elegies*: "Among absent lovers, ardor always fares better."]

The heart may think it knows better: the senses know that absence blots people out. We have really no absent friends. —ELIZABETH BOWEN, *The Death of the Heart*

Absence is to love what wind is to a fire; it puts out the little, it kindles the great. —ROGER DE BUSSY-RABUTIN, *Histoire amoureuse des Gaules*

[This analogy of love to a fire was also made by La Rochefoucauld, in his *Maxims*: "Absence diminishes mediocre passions and increases great ones, as the wind blows out candles and fans fire."]

Absence, that common cure of love. —MIGUEL DE CERVANTES, *Don Quixote de la Mancha*

The absent are always in the wrong. —DESTOUCHES, *L'Obstacle imprévu*

Love reckons hours for months, and days for
    years;
And every little absence is an age.
            —JOHN DRYDEN, *Amphitryon*

Sometimes, only one person is missing, and the whole world seems depopulated. —ALPHONSE DE LAMARTINE, *Premières méditations poétiques*

Abstinence — See MODERATION AND ABSTINENCE

Absurdity

The absurd has meaning only in so far as it is not agreed to. —ALBERT CAMUS, *The Myth of Sisyphus*

2

Those who are serious in ridiculous matters will be ridiculous in serious matters. —CATO THE ELDER, quoted in Plutarch's *Moralia: Sayings of Kings and Commanders*

Life is a jest, and all things show it;
I thought so once, but now I know it.
                    —JOHN GAY, "My Own Epitaph"
[This is inscribed on Gay's monument in Westminster Abbey.]

What is utterly absurd happens in the world. —NIKOLAI GOGOL, "The Nose"

. . . the privilege of absurdity, to which no living creature is subject but men only. —THOMAS HOBBES, *Leviathan*

From the sublime to the ridiculous is but a step. —NAPOLEON I, attributed

Life is full of infinite absurdities, which, strangely enough, do not even need to appear plausible, since they are true. —LUIGI PIRANDELLO, *Six Characters in Search of an Author*

People who cannot recognize a palpable absurdity are very much in the way of civilization. —AGNES REPPLIER, *In Pursuit of Laughter*

Abuse — See INSULTS AND ABUSE

Achievement — See also SUCCESS AND FAILURE

The tree is known by his fruit. —BIBLE, *Matthew* 12:33

I have fought a good fight, I have finished my course, I have kept the faith. —BIBLE, *II Timothy* 4:7

> Measure not the work
> Until the day's out and the labor done.
> —ELIZABETH BARRETT BROWNING, *Aurora
> Leigh*

One never notices what has been done; one can only see what remains to be done. —MARIE CURIE, letter (1894)

The reward of a thing well done is to have done it. —RALPH WALDO EMERSON, *Essays*

We judge ourselves by what we feel capable of doing, while others judge us by what we have already done. —HENRY WADSWORTH LONGFELLOW, *Kavanagh*

> Each morning sees some task begin,
>   Each evening sees it close;
> Something attempted, something done,
>   Has earned a night's repose.
> —HENRY WADSWORTH LONGFELLOW, "The
> Village Blacksmith"

To do all that one is able to do, is to be a man; to do all that one would like to do, is to be a god. —NAPOLEON I, attributed

Let's talk sense to the American people. Let's tell them the truth, that there are no gains without pains. —ADLAI E. STEVENSON, speech (accepting nomination for President, 1952)

[The expression "No pains, no gains" appeared as early as 1670, in John Ray's *English Proverbs*.]

Is there anything in life so disenchanting as attainment? —ROBERT LOUIS STEVENSON, *The New Arabian Nights*

To achieve great things we must live as though we were never going to die. —MARQUIS DE VAUVENARGUES, *Reflections and Maxims*

Acting — See THEATER AND FILM, ACTORS AND ACTING

Action

Whatsoever thy hand findeth to do, do it with thy might; for there is no work, nor device, nor knowledge, nor wisdom, in the grave, whither thou goest. —BIBLE, *Ecclesiastes* 9:10

   [Cicero offered the same advice, in *De Senectute*: "Whatever you do, do with all your might."]

He who desires but acts not breeds pestilence. —WILLIAM BLAKE, *The Marriage of Heaven and Hell*

The world can only be grasped by action, not by contemplation. The hand is more important than the eye. . . . The hand is the cutting edge of the mind. —JACOB BRONOWSKI, *The Ascent of Man*

   Think'st thou existence doth depend on time?
   It doth; but actions are our epochs.
                              —LORD BYRON, *Manfred*

In order to act you must be somewhat insane. A reasonably sensible man is satisfied with thinking. — GEORGES CLEMENCEAU, quoted in *Clemenceau, The Events of His Life As Told by Himself to His Former Secretary, Jean Martet*

Action is consolatory. It is the enemy of thought and the friend of flattering illusions. —JOSEPH CONRAD, *Nostromo*

Our deeds determine us, as much as we determine our deeds. —GEORGE ELIOT, *Adam Bede*

We never do anything well till we cease to think about the manner of doing it. —WILLIAM HAZLITT, *Sketches and Essays*

The great end of life is not knowledge but action.
—THOMAS HENRY HUXLEY, *Technical Education*

I have always thought the actions of men the best interpreters of their thoughts. —JOHN LOCKE, *An Essay Concerning Human Understanding*

Every man feels instinctively that all the beautiful sentiments in the world weigh less than a single lovely action. —JAMES RUSSELL LOWELL, *Among My Books*

Action is eloquence. —SHAKESPEARE, *Coriolanus*

If to do were as easy as to know what were good to do, chapels had been churches and poor men's cottages princes' palaces. —SHAKESPEARE, *The Merchant of Venice*

> Action is transitory—a step, a blow,
> The motion of a muscle, this way or that—
> 'Tis done, and in the after-vacancy
> We wonder at ourselves like men betrayed.
> —WILLIAM WORDSWORTH, *The Borderers*

Adolescence — See also YOUTH

The "teenager" seems to have replaced the Communist as the appropriate target for public controversy and foreboding. —EDGAR Z. FRIEDENBERG, *The Vanishing Adolescent*

The imagination of a boy is healthy, and the mature imagination of a man is healthy; but there is a space of life between, in which the soul is in a ferment, the character undecided, the way of life uncertain, the ambition thick-sighted: thence proceeds mawkishness. —JOHN KEATS, *Endymion*

Oh the innocent girl
in her maiden teens
knows perfectly well
what everything means.
> —D.H. LAWRENCE, "The Jeune Fille"

So much of adolescence is an ill-defined dying,
An intolerable waiting,
A longing for another place and time,
Another condition.
> —THEODORE ROETHKE, "I'm Here"

At sixteen, the adolescent knows about suffering because he himself has suffered, but he barely knows that other beings also suffer. —JEAN-JACQUES ROUSSEAU, *Émile*

Just at the age 'twixt boy and youth,
When thought is speech, and speech is truth.
> —SIR WALTER SCOTT, *Marmion*

I would there were no age between sixteen and three-and-twenty, or that youth would sleep out the rest; for there is nothing in the between but getting wenches with child, wronging the ancientry, stealing, fighting. —SHAKESPEARE, *The Winter's Tale*

Until the rise of American advertising, it never occurred to anyone anywhere in the world that the teenager was a captive in a hostile world of adults. —GORE VIDAL, *Rocking the Boat*

Adultery — See INFIDELITY

Adventure — See also BOLDNESS AND ENTERPRISE

Adventure is the vitaminizing element in histories both individual and social. —WILLIAM BOLITHO, *Twelve Against the Gods*

An adventure is only an inconvenience rightly considered. An inconvenience is only an adventure wrongly considered. —G.K. CHESTERTON, *All Things Considered*

The fruit of my tree of knowledge is plucked, and it is this: "Adventures are to the adventurous." —BENJAMIN DISRAELI, *Ixion in Heaven*

The true adventurer goes forth aimless and uncalculating to meet and greet unknown fate. —O. HENRY, "The Green Door"

Adversity — See also PROBLEMS

Prosperity doth best discover vice, but Adversity doth best discover virtue. —FRANCIS BACON, *Essays*

Most of our misfortunes are more supportable than the comments of our friends upon them. —CHARLES CALEB COLTON, *Lacon*

It is difficulties that show what men are. —EPICTETUS, *Discourses*

The greatest object in the universe, says a certain philosopher, is a good man struggling with adversity; yet there is still a greater, which is the good man that comes to relieve it. —OLIVER GOLDSMITH, *The Vicar of Wakefield*

> [The philosopher was probably Seneca, who wrote in *De Providentia*: "Behold a contest worthy of a god, a brave man matched in conflict with adversity."]

To great evils we submit; we resent little provocations. —WILLIAM HAZLITT, *Literary Remains*

If a man talks of his misfortunes there is something in them that is not disagreeable to him; for where there is nothing but pure misery there never is any recourse to the mention of it. —SAMUEL JOHNSON, quoted in James Boswell's *The Life of Samuel Johnson*

Mishaps are like knives, that either serve us or cut us, as we grasp them by the blade or the handle. —JAMES RUSSELL LOWELL, *Fireside Travels*

Who would have known of Hector, if Troy had been happy? The road to valor is built by adversity. —OVID, *Tristia*

I never knew any man in my life who could not bear another's misfortunes perfectly like a Christian. —ALEXANDER POPE, *Thoughts on Various Subjects*

> [The same thought had occurred to La Rochefoucauld, expressed in his *Maxims*: "We all have strength enough to bear the misfortunes of others."]

Nothing is so bitter that a calm mind cannot find comfort in it. —SENECA, *De Tranquillitate Animi*

> Sweet are the uses of adversity,
> Which, like the toad, ugly and venomous,
> Wears yet a precious jewel in his head.
> —SHAKESPEARE, *As You Like It*

Advertising

Good times, bad times, there will always be advertising. In good times people want to advertise; in bad times they have to. —BRUCE BARTON, in *Town and Country*

You can tell the ideals of a nation by its advertisements. —NORMAN DOUGLAS, *South Wind*

We grew up founding our dreams on the infinite promise of American advertising. —ZELDA FITZGERALD, *Save Me the Waltz*

Advertising may be described as the science of arresting human intelligence long enough to get money from it. —STEPHEN LEACOCK, *Garden of Folly*

The consumer isn't a moron; she is your wife. You insult her intelligence if you assume that a mere slogan and a few vapid adjectives will persuade her to buy anything. —DAVID OGILVY, *Confessions of an Advertising Man*

Advice

Never play cards with a man called Doc. Never eat at a place called Mom's. Never sleep with a woman whose troubles are worse than your own. —NELSON ALGREN, quoted in *Newsweek*

Who cannot give good counsel? 'Tis cheap, it costs them nothing. —ROBERT BURTON, *The Anatomy of Melancholy*

Good but rarely came from good advice. —LORD BYRON, *Don Juan*

Advice is seldom welcome; and those who want it the most always like it the least. —LORD CHESTERFIELD, *Letters to His Son*

We ask advice, but we mean approbation. —CHARLES CALEB COLTON, *Lacon*

The advice of the elders to young men is very apt to be as unreal as a list of the hundred best books. —OLIVER WENDELL HOLMES, JR., speech (1897)

Whatever advice you give, be brief. —HORACE, *Ars Poetica*

Advice is what we ask for when we already know the answer but wish we didn't. —ERICA JONG, *How to Save Your Own Life*

I give myself sometimes admirable advice, but I am incapable of taking it. —LADY MARY WORTLEY MONTAGU, letter (1725)

Many receive advice, few profit by it. —PUBLILIUS SYRUS, *Maxims*

Age and Aging — See also YOUTH

Old age is the verdict of life. —AMELIA BARR, *All the Days of My Life*

To me old age is always fifteen years older than I am. —BERNARD BARUCH, quoted in *Newsweek* (on his 85th birthday)

It is old age, rather than death, that is to be contrasted with life. Old age is life's parody, whereas death transforms life into a destiny. —SIMONE DE BEAUVOIR, *The Coming of Age*

Age is strictly a case of mind over matter. If you don't mind, it doesn't matter. —JACK BENNY, quoted in *New York Times*

With the ancient is wisdom; and in length of days understanding. —BIBLE, *Job* 12:12

> Grow old along with me!
> The best is yet to be,
> The last of life, for which the first was made.
> —ROBERT BROWNING, "Rabbi Ben Ezra"

> As a white candle
> In a holy place,
> So is the beauty
> Of an aged face.
> —JOSEPH CAMPBELL, "The Old Woman"

Old age isn't so bad when you consider the alternative. —MAURICE CHEVALIER, quoted in *New York Times*

Youth is a blunder; manhood a struggle; old age a regret. —BENJAMIN DISRAELI, *Coningsby*

11

If youth knew; if age could. —HENRI ESTIENNE, *Les Prémices*

Whenever a man's friends begin to compliment him about looking young, he may be sure that they think he is growing old. —WASHINGTON IRVING, *Bracebridge Hall*

Old people like to give good advice, as solace for no longer being able to provide bad examples. —LA ROCHEFOUCAULD, *Maxims*

The four stages of man are infancy, childhood, adolescence and obsolescence. —ART LINKLETTER, *A Child's Garden of Misinformation*

Middle age is . . . when a man is always thinking that in a week or two he will feel just as good as ever. —DON MARQUIS, attributed

> I dread no more the first white in my hair,
> Or even age itself, the easy shoe,
> The cane, the wrinkled hands, the special
>   chair:
> Time, doing this to me, may alter too
> My sorrow, into something I can bear.
>   —EDNA ST. VINCENT MILLAY, "Sonnet"

At 50, everyone has the face he deserves. —GEORGE ORWELL (last words written in his notebook)

Don't look back. Something might be gaining on you. —SATCHEL PAIGE, "Formula for Staying Young"

> [This is one of six rules for life that were originally printed in *Collier's* in 1953, the last full year that Paige played Major League baseball. For some time Paige passed out autograph cards with his "rules" printed on the back.]

Growing old is like being increasingly penalized for a crime you haven't committed. —ANTHONY POWELL, *A Dance to the Music of Time: Temporary Kings*

The young have aspirations that never come to pass, the old have reminiscences of what never happened. —SAKI, *Reginald*

Old age is an incurable disease. —SENECA, *Epistulae ad Lucilium*

> Last scene of all,
> That ends this strange eventful history,
> Is second childishness and mere oblivion,
> Sans teeth, sans eyes, sans taste, sans every
> thing.
> —SHAKESPEARE, *As You Like It*

When the age is in, the wit is out. —SHAKESPEARE, *Much Ado About Nothing*

The denunciation of the young is a necessary part of the hygiene of older people, and greatly assists the circulation of their blood. —LOGAN PEARSALL SMITH, *Afterthoughts*

I grow old ever learning many things. —SOLON (fragment)

Nobody loves life like him that's growing old. — SOPHOCLES, *Acrisius*

Every man desires to live long; but no man would be old. —JONATHAN SWIFT, *Thoughts on Various Subjects*

[La Bruyère made the same observation in *Les Caractères:* "We hope to grow old, and we dread old age; that is to say, we love life and flee from death."]

The greatest problem about old age is the fear that it may go on too long. —A.J.P. TAYLOR, quoted in *The Observer*

13

Old age is the most unexpected of all things that happen to a man. —LEON TROTSKY, diary entry (*Diary in Exile*)

> I thought no more was needed
> Youth to prolong
> Than dumbbell and foil
> To keep the body young.
> Oh, who could have foretold
> That the heart grows old?
> —W.B. YEATS, "A Song"

Agnosticism — See ATHEISM AND AGNOSTICISM

Alcohol — See DRINKING

Alienation

I have been a stranger in a strange land. —BIBLE, *Exodus* 2:22

In the nineteenth century the problem was that *God is dead*; in the twentieth century the problem is that *man is dead*. In the nineteenth century inhumanity meant cruelty; in the twentieth century it means schizoid self-alienation. The danger of the past was that men became slaves. The danger of the future is that men may become robots. —ERICH FROMM, *The Sane Society*

> The best
> Thing we can do is to make wherever we're lost
> in
> Look as much like home as we can.
> —CHRISTOPHER FRY, *The Lady's Not for Burning*

> I, a stranger and afraid
> In a world I never made.
> —A.E. HOUSMAN, "The laws of God, the laws of man"

What have I in common with Jews? I have hardly anything in common with myself. —FRANZ KAFKA, diary entry (1914)

To live is to feel oneself lost. —JOSÉ ORTEGA Y GASSET, *The Revolt of the Masses*

Ambition — See also BOLDNESS AND ENTERPRISE

The ambitious climbs up high and perilous stairs, and never cares how to come down; the desire of rising hath swallowed up his fear of a fall. —THOMAS ADAMS, *Diseases of the Soul*

AMBITION, *n.* An overmastering desire to be vilified by enemies while living and made ridiculous by friends when dead. —AMBROSE BIERCE, *The Devil's Dictionary*

> Ah, but a man's reach should exceed his
> grasp,
> Or what's a heaven for?
> —ROBERT BROWNING, "Andrea del Sarto"

Hitch your wagon to a star. —RALPH WALDO EMERSON, *Society and Solitude*

Slight not what's near through aiming at what's far. —EURIPIDES, *Rhesus*

Nothing is so commonplace as to wish to be remarkable. —OLIVER WENDELL HOLMES, SR., *The Autocrat of the Breakfast-Table*

Most people would succeed in small things, if they were not troubled with great ambitions. —HENRY WADSWORTH LONGFELLOW, *Drift-Wood*

Not failure, but low aim, is crime. —JAMES RUSSELL LOWELL, "For an Autograph"

Though ambition is itself a vice, it is often the parent of virtues. —QUINTILIAN, *De Institutione Oratoria*

Fain would I climb, yet fear I to fall. —SIR WALTER RALEIGH, attributed

[This statement is said to have been scratched on a window pane. Under it, Elizabeth I is said to have written as a reply: "If thy heart fails thee, climb not at all."]

Ambition, old as mankind, the immemorial weakness of the strong. —VITA SACKVILLE-WEST, *No Signposts in the Sea*

Vaulting ambition, which o'erleaps itself
And falls on the other [side].
—SHAKESPEARE, *Macbeth*

When that the poor have cried, Caesar hath
wept:
Ambition should be made of sterner stuff.
—SHAKESPEARE, *Julius Caesar*

And he that strives to touch the stars,
Oft stumbles at a straw.
—EDMUND SPENSER, *The Shepherd's Calendar*

America and Americans

Good Americans, when they die, go to Paris. —THOMAS GOLD APPLETON, quoted by Oliver Wendell Holmes, Sr., in *The Autocrat of the Breakfast-Table*

[Oscar Wilde later used this in *A Woman of No Importance*:
MRS. ALLONBY: They say, Lady Hunstanton, that when good Americans die they go to Paris.
LADY HUNSTANTON: Indeed? And when bad Americans die, where do they go?
LORD ILLINGWORTH: Oh, they go to America.]

We expect to eat and stay thin, to be constantly on the move and ever more neighborly . . . to revere God and to be God. —DANIEL J. BOORSTIN, *The Image*

This is America . . .—a brilliant diversity spread like stars, like a thousand points of light in a broad and peaceful sky. —GEORGE BUSH, speech (accepting nomination for President, 1988)

There is nothing the matter with Americans except their ideals. The real American is all right; it is the ideal American who is all wrong. —G.K. CHESTERTON, in *New York Times*

America is the only nation in history which miraculously has gone directly from barbarism to degeneration without the usual interval of civilization. —GEORGES CLEMENCEAU, attributed

The thing that impresses me most about America is the way parents obey their children. —EDWARD, DUKE OF WINDSOR, quoted in *Look*

America is so vast that almost everything said about it is likely to be true, and the opposite is probably equally true. —JAMES T. FARRELL, introduction to H.L. Mencken's *Prejudices: A Selection*

Americans have always been eager for travel, that being how they got to the New World in the first place. —OTTO FRIEDRICH, in *Time*

Our flag is red, white and blue, but our nation is a rainbow—red, yellow, brown, black and white—and we're all precious in God's sight. —JESSE JACKSON, speech (1984)

In America everybody is of the opinion that he has no social superiors, since all men are equal, but he does not admit that he has no social inferiors. —BERTRAND RUSSELL, *Unpopular Essays*

17

America is the greatest of opportunities and the worst of influences. —GEORGE SANTAYANA, *The Last Puritan*

> It's complicated, being an American,
> Having the money and the bad conscience,
>   both at the same time.
> > —LOUIS SIMPSON, "On the Lawn
> > at the Villa"

In the United States there is more space where nobody is than where anybody is. This is what makes America what it is. —GERTRUDE STEIN, *The Geographical History of America*

You will find that the truth is often unpopular and the contest between agreeable fancy and disagreeable fact is unequal. For, in the vernacular, we Americans are suckers for good news. —ADLAI E. STEVENSON, speech (1958)

America is a land of wonders, in which everything is in constant motion and every change seems an improvement. . . . No natural boundary seems to be set to the efforts of man; and in his eyes what is not yet done is only what he has not yet attempted to do. —ALEXIS DE TOCQUEVILLE, *Democracy in America*

The surface of American society is covered with a layer of democratic paint, but from time to time one can see the old aristocratic colors breaking through. —ALEXIS DE TOCQUEVILLE, *Democracy in America*

The youth of America is their oldest tradition. It has been going on now for three hundred years. —OSCAR WILDE, *A Woman of No Importance*

For we must consider that we shall be as a city upon a hill. The eyes of all people are upon us. —JOHN WINTHROP, sermon written during the voyage to Massachusetts (1630)

America. . . . It is a fabulous country, the only fabulous country; it is the only place where miracles not only happen, but where they happen all the time.
—THOMAS WOLFE, *Of Time and the River*

Ancestry — See also FAMILY

I can trace my ancestry back to a protoplasmal primordial atomic globule. Consequently, my family pride is something in-conceivable. I can't help it. I was born sneering. —W.S. GILBERT, *The Mikado*

There is no king who has not had a slave among his ancestors, and no slave who has not had a king among his. —HELEN KELLER, *The Story of My Life*

The man who has not anything to boast of but his illustrious ancestors is like a potato,—the only good belonging to him is under ground. —THOMAS OVERBURY, *Characters*

He who boasts of his ancestry praises the merits of another. —SENECA, *Hercules Furens*

Each has his own tree of ancestors, but at the top of all sits Probably Arboreal. —ROBERT LOUIS STEVENSON, *Memories and Portraits*

> [The reference here is to a statement by Charles Darwin (in *The Descent of Man*): "Man is descended from a hairy, tailed quadruped, probably arboreal in its habits."]

Anger

A soft answer turneth away wrath. —BIBLE, *Proverbs* 15:1

Let not the sun go down upon your wrath. —BIBLE, *Ephesians* 4:26

Heav'n has no rage, like love to hatred turn'd.
Nor Hell a fury, like a woman scorn'd.
—WILLIAM CONGREVE, *The Mourning Bride*

Anger makes dull men witty, but it keeps them poor.
—ELIZABETH I, quoted by Francis Bacon in *Apophthegms*

Spleen can subsist on any kind of food. —WILLIAM HAZLITT, *Lectures on the English Comic Writers*

Anger is a brief madness. —HORACE, *Epistles*

When angry, count ten before you speak; if very angry, an hundred. —THOMAS JEFFERSON, "A Decalogue of Canons for observation in practical life" (in letter, 1825)

[See also Mark Twain, in this section]

Anger is never without an argument, but seldom with a good one. —GEORGE SAVILE, *Political, Moral, and Miscellaneous Thoughts and Reflections*

When angry, count four; when very angry, swear. —MARK TWAIN, *Pudd'nhead Wilson*, "Pudd'nhead Wilson's Calendar"

Animals

The dog was created specially for children. He is a god of frolic. —HENRY WARD BEECHER, *Proverbs from Plymouth Pulpit*

. . . the animal shall not be measured by man. In a world older and more complete than ours they move finished and complete, gifted with extensions of the senses we have lost or never attained, living by voices we shall never hear. They are not brethren, they are not underlings; they are other nations, caught with ourselves in the net of life and time. —HENRY BESTON, *The Outermost House*

A Robin Redbreast in a Cage
Puts all Heaven in a Rage.
> —WILLIAM BLAKE, "Auguries of
> Innocence"

Tyger! Tyger! burning bright
In the forests of the night,
What immortal hand or eye
Could frame thy fearful symmetry?
> —WILLIAM BLAKE, "The Tyger"

That's the wise thrush; he sings each song
twice over,
Lest you should think he never could
recapture
The first fine careless rapture!
> —ROBERT BROWNING, "Home-Thoughts,
> from Abroad"

Wee, sleekit, cow'rin, tim'rous beastie,
O, what a panic's in thy breastie!
> —ROBERT BURNS, "To a Mouse"

The great pleasure of a dog is that you may make a fool of yourself with him and not only will he not scold you, but he will make a fool of himself too. —SAMUEL BUTLER (d 1902), *Note-Books*

Whenever you observe an animal closely, you feel as if a human being sitting inside were making fun of you. —ELIAS CANETTI, *The Human Province*

Animals are such agreeable friends—they ask no questions, they pass no criticisms. —GEORGE ELIOT, *Scenes of Clerical Life*

Cats and monkeys, monkeys and cats—all human life is there. —HENRY JAMES, *The Madonna of the Future*

I never saw a wild thing
Sorry for itself.
> —D.H. LAWRENCE, "Self-Pity"

21

When I play with my cat, who knows whether she isn't amusing herself with me more than I am with her? —MICHEL DE MONTAIGNE, *Essays*

> The trouble with a kitten is
> THAT
> Eventually it becomes a
> CAT.
> —OGDEN NASH, "The Kitten"

> The cow is of the bovine ilk;
> One end is moo, the other, milk.
> —OGDEN NASH, "The Cow"

A horse! a horse! my kingdom for a horse! —SHAKE-SPEARE, *Richard III*

> Hail to thee, blithe spirit!—
> Bird thou never wert,
> That from Heaven, or near it,
> Pourest thy full heart
> In profuse strains of unpremeditated art.
> —PERCY BYSSHE SHELLEY, "To a Skylark"

The bluebird carries the sky on his back. —HENRY DAVID THOREAU, *Journal*

> I think I could turn and live with animals, they
>   are so placid and self-contain'd,
> I stand and look at them long and long.
>
> They do not sweat and whine about their condition,
> They do not lie awake in the dark and weep for
>   their sins,
> They do not make me sick discussing their
>   duty to God,
> Not one is dissatisfied, not one is demented
>   with the mania of owning things,
> Not one kneels to another, nor to his kind that
>   lived thousands of years ago,
> Not one is respectable or unhappy over the
>   whole earth.
> —WALT WHITMAN, *Leaves of Grass*

Anxiety — See also FEAR

We walk in circles, so limited by our own anxieties that we can no longer distinguish between true and false, between the gangster's whim and the purest ideal. —INGMAR BERGMAN, quoted in John Robert Colombo's *Popcorn in Paradise*

But Jesus, when you don't have any money, the problem is food. When you have money, it's sex. When you have both it's health, you worry about getting rupture or something. If everything is simply jake then you're frightened of death. —J.P. DONLEAVY, *The Ginger Man*

How much pain have cost us the evils which have never happened! —THOMAS JEFFERSON, "A Decaloque of Canons for observation in practical life" (in letter, 1825)

Worry, the interest paid by those who borrow trouble. —GEORGE WASHINGTON LYON, in *Judge*

There are more things, Lucilius, that frighten us than injure us, and we suffer more in imagination than in reality. —SENECA, *Epistulae ad Lucilium*

We are, perhaps uniquely among the earth's creatures, the worrying animal. We worry away our lives, fearing the future, discontent with the present, unable to take in the idea of dying, unable to sit still. —LEWIS THOMAS, *The Medusa and the Snail*

Apathy and Indifference

Science may have found a cure for most evils; but it has found no remedy for the worst of them all—the apathy of human beings. —HELEN KELLER, *My Religion*

Nothing is more conducive to peace of mind than not having any opinion at all. —GEORG CHRISTOPH LICHTENBERG, *Aphorisms*

The worst sin towards our fellow creatures is not to hate them, but to be indifferent to them: that's the essence of inhumanity. —GEORGE BERNARD SHAW, *The Devil's Disciple*

The opposite of love is not hate, it's indifference. The opposite of art is not ugliness, it's indifference. The opposite of faith is not heresy, it's indifference. And the opposite of life is not death, it's indifference.
—ELIE WIESEL, quoted in *US News & World Report*

Apologies — See EXCUSES

Appearance

Appearances often are deceiving. —AESOP, *Fables*

Do not hold everything as gold that shines like gold.
—ALAIN DE LILLE (ALANUS DE INSULIS), *Parabolae*
> [This proverbial saying occurs in various forms. Chaucer wrote in *The House of Fame*: "It is not all gold that glareth." Shakespeare made the popularity of the saying evident in *The Merchant of Venice*:
> All that glisters is not gold;
> Often have you heard that told.
> John Dryden used the wording now current in *The Hind and the Panther*: "All, as they say, that glitters is not gold."]

There is less in this than meets the eye. —TALLULAH BANKHEAD, quoted in Alexander Woollcott's *Shouts and Murmurs*
> [Said about a performance of a play by Maeterlinck.]

Judge not according to the appearance. —BIBLE, *John* 7:24

> Keep up appearances; there lies the test;
> The world will give thee credit for the rest.
> —CHARLES CHURCHILL, "Night"

Appearances are not held to be a clue to the truth. . . . But we seem to have no other. —IVY COMPTON-BURNETT, *Manservant and Maidservant*

> Things are seldom what they seem,
> Skim milk masquerades as cream.
> —W.S. GILBERT, *H.M.S. Pinafore*

The Lord prefers common-looking people. That is the reason he makes so many of them. —ABRAHAM LINCOLN, attributed

A fair exterior is a silent recommendation. —PUBLILIUS SYRUS, *Maxims*

Things are entirely what they appear to be—and behind them . . . there is nothing. —JEAN-PAUL SARTRE, *Nausea*

It is only shallow people who do not judge by appearances. The true mystery of the world is the visible, not the invisible. —OSCAR WILDE, *The Picture of Dorian Gray*

Appeasement — See COMPROMISE

Architecture

Architecture is inhabited sculpture. —CONSTANTIN BRANCUSI, quoted in *Themes and Episodes* by Igor Stravinsky and Robert Craft

Architecture, of all the arts, is the one which acts the most slowly, but the most surely, on the soul.
—ERNEST DIMNET, *What We Live By*

I call architecture frozen music. —JOHANN WOLF-GANG VON GOETHE, quoted in Peter Eckermann's *Conversations with Goethe*

> [The phrase had been used earlier, by Friedrich von Schelling, in *Philosophie der Kunst*: "[Architecture] is music in space, as it were a frozen music."]

Architecture is the art of how to waste space. —PHILIP JOHNSON, quoted in *New York Times*

A house is a machine for living in. —LE CORBUSIER, *Towards an Architecture*

When we build, let us think that we build for ever. —JOHN RUSKIN, *The Seven Lamps of Architecture*

Form ever follows function. —LOUIS HENRI SULLIVAN, in *Lippincott's Magazine*

The physician can bury his mistakes, but the architect can only advise his clients to plant vines. —FRANK LLOYD WRIGHT, in *New York Times Magazine*

No house should ever be *on* a hill or *on* anything. It should be *of* the hill. Belonging to it. Hill and house should live together each the happier for the other. —FRANK LLOYD WRIGHT, *An Autobiography*

Arguments and Controversy

The best way I know of to win an argument is to start by being in the right. —QUINTIN McGAREL HOGG, VISCOUNT HAILSHAM, in *New York Times*

We may convince others by our arguments; but we can only persuade them by their own. —JOSEPH JOUBERT, *Pensées*

Quarrels would not last long if the fault were only on one side. —LA ROCHEFOUCAULD, *Maxims*

There is no good in arguing with the inevitable. The only argument available with an east wind is to put on your overcoat. —JAMES RUSSELL LOWELL, *Democracy and Other Addresses*

> We might as well give up the fiction
>   That we can argue any view.
> For what in me is pure Conviction
>   Is simple Prejudice in you.
>   —PHYLLIS MCGINLEY, "Note to My
>   Neighbor"

When men understand what each other mean, they see, for the most part, that controversy is either superfluous or hopeless. —JOHN CARDINAL NEWMAN, sermon (1893)

The most savage controversies are those about matters as to which there is no good evidence either way. —BERTRAND RUSSELL, *Unpopular Essays*

Arguments are to be avoided; they are always vulgar and often convincing. —OSCAR WILDE, *The Importance of Being Earnest*

Art and Artists

A vandal is somebody who throws a brick through a window. An artist is somebody who paints a picture on that window. A great artist is somebody who paints a picture on the window and then throws a brick through it. —A-ONE (a graffiti artist), quoted in *New Yorker*

The object of art is to give life a shape. —JEAN ANOUILH, *The Rehearsal*

PAINTING, *n.* The art of protecting flat surfaces from the weather and exposing them to the critic.
—AMBROSE BIERCE, *The Devil's Dictionary*

Art is meant to upset people, science reassures them.
—GEORGES BRAQUE, *Illustrated Notebooks*

The history of art is the history of revivals. —SAMUEL BUTLER (*d* 1902), *Note-Books*

Art is the unceasing effort to compete with the beauty of flowers—and never succeeding. —MARC CHAGALL, attributed

Art is a jealous mistress. —RALPH WALDO EMERSON, *The Conduct of Life*

All art is autobiographical; the pearl is the oyster's autobiography. —FEDERICO FELLINI, quoted in *Atlantic*

Love art. Of all lies, it is the least untrue. —GUSTAVE FLAUBERT, letter (1846)

The artist, like the God of the creation, remains within or behind or beyond or above his handiwork, invisible, refined out of existence, indifferent, paring his fingernails. —JAMES JOYCE, *A Portrait of the Artist as a Young Man*

Art does not reproduce the visible; rather, it makes visible. —PAUL KLEE, *The Inward Vision*

Art is the objectification of feeling, and the subjectification of nature. —SUZANNE K. LANGER, *Mind*

The whole of art is an appeal to a reality which is not without us but in our minds. —DESMOND MACCARTHY, *Theatre*

Art is a revolt against fate. —ANDRÉ MALRAUX, *Voices of Silence*

A work of art has no importance whatever to society. It is only important to the individual. —VLADIMIR NABOKOV, *Strong Opinions*

There are painters who transform the sun to a yellow spot, but there are others who with the help of their art and their intelligence, transform a yellow spot into sun. —PABLO PICASSO, attributed, quoted by Edith Sitwell in *Fire of the Mind*

We all know that Art is not truth. Art is a lie that makes us realize truth, at least the truth that is given us to understand. —PABLO PICASSO, quoted in Dore Ashton's *Picasso on Art*

Art is the right hand of nature. The latter only gave us being, but the former made us men. —FRIEDRICH VON SCHILLER, *Fiesco*

Contrary to general belief, an artist is never ahead of his time but most people are far behind theirs. —EDGARD VARÈSE, quoted in *New York Herald Tribune*

A work of art has an author and yet, when it is perfect, it has something which is anonymous about it. —SIMONE WEIL, *Gravity and Grace*

Art happens—no hovel is safe from it, no Prince may depend upon it, the vastest intelligence cannot bring it about, and puny efforts to make it universal end in quaint comedy, and coarse farce. —JAMES MCNEILL WHISTLER, *The Gentle Art of Making Enemies*

All art is at once surface and symbol. Those who go beneath the surface do so at their peril. —OSCAR WILDE, *The Picture of Dorian Gray*

All art is quite useless. —OSCAR WILDE, *The Picture of Dorian Gray*

Atheism and Agnosticism

I am an atheist still, thank God. —LUIS BUÑUEL, quoted by Ado Kyrou in *Luis Buñuel: An Introduction*

There are no atheists in the foxholes. —WILLIAM THOMAS CUMMINGS, sermon (1942)

I do not consider it an insult, but rather a compliment to be called an agnostic. I do not pretend to know where many ignorant men are sure—that is all that agnosticism means. —CLARENCE DARROW, courtroom argument (at Scopes trial, 1925)

An atheist is a man who has no invisible means of support. —HARRY EMERSON FOSDICK, attributed

[This has also been attributed to others, including John Buchan and Bishop Fulton Sheen.]

There seems to be a terrible misunderstanding on the part of a great many people to the effect that when you cease to believe you may cease to behave. —LOUIS KRONENBERGER, *Company Manners*

No one is so thoroughly superstitious as the godless man. —HARRIET BEECHER STOWE, *Uncle Tom's Cabin*

By night an atheist half believes a God. —EDWARD YOUNG, *Night Thoughts on Life, Death, and Immortality*

Automobiles

People are broad-minded. They'll accept the fact that a person can be an alcoholic, a dope fiend, a wife beater and even a newspaperman, but if a man doesn't drive, there's something wrong with him. —ART BUCHWALD, *Have I Ever Lied to You?*

To George F. Babbitt, as to most prosperous citizens of Zenith, his motor car was poetry and tragedy, love and heroism. —SINCLAIR LEWIS, *Babbitt*

The car has become a secular sanctuary for the individual, his shrine to the self, his mobile Walden Pond. —EDWARD MCDONAGH, in *Time*

The car has become the carapace, the protective and aggressive shell, of urban and suburban man. —MARSHALL MCLUHAN, *Understanding Media*

Our national flower is the concrete cloverleaf. —LEWIS MUMFORD, quoted in *Quote* magazine

Take most people, they're crazy about cars. They worry if they get a little scratch on them, and they're always talking about how many miles they get to a gallon, and if they get a brand-new car already they start thinking about trading it in for one that's even newer. I don't even like *old* cars. . . . I'd rather have a goddam horse. A horse is at least *human,* for God's sake. —J.D. SALINGER, *The Catcher in the Rye*

Autumn — See SEASONS

Babies — See CHILDREN AND CHILDHOOD

Bargains — See BUYING AND SELLING

Beauty

There is no excellent beauty that hath not some strangeness in the proportion. —FRANCIS BACON, *Essays*

> If you get simple beauty and nought else,
> You get about the best thing God invents.
> —ROBERT BROWNING, "Fra Lippo Lippi"

31

She walks in beauty, like the night
  Of cloudless climes and starry skies;
And all that's best of dark and bright
  Meet in her aspect and her eyes.
      —LORD BYRON, "She Walks in Beauty"

Beauty is in the eye of the beholder. —MARGARET WOLFE HUNGERFORD, *Molly Bawn*

[The idea is an old one, having been used earlier by Shakespeare, Franklin, and Thoreau among others. However Hungerford was the first, apparently, to phrase the notion in such enduring words.]

"Beauty is truth, truth beauty,"—that is all
  Ye know on earth, and all ye need to know.
     —JOHN KEATS, "Ode on a Grecian Urn"

A thing of beauty is a joy forever:
Its loveliness increases; it will never
Pass into nothingness.
      —JOHN KEATS, *Endymion*

Beauty is everlasting
  And dust is for a time.
      —MARIANNE MOORE, "In Distrust
                 of Merits"

Remember that the most beautiful things in the world are the most useless; peacocks and lilies for instance. —JOHN RUSKIN, *The Stones of Venice*

What is beautiful is good, and who is good will soon also be beautiful. —SAPPHO (fragment)

Beauty is all very well at first sight, but who ever looks at it when it has been in the house three days? —GEORGE BERNARD SHAW, *Man and Superman*

Beauty is momentary in the mind—
The fitful tracing of a portal;
But in the flesh it is immortal.

The body dies; the body's beauty lives.
> —WALLACE STEVENS, "Peter Quince
> at the Clavier"

I do not know which to prefer,
The beauty of inflections
Or the beauty of innuendoes,
The blackbird whistling
Or just after.
> —WALLACE STEVENS, "Thirteen Ways of
> Looking at a Blackbird"

Beauty more than bitterness
Makes the heart break.
> —SARA TEASDALE, "Vignettes Overseas:
> Capri"

The perception of beauty is a moral test. —HENRY DAVID THOREAU, *Journal*

It is amazing how complete is the delusion that beauty is goodness. —LEO TOLSTOY, *The Kreutzer Sonata*

The beauty of the world has two edges, one of laughter, one of anguish, cutting the heart asunder.
—VIRGINIA WOOLF, *A Room of One's Own*

Beginnings and Endings

It ain't over till it's over. —YOGI BERRA, widely attributed to and acknowledged by Berra

> [Berra was commenting on the National League pennant race. The remark is quoted in various forms, e.g., "The game isn't over till it's over."]

Better is the end of a thing than the beginning thereof. —BIBLE, *Ecclesiastes* 7:8

> Nothing so difficult as a beginning
> In poesy, unless perhaps the end.
> —LORD BYRON, *Don Juan*

The opera ain't over 'til the fat lady sings. —DAN COOK, in *Washington Post*

In my beginning is my end. —T.S. ELIOT, *Four Quartets*: "East Coker"

A hard beginning maketh a good ending. —JOHN HEYWOOD, *Proverbs*

To have begun is to have done half the task; dare to be wise. —HORACE, *Epistles*

A journey of a thousand miles must begin with a single step. —LAO-TZU, *The Way of Lao-tzu*

Some things are hurrying into existence, and others are hurrying out of it; and of that which is coming into existence part is already extinguished. —MARCUS AURELIUS, *Meditations*

Behavior — See ACTION; MANNERS

Belief

Faith is to believe what you do not yet see; the reward for this faith is to see what you believe. —SAINT AUGUSTINE, *Sermons*

If ye have faith as a grain of mustard-seed, ye shall say unto this mountain, Remove hence to yonder place; and it shall remove. —BIBLE, *Matthew* 17:20

Faith is the substance of things hoped for, the evidence of things not seen. —BIBLE, *Hebrews* 11:1

You can do very little with faith, but you can do nothing without it. —SAMUEL BUTLER (d 1902), *Note-Books*

We are so constituted that we believe the most incredible things; and, once they are engraved upon the memory, woe to him who would endeavor to erase them! —JOHANN WOLFGANG VON GOETHE, *The Sorrows of Young Werther*

Everyone believes very easily whatever he fears or desires. —JEAN DE LA FONTAINE, *Fables*

No amount of manifest absurdity . . . could deter those who wanted to believe from believing. —BERNARD LEVIN, *The Pendulum Years*

Here I stand. I can do no other. —MARTIN LUTHER, speech (1521)

Faith may be defined briefly as an illogical belief in the occurrence of the improbable. —H.L. MENCKEN, *Prejudices*

Nothing is so firmly believed as that which we least know. —MICHEL DE MONTAIGNE, *Essays*

> You're not free
>   until you've been made captive by
>   supreme belief.
>   —MARIANNE MOORE, "Spenser's Ireland"

Convictions are more dangerous enemies of truth than lies. —FRIEDRICH NIETZSCHE, *Human, All-too-Human*

It is certain because it is impossible. —TERTULLIAN, *De Carne Christi*

> [Often quoted as "I believe because it is impossible."]

The people who bind themselves to systems are those who are unable to encompass the whole truth and try to catch it by the tail; a system is like the tail of truth, but truth is like a lizard; it leaves its tail in your fingers and runs away knowing full well that it will grow a new one in a twinkling. —IVAN TURGENEV, quoted in Daniel J. Boorstin's *The Discoverers*

Betrayal

The smiler with the knife under the cloak. —CHAUCER, *The Canterbury Tales*

All a man can betray is his conscience. —JOSEPH CONRAD, *Under Western Eyes*

I hate the idea of causes, and if I had to choose between betraying my country and betraying my friend, I hope I should have the guts to betray my country. —E.M. FORSTER, *Two Cheers for Democracy*

> Treason doth never prosper: what's the
> reason?
> For if it prosper, none dare call it treason.
> —JOHN HARINGTON, *Epigrams*

Caesar had his Brutus, Charles the First his Cromwell, and George the Third—[at this point the speaker is interrupted with cries of "Treason!"] *may profit by their example.* If *this* be treason, make the most of it. —PATRICK HENRY, speech (1765)

Et tu, Brute! —SHAKESPEARE, *Julius Caesar*

> [Julius Caesar's words as he is stabbed by Brutus.]

The Bible — For quotations from the Bible, see under the individual subject categories.

> Both read the Bible day and night,
> But thou read'st black where I read white.
> —WILLIAM BLAKE, *The Everlasting Gospel*

In the twentieth century our highest praise is to call the Bible "The World's Best Seller." And it has come to be more and more difficult to say whether we think it is a best seller because it is great, or vice versa.
—DANIEL J. BOORSTIN, *The Image*

Those who talk of the Bible as a "monument of English prose" are merely admiring it as a monument over the grave of Christianity. —T.S. ELIOT, "Religion and Literature"

The Holy Bible is an abyss. It is impossible to explain how profound it is, impossible to explain how simple it is. —ERNEST HELLO, *Life, Science and Art*

. . . shallows where a lamb could wade and depths where an elephant could drown. —MATTHEW HENRY, *Commentaries*

The English Bible—a book which if everything else in our language should perish, would alone suffice to show the whole extent of its beauty and power.
—THOMAS BABINGTON MACAULAY, in *The Edinburgh Review*

You can learn more about human nature by reading the Bible than by living in New York. —WILLIAM LYON PHELPS, in *New York Times*

The Bible is literature, not dogma. —GEORGE SANTAYANA, *The Ethics of Spinoza*

The devil can cite Scripture for his purpose.
—SHAKESPEARE, *The Merchant of Venice*

I read the book of Job last night—I don't think God comes well out of it. —VIRGINIA WOOLF, letter (1922)

Birds — See ANIMALS

Birth

It is as natural to die as to be born; and to a little infant, perhaps, the one is as painful as the other. —FRANCIS BACON, *Essays*

> My mother groan'd, my father wept—
> Into the dangerous world I leapt,
> Helpless, naked, piping loud,
> Like a fiend hid in a cloud.
> > —WILLIAM BLAKE, "Infant Sorrow"

Being born, we die; our end is consequent on our beginning. —MARCUS MANILIUS, *Astronomica*

The hour which gives us life begins to take it away. —SENECA, *Hercules Furens*

> When we are born, we cry that we are come
> To this great stage of fools.
> > —SHAKESPEARE, *King Lear*

> Our birth is but a sleep and a forgetting:
> The Soul that rises with us, our life's Star,
> > Hath had elsewhere its setting,
> > And cometh from afar.
> > > —WILLIAM WORDSWORTH, "Intimations of
> > > Immortality"

Body and Face

It is the common wonder of all men, how among so many millions of faces, there should be none alike. —THOMAS BROWNE, *Religio Medici*

The countenance is the portrait of the mind, the eyes are its informers. —CICERO, *De Oratore*

Love's mysteries in souls do grow,
But yet the body is his book.
—JOHN DONNE, "The Extasy"

A man finds room in the few square inches of his face for the traits of all his ancestors; for the expression of all his history, and his wants. —RALPH WALDO EMERSON, *The Conduct of Life*

Anatomy is destiny. —SIGMUND FREUD, *Collected Writings*

The human body is a machine which winds its own springs. —JULIEN OFFROY DE LA METTRIE, *L'Homme machine*

How idiotic civilization is! Why be given a body if you have to keep it shut up in a case like a rare, rare fiddle? —KATHERINE MANSFIELD, *Bliss and Other Stories*

This body is not a home but an inn, and that only briefly. —SENECA, *Epistulae ad Lucilium*

Every man is the builder of a temple, called his body, to the god he worships, after a style purely his own, nor can he get off by hammering marble instead. We are all sculptors and painters, and our material is our own flesh and blood and bones. Any nobleness begins at once to refine a man's features, any meanness or sensuality to imbrute them. —HENRY DAVID THOREAU, *Walden*

If any thing is sacred the human body is sacred.
—WALT WHITMAN, *Leaves of Grass*

Boldness and Enterprise

Audacity, more audacity, and always audacity!
—GEORGES JACQUES DANTON, speech (1792)

Bold knaves thrive without one grain of sense,
But good men starve for want of impudence.
　　　—JOHN DRYDEN, "Constantine the Great"

A decent boldness ever meets with friends.
—HOMER, *The Odyssey*

Nothing is too high for the daring of mortals; we storm heaven itself in our folly. —HORACE, *Odes*

If the creator had a purpose in equipping us with a neck, he surely meant us to stick it out. —ARTHUR KOESTLER, in *Encounter*

He either fears his fate too much,
　　Or his deserts are small,
That dares not put it to the touch,
　　To gain or lose it all.
　　　—JAMES GRAHAM, MARQUIS OF MONTROSE,
　　　　　　"I'll Never Love Thee More"

Fortune favors the bold. —VIRGIL, *Aeneid*
　　[But, noted Livy in his history of Rome: "Rashness is not fortunate." See also Terence, under Courage, and Jonson, under Fools and Foolishness.]

Books and Reading

Some books are to be tasted, others to be swallowed, and some few to be chewed and digested. —FRANCIS BACON, *Essays*

The printing press is either the greatest blessing or the greatest curse of modern times, one sometimes forgets which. —JAMES M. BARRIE, *Sentimental Tommy*

Of making many books there is no end; and much study is a weariness of the flesh. —BIBLE, *Ecclesiastes* 12:12

40

There is no Frigate like a Book
To take us Lands away
Nor any Coursers like a Page
Of prancing Poetry.
　　　—EMILY DICKINSON, "There is no Frigate
　　　　　　　　　　　　　　like a Book"

Books are the quietest and most constant of friends; they are the most accessible and wisest of counselors, and the most patient of teachers. —CHARLES W. ELIOT, *The Durable Satisfactions of Life*

Never read any book that is not a year old. —RALPH WALDO EMERSON, *Society and Solitude*

I suggest that the only books that influence us are those for which we are ready, and which have gone a little farther down our particular path than we have yet got ourselves. —E.M. FORSTER, *Two Cheers for Democracy*

All good books are alike in that they are truer than if they had really happened and after you are finished reading one you will feel that all that happened to you and afterwards it all belongs to you: the good and the bad, the ecstasy, the remorse and sorrow, the people and the places and how the weather was. —ERNEST HEMINGWAY, in *Esquire*

We find little in a book but what we put there. But in great books, the mind finds room to put many things. —JOSEPH JOUBERT, *Pensées*

I love to lose myself in other men's minds. When I am not walking, I am reading; I cannot sit and think. Books think for me. —CHARLES LAMB, *Last Essays of Elia*

A book is a mirror: when a monkey looks in, no apostle can look out. —GEORG CHRISTOPH LICHTENBERG, *Aphorisms*

41

Literature is mostly about having sex and not much about having children. Life is the other way around.
—DAVID LODGE, *The British Museum is Falling Down*

> All books are either dreams or swords,
> You can cut, or you can drug, with words.
>   —AMY LOWELL, "Sword Blades and Poppy
>   Seeds"

Literature is news that STAYS news. —EZRA POUND, *ABC of Reading*

People say that life is the thing, but I prefer reading.
—LOGAN PEARSALL SMITH, *Afterthoughts*

Books are good enough in their own way, but they are a mighty bloodless substitute for life. —ROBERT LOUIS STEVENSON, *Virginibus Puerisque*

"Classic": A book which people praise and don't read.
—MARK TWAIN, *Following the Equator*, "Pudd'nhead Wilson's New Calendar"

> [He expressed similar sentiments in a speech in 1900: ". . . a classic—something that everybody wants to have read and nobody wants to read."]

The difference between literature and journalism is that journalism is unreadable, and literature is not read. —OSCAR WILDE, *Intentions*, "The Critic as Artist"

Boredom and Bores

BORE, *n.* A person who talks when you wish him to listen. —AMBROSE BIERCE, *The Devil's Dictionary*

> Society is now one polish'd horde,
> Form'd of two mighty tribes, the *Bores* and
>   *Bored.*
>   —LORD BYRON, *Don Juan*

For I have known them all already, known
    them all—
Have known the evenings, mornings,
    afternoons,
I have measured out my life with coffee
    spoons.
      —T.S. ELIOT, "The Love Song of J. Alfred
                      Prufrock"

The effect of boredom on a large scale in history is underestimated. It is a main cause of revolutions, and would soon bring to an end all the static Utopias and the farmyard civilization of the Fabians. —WILLIAM RALPH INGE, *The End of an Age*

We often forgive those who bore us, but never those whom we bore. —LA ROCHEFOUCAULD, *Maxims*

Boredom is a vital problem for the moralist, since at least half the sins of mankind are caused by the fear of it. —BERTRAND RUSSELL, *The Conquest of Happiness*

A bore is a man who, when you ask him how he is, tells you. —BERT LESTON TAYLOR, *The So-Called Human Race*

. . . the desire for desires—boredom. —LEO TOLSTOY, *Anna Karenina*

One out of three hundred and twelve Americans is a bore . . . and a healthy male adult bore consumes *each year* one and a half times his own weight in other people's patience. —JOHN UPDIKE, *Assorted Prose*

The secret of being a bore is to tell everything. —VOLTAIRE, *Sept discours en vers sur l'homme*

Borrowing and Lending

The borrower is servant to the lender. —BIBLE, *Proverbs* 22:7

ACQUAINTANCE, *n.* A person whom we know well enough to borrow from, but not well enough to lend to. —AMBROSE BIERCE, *The Devil's Dictionary*

If you'd know the value of money, go and borrow some. —BENJAMIN FRANKLIN, *Poor Richard's Almanac*

A bank is a place that will lend you money if you can prove that you don't need it. —BOB HOPE, quoted in *Life in the Crystal Palace* by Alan Harrington

Neither a borrower nor a lender be;
For loan oft loses both itself and friend,
And borrowing dulls the edge of husbandry.
                              —SHAKESPEARE, *Hamlet*

Who goeth a borrowing
Goeth a sorrowing.
Few lend (but fools)
Their working tools.
          —THOMAS TUSSER, *Five Hundred Points
                    of Good Husbandry*

[Benjamin Franklin used this in *Poor Richard's Almanac.*]

Bravery — See COURAGE

Brevity

Let thy speech be short, comprehending much in few words. —BIBLE, *Ecclesiasticus* 32:8

Good things, when short, are twice as good. —BALTASAR GRACIÁN, *The Art of Worldly Wisdom*

I struggle to be brief, and I become obscure. —HORACE, *Ars Poetica*

It is my ambition to say in ten sentences what other men say in whole books—what other men do *not* say in whole books. —FRIEDRICH NIETZSCHE, *Twilight of the Idols*

Brevity is the soul of lingerie. —DOROTHY PARKER, attributed

[See also Shakespeare, below.]

Therefore, since brevity is the soul of wit,
And tediousness the limbs and outward
 flourishes,
I will be brief.

—SHAKESPEARE, *Hamlet*

Brotherhood

Have we not all one father? hath not one God created us? —BIBLE, *Malachi* 2:10

While there is a lower class I am in it, while there is a criminal element I am of it; while there is a soul in prison, I am not free. —EUGENE V. DEBS, speech (1917)

No man is an island, entire of itself; every man is a piece of the continent, a part of the main; if a clod be washed away by the sea, Europe is the less, . . . Any man's death diminishes me, because I am involved in mankind; And therefore never send to know for whom the bell tolls; it tolls for thee. —JOHN DONNE, *Devotions upon Emergent Occasions*

A low capacity for getting along with those near us often goes hand in hand with a high receptivity to the idea of the brotherhood of men. —ERIC HOFFER, *The Ordeal of Change*

The world has narrowed to a neighborhood before it has broadened to a brotherhood. —LYNDON B. JOHNSON, speech (1963)

I want to be the white man's brother, not his brother-in-law. —MARTIN LUTHER KING, JR., quoted in *New York Journal-American*

We must learn to live together as brothers or perish together as fools. —MARTIN LUTHER KING, JR., speech (1964)

> Whoever degrades another degrades me,
> And whatever is done or said returns at last to me.
> —WALT WHITMAN, *Leaves of Grass*

Bureaucracy

Bureaucracy, the gigantic power set in motion by dwarves, was thus born. —HONORÉ DE BALZAC, *Les Employés*

Bureaucrats are the only people in the world who can say absolutely nothing and mean it. —JAMES H. BOREN, quoted in *Time*

We can lick gravity, but sometimes the paperwork is overwhelming. —WERNHER VON BRAUN, in *Chicago Sun Times*

Too often I find that the volume of paper expands to fill the available briefcases. —JERRY BROWN, quoted in *Wall Street Journal*

. . . skewered through and through with office-pens, and bound hand and foot with red tape. —CHARLES DICKENS, *David Copperfield*

A civil servant doesn't make jokes. —EUGÈNE IONESCO, *The Killer*

Bureaucracy, the rule of no one, has become the modern form of despotism. —MARY MCCARTHY, in *New Yorker*

Business — See also BUYING AND SELLING; CAPITALISM

CORPORATION, *n.* An ingenious device for obtaining individual profit without individual responsibility. —AMBROSE BIERCE, *The Devil's Dictionary*

What is robbing a bank compared with founding a bank? —BERTOLT BRECHT, *The Threepenny Opera*

Keep thy shop, and thy shop will keep thee.
—GEORGE CHAPMAN, BEN JONSON, AND JOHN MARSTON, *Eastward Ho*

> [Used later by Benjamin Franklin in *Poor Richard's Almanac*.]

Corporations cannot commit treason, nor be outlawed, nor excommunicated, for they have no souls. —EDWARD COKE, *Reports*, "Case of Sutton's Hospital"

The chief business of the American people is business. —CALVIN COOLIDGE, speech (1925)

> [Often quoted as: "The business of America is business."]

Here's the rule for bargains—"Do other men, for they would do you." That's the true business precept. —CHARLES DICKENS, *Martin Chuzzlewit*

Business? That's very simple—it's other people's money. —ALEXANDRE DUMAS, FILS, *La Question d'argent*

No nation was ever ruined by trade. —BENJAMIN FRANKLIN, *Thoughts on Commercial Subjects*

Drive thy Business, or it will drive thee. —BENJAMIN FRANKLIN, *Poor Richard's Almanac*

Boldness in business is the first, second, and third thing. —THOMAS FULLER, *Gnomologia*

The salary of the chief executive of the large corporation is not a market award for achievement. It is frequently in the nature of a warm personal gesture by the individual to himself. —JOHN KENNETH GALBRAITH, *Annals of an Abiding Liberal*

He's a businessman. I'll make him an offer he can't refuse. —MARIO PUZO, *The Godfather*

People of the same trade seldom meet together, even for merriment and diversion, but the conversation ends in a conspiracy against the public, or in some contrivance to raise prices. —ADAM SMITH, *The Wealth of Nations*

For years I thought what was good for our country was good for General Motors, and vice versa.
—CHARLES E. WILSON, said in testimony before a U.S. Senate hearing

> [Wilson, former president of General Motors, said this in his confirmation hearings for Secretary of Defense. It is often misquoted as: "What's good for General Motors is good for the country."]

Business underlies everything in our national life, including our spiritual life. Witness the fact that in the Lord's Prayer the first petition is for daily bread. No one can worship God or love his neighbor on an empty stomach. —WOODROW WILSON, speech (1912)

Buying and Selling

It is naught, it is naught, saith the buyer: but when he is gone his way, then he boasteth. —BIBLE, *Proverbs* 20:14

Good bargains are pick-pockets. —THOMAS FULLER, *Gnomologia*

The buyer needs a hundred eyes, the seller not one.
—GEORGE HERBERT, *Jacula Prudentum*

In a consumer society there are inevitably two kinds of slaves: the prisoners of addiction and the prisoners of envy. —IVAN ILLICH, *Tools for Conviviality*

Conspicuous consumption of valuable goods is a means of reputability to the gentleman of leisure. —THORSTEIN VEBLEN, *The Theory of the Leisure Class*

Candor and Sincerity

Men are always sincere. They change sincerities, that's all. —TRISTAN BERNARD, *Ce que l'on dit aux femmes*

> Give me the avowed, erect and manly foe;
> Firm I can meet, perhaps return the blow;
> But of all plagues, good Heaven, thy wrath can
>   send,
> Save me, oh, save me, from the candid friend.
>   —GEORGE CANNING, *New Morality*

Nothing astonishes men so much as common sense and plain dealing. —RALPH WALDO EMERSON, *Essays*

Civility is not a sign of weakness, and sincerity is always subject to proof. —JOHN F. KENNEDY, speech (inaugural address, 1961)

The greatest horrors of our world, from the executions in Iran to the brutalities of the IRA, are committed by people who are totally sincere. —JOHN MORTIMER, quoted in *The Observer*

Talking much about oneself may be a way of hiding oneself. —FRIEDRICH NIETZSCHE, *Beyond Good and Evil*

Plain-dealing is a jewel, and he that useth it shall die a beggar. —HENRY PORTER, *The Two Angrie Women of Abington*

A little sincerity is a dangerous thing, and a great deal of it is absolutely fatal. —OSCAR WILDE, *Intentions*, "The Critic as Artist"

All cruel people describe themselves as paragons of frankness. —TENNESSEE WILLIAMS, *The Milk Train Doesn't Stop Here Anymore*

Capitalism — See also BUSINESS

Laissez-faire, Supply-and-demand,—one begins to be weary of all that. Leave all to egoism, to ravenous greed of money, of pleasure, of applause:—it is the Gospel of Despair! —THOMAS CARLYLE, *Past and Present*

The basic law of capitalism is you or I, not both you and I. —KARL LIEBKNECHT, speech (1907)

The revolution eats its own. Capitalism re-creates itself. —MORDECAI RICHLER, *Cocksure*

The trouble with the profit system has always been that it was highly unprofitable to most people. —E.B. WHITE, *One Man's Meat*

Cats — See ANIMALS

Caution — See PRUDENCE AND FORESIGHT

Celebrity — See FAME

Censorship

We are willing enough to praise freedom when she is safely tucked away in the past and cannot be a nuisance. In the present, amidst dangers whose outcome we cannot foresee, we get nervous about her, and admit censorship. —E.M. FORSTER, *Two Cheers for Democracy*

Books won't stay banned. They won't burn. Ideas won't go to jail. In the long run of history, the censor and the inquisitor have always lost. The only sure weapon against bad ideas is better ideas. —A. WHITNEY GRISWOLD, speech (1952)

Wherever they burn books they will also, in the end, burn human beings. —HEINRICH HEINE, *Almansor: A Tragedy*

As good almost kill a man as kill a good book: who kills a man kills a reasonable creature, God's image; but he who destroys a good book, kills reason itself, kills the image of God, as it were, in the eye. —JOHN MILTON, *Areopagitica*

It may be said that artist and censor differ in this wise: that the first is a decent mind in an indecent body and that the second is an indecent mind in a decent body. —GEORGE JEAN NATHAN, *The Autobiography of an Attitude*

Assassination is the extreme form of censorship. —GEORGE BERNARD SHAW, *The Rejected Statement*

Certainty

If a man will begin with certainties, he shall end in doubts, but if he will be content to begin with doubts, he shall end in certainties. —FRANCIS BACON, *The Advancement of Learning*

Oh! let us never, never doubt
What nobody is sure about!
        —HILAIRE BELLOC, "The Microbe"

POSITIVE, *adj.* Mistaken at the top of one's voice. —AMBROSE BIERCE, *The Devil's Dictionary*

In this world nothing is certain but death and taxes. —BENJAMIN FRANKLIN, letter (1789)

We can be absolutely certain only about things we do not understand. —ERIC HOFFER, *The True Believer*

Certainty generally is illusion, and repose is not the destiny of man. —OLIVER WENDELL HOLMES, JR., speech (1897)

[Edward Coke had written in *The First Part of the Institutes of the Laws of England*: "Certainty is the mother of quiet and repose, and uncertainty the cause of variance and contentions."]

Certitude is not the test of certainty. —OLIVER WENDELL HOLMES, JR., *Natural Law*

It is the dull man who is always sure, and the sure man who is always dull. —H.L. MENCKEN, *Prejudices*

The only certainty is that nothing is certain. —PLINY THE ELDER, *Natural History*

Doubt is not a pleasant condition, but certainty is an absurd one. —VOLTAIRE, letter (to Frederick the Great, 1767)

Chance — See FORTUNE AND CHANCE

Change

Weep not that the world changes—did it keep
A stable, changeless state, 'twere cause indeed
    to weep.
        —WILLIAM CULLEN BRYANT, "Mutation"

It is only the wisest and the very stupidest who cannot change. —CONFUCIUS, *Analects*

The world's a scene of changes, and to be
Constant, in Nature were inconstancy.
        —ABRAHAM COWLEY, "Inconstancy"

In a progressive country change is constant; change is inevitable. —BENJAMIN DISRAELI, speech (1867)

Most of the change we think we see in life
Is due to truths being in and out of favor.
        —ROBERT FROST, "The Black Cottage"

Happiness is never really so welcome as changelessness. —GRAHAM GREENE, *The Heart of the Matter*

There is nothing permanent except change. —HERACLITUS, quoted by Diogenes Laertius in *Lives of the Philosophers*

All is flux, nothing stays still. —HERACLITUS, quoted by Plato in *Cratylus*

There is a certain relief in change, even though it be from bad to worse; as I have found in travelling in a stagecoach, that it is often a comfort to shift one's position and be bruised in a new place. —WASHINGTON IRVING, *Tales of a Traveller*

The more things change, the more they remain the same. (*Plus ça change, plus c'est la même chose.*) —ALPHONSE KARR, in *Les Guêpes*

Is any man afraid of change? Why what can take place without change? What then is more pleasing or more suitable to the universal nature? —MARCUS AURELIUS, *Meditations*

All things change; nothing perishes. —OVID, *Metamorphoses*

Character and Personality

Don't *say* things. What you *are* stands over you the while, and thunders so that I cannot hear what you say to the contrary. —RALPH WALDO EMERSON, *Letters and Social Aims*

Character is that which can do without success. —RALPH WALDO EMERSON, *Uncollected Lectures*

Talent develops in quiet,
Character in the torrent of the world.
—JOHANN WOLFGANG VON GOETHE,
Torquato Tasso

Character is destiny. —HERACLITUS (fragment)

Character is what a man is in the dark. —DWIGHT L. MOODY, quoted in William R. Moody's *D.L. Moody*

Character is simply habit long continued. —PLUTARCH, *Morals*

Everyone is a moon, and has a dark side which he never shows to anybody. —MARK TWAIN, *Following the Equator*, "Pudd'nhead Wilson's New Calendar"

Charity

> The desire of power in excess caused the angels to fall; the desire of knowledge in excess caused man to fall: but in charity there is no excess; neither can angel or man come in danger by it.
> —FRANCIS BACON, *Essays*

Though I speak with the tongues of men and of angels, and have not charity, I am become as sounding brass, or a tinkling cymbal. —BIBLE, *I Corinthians* 13:1

[The Revised Standard Version translates this with *love* in place of *charity*.]

And now abideth faith, hope, charity, these three; but the greatest of these is charity. —BIBLE, *I Corinthians* 13:13

Charity shall cover the multitude of sins. —BIBLE, *I Peter* 4:8

[Commonly quoted in the proverbial form: "Charity covers a multitude of sins." Oscar Wilde's anti-proverb, in *The Soul of Man under Socialism*: "Charity creates a multitude of sins."]

When thou doest alms, let not thy left hand know what thy right hand doeth. —BIBLE, *Matthew* 6:3

Too many have dispensed with generosity in order to practice charity. —ALBERT CAMUS, *The Fall*

Philanthropy is commendable, but it must not cause the philanthropist to overlook the circumstances of economic injustice which make philanthropy necessary. —MARTIN LUTHER KING, JR., *Strength to Love*

Anticipate charity by preventing poverty. —MAIMONIDES, *Guide to the Perplexed*

> Our charity begins at home,
> And mostly ends where it begins.
> —HORACE SMITH, *Horace in London*

No one would remember the Good Samaritan if he'd only had good intentions. He had money as well. —MARGARET THATCHER, television interview

Philanthropy is almost the only virtue which is sufficiently appreciated by mankind. Nay, it is greatly overrated; and it is our selfishness which overrates it. —HENRY DAVID THOREAU, *Walden*

Charm

Charm: the quality in others that makes us more satisfied with ourselves. —HENRI-FRÉDÉRIC AMIEL, *Journal intime*

It's a sort of bloom on a woman. If you have it, you don't need to have anything else; and if you don't have it, it doesn't much matter what else you have. —JAMES M. BARRIE, *What Every Woman Knows*

You know what charm is: a way of getting the answer yes without having asked any clear question. —ALBERT CAMUS, *The Fall*

All charming people have something to conceal, usually their total dependence on the appreciation of others. —CYRIL CONNOLLY, *Enemies of Promise*

55

Cheating — See DECEPTION AND FRAUD

Cheerfulness

Health and cheerfulness mutually beget each other.
—JOSEPH ADDISON, *The Spectator*

A merry heart doeth good like a medicine. —BIBLE, *Proverbs* 17:22

So of cheerfulness, or a good temper—the more it is spent, the more of it remains. —RALPH WALDO EMERSON, *The Conduct of Life*

The plainest sign of wisdom is a continual cheerfulness: her state is like that of things in the regions above the moon, always clear and serene. —MICHEL DE MONTAIGNE, *Essays*

Children and Childhood — See also ADOLESCENCE; YOUTH

Children sweeten labors, but they make misfortunes more bitter. They increase the cares of life, but they mitigate the remembrance of death. —FRANCIS BACON, *Essays*

Children have never been very good at listening to their elders, but they have never failed to imitate them. —JAMES BALDWIN, *Nobody Knows My Name*

Out of the mouth of babes and sucklings hast thou ordained strength. —BIBLE, *Psalms* 8:2

Suffer the little children to come unto me, and forbid them not: for of such is the kingdom of God. —BIBLE, *Mark* 10:14

There is no end to the violations committed by children on children, quietly talking alone. —ELIZABETH BOWEN, *The House in Paris*

There is no finer investment for any community than putting milk into babies. —WINSTON CHURCHILL, speech (1943)

In the little world in which children have their existence, whosoever brings them up, there is nothing so finely perceived and so finely felt as injustice. —CHARLES DICKENS, *Great Expectations*

Little children are still the symbol of the eternal marriage between love and duty. —GEORGE ELIOT, *Romola*

We find delight in the beauty and happiness of children that makes the heart too big for the body. —RALPH WALDO EMERSON, *The Conduct of Life*

Your children are not your children.
They are the sons and daughters of Life's
    longing for itself. . . .
You may house their bodies but not their
    souls,
For their souls dwell in the house of tomorrow,
    which you cannot visit, not even in your
    dreams.
                    —KAHLIL GIBRAN, *The Prophet*

We can't form our children on our own concepts; we must take them and love them as God gives them to us. —JOHANN WOLFGANG VON GOETHE, *Hermann und Dorothea*

There is always one moment in childhood when the door opens and lets the future in. —GRAHAM GREENE, *The Power and the Glory*

Children need models more than they need critics. —JOSEPH JOUBERT, *Pensées*

Childhood is not from birth to a certain age
  and at a certain age
The child is grown, and puts away childish
  things.
Childhood is the kingdom where nobody dies.
Nobody that matters, that is.
> —EDNA ST. VINCENT MILLAY, "Childhood
> Is the Kingdom Where Nobody Dies"

How sharper than a serpent's tooth it is
To have a thankless child!
> —SHAKESPEARE, *King Lear*

A baby is an inestimable blessing and bother.
—MARK TWAIN, letter (1876)

Childhood is frequently a solemn business for those
inside it. —GEORGE F. WILL, in *Newsweek*

The Child is father of the Man. —WILLIAM WORDS-
WORTH, "My Heart Leaps Up"

Choice

White shall not neutralize the black, nor good
Compensate bad in man, absolve him so:
Life's business being just the terrible choice.
> —ROBERT BROWNING, "The Pope"

Every act of will is an act of self-limitation. To desire
action is to desire limitation. In that sense, every act
is an act of self-sacrifice. When you choose anything,
you reject everything else. —G.K. CHESTERTON,
Orthodoxy

Guess if you can, choose if you dare. —PIERRE COR-
NEILLE, *Héraclius*

The strongest principle of growth lies in the human
choice. —GEORGE ELIOT, *Daniel Deronda*

I shall be telling this with a sigh
Somewhere ages and ages hence:
Two roads diverged in a wood, and I—
I took the one less traveled by,
And that has made all the difference.
>   —ROBERT FROST, "The Road Not Taken"

There's small choice in rotten apples. —SHAKE-SPEARE, *The Taming of the Shrew*

Christians — See RELIGION

Christmas — See HOLIDAYS

Church — See RELIGION

Cigarettes — See SMOKING

City and Country

Match me such marvel save in Eastern clime,
A rose-red city "half as old as Time!"
>   —JOHN WILLIAM BURGON, "Petra"

If you would be known, and not know, vegetate in a village; if you would know, and not be known, live in a city. —CHARLES CALEB COLTON, *Lacon*

It is my belief, Watson, founded upon my experience, that the lowest and vilest alleys of London do not present a more dreadful record of sin than does the smiling and beautiful countryside. —ARTHUR CONAN DOYLE, *The Adventures of Sherlock Holmes*

When I am in the country I wish to vegetate like the country. —WILLIAM HAZLITT, *Table Talk*

There is nothing good to be had in the country, or, if there be, they will not let you have it. —WILLIAM HAZLITT, *Lectures*

In Rome you long for the country; in the country—oh inconstant!—you praise the distant city to the stars. —HORACE, *Satires*

All cities are mad: but the madness is gallant. All cities are beautiful: but the beauty is grim. —CHRISTOPHER MORLEY, *Where the Blue Begins*

Clearly, then, the city is not a concrete jungle, it is a human zoo. —DESMOND MORRIS, *The Human Zoo*

Cities are the abyss of the human species. —JEAN-JACQUES ROUSSEAU, *Émile*

I suppose the pleasure of country life lies really in the eternally renewed evidences of the determination to live. —VITA SACKVILLE-WEST, *Country Notes*

Anybody can be good in the country. —OSCAR WILDE, *The Picture of Dorian Gray*

Civilization

The three great elements of modern civilization, gunpowder, printing, and the Protestant religion. —THOMAS CARLYLE, *Critical and Miscellaneous Essays*

Increased means and increased leisure are the two civilizers of man. —BENJAMIN DISRAELI, speech (1872)

Our civilization is still in a middle stage, scarcely beast, in that it is no longer wholly guided by instinct; scarcely human, in that it is not yet wholly guided by reason. —THEODORE DREISER, *Sister Carrie*

what man calls civilization
always results in deserts
—DON MARQUIS, *archy and mehitabel*

If a test of civilization be sought, none can be so sure as the condition of that half of society over which the other half has power. —HARRIET MARTINEAU, *Society in America*

Civilization is nothing else than the attempt to reduce force to being the *ultima ratio* [last resort]. —JOSÉ ORTEGA Y GASSET, *The Revolt of the Masses*

You can't say civilization don't advance, however, for in every war they kill you in a new way. —WILL ROGERS, *The Autobiography of Will Rogers*

Civilization advances by extending the number of important operations which we can perform without thinking about them. —ALFRED NORTH WHITEHEAD, *An Introduction to Mathematics*

Class

When Adam delved and Eve span,
Who was then the gentleman?
—JOHN BALL, speech (1381)

Dialect words—those terrible marks of the beast to the truly genteel. —THOMAS HARDY, *The Mayor of Casterbridge*

The bourgeois prefers comfort to pleasure, convenience to liberty, and a pleasant temperature to the deathly inner consuming fire. —HERMANN HESSE, *Der Steppenwolf*

How beastly the bourgeois is
Especially the male of the species.
—D.H. LAWRENCE, "How Beastly the
Bourgeois Is"

An aristocracy in a republic is like a chicken whose head has been cut off; it may run about in a lively way, but in fact it is dead. —NANCY MITFORD, *Noblesse Oblige*

Common sense, in so far as it exists, is all for the bourgeoisie. Nonsense is the privilege of the aristocracy. The worries of the world are for the common people. —GEORGE JEAN NATHAN, *Autobiography of an Attitude*

There is no stronger craving in the world than that of the rich for titles, except that of the titled for riches. —HESKETH PEARSON, *The Marrying Americans*

I can't help feeling wary when I hear anything said about the masses. First, you take their faces away from 'em by calling them masses, and then you accuse 'em of not having any faces. —J.B. PRIESTLEY, *Saturn Over the Water*

To have a horror of the bourgeois is bourgeois. —JULES RENARD, *The Journal of Jules Renard*, ed. Louise Bogan and Elizabeth Roget

A moderately honest man with a moderately faithful wife, moderate drinkers both, in a moderately healthy house: that is the true middle class unit. —GEORGE BERNARD SHAW, *Man and Superman*

Clothing — See also FASHION

A little of what you call frippery is very necessary towards looking like the rest of the world. —ABIGAIL ADAMS, letter (1780)

Any man may be in good spirits and good temper when he's well dressed. There ain't much credit in that. —CHARLES DICKENS, *Martin Chuzzlewit*

Probably every new and eagerly expected garment ever put on since clothes came in fell a trifle short of the wearer's expectation. —CHARLES DICKENS, *Great Expectations*

I have heard with admiring submission the experience of the lady who declared that the sense of being perfectly well-dressed gives a feeling of inward tranquillity which religion is powerless to bestow.
—RALPH WALDO EMERSON, *Letters and Social Aims*

If all your clothes are worn to the same state, it means you go out too much. —F. SCOTT FITZGERALD, *The Crack-Up*, ed. Edmund Wilson

All women's dresses, in every age and country, are merely variations on the eternal struggle between the admitted desire to dress and the unadmitted desire to undress. —LIN YUTANG, quoted in *Ladies' Home Journal*

> Where's the man could ease a heart
> Like a satin gown?
> —DOROTHY PARKER, "The Satin Dress"

> Costly thy habit as thy purse can buy,
> But not express'd in fancy; rich, not gaudy;
> For the apparel oft proclaims the man.
> —SHAKESPEARE, *Hamlet*

I say, beware of all enterprises that require new clothes, and not rather a new wearer of clothes.
—HENRY DAVID THOREAU, *Walden*

Committees

A committee is a cul-de-sac down which ideas are lured and then quietly strangled. —BARNETT COCKS, attributed

No grand idea was ever born in a conference, but a lot of foolish ideas have died there. —F. SCOTT FITZGERALD, *The Crack-Up*, ed. Edmund Wilson

Could *Hamlet* have been written by a committee, or the *Mona Lisa* painted by a club? Could the New Testament have been composed as a conference report? Creative ideas do not spring from groups. They spring from individuals. The divine spark leaps from the finger of God to the finger of Adam. —A. WHITNEY GRISWOLD, speech (1957)

A committee is an animal with four back legs. —JOHN LE CARRÉ, *Tinker Tailor Soldier Spy*

Common Sense — See WISDOM AND SENSE

Communication

We shall never understand one another until we reduce the language to seven words. —KAHLIL GIBRAN, *Sand and Foam*

No one would talk much in society, if he knew how often he misunderstands others. —JOHANN WOLFGANG VON GOETHE, *Elective Affinities*

After all, when you come right down to it, how many people speak the same language even when they speak the same language? —RUSSELL HOBAN, *The Lion of Boaz-Jachin and Jachin-Boaz*

The medium is the message. —MARSHALL MCLUHAN, *Understanding Media*

To use the same words is not a sufficient guarantee of understanding; one must use the same words for the same genus of inward experience; ultimately one must have one's experiences in *common*. —FRIEDRICH NIETZSCHE, *Beyond Good and Evil*

I have made this letter longer than usual, only because I have not had the time to make it shorter. —BLAISE PASCAL, *Provincial Letters*

I distrust the incommunicable; it is the source of all violence. —JEAN-PAUL SARTRE, *What is Literature?*

Humanity is never more sphinxlike than when it is expressing itself. —REBECCA WEST, *The Court and the Castle*

Communism and Socialism

> What is a communist? One who hath
>   yearnings
> For equal division of unequal earnings.
>   —EBENEZER ELLIOTT, "Epigram"

Leninism is a combination of two things which Europeans have kept for some centuries in different compartments of their soul—religion and business. —JOHN MAYNARD KEYNES, *Essays in Persuasion*

If anyone believes that our smiles involve abandonment of the teaching of Marx, Engels, and Lenin he deceives himself poorly. Those who wait for that must wait until a shrimp learns to whistle. —NIKITA KHRUSHCHEV, speech (1955)

From each according to his abilities, to each according to his needs. —KARL MARX, *Critique of the Gotha Program*

A specter is haunting Europe—the specter of Communism. —KARL MARX AND FRIEDRICH ENGELS, *The Communist Manifesto*

As with the Christian religion, the worst advertisement for Socialism is its adherents. —GEORGE ORWELL, *The Road to Wigan Pier*

Communism is inequality, but not as property is. Property is the exploitation of the weak by the strong. Communism is the exploitation of the strong by the weak. —PIERRE-JOSEPH PROUDHON, *What Is Property?*

Communism is like Prohibition, it's a good idea but it won't work. —WILL ROGERS, *Autobiography*

Communism is the corruption of a dream of justice. —ADLAI E. STEVENSON, speech (1951)

Companionship

Tell me what company you keep, and I'll tell you what you are. —MIGUEL DE CERVANTES, *Don Quixote de la Mancha*

If a man could mount to heaven and survey the mighty universe, his admiration of its beauties would be much diminished unless he had some one to share in his pleasure. —CICERO, *De Amicitia*

Men who know the same things are not long the best company for each other. —RALPH WALDO EMERSON, *Representative Men*

Man loves company even if only that of a small burning candle. —GEORG CHRISTOPH LICHTENBERG, *Aphorisms*

It is a consolation to the wretched to have companions in misery. —PUBLILIUS SYRUS, *Maxims*

[An early version of "Misery loves company." See also Thoreau, under Unhappiness.]

What men call social virtue, good fellowship, is commonly but the virtue of pigs in a litter, which lie close together to keep each other warm. —HENRY DAVID THOREAU, *Journal*

Good company and good discourse are the very sinews of virtue. —IZAAK WALTON, *The Compleat Angler*

Comparison

Comparisons are odious. —JOHN FORTESCUE, *De laudibus legum Angliae*

[This appears in the works of many 15th and 16th century authors. Shakespeare used it in a play on words in *Much Ado About Nothing*: "Comparisons are odorous."]

Analogies, it is true, decide nothing, but they can make one feel more at home. —SIGMUND FREUD, *New Introductory Lectures of Psychoanalysis*

Nothing is good or bad but by comparison.
—THOMAS FULLER, *Gnomologia*

Compassion — See MERCY AND COMPASSION

Competence — See ABILITY

Competition

Rivalry adds so much to the charms of one's conquests. —LOUISA MAY ALCOTT, *Behind a Mask*

> Thou shalt not covet; but tradition
> Approves all forms of competition.
> —ARTHUR HUGH CLOUGH, "The Latest
> Decalogue"

Competition brings out the best in products and the worst in people. —DAVID SARNOFF, quoted in *Esquire*

The trouble with the rat race is that even if you win, you're still a rat. —LILY TOMLIN, attributed

Complaint

Never complain and never explain. —BENJAMIN DISRAELI, quoted in John Morley's *The Life of William Ewart Gladstone*

To have a grievance is to have a purpose in life.
—ERIC HOFFER, *The Passionate State of Mind*

If you are foolish enough to be contented, don't show it, but grumble with the rest. —JEROME K. JEROME, *The Idle Thoughts of an Idle Fellow*

Compliments — See PRAISE AND FLATTERY

Compromise

All government—indeed, every human benefit and enjoyment, every virtue and every prudent act—is founded on compromise and barter. —EDMUND BURKE, speech (1775)

Compromise used to mean that half a loaf was better than no bread. Among modern statesmen it really seems to mean that half a loaf is better than a whole loaf. —G.K. CHESTERTON, *What's Wrong with the World*

Truth is the glue that holds government together. Compromise is the oil that makes governments go. —GERALD R. FORD, comment during U.S. House committee hearing (1973)

Compromise is never anything but an ignoble truce between the duty of a man and the terror of a coward. —REGINALD WRIGHT KAUFFMAN, *The Way of Peace*

Compromise, if not the spice of life, is its solidity. It is what makes nations great and marriages happy. —PHYLLIS McGINLEY, *The Province of the Heart*

If you want to get along, go along. —SAM RAYBURN, quoted in Neil MacNeil's *Forge of Democracy*

Computers — See also TECHNOLOGY

They can rattle off the Manhattan telephone directory unerringly time after time, which no human can do, but they cannot begin to distinguish one face from another, as babies can do. —LEE DEMBART, in *New York Times*

Man is still the most extraordinary computer of all.
—JOHN F. KENNEDY, speech (1963)

A computer does not substitute for judgment any more than a pencil substitutes for literacy. But writing without a pencil is no particular advantage.
—ROBERT S. MCNAMARA, *The Essence of Security*

All a computer does is tell a consistent story: a consistent truth or, if the programmer's guesses are unlikely, a consistent fiction. —PAUL A. SAMUELSON, in *Newsweek*

The real question is not whether machines think but whether men do. The mystery which surrounds a thinking machine already surrounds a thinking man. —B.F. SKINNER, *Contingencies of Reinforcement*

A computer will do what you tell it to do, but that may be much different from what you had in mind.
—JOSEPH WEIZENBAUM, quoted in *Time*

Conceit, Egotism, and Vanity

To say that a man is vain means merely that he is pleased with the effect he produces on other people. A conceited man is satisfied with the effect he produces on himself. —MAX BEERBOHM, *And Even Now*

Seest thou a man wise in his own conceit? there is more hope of a fool than of him. —BIBLE, *Proverbs* 26:12

Vanity plays lurid tricks with our memory. —JOSEPH CONRAD, *Lord Jim*

Vanity, like murder, will out. —HANNAH COWLEY, *The Belle's Stratagem*

We are so vain that we even care for the opinion of those we don't care for. —MARIE VON EBNER-ESCHENBACH, *Aphorisms*

I've never any pity for conceited people, because I think they carry their comfort about with them.
—GEORGE ELIOT, *The Mill on the Floss*

Half of the harm that is done in this world
Is due to people who want to feel important.
　　　　　　　　—T.S. ELIOT, *The Cocktail Party*

He that falls in love with himself will have no rivals.
—BENJAMIN FRANKLIN, *Poor Richard's Almanac*

Conceit is the finest armor a man can wear.
—JEROME K. JEROME, *The Idle Thoughts of an Idle Fellow*

We would rather speak ill of ourselves than not talk about ourselves at all. —LA ROCHEFOUCAULD, *Maxims*

Self-love is the greatest of all flatterers. —LA ROCHEFOUCAULD, *Maxims*

The vanity of others runs counter to our taste only when it runs counter to our vanity. —FRIEDRICH NIETZSCHE, *Beyond Good and Evil*

Self-love seems so often unrequited. —ANTHONY POWELL, *A Dance to the Music of Time: The Acceptance World*

Self-love, my liege, is not so vile a sin
As self-neglecting.
　　　　　　　　—SHAKESPEARE, *Henry V*

No man thinks there is much ado about nothing when the ado is about himself. —ANTHONY TROLLOPE, *The Bertrams*

To love one's self is the beginning of a life-long romance. —OSCAR WILDE, *An Ideal Husband*

Confidence

You can have anything in this world you want, if you want it badly enough and you're willing to pay the price. —MARY KAY ASH, quoted in *New York Times*

Trust thyself: every heart vibrates to that iron string. —RALPH WALDO EMERSON, *Essays*, "Self-Reliance"

Skill and confidence are an unconquered army. —GEORGE HERBERT, *Jacula Prudentum*

Those who believe that they are exclusively in the right are generally those who achieve something. —ALDOUS HUXLEY, *Proper Studies*

The confidence which we have in ourselves engenders the greatest part of that which we have in others. —LA ROCHEFOUCAULD, *Maxims*

They can because they think they can. —VIRGIL, *Aeneid*

Conformity

When I am at Rome, I fast on a Saturday; when I am at Milan, I do not. Follow the custom of the church where you are. —SAINT AMBROSE, advice to St. Augustine, quoted by St. Augustine in *Epistle to Januarius*

[This appears to be the antecedent for the saying "When in Rome, do as the Romans do."]

For one man who thanks God that he is not as other men there are a thousand to offer thanks that they are as other men, sufficiently as others are to escape attention. —JOHN DEWEY, *Human Nature and Conduct*

Conform and be dull. —JAMES FRANK DOBIE, *The Voice of the Coyote*

. . . conformity is the jailer of freedom and the enemy of growth. —JOHN F. KENNEDY, speech (1961)

It is not difficult to be unconventional in the eyes of the world when your unconventionality is but the convention of your set. —W. SOMERSET MAUGHAM, *The Moon and Sixpence*

One should respect public opinion in so far as is necessary to avoid starvation and to keep out of prison, but anything that goes beyond this is voluntary submission to an unnecessary tyranny. —BERTRAND RUSSELL, *The Conquest of Happiness*

Conscience

A good conscience is a continual feast. —ROBERT BURTON, *The Anatomy of Melancholy*

> [Benjamin Franklin wrote in *Poor Richard's Almanac*: "A good conscience is a continual Christmas."]

Conscience is thoroughly well-bred and soon leaves off talking to those who do not wish to hear it. —SAMUEL BUTLER (d 1902), *Note-Books*

> There is one thing alone
> that stands the brunt of life throughout its
>   course:
> a quiet conscience.
> —EURIPIDES, *Hippolytus*

The paradoxical—and tragic—situation of man is that his conscience is weakest when he needs it most. —ERICH FROMM, *Man for Himself*

Conscience is a coward, and those faults it has not strength enough to prevent it seldom has justice enough to accuse. —OLIVER GOLDSMITH, *The Vicar of Wakefield*

I cannot and will not cut my conscience to fit this year's fashions. —LILLIAN HELLMAN, letter (1952)

Conscience is the inner voice which warns us that someone may be looking. —H.L. MENCKEN, *A Little Book in C Major*

> There is only one way to achieve happiness on
>   this terrestrial ball,
> And that is to have either a clear conscience,
>   or none at all.
>   —OGDEN NASH, "Interoffice
>   Memorandum"

Don't you see that that blessed conscience of yours is nothing but other people inside you? —LUIGI PIRANDELLO, *Each in His Own Way*

> Conscience is but a word that cowards use,
> Devised at first to keep the strong in awe.
>   —SHAKESPEARE, *Richard III*

Thus conscience does makes cowards of us all. —SHAKESPEARE, *Hamlet*

Consequences

They have sown the wind, and they shall reap the whirlwind. —BIBLE, *Hosea* 8:7

Don't wait for the Last Judgment. It takes place every day. —ALBERT CAMUS, *The Fall*

Logical consequences are the scarecrows of fools and the beacons of wise men. —THOMAS HENRY HUXLEY, *Science and Culture*

You can do anything in this world if you're prepared to take the consequences. —W. SOMERSET MAUGHAM, *The Circle*

Nothing exists from whose nature some effect does not follow. —BENEDICT DE SPINOZA, *Ethics*

Conservatives — See LIBERALS AND CONSERVATIVES

Consistency

Consistency requires you to be as ignorant today as you were a year ago. —BERNARD BERENSON, *Notebook*

A foolish consistency is the hobgoblin of little minds, adored by little statesmen and philosophers and divines. With consistency a great soul has simply nothing to do. —RALPH WALDO EMERSON, *Essays*, "Self-Reliance"

Consistency is contrary to nature, contrary to life. The only completely consistent people are the dead. —ALDOUS HUXLEY, *Do What You Will*

Like all weak men he laid an exaggerated stress on not changing one's mind. —W. SOMERSET MAUGHAM, *Of Human Bondage*

> Do I contradict myself?
> Very well then I contradict myself,
> (I am large, I contain multitudes.)
> —WALT WHITMAN, *Leaves of Grass*

Contentment — See HAPPINESS

Controversy — See ARGUMENTS AND CONTROVERSY

Conversation

It is greed to do all the talking but not to want to listen at all. —DEMOCRITUS OF ABDERA (fragment)

Conversation is an art in which a man has all mankind for his competitors, for it is that which all are practicing every day while they live. —RALPH WALDO EMERSON, *The Conduct of Life*

Nature has given men one tongue and two ears, that we may hear twice as much as we speak. —EPICTETUS (fragment)

A civil guest
Will no more talk all, than eat all the feast.
—GEORGE HERBERT, "The Church-Porch"

The happiest conversation is that of which nothing is distinctly remembered, but a general effect of pleasing impression. —SAMUEL JOHNSON, quoted in James Boswell's *The Life of Samuel Johnson*

A gossip is one who talks to you about others; a bore is one who talks to you about himself; and a brilliant conversationalist is one who talks to you about yourself. —LISA KIRK, quoted in *New York Journal-American*

Confidence contributes more to conversation than wit. —LA ROCHEFOUCAULD, *Maxims*

If you can't say something good about someone, sit right here by me. —ALICE ROOSEVELT LONGWORTH, quoted in *Time*

   [This was her motto for a successful party, embroidered on a pillow.]

One person seeks a midwife for his thoughts; the other, someone he can assist. Here is the origin of a good conversation. —FRIEDRICH NIETZSCHE, *Beyond Good and Evil*

Ideal conversation must be an exchange of thought, and not, as many of those who worry most about their shortcomings believe, an eloquent exhibition of wit or oratory. —EMILY POST, *Etiquette*

Conversation has a kind of charm about it, an insinuating and insidious something that elicits secrets from us just like love or liquor. —SENECA, *Epistulae ad Lucilium*

No syren did ever so charm the ear of the listener, as the listening ear has charmed the soul of the syren. —HENRY TAYLOR, *The Statesman*

There is no such thing as conversation. It is an illusion. There are intersecting monologues, that is all. —REBECCA WEST, *There Is No Conversation*

Country — See CITY AND COUNTRY

Courage

Until the day of his death, no man can be sure of his courage. —JEAN ANOUILH, *Becket*

The coward calls the brave man rash, the rash man calls him a coward. —ARISTOTLE, *Nichomachean Ethics*

> The brave man is not he who feels no fear,
> For that were stupid and irrational;
> But he, whose noble soul its fear subdues,
> And bravely dares the danger nature shrinks
> from.
> —JOANNA BAILLIE, *Basil*

Where life is more terrible than death, it is then the truest valor to dare to live. —THOMAS BROWNE, *Religio Medici*

Courage is almost a contradiction in terms. It means a strong desire to live taking the form of a readiness to die. —G.K. CHESTERTON, *Orthodoxy*

To see what is right and not to do it is want of courage. —CONFUCIUS, *Analects*

None but the brave deserves the fair. —JOHN DRYDEN, "Alexander's Feast"

Courage is the price that life exacts for granting peace. —AMELIA EARHART, "Courage"

[by "guts" I mean] grace under pressure. —ERNEST HEMINGWAY, quoted in *New Yorker*

It is better to die on your feet than to live on your knees. —DOLORES IBARRURI, speech (1936)
  [Sometimes attributed to Emiliano Zapata]

Perfect courage is to do without witnesses what one would be capable of doing before all the world. —LA ROCHEFOUCAULD, *Maxims*

Fighting is like champagne. It goes to the heads of cowards as quickly as of heroes. Any fool can be brave on a battlefield when it's be brave or else be killed. —MARGARET MITCHELL, *Gone with the Wind*

Life shrinks or expands in proportion to one's courage. —ANAÏS NIN, diary entry (*The Diary of Anaïs Nin*)

Courage mounteth with occasion. —SHAKESPEARE, *King John*

  But screw your courage to the sticking-place,
  And we'll not fail.
                              —SHAKESPEARE, *Macbeth*

Courage, the footstool of the Virtues, upon which they stand. —ROBERT LOUIS STEVENSON, "The Great North Road"

Fortune favors the brave. —TERENCE, *Phormio*
  [This appears in the works of several ancient writers, including Cicero. See also Virgil, under Boldness and Enterprise, for a very similar thought.]

Courage is resistance to fear, mastery of fear—not absence of fear. —MARK TWAIN, *Pudd'nhead Wilson*, "Pudd'nhead Wilson's Calendar"

Courtesy — See MANNERS

Cowardice

Many would be cowards if they had courage enough. —THOMAS FULLER, *Gnomologia*

> [Stated more strongly by John Wilmot, Earl of Rochester: "For all men would be cowards if they durst."—*A Satyr Against Mankind*.]

Cowardice, as distinguished from panic, is almost always simply a lack of ability to suspend the functioning of the imagination. —ERNEST HEMINGWAY, *Men at War*

It is thus that mutual cowardice keeps us in peace. Were one half of mankind brave, and one half cowards, the brave would be always beating the cowards. Were all brave, they would lead a very uneasy life; all would be continually fighting: but being all cowards, we go on very well. —SAMUEL JOHNSON, quoted in James Boswell's *The Life of Samuel Johnson*

Fear even when morbid is not cowardice. That is the label we reserve for something that a man does. What passes through his mind is his own affair. —LORD MORAN, *The Anatomy of Courage*

> Cowards die many times before their deaths;
> The valiant never taste of death but once.
> —SHAKESPEARE, *Julius Caesar*

Craftiness

The fox has many tricks, and the hedgehog only one, but that is the best of all. —ARCHILOCHUS (fragment)

Nothing doth more hurt in a state than that cunning men pass for wise. —FRANCIS BACON, *Essays*

"Frank and explicit;" that is the right line to take when you wish to conceal your own mind and to confuse the minds of others. —BENJAMIN DISRAELI, *Sybil*

Every man wishes to be wise, and they who cannot be wise are almost always cunning. —SAMUEL JOHNSON, *The Idler*

No man is so much a fool as not to have wit enough sometimes to be a knave; nor any so cunning a knave as not to have the weakness sometimes to play the fool. —GEORGE SAVILE, *Political, Moral and Miscellaneous Thoughts and Reflections*

Creation and Creativity

All things bright and beautiful,
All creatures great and small,
All things wise and wonderful,
The Lord God made them all.
—MRS. CECIL FRANCES ALEXANDER, "All
Things Bright"

Every animal leaves traces of what it was; man alone leaves traces of what he created. —JACOB BRONOWSKI, *The Ascent of Man*

GABRIEL: How about cleanin' up de whole mess of 'em and sta'tin' all over ag'in wid some new kind of animal?
GOD: An' admit I'm licked?
—MARCUS COOK CONNELLY, *The Green
Pastures*

Think before you speak is criticism's motto; speak before you think creation's. —E.M. FORSTER, *Two Cheers for Democracy*

79

In creating, the only hard thing's to begin;
A grass-blade's no easier to make than an oak.
—JAMES RUSSELL LOWELL, "A Fable for
Critics"

Nothing can be created out of nothing. —LUCRETIUS,
De Rerum Natura

We live at a time when man believes himself fabulously capable of creation, but does not know what to create. Lord of all things, he is not lord of himself.
—JOSÉ ORTEGA Y GASSET, *The Revolt of the Masses*

Crime

Murder will out, certain, it will not fail. —CHAUCER,
The Canterbury Tales

> [Chaucer also used the proverb "murder will out"
> in another of the *Canterbury Tales*. Shakespeare
> expressed this idea in several plays, including
> *Hamlet*:
>> For murder, though it have no tongue, will
>> speak
>> With most miraculous organ.]

Thieves respect property. They merely wish the property to become their property that they may more perfectly respect it. —G.K. CHESTERTON, *The Man who was Thursday*

Everybody is a potential murderer. I've never killed anyone, but I frequently get satisfaction reading the obituary notices. —CLARENCE DARROW, quoted in *New York Times Magazine*

Singularity is almost invariably a clue. The more featureless and commonplace a crime is, the more difficult is it to bring it home. —ARTHUR CONAN DOYLE, *The Adventures of Sherlock Holmes*

There is no den in the wide world to hide a rogue. . . .
Commit a crime, and the earth is made of glass.
—RALPH WALDO EMERSON, *Essays*

Crimes, like virtues, are their own rewards.
—GEORGE FARQUHAR, *The Inconstant*

> As some day it may happen that a victim must
>   be found,
>   I've got a little list, I've got a little list
> Of society offenders who might well be
>   underground
>   And who never would be missed, who never
>   would be missed!
>   —W.S. GILBERT, *The Mikado*

What man was ever content with one crime? —JUVE-
NAL, *Satires*

> One murder made a villain,
>   Millions a hero.
>   —BEILBY PORTEUS, "Death"

Successful and fortunate crime is called virtue.
—SENECA, *Hercules Furens*

The robb'd that smiles steals something from the
thief. —SHAKESPEARE, *Othello*

I came to the conclusion many years ago that almost
all crime is due to the repressed desire for aesthetic
expression. —EVELYN WAUGH, *Decline and Fall*

Crisis and Upheaval

> In the nightmare of the dark
> All the dogs of Europe bark,
> And the living nations wait,
> Each sequestered in its hate.
>   —W.H. AUDEN, "In Memory of W.B.
>   Yeats"

It was the best of times, it was the worst of times, it
was the age of wisdom, it was the age of foolishness,

it was the epoch of belief, it was the epoch of incredulity, it was the season of Light, it was the season of Darkness, it was the spring of hope, it was the winter of despair, we had everything before us, we had nothing before us, we were all going direct to Heaven, we were all going direct the other way. —CHARLES DICKENS, *A Tale of Two Cities*

When written in Chinese the word *crisis* is composed of two characters. One represents danger and the other represents opportunity. —JOHN F. KENNEDY, speech (1959)

If you can keep your head when all about you are losing theirs, it's just possible you haven't grasped the situation. —JEAN KERR, *Please Don't Eat the Daisies*

These are the times that try men's souls. The summer soldier and the sunshine patriot will, in this crisis, shrink from the service of their country; but he that stands it *now*, deserves the love and thanks of man and woman. —THOMAS PAINE, "The American Crisis"

After us the deluge. (*Après nous le déluge.*)
—MADAME DE POMPADOUR, attributed (comment reportedly made after the defeat of the French by Frederick the Great at Rossbach)
[This was a proverbial saying in French, already in existence at the time.]

Things fall apart; the center cannot hold;
Mere anarchy is loosed upon the world,
The blood-dimmed tide is loosed, and
    everywhere
The ceremony of innocence is drowned;
The best lack all conviction, while the worst
Are full of passionate intensity.
     —W.B. YEATS, "The Second Coming"

Criticism and Critics

To be a critic, you have to have maybe three percent education, five percent intelligence, two percent style, and ninety percent gall and egomania in equal parts. —JUDITH CRIST, quoted in John Robert Colombo's *Popcorn in Paradise*

A man is a critic when he cannot be an artist, in the same way that a man becomes an informer when he cannot be a soldier. —GUSTAVE FLAUBERT, letter (1846)

The good critic is he who relates the adventures of his soul among masterpieces. —ANATOLE FRANCE, *La Vie littéraire*

You *may* abuse a tragedy, though you cannot write one. You may scold a carpenter who has made you a bad table, though you cannot make a table. It is not your trade to make tables. —SAMUEL JOHNSON, quoted in James Boswell's *The Life of Samuel Johnson*

The pleasure of criticizing robs us of the pleasure of being moved by some very fine things. —LA BRUYÈRE, *Les Caractères*

> Nature fits all her children with something to
>   do,
> He who would write and can't write, can
>   surely review.
>   —JAMES RUSSELL LOWELL, "A Fable for
>   Critics"

> You puff the poets of other days,
> The living you deplore.
> Spare me the accolade: your praise
> Is not worth dying for.
>   —MARTIAL, *Epigrams*

83

People ask you for criticism, but they only want praise. —W. SOMERSET MAUGHAM, *Of Human Bondage*

> Damn with faint praise, assent with civil leer,
> And without sneering, teach the rest to sneer;
> Willing to wound, and yet afraid to strike,
> Just hint a fault, and hesitate dislike.
> —ALEXANDER POPE, *Epistle to Dr. Arbuthnot*

Works of art are of an infinite loneliness and with nothing so little to be reached as with criticism. Only love can grasp and hold and be just toward them. —RAINER MARIA RILKE, *Letters to a Young Poet*

Never pay attention to what critics say. Remember, a statue has never been set up in honor of a critic. —JEAN SIBELIUS, quoted in *Sibelius: A Close-Up* by Bengt de Törne

Interpretation is the revenge of the intellect upon art. —SUSAN SONTAG, *Against Interpretation*

A critic is a man who knows the way but can't drive the car. —KENNETH TYNAN, in *New York Times Magazine*

Crowds

You cannot make a man by standing a sheep on its hind-legs. But by standing a flock of sheep in that position you can make a crowd of men. —MAX BEERBOHM, *Zuleika Dobson*

If it has to choose who is to be crucified, the crowd will always save Barabbas. —JEAN COCTEAU, *Cock and Harlequin*

84

"It's always best on these occasions to do what the mob do."

"But suppose there are two mobs?" suggested Mr. Snodgrass.

"Shout with the largest," replied Mr. Pickwick.
　　　　　　　—CHARLES DICKENS, *Pickwick Papers*

The best university that can be recommended to a man of ideas is the gauntlet of the mob. —RALPH WALDO EMERSON, *Society and Solitude*

The mob has many heads, but no brains. —THOMAS FULLER, *Gnomologia*

Every one in a crowd has the power to throw dirt: nine out of ten have the inclination. —WILLIAM HAZLITT, "On Reading New Books"

Every man has a mob self and an individual self, in varying proportions. —D.H. LAWRENCE, *Pornography and Obscenity*

Cruelty

The wish to hurt, the momentary intoxication with pain, is the loophole through which the pervert climbs into the minds of ordinary men. —JACOB BRONOWSKI, *The Face of Violence*

Man's inhumanity to man
　Makes countless thousands mourn!
　　　　　　　—ROBERT BURNS, "Man was Made
　　　　　　　　　　　　to Mourn"

Cruelty is a tyrant that's always attended with fear.
—THOMAS FULLER, *Gnomologia*

Cruelty is the law pervading all nature and society; and we can't get out of it if we would. —THOMAS HARDY, *Jude the Obscure*

Scarcely anything awakens attention like a tale of cruelty. The writer of news never fails . . . to tell how the enemies murdered children and ravished virgins; and, if the scene of action be somewhat distant, scalps half the inhabitants of a province. —SAMUEL JOHNSON, *The Idler*

Cruelty is fed, not weakened, by tears. —PUBLILIUS SYRUS, *Maxims*

Culture

Culture has one great passion—the passion for sweetness and light. It has one even yet greater, the passion for making them *prevail.* —MATTHEW ARNOLD, *Culture and Anarchy*

> [Arnold borrowed the phrase "sweetness and light" from Jonathan Swift, who used it in *The Battle of the Books.*]

The great law of culture is: Let each become all that he was created capable of being. —THOMAS CARLYLE, *Critical and Miscellaneous Essays*

Culture is one thing, and varnish another. —RALPH WALDO EMERSON, *Journals*

One ought every day at least, to hear a little song, read a good poem, see a fine picture, and, if it were possible, to speak a few reasonable words. —JOHANN WOLFGANG VON GOETHE, *Wilhelm Meister's Apprenticeship*

When I hear the word *culture* . . . I release the safety-catch of my Browning. —HANNS JOHST, *Schlageter*

> [Often quoted as ". . . I reach for my revolver," and often attributed to Hermann Göring.]

Culture is on the horns of this dilemma: if profound and noble it must remain rare, if common it must become mean. —GEORGE SANTAYANA, *The Life of Reason*

Culture is an instrument wielded by professors to manufacture professors, who when their turn comes will manufacture professors. —SIMONE WEIL, *The Need for Roots*

Mrs. Ballinger is one of the ladies who pursue Culture in bands, as though it were dangerous to meet it alone. —EDITH WHARTON, "Xingu"

Cunning — See CRAFTINESS

Curiosity

Remember Lot's wife. —BIBLE, *Luke* 17:32

Be not curious in unnecessary matters: for more things are shewed unto thee than men understand. —BIBLE, *Ecclesiasticus* 3:23

Curiosity is, in great and generous minds, the first passion and the last. —SAMUEL JOHNSON, *The Rambler*

Curiosity is only vanity. Most frequently we wish not to know, but to talk. We would not take a sea voyage for the sole pleasure of seeing without hope of ever telling. —BLAISE PASCAL, *Pensées*

Curiosity is a willing, a proud, an eager confession of ignorance. —S. LEONARD RUBINSTEIN, quoted in *Reader's Digest*

Curiosity will conquer fear even more than bravery will. —JAMES STEPHENS, *The Crock of Gold*

Disinterested intellectual curiosity is the life-blood of real civilization. —G.M. TREVELYAN, *English Social History*

Custom and Tradition

What custom hath endeared
We part with sadly, though we prize it not.
—JOANNA BAILLIE, *Basil*

Custom reconciles us to everything. —EDMUND BURKE, *On the Sublime and Beautiful*

Tradition may be defined as an extension of the franchise. Tradition means giving votes to the most obscure of all classes, our ancestors. It is the democracy of the dead.
—G.K. CHESTERTON, *Orthodoxy*

Oh, the times! Oh, the customs! (*O tempora! O mores!*) —CICERO, *In Catilinam*

[Sometimes translated with *manners* in place of *customs*.]

A precedent embalms a principle. —BENJAMIN DISRAELI, speech (1848)

[This has also been attributed to William Scott (Lord Stowell).]

Tradition becomes our security, and when the mind is secure it is in decay. —KRISHNAMURTI, "The Only Revolution: India"

Custom has furnished the only basis which ethics have ever had, and there is no conceivable human action which custom has not at one time justified and at another condemned. —JOSEPH WOOD KRUTCH, *The Modern Temper*

We are all convention; convention carries us away, and we neglect the substance of things. . . . We dare not call our parts by their right names, but are not afraid to use them for every sort of debauchery.
—MICHEL DE MONTAIGNE, *Essays*

We are more sensible of what is done against custom than against nature. —PLUTARCH, *Morals*

But to my mind, though I am native here
And to the manner born, it is a custom
More honor'd in the breach than the
    observance.
—SHAKESPEARE, *Hamlet*

Cynicism

A cynic is not merely one who reads bitter lessons from the past; he is one who is prematurely disappointed in the future. —SYDNEY J. HARRIS, *On the Contrary*

Cynicism is an unpleasant way of saying the truth. —LILLIAN HELLMAN, *The Little Foxes*

Cynicism is intellectual dandyism. —GEORGE MEREDITH, *The Egoist*

The worst cynicism: a belief in luck. —JOYCE CAROL OATES, *Do with Me What You Will*

What is a cynic? A man who knows the price of everything, and the value of nothing. —OSCAR WILDE, *Lady Windermere's Fan*

Dance

The truest expression of a people is in its dances and its music. . . . Bodies never lie. —AGNES DE MILLE, in *New York Times Magazine*

The poetry of the foot. —JOHN DRYDEN, *The Rival Ladies*

Dance is the hidden language of the soul, of the body. —MARTHA GRAHAM, quoted in *New York Times*

> Come and trip it as ye go,
> On the light fantastic toe.
> —JOHN MILTON, *L'Allegro*

Dancing is a perpendicular expression of a horizontal desire. —GEORGE BERNARD SHAW, attributed

Dance is the only art of which we ourselves are the stuff of which it is made. —TED SHAWN, quoted in *Time*

O body swayed to music, O brightening
   glance,
How can we know the dancer from the dance?
      —W.B. YEATS, "Among School Children"

Danger

Dangers by being despised grow great. —EDMUND
BURKE, speech (1792)

Nothing in life is so exhilarating as to be shot at without result. —WINSTON CHURCHILL, *The Story of the Malakand Field Force*

 [Ronald Reagan alluded to Churchill's comment after an attempt was made on Reagan's life in 1981.]

We triumph without glory when we conquer without danger. —PIERRE CORNEILLE, *Le Cid*

Believe me, the secret of the greatest fruitfulness and the greatest enjoyment of existence is: to *live dangerously!* —FRIEDRICH NIETZSCHE, *The Joyful Wisdom* (also known as *The Gay Science*)

There is no person who is not dangerous for someone. —MARIE DE SÉVIGNÉ, letter

Out of this nettle, danger, we pluck this flower, safety. —SHAKESPEARE, *Henry IV, Part I*

Daring — See BOLDNESS AND ENTERPRISE

Day — See TIMES OF DAY

Death

Men fear Death, as children fear to go in the dark; and as that natural fear in children is increased with tales, so is the other. —FRANCIS BACON, *Essays*

To die will be an awfully big adventure. —JAMES M. BARRIE, *Peter Pan*

For dust thou art, and unto dust thou shalt return. —BIBLE, *Genesis* 3:19

And I looked, and behold, a pale horse: and his name that sat on him was Death. —BIBLE, *Revelation* 6:8

O death, where is thy sting? O grave, where is thy victory? —BIBLE, *I Corinthians* 15:55

The long habit of living indisposeth us for dying. —THOMAS BROWNE, *Urn Burial*

> Even throughout life, 'tis death that makes life
>   live,
> Gives it whatever the significance.
> > —ROBERT BROWNING, *The Ring*
> >   *and the Book*

> Because I could not stop for Death,
> He kindly stopped for me—
> The Carriage held but just Ourselves
> And Immortality.
> > —EMILY DICKINSON, "Because I could not
> >   stop for Death"

> Death be not proud, though some have called
>   thee
> Mighty and dreadful, for thou art not so,
> For those whom thou think'st thou dost
>   overthrow,
> Die not, poor death, nor yet canst thou kill
>   me.
> > —JOHN DONNE, *Holy Sonnets*

> Death, in itself, is nothing; but we fear
> To be we know not what, we know not where.
> > —JOHN DRYDEN, *Aureng-Zebe*

It hath been often said, that it is not death, but dying, which is terrible. —HENRY FIELDING, *Amelia*

Depend upon it, Sir, when a man knows he is to be hanged in a fortnight, it concentrates his mind wonderfully. —SAMUEL JOHNSON, quoted in James Boswell's *The Life of Samuel Johnson*

A man's dying is more the survivors' affair than his own. —THOMAS MANN, *The Magic Mountain*

> The grave's a fine and private place,
> But none, I think, do there embrace.
> > —ANDREW MARVELL, "To His
> > Coy Mistress"

Death has a thousand doors to let out life: I shall find one. —PHILIP MASSINGER, *A Very Young Woman*

> [Other writers have used this image. See, for example, Seneca, in this section.]

Whom the gods love dies young. —MENANDER, *Dis Exapaton*

> [Plautus used this in *Bacchides*, noting one of the advantages of an early death: "He whom the gods love dies young, while he has his strength and senses and wits."]

One should part from life as Odysseus parted from Nausicaa: with a blessing rather than in love. —FRIEDRICH NIETZSCHE, *Beyond Good and Evil*

> It costs me never a stab nor squirm
> To tread by chance upon a worm.
> "Aha, my little dear," I say,
> "Your clan will pay me back one day."
> > —DOROTHY PARKER, "Thought for a
> > Sunshiny Morning"

> Dying
> Is an art, like everything else.
> I do it exceptionally well.
> > —SYLVIA PLATH, "Lady Lazarus"

I am going to seek a great perhaps. —FRANÇOIS RABELAIS, reputed last words

> When I am dead, my dearest,
>   Sing no sad songs for me.
>   —CHRISTINA ROSSETTI, "Song"

Death is an evil; the gods have so judged; had it been good, they would die. —SAPPHO (fragment)

> I have a rendezvous with Death
> At some disputed barricade,
> When Spring comes back with rustling shade
> And apple blossoms fill the air.
>   —ALAN SEEGER, "I Have a Rendezvous
>   with Death"

Anyone can stop a man's life, but no one his death; a thousand doors open on to it. —SENECA, *Phoenissae*

> Death is the veil which those who live call life;
> They sleep, and it is lifted.
>   —PERCY BYSSHE SHELLEY, *Prometheus
>   Unbound*

> Here he lies where he long'd to be;
> Home is the sailor, home from sea,
>   And the hunter home from the hill.
>   —ROBERT LOUIS STEVENSON, "Requiem"

> Sunset and evening star,
>   And one clear call for me!
> And may there be no moaning of the bar,
>   When I put out to sea.
>   —ALFRED, LORD TENNYSON,
>   "Crossing the Bar"

> Do not go gentle into that good night,
> Old age should burn and rave at close of day;
> Rage, rage against the dying of the light.
>   —DYLAN THOMAS, "Do Not Go Gentle into
>   that Good Night"

The report of my death was an exaggeration. —MARK TWAIN, cable from London to a New York newspaper

[Often quoted as "Reports of my death are greatly exaggerated."]

The good die first,
And they whose hearts are dry as summer
    dust
Burn to the socket.
> —WILLIAM WORDSWORTH, *The Excursion*

Debt — See BORROWING AND LENDING

Deception and Fraud

Full of wiles, full of guile, at all times, in all
    ways,
Are the children of Men.
> —ARISTOPHANES, *The Birds*

'Tis my opinion every man cheats in his way, and he is only honest who is not discovered. —SUSANNAH CENTLIVRE, *The Artifice*

Thou shalt not steal; an empty feat,
When it's so lucrative to cheat.
> —ARTHUR HUGH CLOUGH, "The Latest
>   Decalogue"

No man, for any considerable period, can wear one face to himself, and another to the multitude, without finally getting bewildered as to which may be the true. —NATHANIEL HAWTHORNE, *The Scarlet Letter*

It is a double pleasure to deceive the deceiver.
—JEAN DE LA FONTAINE, *Fables*

You may fool all the people some of the time; you can even fool some of the people all the time; but you can't fool all of the people all the time. —ABRAHAM LINCOLN, attributed

[Although this is one of the most frequently quoted remarks attributed to Lincoln, it has never been found in his writings. It appears in Alexander K. McClure's *"Abe" Lincoln's Yarns and Stories*, published in 1904. It has also sometimes been attributed to P.T. Barnum.]

Everything that deceives may be said to enchant.
—PLATO, *The Republic*

That which deceives us and does us harm, also undeceives us and does us good. —JOSEPH ROUX, *Meditations of a Parish Priest*

Oh, what a tangled web we weave,
When first we practice to deceive!
—SIR WALTER SCOTT, *Marmion*

Decision

It is the advantage and the nature of the strong that they can bring crucial issues to the fore and take a clear position regarding them. The weak always have to choose between alternatives that are not their own.
—DIETRICH BONHOEFFER, *Letters and Papers from Prison*

The die is cast. —JULIUS CAESAR, quoted by Suetonius in *Lives of the Caesars*

[Said by Julius Caesar upon deciding to cross the Rubicon from Gaul into Italy to march against Pompey.]

If someone tells you he is going to make a "realistic decision," you immediately understand that he has resolved to do something bad. —MARY McCARTHY, *On the Contrary*

To live is to feel ourselves *fatally* obliged to exercise our *liberty*, to decide what we are going to be in this world. Not for a single moment is our activity of decision allowed to rest. —JOSÉ ORTEGA Y GASSET, *The Revolt of the Masses*

It is always thus, impelled by a state of mind which is destined not to last, that we make our irrevocable decisions. —MARCEL PROUST, *Remembrance of Things Past: Within a Budding Grove*

Deeds — See ACHIEVEMENT

Defeat — See VICTORY AND DEFEAT

Democracy

Remember, democracy never lasts long. It soon wastes, exhausts, and murders itself. There never was a democracy yet that did not commit suicide. —JOHN ADAMS, letter (1814)

Democracy means despair of finding any heroes to govern you, and contented putting up with the want of them. —THOMAS CARLYLE, *Past and Present*

No one pretends that democracy is perfect or all-wise. Indeed, it has been said that democracy is the worst form of government except all those other forms that have been tried from time to time. —WINSTON CHURCHILL, speech (1947)

> I swear to the Lord
>   I still can't see
> Why Democracy means
>   Everybody but me.
>   —LANGSTON HUGHES, "The Black
>   Man Speaks"

. . . government of the people, by the people, for the people, shall not perish from the earth. —ABRAHAM LINCOLN, speech (address at Gettysburg, 1863)

[Lincoln's famous description of democracy echoed earlier speakers, including Daniel Webster, in a speech in 1830: ". . . the people's government made for the people, made by the people, and answerable to the people," and Theodore Parker, also in a speech (1850): "A democracy—that is, a government of all the people, by all the people, for all the people."]

Among free men there can be no successful appeal from the ballot to the bullet. —ABRAHAM LINCOLN, letter (1863)

[Lincoln is sometimes quoted as having said "The ballot is stronger than the bullet," in a speech in 1856, but there does not seem to be any contemporary record to substantiate this.]

Democracy is the theory that the common people know what they want, and deserve to get it good and hard. —H.L. MENCKEN, *A Little Book in C Major*

Man's capacity for justice makes democracy possible, but man's inclination to injustice makes democracy necessary. —REINHOLD NIEBUHR, *The Children of Light and the Children of Darkness*

Democracy . . . is a charming form of government, full of variety and disorder, and dispensing a sort of equality to equals and unequals alike. —PLATO, *The Republic*

Democracy substitutes election by the incompetent many for appointment by the corrupt few. —GEORGE BERNARD SHAW, *Man and Superman*, "The Revolutionist's Handbook"

All the ills of democracy can be cured by more democracy. —ALFRED E. SMITH, speech (1933)

It's not the voting that's democracy; it's the counting. —TOM STOPPARD, *Jumpers*

People who want to understand democracy should spend less time in the library with Aristotle and more time on the buses and in the subway. —SIMEON STRUNSKY, *No Mean City*

Democracy is the recurrent suspicion that more than half of the people are right more than half of the time. —E.B. WHITE, in *New Yorker*

The world must be made safe for democracy. —WOODROW WILSON, speech (to Congress, seeking a declaration of war, 1917)

Depression — See DESPAIR

Desire

Modern man lives under the illusion that he knows what he wants, while he actually wants what he is supposed to want. —ERICH FROMM, *Escape from Freedom*

> Man wants but little here below,
> Nor wants that little long.
> —OLIVER GOLDSMITH, *The Vicar of Wakefield*

> [Edward Young had said this, in 1742: "Man wants but little; nor that little, long."—*Night Thoughts on Life, Death, and Immortality*.]

A short cut to riches is to subtract from our desires. —PETRARCH, *Epistolae de Rebus Familiaribus*

> [Jonathan Swift observed, in *Thoughts on Various Subjects*: "The stoical scheme of supplying our wants by lopping off our desires, is like cutting off our feet, when we want shoes."]

As long as I have a want, I have a reason for living. Satisfaction is death. —GEORGE BERNARD SHAW, *Overruled*

Desire is the very essence of man. —BENEDICT DE SPINOZA, *Ethics*

An aspiration is a joy for ever, a possession as solid as a landed estate. —ROBERT LOUIS STEVENSON, *Virginibus Puerisque*

> In this world there are only two tragedies. One
> is not getting what one wants, and the
> other is getting it.
> —OSCAR WILDE, *Lady Windermere's Fan*

[Others have made similar observations. George Bernard Shaw, in fact used almost the same words in his play *Man and Superman*: "There are two tragedies in life. One is not to get your heart's desire. The other is to get it." See also Vanbrugh, under Possessions and Property]

Despair

> And we are here as on a darkling plain
> Swept with confused alarms of struggle and
>   flight,
> Where ignorant armies clash by night.
>   —MATTHEW ARNOLD, "Dover Beach"

Abandon all hope, ye who enter here! —DANTE, *The Divine Comedy*

[These words are inscribed over the gates of Hell.]

But what we call our despair is often only the painful eagerness of unfed hope. —GEORGE ELIOT, *Middlemarch*

In a real dark night of the soul it is always three o'clock in the morning, day after day. —F. SCOTT FITZGERALD, in *Esquire*

["The Dark Night of the Soul" is the title of a 16th century work by St. John of the Cross.]

Despair is the price one pays for setting oneself an impossible aim. —GRAHAM GREENE, *The Heart of the Matter*

> I was much further out than you thought
> And not waving but drowning.
> —STEVIE SMITH, "Not Waving But Drowning"

The mass of men lead lives of quiet desperation. What is called resignation is confirmed desperation. —HENRY DAVID THOREAU, *Walden*

Destiny — See FATE

Determination

. . . resolved to take fate by the throat and shake a living out of her. —LOUISA MAY ALCOTT, quoted by Ednah D. Cheney in *Louisa May Alcott, Her Life, Letters, and Journals*

Let's meet, and either do or die. —JOHN FLETCHER, *The Island Princess*

> [Also in Robert Burns' "Scots Wha Hae":
>   Liberty's in every blow!
>   Let us do or die!]

I have not yet begun to fight. —JOHN PAUL JONES, reply to a demand by the British that he surrender when his ship, the *Bonhomme Richard*, was sinking (1779)

> He who breaks a resolution is a weakling;
> He who makes one is a fool.
> —F.M. KNOWLES, *A Cheerful Year Book*

> Let us, then, be up and doing,
>   With a heart for any fate;
> Still achieving, still pursuing,
>   Learn to labor and to wait.
> —HENRY WADSWORTH LONGFELLOW, "A Psalm of Life"

What though the field be lost?
All is not lost; the unconquerable Will,
And study of revenge, immortal hate,
And courage never to submit or yield:
And what else is not to be overcome?
—JOHN MILTON, *Paradise Lost*

The Devil — See also EVIL

The devil's most devilish when respectable. —ELIZABETH BARRETT BROWNING, *Aurora Leigh*

An Apology for the Devil: It must be remembered that we have only heard one side of the case. God has written all the books. —SAMUEL BUTLER (d 1902), *Note-Books*

Wherever God erects a house of prayer,
The Devil always builds a chapel there;
And 'twill be found, upon examination,
The latter has the largest congregation.
—DANIEL DEFOE, *The True-Born Englishman*

. . . if the devil does not exist, and man has therefore created him, he has created him in his own image and likeness. —FYODOR DOSTOYEVSKY, *The Brothers Karamozov*

It is stupid of modern civilization to have given up believing in the devil, when he is the only explanation of it. —RONALD KNOX, *Let Dons Delight*

The spirit that I have seen
May be the devil: and the devil hath power
To assume a pleasing shape.
—SHAKESPEARE, *Hamlet*

Dictators — See TYRANNY

Diplomacy

Diplomacy—The art of saying "Nice doggie" till you can find a rock. —WYNN CATLIN, attributed, by Bennett Cerf in *The Laugh's on Me*

All diplomacy is a continuation of war by other means. —CHOU EN-LAI, quoted in *Saturday Evening Post*

> [See Clausewitz, under War, for the statement on which this is based.]

To jaw-jaw is always better than to war-war. —WINSTON CHURCHILL, speech (1954)

> Diplomacy is to do and say
> The nastiest thing in the nicest way.
> —ISAAC GOLDBERG, in *The Reflex*

Let us never negotiate out of fear. But let us never fear to negotiate. —JOHN F. KENNEDY, speech (inaugural address, 1961)

[A Foreign Secretary] is forever poised between the cliché and the indiscretion. —HAROLD MACMILLAN, comment made in Parliament

A diplomat is a person who can tell you to go to hell in such a way that you actually look forward to the trip. —CASKIE STINNETT, *Out of the Red*

An ambassador is an honest man sent to lie abroad for the commonwealth. —HENRY WOTTON, written in the autograph album of Christopher Fleckmore (1604)

Disappointment

Nothing is so good as it seems beforehand.
—GEORGE ELIOT, *Silas Marner*

The mountains will be in labor, and a ridiculous mouse will be born. —HORACE, *Ars Poetica*

"Blessed is the man who expects nothing, for he shall never be disappointed" was the ninth beatitude.
—ALEXANDER POPE, letter (1725)

The pain of a disappointed wish necessarily produces less effect upon the mind if a man has not certainly promised himself success. —SENECA, *De Tranquillitate Animi*

> Oft expectation fails and most oft there
> Where most it promises, and oft it hits
> Where hope is coldest and despair most fits.
> —SHAKESPEARE, *All's Well*
> *That Ends Well*

Disaster

Calamity is man's true touchstone. —FRANCIS BEAUMONT AND JOHN FLETCHER, *Four Plays in One: The Triumph of Honor*

Calamities are of two kinds: misfortune to ourselves, and good fortune to others. —AMBROSE BIERCE, *The Devil's Dictionary*

Public calamity is a mighty leveller. —EDMUND BURKE, speech (1775)

The man does better who runs from disaster than he who is caught by it. —HOMER, *The Iliad*

Fate is not satisfied with inflicting one calamity. —PUBLILIUS SYRUS, *Maxims*

Discontent

> And sigh that one thing only has been lent
> To youth and age in common—discontent.
> —MATTHEW ARNOLD, "Youth's Agitations"

> Does he paint? he fain would write a poem,—
> Does he write?—he fain would paint a picture.
> —ROBERT BROWNING, "One Word More"

Let thy discontents be thy secrets;—if the world knows them 't will despise thee and increase them. —BENJAMIN FRANKLIN, *Poor Richard's Almanac*

> The idiot who praises, with enthusiastic tone,
> All centuries but this and every country but
>   his own.
>   —W.S. GILBERT, *The Mikado*

> Ever let the Fancy roam,
> Pleasure never is at home.
>   —JOHN KEATS, "Fancy"

"A cucumber is bitter." Throw it away. "There are briars in the road." Turn aside from them. This is enough. Do not add, "And why were such things made in the world?" —MARCUS AURELIUS, *Meditations*

> The splendid discontent of God
>   With Chaos, made the world; . . .
> And from the discontent of man
>   The world's best progress springs.
>   —ELLA WHEELER WILCOX, "Discontent"

[Oscar Wilde also saw discontent as a spur to progress. In *A Woman of No Importance*, he wrote: "Discontent is the first step in the progress of a man or a nation."]

Discovery — See INVENTION AND DISCOVERY

Disease — See ILLNESS

Dishonesty — See DECEPTION AND FRAUD; LYING AND LIARS

Dislike — See HATRED AND DISLIKE

Divorce — See also MARRIAGE

So many persons think divorce a panacea for every ill, who find out, when they try it, that the remedy is worse than the disease. —DOROTHY DIX, *Dorothy Dix, Her Book*

Alimony—The ransom that the happy pay to the devil. —H.L. MENCKEN, *A Mencken Chrestomathy*

Judges, as a class, display, in the matter of arranging alimony, that reckless generosity that is found only in men who are giving away somebody else's cash. —P.G. WODEHOUSE, *Louder and Funnier*

Doctors — See MEDICINE AND DOCTORS

Dogs — See ANIMALS

Doubt and Skepticism

O thou of little faith, wherefore didst thou doubt? —BIBLE, *Matthew* 14:31

> All we have gained then by our unbelief
> Is a life of doubt diversified by faith,
> For one of faith diversified by doubt:
> We called the chess-board white,—we call it
> black.
> —ROBERT BROWNING, "Bishop
Blougram's Apology"

If you would be a real seeker after truth, it is necessary that at least once in your life you doubt, as far as possible, all things. —RENÉ DESCARTES, *Principles of Philosophy*

The first step towards philosophy is incredulity. —DENIS DIDEROT, attributed (last words)

Doubt grows with knowledge. —JOHANN WOLFGANG VON GOETHE, *Proverbs in Prose*

> Modest doubt is call'd
> The beacon of the wise.
> —SHAKESPEARE, *Troilus and Cressida*

Our doubts are traitors
And make us lose the good we oft might win
By fearing to attempt.
   —SHAKESPEARE, *Measure for Measure*

There lives more faith in honest doubt,
Believe me, than in half the creeds.
   —ALFRED, LORD TENNYSON, *In Memoriam*

Life is doubt,
And faith without doubt is nothing but death.
   —MIGUEL DE UNAMUNO, "Salmo II"

Dreams and Dreamers

If there were dreams to sell,
What would you buy?
   —THOMAS LOVELL BEDDOES, "Dream-
         Pedlary"

All the things one has forgotten scream for help in dreams. —ELIAS CANETTI, *The Human Province*

Dreaming permits each and every one of us to be quietly and safely insane every night of our lives.
—CHARLES FISHER, in *Newsweek*

Only the dreamer shall understand realities, though, in truth, his dreaming must not be out of proportion to his waking! —MARGARET FULLER, *Summer on the Lakes*

We are not hypocrites in our sleep. —WILLIAM HAZLITT, "On Dreams"

What happens to a dream deferred?
Does it dry up
like a raisin in the sun?
Or fester like a sore—
And then run?
 . . . .
Or does it explode?
   —LANGSTON HUGHES, "Harlem"

All men dream: but not equally. Those who dream by night in the dusty recesses of their minds wake in the day to find that it was vanity: but the dreamers of the day are dangerous men, for they may act their dreams with open eyes, to make it possible. —T.E. LAWRENCE, *Seven Pillars of Wisdom*

The republic is a dream.
Nothing happens unless first a dream.
      —CARL SANDBURG, "Washington
                    Monument by Night"

In a dream you are never eighty. —ANNE SEXTON, "Old"

Dreams are true while they last, and do we not live in dreams? —ALFRED, LORD TENNYSON, "The Higher Pantheism"

In dreams begins responsibility. —W.B. YEATS, *Responsibilities*

Dress — See CLOTHING; FASHION

Drinking

If all be true that I do think,
There are five reasons we should drink:
Good wine—a friend—or being dry—
Or lest we should be by and by—
Or any other reason why.
      —HENRY ALDRICH, "Five Reasons for
                    Drinking"

No animal ever invented anything so bad as drunkenness—or so good as drink. —G.K. CHESTERTON, *All Things Considered*

I have taken more out of alcohol than alcohol has taken out of me. —WINSTON CHURCHILL, quoted in Quentin Reynolds' *By Quentin Reynolds*

Then trust me there's nothing like drinking,
  So pleasant on this side of the grave:
It keeps the unhappy from thinking,
  And makes e'en the valiant more brave.
      —CHARLES DIBDIN, "Nothing Like Grog"

I always keep a supply of stimulant handy in case I see a snake—which I also keep handy. —W.C. FIELDS, quoted in Corey Ford's *Time of Laughter*

YESTERDAY *This* Day's Madness did prepare;
TOMORROW'S Silence, Triumph, or Despair:
  Drink! for you know not whence you came,
    nor why:
Drink! for you know not why you go, nor
    where.
      —EDWARD FITZGERALD, *The Rubáiyát of
                  Omar Khayyám*

Drink today, and drown all sorrow;
You shall perhaps not do it tomorrow; Best,
  while you have it, use your breath;
There is no drinking after death.
      —JOHN FLETCHER, PHILIP MASSINGER, BEN
          JONSON, AND GEORGE CHAPMAN, *The
                  Bloody Brother*

It is better to hide ignorance, but it is hard to do this when we relax over wine. —HERACLITUS (fragment)

And malt does more than Milton can
To justify God's ways to man.
      —A.E. HOUSMAN, "Terence, this is
                stupid stuff:"
[The reference is to Milton's invocation in *Paradise Lost*:
  What in me is dark
  Illumine, what is low raise and support;
  That to the highth of this great Argument
  I may assert Eternal Providence,
  And justify the ways of God to men.]

If merely "feeling good" could decide, drunkenness would be the supremely valid human experience. —WILLIAM JAMES, *The Varieties of Religious Experience*

Claret is the liquor for boys; port for men; but he who aspires to be a hero must drink brandy. —SAMUEL JOHNSON, quoted in James Boswell's *The Life of Samuel Johnson*

Long quaffing maketh a short life. —JOHN LYLY, *Euphues*

Candy
Is dandy
But liquor
Is quicker.
        —OGDEN NASH, "Reflections on Ice-
                              breaking"

There are two reasons for drinking: one is, when you are thirsty, to cure it; the other, when you are not thirsty, to prevent it. —THOMAS LOVE PEACOCK, *Melincourt*

'Tis not the drinking that is to be blamed, but the excess. —JOHN SELDEN, *Table Talk*

Drunkenness is nothing but voluntary madness. —SENECA, *Epistulae ad Lucilium*

There are two things that will be believed of any man whatsoever, and one of them is that he has taken to drink. —BOOTH TARKINGTON, *Penrod*

Drugs

Cocaine habit-forming? Of course not. I ought to know. I've been using it for years. —TALLULAH BANKHEAD, *Tallulah*

OPIATE, *n.* An unlocked door in the prison of Identity. It leads into the jail yard. —AMBROSE BIERCE, *The Devil's Dictionary*

Thou hast the keys of Paradise, O just, subtle, and mighty opium! —THOMAS DE QUINCEY, *Confessions of an English Opium Eater*

If you take the game of life seriously, if you take your nervous system seriously, if you take your sense organs seriously, if you take the energy process seriously, you must turn on, tune in and drop out. —TIMOTHY LEARY, speech (1967)

What is dangerous about the tranquilizers is that whatever peace of mind they bring is a packaged peace of mind. Where you buy a pill and buy peace with it, you get conditioned to cheap solutions instead of deep ones. —MAX LERNER, *The Unfinished Country*

Drunkenness — See DRINKING

Duty and Responsibility

For unto whomsoever much is given, of him shall be much required. —BIBLE, *Luke* 12:48

> [John F. Kennedy paraphrased this in a speech in 1961: "For of those to whom much is given, much is required."]

Do your duty, and leave the rest to the gods. —PIERRE CORNEILLE, *Horace*

> So nigh is grandeur to our dust,
> So near is God to man,
> When Duty whispers low, *Thou must,*
> The youth replies, *I can.*
>   —RALPH WALDO EMERSON, "Voluntaries"

[Ogden Nash parodied this in "Kind of an Ode to Duty": "In the words of the poet, When Duty whispers low, Thou must, this erstwhile youth replies, I just can't."]

Duty largely consists of pretending that the trivial is critical. —JOHN FOWLES, *The Magus*

Man's responsibility increases as that of the gods decreases. —ANDRÉ GIDE, *Journals*

What, then, is your duty? What the day demands.
—JOHANN WOLFGANG VON GOETHE, *Proverbs in Prose*

> I slept, and dreamed that life was Beauty;
> I woke, and found that life was Duty.
> —ELLEN STURGIS HOOPER, "Beauty and
> Duty"

> O Duty,
> Why hast thou not the visage of a sweetie or a
> cutie?
> Why glitter thy spectacles so ominously?
> Why art thou clad so abominously?
> —OGDEN NASH, "Kind of an Ode to Duty"

I believe that every right implies a responsibility; every opportunity, an obligation; every possession, a duty. —JOHN D. ROCKEFELLER, JR., speech (1941)

To be a man is, precisely, to be responsible.
—ANTOINE DE SAINT-EXUPÉRY, *Wind, Sand, and Stars*

When a stupid man is doing something he is ashamed of, he always declares that it is his duty.
—GEORGE BERNARD SHAW, *Caesar and Cleopatra*

The Buck Stops Here —HARRY S TRUMAN, motto on his desk when President

Dying — See DEATH

Earth — See THE WORLD

Eating — See FOOD AND EATING

Economizing — See THRIFT

The Economy

If successful prediction were the sole criterion of the merit of a science, economics should long since have ceased to exist as a serious intellectual pursuit. Accurate prognosis is not its forte. The real strength of the discipline lies in another direction—namely in its apparently limitless capacity to rationalize events after they happen. —ROBERT W. CLOWER, in *Journal of Economic History*

Production only fills a void that it has itself created. —JOHN KENNETH GALBRAITH, *The Affluent Society*

The individual serves the industrial system not by supplying it with savings and the resulting capital; he serves it by consuming its products. —JOHN KENNETH GALBRAITH, *The New Industrial State*

The fundamental principle of human action—the law that is to political economy what the law of gravitation is to physics—is that men seek to gratify their desires with the least exertion. —HENRY GEORGE, *Progress and Poverty*

Inflation is like sin; every government denounces it and every government practices it. —FREDERICK LEITH-ROSS, quoted in *The Observer*

Labor is prior to, and independent of, capital. Capital is only the fruit of labor, and could never have existed if labor had not first existed. Labor is the superior of capital, and deserves much the higher consideration. —ABRAHAM LINCOLN, speech (1861)

No profit whatever can possibly be made but at the expense of another. . . . The Merchant only thrives, and grows rich, by the pride, wantonness and debauchery of youth; the husbandman by the price and scarcity of grain; the architect by the ruin of buildings; lawyers, and officers of Justice, by the suits and contentions of men; nay even the honor and office of Divines are derived from our death and vices. A physician takes no pleasure in the health even of his friends . . . nor a soldier in the peace of his country and so of the rest. —MICHEL DE MONTAIGNE, *Essays*

It's a recession when your neighbor loses his job; it's a depression when you lose your own. —HARRY S TRUMAN, quoted in *The Observer*

One man's wage rise is another man's price increase. —HAROLD WILSON, quoted in *The Observer*

Education — See also KNOWLEDGE AND LEARNING

Nothing in education is so astonishing as the amount of ignorance it accumulates in the form of inert facts. —HENRY ADAMS, *The Education of Henry Adams*

The roots of education are bitter, but the fruit is sweet. —ARISTOTLE, quoted by Diogenes Laertius in *Lives of the Philosophers*

The test and the use of man's education is that he finds pleasure in the exercise of his mind. —JACQUES BARZUN, in *Saturday Evening Post*

Education makes a people easy to lead, but difficult to drive; easy to govern, but impossible to enslave. —HENRY PETER BROUGHAM, BARON BROUGHAM AND VAUX, speech (1828)

"Reeling and Writhing, of course, to begin with," the Mock Turtle replied, "and then the different branches of Arithmetic—Ambition, Distraction, Uglification, and Derision." —LEWIS CARROLL, *Alice's Adventures in Wonderland*

Ye can lead a man up to the university, but ye can't make him think. —FINLEY PETER DUNNE, *Mr. Dooley's Opinions*

Only the educated are free. —EPICTETUS, *Discourses*

The purpose of education is to replace an empty mind with an open one. —MALCOLM FORBES, attributed, in Ann Landers' syndicated column

Education, then, beyond all other devices of human origin, is the great equalizer of the conditions of men,—the balance-wheel of the social machinery. —HORACE MANN, education report (1848)

I have long since abandoned the notion that higher education is essential to either success or happiness. Hothouses of learning do not always grow anything edible. —ROBERT MOSES, speech (1971)

'Tis Education forms the common mind,
Just as the Twig is bent, the Tree's inclin'd.
—ALEXANDER POPE, *Moral Essays*

In Examinations those who do not wish to know ask questions of those who cannot tell. —SIR WALTER RALEIGH, *Laughter from a Cloud*

Education is what survives when what has been learned has been forgotten. —B.F. SKINNER, in *New Scientist*

Education . . . has produced a vast population able to read but unable to distinguish what is worth reading. —G.M. TREVELYAN, *English Social History*

Education is an admirable thing, but it is well to remember from time to time that nothing that is worth knowing can be taught. —OSCAR WILDE, *Intentions*

Efficiency — See ORDER AND EFFICIENCY

Effort — See PERSEVERANCE AND EFFORT

Egotism — See CONCEIT, EGOTISM, AND VANITY

Emotion — See THE HEART AND EMOTION

Endings — See BEGINNINGS AND ENDINGS

Endurance — See also PATIENCE

The manner in which one endures what must be endured is more important than the thing that must be endured. —DEAN ACHESON, quoted by Merle Miller in *Plain Speaking*

> Endurance is the crowning quality,
> And patience all the passion of great hearts.
> —JAMES RUSSELL LOWELL, "Columbus"

Nothing happens to any man which he is not formed by nature to bear. —MARCUS AURELIUS, *Meditations*

> Does the road wind uphill all the way?
>   Yes, to the very end.
> Will the day's journey take the whole long day?
>   From morn to night, my friend.
> —CHRISTINA ROSSETTI, "Up-Hill"

Whatever it be, every fortune is to be overcome by bearing it. —VIRGIL, *Aeneid*

Enemies

The haft of the arrow had been feathered with one of the eagle's own plumes. We often give our enemies the means of our own destruction. —AESOP, *Fables*

115

He who has a thousand friends has not a
    friend to spare,
And he who has one enemy will meet him
    everywhere.
        —ALĪ IBN ABĪ ṬĀLIB, *A Hundred Sayings*

Pay attention to your enemies, for they are the first to discover your mistakes. —ANTISTHENES, quoted by Diogenes Laertius in *Lives of the Philosophers*

    [Others have also remarked on the wisdom of learning from one's enemies. See, for example, Baltasar Gracián, in this section.]

Call no man foe, but never love a stranger. —STELLA BENSON, "To the Unborn"

If thine enemy be hungry, give him bread to eat; and if he be thirsty, give him water to drink: For thou shalt heap coals of fire upon his head, and the Lord shall reward thee. —BIBLE, *Proverbs* 25:21–22

Love your enemies, bless them that curse you, do good to them that hate you, and pray for them which despitefully use you, and persecute you. —BIBLE, *Matthew* 5:44

Yet is every man his greatest enemy, and, as it were, his own executioner. —THOMAS BROWNE, *Religio Medici*

    [This idea dates back to ancient times. In *Epistolae Ad Atticum*, Cicero said of Julius Caesar: "He is his own worst enemy."]

You shall judge of a man by his foes as well as by his friends. —JOSEPH CONRAD, *Lord Jim*

There is no little enemy. —BENJAMIN FRANKLIN, *Poor Richard's Almanac*

If you have no enemies, it is a sign fortune has forgot you. —THOMAS FULLER, *Gnomologia*

[An earlier version: "It is an unhappy lot which finds no enemies."—Publilius Syrus, *Maxims*.]

A wise man gets more use from his enemies than a fool from his friends. —BALTASAR GRACIÁN, *The Art of Worldly Wisdom*

We have met the enemy and he is us. —WALT KELLY, comic strip *Pogo*

[Inspired by Oliver Perry's words, in this section.]

Even a paranoid can have enemies. —HENRY A. KISSINGER, quoted in *Time*

We have met the enemy and they are ours. —OLIVER HAZARD PERRY, military communique (1813)

He makes no friend who never made a foe. —ALFRED, LORD TENNYSON, *The Idylls of the King*

[Similarly: "He will never have true friends who is afraid of making enemies"—William Hazlitt, *Characteristics*.]

I have never made but one prayer to God, a very short one: "O Lord, make my enemies ridiculous." And God granted it. —VOLTAIRE, letter (1767)

A man cannot be too careful in the choice of his enemies. —OSCAR WILDE, *The Picture of Dorian Gray*

England and the English

Great Britain has lost an Empire and has not yet found a role. —DEAN ACHESON, speech (1962)

If I should die, think only this of me:
That there's some corner of a foreign field
That is for ever England.
—RUPERT BROOKE, "The Soldier"

Oh, to be in England
Now that April's there.
—ROBERT BROWNING, "Home-Thoughts,
from Abroad"

In England there are sixty different religions, and only one sauce. —DOMENICO CARACCIOLO, attributed

The maxim of the British people is "Business as usual." —WINSTON CHURCHILL, speech (1914)

England is the paradise of women, the purgatory of men, and the hell of horses. —JOHN FLORIO, *Second Frutes*

It is not that the Englishman can't feel—it is that he is afraid to feel. He has been taught at his public school that feeling is bad form. He must not express great joy or sorrow, or even open his mouth too wide when he talks—his pipe might fall out if he did. —E.M. FORSTER, *Arbinger Harvest*

An Englishman, even if he is alone, forms an orderly queue of one. —GEORGE MIKES, *How to be an Alien*

England is a nation of shopkeepers. —NAPOLEON I, quoted in Barry O'Meara's *Napoleon at St. Helena*
[Samuel Adams is also reputed to have called England a nation of shopkeepers, in a speech in 1776. Both may have been inspired by Adam Smith, who wrote in *The Wealth of Nations*: "To found a great empire for the sole purpose of raising up a people of customers, may at first sight appear a project fit only for a nation of shopkeepers. It is, however, a project altogether unfit for a nation of shopkeepers; but extremely fit for a nation whose government is influenced by shopkeepers."]

England is the paradise of individuality, eccentricity, heresy, anomalies, hobbies, and humors. —GEORGE SANTAYANA, *Soliloquies in England*

This royal throne of kings, this scepter'd isle,
This earth of majesty, this seat of Mars,
This other Eden, demi-paradise,
This fortress built by Nature for herself
Against infection and the hand of war,
This happy breed of men, this little world,
This precious stone set in the silver sea, . . .
This blessed plot, this earth, this realm, this
    England.
              —SHAKESPEARE, *Richard II*

An Englishman thinks he is moral when he is only uncomfortable. —GEORGE BERNARD SHAW, *Man and Superman*

There is nothing so bad or so good that you will not find an Englishman doing it; but you will never find an Englishman in the wrong. He does everything on principle. He fights you on patriotic principles; he robs you on business principles; he enslaves you on imperial principles. —GEORGE BERNARD SHAW, *The Man of Destiny*

The English have no respect for their language, and will not teach their children to speak it. . . . It is impossible for an Englishman to open his mouth, without making some other Englishman despise him. —GEORGE BERNARD SHAW, *Pygmalion*

What two ideas are more inseparable than Beer and Britannia? —SYDNEY SMITH, quoted in Hesketh Pearson's *The Smith of Smiths*

Enjoyment — See PLEASURE AND INDULGENCE

Enterprise — See BOLDNESS AND ENTERPRISE

Enthusiasm and Zeal

It is unfortunate, considering that enthusiasm moves the world, that so few enthusiasts can be trusted to speak the truth. —ARTHUR JAMES BALFOUR, letter (1891)

In things pertaining to enthusiasm, no man is sane who does not know how to be insane on proper occasions. —HENRY WARD BEECHER, *Proverbs from Plymouth Pulpit*

You can't sweep other people off their feet, if you can't be swept off your own. —CLARENCE DAY, "A Wild Polish Hero"

Nothing great was ever achieved without enthusiasm. —RALPH WALDO EMERSON, *Essays*

Zeal without knowledge is fire without light.
—THOMAS FULLER, *Gnomologia*

[This statement also appears in John Ray's *English Proverbs*.]

I would remind you that extremism in the defense of liberty is no vice! And let me remind you also that moderation in the pursuit of justice is no virtue!
—BARRY GOLDWATER, speech (accepting nomination for President, 1964)

Life is a romantic business. It is painting a picture, not doing a sum—but you have to make the romance, and it will come to the question how much fire you have in your belly. —OLIVER WENDELL HOLMES, JR., letter (1911)

We act as though comfort and luxury were the chief requirements of life, when all that we need to make us really happy is something to be enthusiastic about. —CHARLES KINGSLEY, quoted in *Reader's Digest*

What hunger is in relation to food, zest is in relation to life. —BERTRAND RUSSELL, *The Conquest of Happiness*

The Environment

Do no dishonor to the earth lest you dishonor the spirit of man. —HENRY BESTON, *The Outermost House*

Not one cent for scenery. —JOSEPH G. CANNON, quoted in *Tyrant from Illinois* by Blair Bolles

[This comment was made by the congressman in the course of denying funds for conservation.]

As crude a weapon as the cave man's club, the chemical barrage has been hurled against the fabric of life. —RACHEL CARSON, *Silent Spring*

Man has been endowed with reason, with the power to create, so that he can add to what he's been given. But up to now he hasn't been a creator, only a destroyer. Forests keep disappearing, rivers dry up, wild life's become extinct, the climate's ruined and the land grows poorer and uglier every day. —ANTON CHEKHOV, *Uncle Vanya*

We are the children of our landscape; it dictates behavior and even thought in the measure to which we are responsive to it. —LAWRENCE DURRELL, *Justine*

Now there is one outstandingly important fact regarding Spaceship Earth, and that is that no instruction book came with it. —R. BUCKMINSTER FULLER, *Operating Manual for Spaceship Earth*

Civilization is being poisoned by its own waste products. —WILLIAM RALPH INGE, in *Wit and Wisdom of Dean Inge*, ed. James Marchant

Like winds and sunsets, wild things were taken for granted until progress began to do away with them. Now we face the question whether a still higher "standard of living" is worth its cost in things natural, wild, and free. For us of the minority, the opportunity to see geese is more important than television. —ALDO LEOPOLD, *A Sand County Almanac*

The earth we abuse and the living things we kill will, in the end, take their revenge; for in exploiting their presence we are diminishing our future. —MARYA MANNES, *More in Anger*

Many people live in ugly wastelands, but in the absence of imaginative standards, most of them do not even know it. —C. WRIGHT MILLS, *Power, Politics and People*

Approximately 80% of our air pollution stems from hydrocarbons released by vegetation, so let's not go overboard in setting and enforcing tough emission standards from man-made sources. —RONALD REAGAN, quoted in *Ronald Reagan's Reign of Error* by Mark Green and Gail MacColl

The Nation that destroys its soil destroys itself. —FRANKLIN D. ROOSEVELT, letter (1937)

The emergence of intelligence, I am convinced, tends to unbalance the ecology. In other words, intelligence is the great polluter. It is not until a creature begins to manage its environment that nature is thrown into disorder. —CLIFFORD D. SIMAK, *Shakespeare's Planet*

In Wildness is the preservation of the world. —HENRY DAVID THOREAU, "Walking"

Envy — See JEALOUSY AND ENVY

Equality

It is not the possessions but the desires of mankind which require to be equalized. —ARISTOTLE, *Politics*

The defect of equality is that we only desire it with our superiors. —HENRY BECQUE, *Querelles littéraires*

It was a wise man who said that there is no greater inequality than the equal treatment of unequals. —FELIX FRANKFURTER, judicial opinion (1949)

That all men are equal is a proposition to which, at ordinary times, no sane individual has ever given his assent. —ALDOUS HUXLEY, *Proper Studies*

We hold these truths to be self-evident: that all men are created equal; that they are endowed by their creator with inherent and inalienable rights; that among these are life, liberty, and the pursuit of happiness. —THOMAS JEFFERSON, draft of the *Declaration of Independence*

[Jefferson's early draft had the words "with inherent and inalienable rights." The Continental Congress revised it to "with certain unalienable rights" before adopting it.]

Your levellers wish to level *down* as far as themselves; but they cannot bear levelling *up* to themselves. —SAMUEL JOHNSON, quoted in James Boswell's *The Life of Samuel Johnson*

All of us do not have equal talent, but all of us should have an equal opportunity to develop our talents. —JOHN F. KENNEDY, speech (1963)

I have a dream that my four little children will one day live in a nation where they will not be judged by the color of their skin but by the content of their character. I have a dream today. —MARTIN LUTHER KING, JR., speech (at the March on Washington, 1963)

I have a dream that one day this nation will rise up and live out the true meaning of its creed:—"We hold these truths to be self-evident, that all men are created equal." —MARTIN LUTHER KING, JR., speech (at the March on Washington, 1963)

All animals are equal, but some animals are more equal than others. —GEORGE ORWELL, *Animal Farm*

We hold these truths to be self-evident: that all men and women are created equal. —ELIZABETH CADY STANTON, "Declaration of Sentiments" (First Woman's Rights Convention, 1848)

Error — See also FAULTS AND WEAKNESSES

An error is the more dangerous in proportion to the degree of truth which it contains. —HENRI-FRÉDÉRIC AMIEL, *Journal intime*

Truth lies within a little and certain compass, but error is immense. —HENRY ST. JOHN, VISCOUNT BOLINGBROKE, *Reflections upon Exile*

Every great mistake has a halfway moment, a split second when it can be recalled and perhaps remedied. —PEARL S. BUCK, *What America Means to Me*

You can create a good impression on yourself by being right, he realizes, but for creating a good impression on others there's nothing to beat being totally and catastrophically wrong. —MICHAEL FRAYN, *Sweet Dreams*

All men are liable to error; and most men are, in many points, by passion or interest, under temptation to it. —JOHN LOCKE, *An Essay Concerning Human Understanding*

It is one thing to show a man that he is in an error, and another to put him in possession of truth. —JOHN LOCKE, *An Essay Concerning Human Understanding*

The man who makes no mistakes does not usually make anything. —WILLIAM CONNOR MAGEE, sermon (1868)

A man should never be ashamed to own he has been in the wrong, which is but saying, in other words, that he is wiser today than he was yesterday.
—ALEXANDER POPE, *Thoughts on Various Subjects*

Love truth, but pardon error. —VOLTAIRE, *Sept discours en Vers sur l'homme*

Ethics — See MORALITY AND ETHICS

Ethnic Heritage — See RACE AND ETHNIC HERITAGE

Evidence

One swallow does not make a spring, nor does one fine day. —ARISTOTLE, *Nichomachean Ethics*
[A proverbial saying, usually given in the form "One swallow does not make a summer."]

"Is there any other point to which you would wish to draw my attention?"
"To the curious incident of the dog in the night-time."
"The dog did nothing in the nighttime."
"That was the curious incident," remarked Sherlock Holmes.
—ARTHUR CONAN DOYLE, *Memoirs of Sherlock Holmes*

Youk'n hide de fier, but w'at you gwine do wid de smoke? —JOEL CHANDLER HARRIS, *Uncle Remus*

Some circumstantial evidence is very strong, as when you find a trout in the milk. —HENRY DAVID THOREAU, *Journal*

Evil — See also THE DEVIL

It was as though in those last minutes he [Eichmann] was summing up the lessons that this long course in human wickedness had taught us—the lesson of the fearsome, word-and-thought-defying *banality of evil.*
—HANNAH ARENDT, *Eichmann in Jerusalem*

Good can imagine Evil; but Evil cannot imagine Good. —W.H. AUDEN, *A Certain World*

> Evil is unspectacular and always human
> And shares our bed and eats at our own table.
> —W.H. AUDEN, "Herman Melville"

The only thing necessary for the triumph of evil is for good men to do nothing. —EDMUND BURKE, attributed

[This has not been found in Burke's writings.]

The belief in a supernatural source of evil is not necessary; men alone are quite capable of every wickedness. —JOSEPH CONRAD, *Under Western Eyes*

The resolution to avoid an evil is seldom framed till the evil is so far advanced as to make avoidance impossible. —THOMAS HARDY, *Far from the Madding Crowd*

No one ever suddenly became depraved. —JUVENAL, *Satires*

Nothing is evil which is according to nature. —MARCUS AURELIUS, *Meditations*

It is a sin to believe evil of others, but it is seldom a mistake. —H.L. MENCKEN, *A Mencken Chrestomathy*

> So farewell Hope, and with Hope farewell Fear,
> Farewell Remorse: all Good to me is lost;
> Evil be thou my Good.
> —JOHN MILTON, *Paradise Lost*

Between two evils, I always pick the one I never tried before. —MAE WEST, in the film *Klondike Annie*

No man chooses evil because it is evil; he only mistakes it for happiness, the good he seeks. —MARY WOLLSTONECRAFT, *A Vindication of the Rights of Men*

Evolution

A hen is only an egg's way of making another egg.
—SAMUEL BUTLER (d 1902), *Life and Habit*

> "The unfit die—the fit both live and thrive."
> Alas, who says so? They who do survive.
> —SARAH NORCLIFFE CLEGHORN, "The
> Survival of the Fittest"

I confess freely to you, I could never look long upon a monkey, without very mortifying reflections.
—WILLIAM CONGREVE, *Letters upon Several Occasions*, ed. John Dennis

Is man an ape or an angel? I, my lord, I am on the side of the angels. —BENJAMIN DISRAELI, speech (1864)

It's more comfortable to feel that we're a slight improvement on a monkey thin such a fallin' off fr'm th'angels. —FINLEY PETER DUNNE, *Mr. Dooley On Making a Will*

> Darwinian Man, though well-behaved,
> At best is only a monkey shaved!
> —W.S. GILBERT, *Princess Ida*

Example

Example is the school of mankind, and they will learn at no other. —EDMUND BURKE, *Letters on a Regicide Peace*

Setting too good an example is a kind of slander seldom forgiven. —BENJAMIN FRANKLIN, *Poor Richard's Almanac*

A good example is the best sermon. —THOMAS FULLER, *Gnomologia*
> [This also appears in Benjamin Franklin's *Poor Richard's Almanac*.]

127

I have learned silence from the talkative, toleration from the intolerant, and kindness from the unkind; yet strange, I am ungrateful to those teachers.
—KAHLIL GIBRAN, *Sand and Foam*

It is the true nature of mankind to learn from mistakes, not from example. —FRED HOYLE, *Into Deepest Space*

Everyone is bound to bear patiently the results of his own example. —PHAEDRUS, *Fables*

Few things are harder to put up with than the annoyance of a good example. —MARK TWAIN, *Pudd'nhead Wilson*, "Pudd'nhead Wilson's Calendar"

Excess

The road of excess leads to the palace of wisdom.
—WILLIAM BLAKE, *The Marriage of Heaven and Hell*

Excess on occasion is exhilarating. It prevents moderation from acquiring the deadening effect of a habit. —W. SOMERSET MAUGHAM, *The Summing Up*

Our nature hardly allows us to have enough of anything without having too much. —GEORGE SAVILE, *Character of Bishop Burnet*

> [This work has been attributed to George Savile, but the authorship is in doubt.]

> To gild refined gold, to paint the lily,
> To throw a perfume on the violet,
> To smooth the ice, or add another hue
> Unto the rainbow, or with taper light
> To seek the beauteous eye of heaven to garnish,
> Is wasteful and ridiculous excess.
> —SHAKESPEARE, *King John*

> [The two halves of the first line have merged to form the phrase "to gild the lily."]

They are as sick that surfeit with too much as they that starve with nothing. —SHAKESPEARE, *The Merchant of Venice*

Moderation is a fatal thing. Nothing succeeds like excess. —OSCAR WILDE, *A Woman of No Importance*
   [See Alexander Dumas, under Success and Failure.]

Excuses

Apology is only egotism wrong side out. —OLIVER WENDELL HOLMES, SR., *The Professor at the Breakfast-Table*

Never explain—your friends do not need it and your enemies will not believe you anyway. —ELBERT HUBBARD, *The Note Book*

He who excuses himself accuses himself. —GABRIEL MEURIER, *Trésor des sentences*
   [A French proverb: *Qui s'excuse, s'accuse.*]

   And oftentimes excusing of a fault
   Doth make the fault the worse by the excuse.
                    —SHAKESPEARE, *King John*

Two wrongs don't make a right, but they make a good excuse. —THOMAS SZASZ, *The Second Sin*

It is a good rule in life never to apologize. The right sort of people do not want apologies, and the wrong sort take a mean advantage of them. —P.G. WODEHOUSE, *The Man Upstairs*

Exercise — See HEALTH AND FITNESS

Experience

Experience isn't interesting till it begins to repeat itself—in fact, till it does that, it hardly *is* experience. —ELIZABETH BOWEN, *The Death of the Heart*

To most men, experience is like the stern lights of a ship, which illumine only the track it has passed. —Samuel Taylor Coleridge, *Table Talk*

Experience keeps a dear school, yet fools will learn in no other. —Benjamin Franklin, *Poor Richard's Almanac*

I have but one lamp by which my feet are guided, and that is the lamp of experience. I know of no way of judging the future but by the past. —Patrick Henry, speech (1775)

Experience is not what happens to a man; it is what a man does with what happens to him. —Aldous Huxley, *Texts and Pretexts*

Experience is never limited, and it is never complete; it is an immense sensibility, a kind of huge spider-web of the finest silken threads suspended in the chamber of consciousness, and catching every air-borne particle in its tissue. —Henry James, *Partial Portraits*

Experience is a hard teacher because she gives the test first, the lesson afterwards. —Vernon Law, in *This Week*

Experience does not ever err; it is only your judgment that errs in promising itself results which are not caused by your experiments. —Leonardo Da Vinci, *Notebooks*

> I am a part of all that I have met;
> Yet all experience is an arch wherethro'
> Gleams that untravell'd world whose margin fades
> For ever and for ever when I move.
> —Alfred, Lord Tennyson, "Ulysses"

We should be careful to get out of an experience only the wisdom that is in it—and stop there; lest we be like the cat that sits down on a hot stove lid. She will never sit down on a hot stove lid again—and that is well; but also she will never sit down on a cold one anymore. —MARK TWAIN, *Following the Equator*, "Pudd'nhead Wilson's New Calendar"

Experience is the name everyone gives to their mistakes. —OSCAR WILDE, *Lady Windermere's Fan*

Experts

An expert is one who knows more and more about less and less. —NICHOLAS MURRAY BUTLER, attributed

A consultant is someone who takes your watch away to tell you what time it is. —ED FINKELSTEIN, in *New York Times Magazine*

An expert is someone who knows some of the worst mistakes that can be made in his subject, and how to avoid them. —WERNER HEISENBERG, *Physics and Beyond*

The trouble with specialists is that they tend to think in grooves. —ELAINE MORGAN, *The Descent of Woman*

Face — See BODY AND FACE

Facts

I often wish . . . that I could rid the world of the tyranny of facts. What are facts but compromises? A fact merely marks the point where we have agreed to let investigation cease. —BLISS CARMAN, attributed

[These words appear in an unsigned article in *Atlantic* (in 1906) thought to have been written by Carman.]

Now, what I want is, Facts . . . Facts alone are wanted in life. —CHARLES DICKENS, *Hard Times*

> [These opening lines from the book set forth Thomas Gradgrind's educational philosophy.]

Facts are stubborn things. —EBENEZER ELLIOTT, *Field Husbandry*

Time dissipates to shining ether the solid angularity of facts. —RALPH WALDO EMERSON, *Essays*

The way to do research is to attack the facts at the point of greatest astonishment. —CELIA GREEN, *The Decline and Fall of Science*

Facts do not cease to exist because they are ignored. —ALDOUS HUXLEY, *Proper Studies*

Facts are ventriloquists' dummies. Sitting on a wise man's knee they may be made to utter words of wisdom; elsewhere they say nothing or talk nonsense. —ALDOUS HUXLEY, *Time Must Have a Stop*

Sit down before fact as a little child, be prepared to give up every preconceived notion, follow humbly wherever and to whatever abysses nature leads, or you shall learn nothing. —THOMAS HENRY HUXLEY, letter (1860)

Facts, or what a man believes to be facts, are always delightful. . . . Get your facts first, and . . . then you can distort 'em as much as you please. —MARK TWAIN, quoted in Rudyard Kipling's *From Sea to Sea*

It is the spirit of the age to believe that any fact, no matter how suspect, is superior to any imaginative exercise, no matter how true. —GORE VIDAL, in *Encounter*

Failure — See SUCCESS AND FAILURE

Faith — See BELIEF

Faithfulness and Loyalty

Wither thou goest, I will go; and where thou lodgest, I will lodge: thy people shall be my people, and thy God my God: Where thou diest, will I die, and there will I be buried: the Lord do so to me, and more also, if aught but death part thee and me. —BIBLE, *Ruth 1:16*

I have been faithful to thee, Cynara! in my fashion. —ERNEST DOWSON, *Non Sum Qualis Eram*

Faithful women are all alike. They think only of their fidelity and never of their husbands. —JEAN GIRAUDOUX, *Amphitryon 38*

An ounce of loyalty is worth a pound of cleverness. —ELBERT HUBBARD, *The Note Book*

> O heaven! were man
> But constant, he were perfect.
> > —SHAKESPEARE, *The Two Gentlemen of
> > Verona*

The fickleness of the women I love is only equalled by the infernal constancy of the women who love me. —GEORGE BERNARD SHAW, *The Philanderer*

> Out upon it, I have loved
> > Three whole days together;
> And am like to love three more,
> > If it prove fair weather.
> > > —JOHN SUCKLING, "A Poem with the
> > > Answer"

Those who are faithless know the pleasures of love; it is the faithful who know love's tragedies. —OSCAR WILDE, *The Picture of Dorian Gray*

Fall — See SEASONS

Fame

A celebrity is a person who works hard all his life to become well known, then wears dark glasses to avoid being recognized. —FRED ALLEN, *Treadmill to Oblivion*

Fame is like a river, that beareth up things light and swollen, and drowns things weighty and solid. —FRANCIS BACON, *Essays*

Live by publicity, you'll probably die by publicity. —RUSSELL BAKER, in *New York Times*

Fame always brings loneliness. Success is as ice cold and lonely as the north pole. —VICKI BAUM, *Grand Hotel*

[See also Friedrich Nietzsche, under Greatness.]

The celebrity is a person who is known for his well-knownness. —DANIEL J. BOORSTIN, *The Image*

I would much rather have men ask why I have no statue, than why I have one. —CATO THE ELDER, quoted in Plutarch's *Parallel Lives*

In the very books in which philosophers bid us scorn fame, they inscribe their names. —CICERO, *Pro Archia Poeta*

Fame is a bee.
It has a song—
It has a sting—
Ah, too, it has a wing.
　　　　—EMILY DICKINSON, "Fame is a bee"

If a man can write a better book, preach a better sermon, or make a better mousetrap than his neighbor, though he build his house in the woods, the world will make a beaten path to his door. —RALPH WALDO EMERSON, attributed, quoted by Sarah Yule and Mary S. Keene in *Borrowings* (1889)

[This quotation has not been found in Emerson's writings. Sarah Yule said she wrote the statement down from a lecture Emerson gave in 1871.]

Fame usually comes to those who are thinking about something else. —OLIVER WENDELL HOLMES, SR., *The Autocrat of the Breakfast-Table*

Many brave men lived before Agamemnon, but all are weighed down in unending night, unwept and unknown, because they lacked a sacred bard. —HORACE, *Odes*

A celebrity is one who is known to many persons he is glad he doesn't know. —H.L. MENCKEN, *A Mencken Chrestomathy*

Fame is the spur that the clear spirit doth
raise
(That last infirmity of noble mind)
To scorn delights, and live laborious days.
　　　　　　　—JOHN MILTON, *Lycidas*

Love of fame is the last thing even the wise give up. —TACITUS, *Histories*

In the future everyone will be world-famous for fifteen minutes. —ANDY WARHOL, widely attributed to and acknowledged by Warhol

[Warhol's later comment: "I'm bored with that line. I never use it anymore. My new line is, 'In fifteen minutes everybody will be famous.'"]

If you want a place in the sun, you have to expect a few blisters. —LORETTA YOUNG, quoted in John Robert Colombo's *Popcorn in Paradise*

Familiarity

No man is a hero to his valet. —MADAME DE CORNUEL, quoted in *Lettres de Mlle. Aïssé*

Though familiarity may not breed contempt, it takes the edge off admiration. —WILLIAM HAZLITT, *Characteristics*

[The proverb "Familiarity breeds contempt" dates back at least to Roman times. Publilius Syrus included it in his *Maxims*.]

Sweets grown common lose their dear delight. —SHAKESPEARE, *Sonnet CII*

Familiar acts are beautiful through love. —PERCY BYSSHE SHELLEY, *Prometheus Unbound*

Familiarity breeds contempt—and children. —MARK TWAIN, *Notebooks*

Family — See also ANCESTRY

It is a melancholy truth that even great men have their poor relations. —CHARLES DICKENS, *Bleak House*

Accidents will occur in the best-regulated families. —CHARLES DICKENS, *David Copperfield*

The greatest thing in family life is to take a hint when a hint is intended—and not to take a hint when a hint isn't intended. —ROBERT FROST, quoted in *Vogue*

He that has no fools, knaves, nor beggars in his family, was begot by a flash of lightning. —THOMAS FULLER, *Gnomologia*

136

Families, I hate you! Shut-in homes, closed doors, jealous possessors of happiness. —ANDRÉ GIDE, *Fruits of the Earth*

A group of closely related persons living under one roof; it is a convenience, often a necessity, sometimes a pleasure, sometimes the reverse; but who first exalted it as admirable, an almost religious ideal? —ROSE MACAULAY, *The World My Wilderness*

> One would be in less danger
> From the wiles of the stranger
> If one's own kin and kith
> Were more fun to be with.
> —OGDEN NASH, "Family Court"

The family is one of nature's masterpieces. —GEORGE SANTAYANA, *The Life of Reason*

To the family—that dear octopus from whose tentacles we never quite escape, nor, in our inmost hearts, ever quite wish to. —DODIE SMITH, *Dear Octopus*

All happy families are like one another; each unhappy family is unhappy in its own way. —LEO TOLSTOY, *Anna Karenina*

Fanaticism

A fanatic is one who can't change his mind and won't change the subject. —WINSTON CHURCHILL, quoted in *New York Times*

A fanatic is a man that does what he thinks th' Lord wud do if He knew th' facts iv th' case. —FINLEY PETER DUNNE, *Mr. Dooley's Opinions*

There is no strong performance without a little fanaticism in the performer. —RALPH WALDO EMERSON, *Journals*

Fanatics have their dreams, wherewith they
weave
A paradise for a sect.
>—JOHN KEATS, "The Fall of Hyperion"

Fanaticism consists in redoubling your efforts when you have forgotten your aim. —GEORGE SANTAYANA, *The Life of Reason*

Fashion — See also CLOTHING

FASHION, *n.* A despot whom the wise ridicule and obey. —AMBROSE BIERCE, *The Devil's Dictionary*

One had as good be out of the world, as out of the fashion. —COLLEY CIBBER, *Love's Last Shift*

Fashion is gentility running away from vulgarity and afraid of being overtaken. —WILLIAM HAZLITT, *The Conversations of James Northcote*

There are few who would not rather be taken in adultery than in provincialism. —ALDOUS HUXLEY, *Antic Hay*

Be not the first by whom the new are tried,
Nor yet the last to lay the old aside.
>—ALEXANDER POPE, *An Essay on
Criticism*

The fashion wears out more apparel than the man. —SHAKESPEARE, *Much Ado About Nothing*

Fashions, after all, are only induced epidemics. —GEORGE BERNARD SHAW, *The Doctor's Dilemma*

To call a fashion wearable is the kiss of death. No new fashion worth its salt is ever wearable. —EUGENIA SHEPPARD, in *New York Herald Tribune*

You cannot be both fashionable and first-rate.
—LOGAN PEARSALL SMITH, *Afterthoughts*

Every generation laughs at the old fashions, but follows religiously the new. —HENRY DAVID THOREAU, *Walden*

A fashion is merely a form of ugliness so unbearable that we are compelled to alter it every six months. —OSCAR WILDE, quoted in Richard Ellmann's *Oscar Wilde*

Fate — See also FORTUNE AND CHANCE

Fate is not an eagle, it creeps like a rat. —ELIZABETH BOWEN, *The House in Paris*

I do not believe in a fate that falls on men however they act; but I do believe in a fate that falls on them unless they act. —G.K. CHESTERTON, *Generally Speaking*

> The Moving Finger writes; and, having writ,
> Moves on: nor all your Piety nor Wit
>   Shall lure it back to cancel half a Line,
> Nor all your Tears wash out a Word of it.
>   —EDWARD FITZGERALD, *The Rubáiyát of*
>   *Omar Khayyám*

> It matters not how strait the gate,
> How charged with punishments the scroll,
> I am the master of my fate:
> I am the captain of my soul.
>   —W.E. HENLEY, "Invictus"

Human reason needs only to will more strongly than fate, and she *is* fate. —THOMAS MANN, *The Magic Mountain*

We may become the makers of our fate when we have ceased to pose as its prophets. —KARL POPPER, *The Open Society and Its Enemies*

Fate leads the willing and drags along the unwilling.
—SENECA, *Epistulae ad Lucilium*

Men at some time are masters of their fates:
The fault, dear Brutus, is not in our stars,
But in ourselves, that we are underlings.
—SHAKESPEARE, *Julius Caesar*

There is no armor against fate;
Death lays his icy hand on kings.
—JAMES SHIRLEY, *The Contention of Ajax
and Ulysses*

Every bullet has its billet. —WILLIAM III, attributed

Fathers — See PARENTS AND PARENTHOOD

Fatness — See WEIGHT

Faults and Weaknesses — See also ERROR

The greatest of faults, I should say, is to be conscious of none. —THOMAS CARLYLE, *On Heroes, Hero-Worship and the Heroic in History*

Men are much more unwilling to have their weaknesses and their imperfections known than their crimes. —LORD CHESTERFIELD, *Letters to His Son*

People who have no weaknesses are terrible; there is no way of taking advantage of them. —ANATOLE FRANCE, *The Crime of Sylvestre Bonnard*

It is well that there is no one without a fault; for he would not have a friend in the world. —WILLIAM HAZLITT, *Characteristics*

Sometimes even excellent Homer nods. —HORACE, *Ars Poetica*

We confess to little faults only to persuade others that we have no great ones. —LA ROCHEFOUCAULD, *Maxims*

Men always try to make virtues of their weaknesses. Fear of death and fear of life both become piety. —H.L. MENCKEN, *Minority Report: H.L. Mencken's Notebooks*

> They say, best men are moulded out of faults;
> And, for the most, become much more the
>   better
> For being a little bad.
>   —SHAKESPEARE, *Measure for Measure*

The mystery of existence is the connection between our faults and our misfortunes. —MADAME DE STAËL, quoted in Samuel Griswold Goodrich's *Lives of Celebrated Women*

People mistake their limitations for high standards. —JEAN TOOMER, in *Essentials: Definitions and Aphorisms*, ed. Rudolph P. Byrd

Fear — See also ANXIETY

Early and provident fear is the mother of safety. —EDMUND BURKE, speech (1792)

Fear is sharp-sighted, and can see things underground, and much more in the skies. —MIGUEL DE CERVANTES, *Don Quixote de la Mancha*

A door slamming makes one jump, but it doesn't make one afraid. What one fears is the serpent that crawls underneath it. —COLETTE, *Cheri*

> And I will show you something different from
>   either
> Your shadow at morning striding behind you
> Or your shadow at evening rising to meet you;
> I will show you fear in a handful of dust.
>   —T.S. ELIOT, *The Waste Land*

Since love and fear can hardly exist together, if we must choose between them, it is far safer to be feared than loved. —NICCOLÓ MACHIAVELLI, *The Prince*

Let me assert my firm belief that the only thing we have to fear is fear itself—nameless, unreasoning, unjustified terror which paralyzes needed efforts to convert retreat into advance. —FRANKLIN D. ROOSEVELT, speech (inaugural address, 1933)

[Others had expressed similar thoughts. Thoreau, for example, had written in his *Journal*: "Nothing is so much to be feared as Fear." And the Duke of Wellington, referring to the outbreak of cholera in London in 1831, said: "The only thing I am afraid of is fear" (quoted in Philip Henry Stanhope's *Notes of Conversations with the Duke of Wellington*).]

Fear is the main source of superstition, and one of the main sources of cruelty. To conquer fear is the beginning of wisdom. —BERTRAND RUSSELL, *Unpopular Essays*

Present fears
Are less than horrible imaginings.
　　　　　　—SHAKESPEARE, *Macbeth*

When our actions do not,
Our fears do make us traitors.
　　　　　　—SHAKESPEARE, *Macbeth*

To him who is afraid everything rustles. —SOPHOCLES, *Acrisius*

Fear cannot be without hope nor hope without fear. —BENEDICT DE SPINOZA, *Ethics*

Feelings — See THE HEART AND EMOTION

Film — See THEATER AND FILM, ACTORS AND ACTING

Fitness — See HEALTH AND FITNESS

Flattery — See PRAISE AND FLATTERY

Flirtation and Romance

His designs were strictly honorable, as the phrase is: that is, to rob a lady of her fortune by way of marriage. —HENRY FIELDING, *Tom Jones*

The coquets of both sexes are self-lovers, and that is a love no other whatever can dispossess. —JOHN GAY, *The Beggar's Opera*

> O Polly, you might have toyed and kissed:
> By keeping men off, you keep them on.
> —JOHN GAY, *The Beggar's Opera*

The greatest miracle of love is the cure of coquetry. —LA ROCHEFOUCAULD, *Maxims*

Kissing your hand may make you feel very very good but a diamond and safire bracelet lasts forever. —ANITA LOOS, *Gentlemen Prefer Blondes*

> Had we but world enough, and time,
> This coyness, Lady, were no crime.
> —ANDREW MARVELL, "To His Coy
> Mistress"

Whether they yield or refuse, it delights women to have been asked. —OVID, *Ars Amatoria*

> Men seldom make passes
> At girls who wear glasses.
> —DOROTHY PARKER, "News Item"

143

Brevity may be the soul of wit, but not when someone's saying, "I love you." —JUDITH VIORST, in *Redbook*

When one is in love, one always begins by deceiving oneself, and one always ends by deceiving others. That is what the world calls a romance. —OSCAR WILDE, *The Picture of Dorian Gray*

Nothing spoils a romance so much as a sense of humor in the woman. —OSCAR WILDE, *A Woman of No Importance*

Flowers and Trees — See also GARDENS; NATURE

Flowers are the sweetest things that God ever made, and forgot to put a soul into. —HENRY WARD BEECHER, *Life Thoughts*

Consider the lilies of the field how they grow; they toil not, neither do they spin;
  And yet I say unto you, That even Solomon in all his glory was not arrayed like one of these. —BIBLE, *Matthew* 6:28–29

To create a little flower is the labor of ages. —WILLIAM BLAKE, *The Marriage of Heaven and Hell*

> Any nose
> May ravage with impunity a rose.
> —ROBERT BROWNING, *Sordello*

I like trees because they seem more resigned to the way they have to live than other things do. —WILLA CATHER, *O Pioneers!*

> I sometimes think that never blows so red
> The Rose as where some buried Caesar bled;
> That every Hyacinth the Garden wears
> Dropt in her Lap from some once lovely Head.
> —EDWARD FITZGERALD, *The Rubáiyát of Omar Khayyám*

He that plants trees, loves others besides himself. — THOMAS FULLER, *Gnomologia*

The flower is the poetry of reproduction. It is an example of the eternal seductiveness of life. —JEAN GIRAUDOUX, *The Enchanted*

> I think that I shall never see
> A poem lovely as a tree
>
> . . . .
> Poems are made by fools like me,
> But only God can make a tree.
> > —JOYCE KILMER, "Trees"

> [Ogden Nash wrote in "Song of the Open Road":
> > I think that I shall never see
> > A billboard lovely as a tree.
> > Indeed, unless the billboards fall
> > I'll never see a tree at all.]

> 'Tis the last rose of summer
> > Left blooming alone;
> All her lovely companions
> > Are faded and gone.
> > —THOMAS MOORE, "'Tis the Last Rose"

> Woodman, spare that tree!
> Touch not a single bough!
> In youth it sheltered me,
> And I'll protect it now.
> > —GEORGE POPE MORRIS, "Woodman,
> > > Spare That Tree"

People from a planet without flowers would think we must be mad with joy the whole time to have such things about us. —IRIS MURDOCH, *A Fairly Honorable Defeat*

Rose is a rose is a rose is a rose. —GERTRUDE STEIN, *Sacred Emily*

I wandered lonely as a cloud
That floats on high o'er vales and hills,
When all at once I saw a crowd,
A host, of golden daffodils.
—WILLIAM WORDSWORTH, "I Wandered
Lonely as a Cloud"

To me the meanest flower that blows can give
Thoughts that do often lie too deep for tears.
—WILLIAM WORDSWORTH, "Intimations of
Immortality"

Fog — See WEATHER

Food and Eating

EDIBLE, *adj.* Good to eat, and wholesome to digest, as
a worm to a toad, a toad to a snake, a snake to a pig,
a pig to a man, and a man to a worm. —AMBROSE
BIERCE, *The Devil's Dictionary*

Tell me what you eat, and I will tell you what you are.
—ANTHELME BRILLAT-SAVARIN, *The Physiology of
Taste*

The discovery of a new dish does more for human
happiness than the discovery of a new star.
—ANTHELME BRILLAT-SAVARIN, *The Physiology of Taste*

There's no sauce in the world like hunger. —MIGUEL
DE CERVANTES, *Don Quixote de la Mancha*

It's a very odd thing—
As odd as can be—
That whatever Miss T. eats
Turns into Miss T.
—WALTER DE LA MARE, "Miss T."

. . . cheese, milk's leap toward immortality. —CLIF-
TON FADIMAN, *Any Number Can Play*

More die in the United States of too much food than of too little. —JOHN KENNETH GALBRAITH, *The Affluent Society*

He was a very valiant man who first adventured on eating of oysters. —JAMES I, quoted in Thomas Fuller's *Worthies of England*

> [Jonathan Swift listed this as a cliché in his *Polite Conversation*: "He was a bold man that first eat an oyster."]

A cucumber should be well sliced, and dressed with pepper and vinegar, and then thrown out, as good for nothing. —SAMUEL JOHNSON, quoted in James Boswell's *Tour to the Hebrides*

Some people have a foolish way of not minding, or pretending not to mind, what they eat. For my part, I mind my belly very studiously, and very carefully; for I look upon it, that he who does not mind his belly will hardly mind anything else. —SAMUEL JOHNSON, quoted in James Boswell's *The Life of Samuel Johnson*

> We may live without poetry, music and art;
> We may live without conscience, and live
>   without heart;
> We may live without friends; we may live
>   without books;
> But civilized man cannot live without cooks.
>   —OWEN MEREDITH, *Lucile*

According to the saying of an ancient philosopher, one should eat to live, and not live to eat. —MOLIÈRE, *L'Avare*

> [The ancient philosopher was Socrates, as quoted in Plutarch's *How a Young Man Ought to Hear Poems*: "Bad men live that they may eat and drink, whereas good men eat and drink that they may live." This ascetic advice also appears in Benjamin Franklin's *Poor Richard's Almanac*: "Eat to live, and not live to eat."]

There is no love sincerer than the love of food.
—GEORGE BERNARD SHAW, *Man and Superman*

Serenely full, the epicure would say,
Fate cannot harm me, I have dined today.
—SYDNEY SMITH, quoted in Lady
Holland's *Memoir*

MOTHER: It's broccoli, dear.
CHILD: I say it's spinach, and I say the hell with it.
—E.B. WHITE, cartoon caption in *New Yorker*

One cannot think well, love well, sleep well, if one has not dined well. —VIRGINIA WOOLF, *A Room of One's Own*

Fools and Foolishness

Answer not a fool according to his folly, lest thou also be like unto him. Answer a fool according to his folly, lest he be wise in his own conceit. —BIBLE, *Proverbs* 26:4–5

A fool sees not the same tree that a wise man sees.
—WILLIAM BLAKE, *The Marriage of Heaven and Hell*

A fool always finds a bigger fool to admire him.
—NICOLAS BOILEAU, *L'Art poétique*

Wise men profit more from fools than fools from wise men; for the wise men shun the mistakes of fools, but fools do not imitate the successes of the wise. —CATO THE ELDER, quoted in Plutarch's *Parallel Lives*

A fool must now and then be right, by chance.
—WILLIAM COWPER, "Conversation"

None is a fool always, everyone sometimes.
—GEORGE HERBERT, *Jacula Prudentum*

Fortune, that favors fools. —BEN JONSON, *The Alchemist*

> [John Gay wrote in his *Fables*:
> Tis a gross error held in schools,
> That Fortune always favors fools.]

Fools rush in where angels fear to tread. —ALEXANDER POPE, *An Essay on Criticism*

The follies which a man regrets most in his life are those which he didn't commit when he had the opportunity. —HELEN ROWLAND, *Reflections of a Bachelor Girl*

The fool doth think he is wise, but the wise man knows himself to be a fool. —SHAKESPEARE, *As You Like It*

Lord, what fools these mortals be! —SHAKESPEARE, *A Midsummer Night's Dream*

> [Seneca had made exactly the same observation in his *Epistulae ad Lucilium*.]

Let us be thankful for the fools. But for them the rest of us could not succeed. —MARK TWAIN, *Following the Equator*, "Pudd'nhead Wilson's New Calendar"

The Forbidden

Stolen waters are sweet, and bread eaten in secret is pleasant. —BIBLE, *Proverbs* 9:17

Forbid us [some]thing, and that [thing] we desire. —CHAUCER, *The Canterbury Tales*

Stolen sweets are best. —COLLEY CIBBER, *The Rival Fools*

The illicit has an added charm. —TACITUS, *Annals*

149

Adam was but human—this explains it all. He did not want the apple for the apple's sake, he wanted it only because it was forbidden. The mistake was in not forbidding the serpent; then he would have eaten the serpent. —MARK TWAIN, *Pudd'nhead Wilson*, "Pudd'nhead Wilson's Calendar"

Force — See VIOLENCE AND FORCE

Foreigners and Foreignness

Everyone's quick to blame the alien. —AESCHYLUS, *The Suppliant Maidens*

I don't hold with abroad and think that foreigners speak English when our backs are turned. —QUENTIN CRISP, *The Naked Civil Servant*

They spell it Vinci and pronounce it Vinchy; foreigners always spell better than they pronounce. —MARK TWAIN, *Innocents Abroad*

Foresight — See PRUDENCE AND FORESIGHT

Forgiveness

You ought certainly to forgive them as a Christian, but never to admit them in your sight, or allow their names to be mentioned in your hearing. —JANE AUSTEN, *Pride and Prejudice*

And forgive us our debts, as we forgive our debtors. —BIBLE, *Matthew* 6:12

[This line from The Lord's Prayer is perhaps better known as given in the *Book of Common Prayer*: "And forgive us our trespasses, as we forgive those who trespass against us."]

Forgiveness to the injured does belong;
But they ne'er pardon who have done the
    wrong.
                    —JOHN DRYDEN, *The Conquest of*
                                            Granada

[This is expressed more tersely by George Herbert
in *Jacula Prudentum*: "The offender never par-
dons."]

If you forgive people enough you belong to them, and
they to you, whether either person likes it or not—
squatter's rights of the heart. —JAMES HILTON, *Time*
and Time Again

Nobuddy ever fergits where he buried a hatchet.
—KIN HUBBARD, *Abe Martin's Broadcast*

He, who cannot forgive a trespass of malice to his
enemy, has never yet tasted the most sublime enjoyment of love. —JOHANN KASPAR LAVATER, *Aphorisms*
on Man

To err is human, to forgive, divine. —ALEXANDER
POPE, *An Essay on Criticism*

["To err is human" was a much older saying, dating
back at least to Roman times. It is found in the
works of Seneca and others. Benjamin Franklin
used it as the starting point for a saying in *Poor*
Richard's Almanac: "To err is human, to repent
divine, to persist devilish."]

Fortune and Chance — See also FATE

I returned, and saw under the sun, that the race is
not to the swift, nor the battle to the strong, neither
yet bread to the wise, nor yet riches to men of
understanding, nor yet favor to men of skill; but time
and chance happeneth to them all. —BIBLE, *Eccle-*
siastes 9:11

151

> Luck is not chance—
> It's Toil—Fortune's expensive smile
> Is earned—.
> —EMILY DICKINSON, "Luck is not chance"

Fortune's wheel never stands still—the highest point is therefore the most perilous. —MARIA EDGEWORTH, *Patronage*

Chance is perhaps the pseudonym of God when He did not want to sign. —ANATOLE FRANCE, *Le Jardin d'épicure*

Fortune gives many too much, but none enough. —MARTIAL, *Epigrams*

Where observation is concerned, chance favors only the prepared mind. —LOUIS PASTEUR, speech (1854)

When Fortune flatters, she does it to betray. —PUBLILIUS SYRUS, *Maxims*

Those whom fortune has never favored are more joyful than those whom she has deserted. —SENECA, *De Tranquillitate Animi*

The power of fortune is confessed only by the miserable; for the happy impute all their success to prudence and merit. —JONATHAN SWIFT, *Thoughts on Various Subjects*

France and the French

France was long a despotism tempered by epigrams. —THOMAS CARLYLE, *The French Revolution*

France has cherished words to the point of vice, and at the expense of *things*. Dubious of our possibilities of knowing, she is not so of our possibilities of *formulating* our doubts. —E.M. CIORAN, *The Temptation to Exist*

How can you be expected to govern a country that has 246 kinds of cheese? —CHARLES DE GAULLE, quoted in *Newsweek*

[This image of France's diversity was apparently a favorite of de Gaulle's, used by him on several occasions.]

Bouillabaisse is only good because cooked by the French, who, if they cared to try, could produce an excellent and nutritious substitute out of cigar stumps and empty matchboxes. —NORMAN DOUGLAS, *Siren Lands*

The French woman says, "I am a woman and a Parisienne, and nothing foreign to me appears altogether human." —RALPH WALDO EMERSON, *Uncollected Lectures*

[Compare Terence, under Humans and Human Nature.]

It's true that the French have a certain obsession with sex, but it's a particularly adult obsession. France is the thriftiest of all nations; to a Frenchman sex provides the most economical way to have fun. —ANITA LOOS, *Kiss Hollywood Goodbye*

Yet, who can help loving the land that has
　　taught us
Six hundred and eighty-five ways to dress
　　eggs?
　　　　　　—THOMAS MOORE, *The Fudge Family in
　　　　　　　　　　　　　　　Paris*

Frankness — See CANDOR AND SINCERITY

Fraud — See DECEPTION AND FRAUD

Freedom and Liberty

A man is either free or he is not. There cannot be any apprenticeship for freedom. —IMAMU AMIRI BARAKA, in *Kulchur*

Who would be free themselves must strike the blow.
—LORD BYRON, *Childe Harold's Pilgrimage*

I only ask to be free. The butterflies are free.
—CHARLES DICKENS, *Bleak House*

The cost of liberty is less than the price of repression.
—W.E.B. DU BOIS, *John Brown*

Liberty lies in the hearts of men and women; when it dies there, no constitution, no law . . . no court can save it. . . . The spirit of liberty is the spirit which is not too sure that it is right; the spirit of liberty is the spirit which seeks to understand the minds of other men and women. —LEARNED HAND, speech (1944)

Is life so dear, or peace so sweet, as to be purchased at the price of chains and slavery? Forbid it, Almighty God!—I know not what course others may take; but as for me, give me liberty, or give me death! —PATRICK HENRY, speech (1775)

There can be no real freedom without the freedom to fail. —ERIC HOFFER, *The Ordeal of Change*

I would rather be exposed to the inconveniencies attending too much liberty than those attending too small a degree of it. —THOMAS JEFFERSON, letter (1791)

It's often safer to be in chains than to be free.
—FRANZ KAFKA, *The Trial*

Let every nation know, whether it wishes us well or ill, that we shall pay any price, bear any burden, meet any hardship, support any friend, oppose any foe to assure the survival and the success of liberty.
—JOHN F. KENNEDY, speech (inaugural address, 1961)

Those who deny freedom to others deserve it not for themselves. —ABRAHAM LINCOLN, letter (1859)

Freedom is always and exclusively freedom for the one who thinks differently. —ROSA LUXEMBURG, *The Russian Revolution*

None can love freedom heartily, but good men; the rest love not freedom, but license. —JOHN MILTON, *The Tenure of Kings and Magistrates*

Liberty is the right to do whatever the laws permit. —BARON DE MONTESQUIEU, *De l'esprit des lois*

Those who expect to reap the blessings of freedom, must, like men, undergo the fatigues of supporting it. —THOMAS PAINE, "The American Crisis"

Eternal vigilance is the price of liberty—power is ever stealing from the many to the few. —WENDELL PHILLIPS, speech (1852)

[John Philpot Curran earlier expressed this idea in a speech (1790): "The condition upon which God hath given liberty to man is eternal vigilance."]

A Country can get more real joy out of just Hollering for their Freedom than they can if they get it. —WILL ROGERS, *The Autobiography of Will Rogers*

O liberty! O liberty! What crimes are committed in thy name! —(MADAME) JEANNE-MARIE ROLAND, attributed, quoted in Alphonse de Lamartine's *Histoire des Girondins*

[Madame Roland is said to have uttered these words just before being guillotined.]

We look forward to a world founded upon four essential human freedoms. The first is freedom of speech and expression—everywhere in the world. The second is freedom of every person to worship God in his own way—everywhere in the world. The third is freedom from want . . . everywhere in the world. The fourth is freedom from fear . . . anywhere in the world. —FRANKLIN D. ROOSEVELT, speech (1941)

Man is born free, and everywhere he is in chains.
—JEAN-JACQUES ROUSSEAU, *The Social Contract*

Man is condemned to be free. —JEAN-PAUL SARTRE, *Existentialism and Humanism*

Liberty means responsibility. That is why most men dread it. —GEORGE BERNARD SHAW, *Man and Superman*, "The Revolutionist's Handbook"

My definition of a free society is a society where it is safe to be unpopular. —ADLAI E. STEVENSON, speech (1952)

It is by the goodness of God that in our country we have those three unspeakably precious things: freedom of speech, freedom of conscience, and the prudence never to practice either of them. —MARK TWAIN, *Following the Equator*, "Pudd'nhead Wilson's New Calendar"

Freedom of Speech and the Press

A free press can of course be good or bad, but, most certainly, without freedom it will never be anything but bad. —ALBERT CAMUS, *Resistance, Rebellion and Death*

You can muffle the drum, and you can loosen the strings of the lyre, but who shall command the skylark not to sing? —KAHLIL GIBRAN, *The Prophet*

The most stringent protection of free speech would not protect a man in falsely shouting fire in a theater and causing a panic. —OLIVER WENDELL HOLMES, JR., judicial decision (1919)

The right to be heard does not automatically include the right to be taken seriously. —HUBERT H. HUMPHREY, speech (1965)

156

No government ought to be without censors; and where the press is free, no one ever will. —THOMAS JEFFERSON, letter (to George Washington, 1792)

If all mankind minus one, were of one opinion, and only one person were of the contrary opinion, mankind would be no more justified in silencing that one person, than he, if he had the power, would be justified in silencing mankind. —JOHN STUART MILL, *On Liberty*

The only way to make sure people you agree with can speak is to support the rights of people you don't agree with. —ELEANOR HOLMES NORTON, quoted in *New York Post*

I detest what you write, but I would give my life to make it possible for you to continue to write. —VOLTAIRE, letter (1770)

> [This seems to be the closest thing Voltaire ever actually said to the statement often attributed to him: "I disapprove of what you say, but I will defend to the death your right to say it." Those words were used by S.G. Tallentyre in *The Friends of Voltaire* (1906) to paraphrase Voltaire's reaction to the condemnation of Helvétius's *De l'esprit* (*On the Mind*).]

I have always been among those who believed that the greatest freedom of speech was the greatest safety, because if a man is a fool, the best thing to do is to encourage him to advertise the fact by speaking. —WOODROW WILSON, speech (1919)

Friends and Friendship

One friend in a lifetime is much; two are many; three are hardly possible. —HENRY ADAMS, *The Education of Henry Adams*

What is a friend? A single soul dwelling in two bodies.
—ARISTOTLE, quoted by Diogenes Laertius in *Lives of the Philosophers*

This communicating of a man's self to his friend works two contrary effects, for it redoubleth joys, and cutteth griefs in half. —FRANCIS BACON, *Essays*

A faithful friend is the medicine of life. —BIBLE, *Ecclesiasticus* 6:16

Greater love hath no man than this, that a man lay down his life for his friends. —BIBLE, *John* 15:13

Forsake not an old friend; for the new is not comparable to him: a new friend is as new wine; when it is old, thou shalt drink it with pleasure. —BIBLE, *Ecclesiasticus* 9:10

When the sun shines on you, you see your friends. Friends are the thermometers by which one may judge the temperature of our fortunes. —MARGUERITE BLESSINGTON, *Commonplace Book*

There is no man so friendless but what he can find a friend sincere enough to tell him disagreeable truths. —EDWARD BULWER-LYTTON, *What Will He Do With It?*

A friend is, as it were, a second self. —CICERO, *De Amicitia*

In prosperity our friends know us; in adversity we know our friends. —CHURTON COLLINS, *Aphorisms*

Have no friends not equal to yourself. —CONFUCIUS, *Analects*

Fate makes our relatives, choice makes our friends. —JACQUES DELILLE, *Malheur et pitié*

[Addison Mizner expressed this in a more opinionated way in *The Cynic's Calendar*: "God gives us relatives; thank God, we can choose our friends."]

A friend may well be reckoned the masterpiece of Nature. —RALPH WALDO EMERSON, *Essays*, "Friendship"

The only reward of virtue is virtue; the only way to have a friend is to be one. —RALPH WALDO EMERSON, *Essays*, "Friendship"

When a friend asks there is no tomorrow. —GEORGE HERBERT, *Jacula Prudentum*

A true friend is the greatest of all blessings, and the one that we take the least care of all to acquire. —LA ROCHEFOUCAULD, *Maxims*

Each friend represents a world in us, a world possibly not born until they arrive, and it is only by this meeting that a new world is born. —ANAÏS NIN, diary entry (*The Diary of Anaïs Nin*)

True friendship is never serene. —MARIE DE SÉVIGNÉ, letter (1671)

The holy passion of Friendship is of so sweet and steady and loyal and enduring a nature that it will last through a whole lifetime, if not asked to lend money. —MARK TWAIN, *Pudd'nhead Wilson*, "Pudd'nhead Wilson's Calendar"

> Think where man's glory most begins and
>   ends
> And say my glory was I had such friends.
>   —W.B. YEATS, "The Municipal Gallery
>   Re-visited"

The Future

"We are always doing," says he, "something for Posterity, but I would fain see Posterity do something for us." —JOSEPH ADDISON, *The Spectator*

Take therefore no thought for the morrow: for the morrow shall take thought for the things of itself. Sufficient unto the day is the evil thereof. —BIBLE, *Matthew* 6:34

Boast not thyself of to-morrow; for thou knowest not what a day may bring forth. —BIBLE, *Proverbs* 27:1

FUTURE, *n.* That period of time in which our affairs prosper, our friends are true and our happiness is assured. —AMBROSE BIERCE, *The Devil's Dictionary*

If you do not think about the future, you cannot have one. —JOHN GALSWORTHY, *Swan Song*

An idealist believes the short run doesn't count. A cynic believes the long run doesn't matter. A realist believes that what is done or left undone in the short run determines the long run. —SYDNEY J. HARRIS, quoted in *Reader's Digest*

But this *long run* is a misleading guide to current affairs. *In the long run* we are all dead. —JOHN MAYNARD KEYNES, *The Tract on Monetary Reform*

The Future . . . something which everyone reaches at the rate of sixty minutes an hour, whatever he does, whoever he is. —C.S. LEWIS, *The Screwtape Letters*

I have been over into the future, and it works. —LINCOLN STEFFENS, *Autobiography*

  [Steffens was reporting on his visit to Russia in 1919. His remark is sometimes quoted as: "I have seen the future, and it works."]

The future is made of the same stuff as the present. —SIMONE WEIL, in *On Science, Necessity and the Love of God*, ed. Richard Rees

Games and Gambling

The gambling known as business looks with austere disfavor upon the business known as gambling.
—AMBROSE BIERCE, *The Devil's Dictionary*

I had always been fascinated by the bizarre world of cards. It was a world of pure power politics where rewards and punishments were meted out immediately. —ELY CULBERTSON, *Total Peace*

Death and dice level all distinction. —SAMUEL FOOTE, *The Minor*

Most amusements only mean trying to win another person's money. —RUDYARD KIPLING, *Plain Tales from the Hills*

Man is a gaming animal. He must be always trying to get the better in something or other. —CHARLES LAMB, *Essays of Elia*

It should be noted that the games of children are not games, and must be considered as their most serious actions. —MICHEL DE MONTAIGNE, *Essays*

The race is not always to the swift, nor the battle to the strong—but that's the way to bet. —DAMON RUNYON, attributed

> [See Bible *Ecclesiastes*, under Fortune and Chance]

Gambling promises the poor what Property performs for the rich. —GEORGE BERNARD SHAW, *Man and Superman*, "The Revolutionist's Handbook"

To play billiards well was a sign of an ill-spent youth. —HERBERT SPENCER, letter (to Beatrice Potter, 1890)

Gardens — See also FLOWERS AND TREES; NATURE

God Almighty first planted a garden. And indeed it is the purest of human pleasures. —FRANCIS BACON, *Essays*

A Garden is a lovesome thing, God wot! —THOMAS EDWARD BROWN, "My Garden"

The kiss of sun for pardon,
    The song of the birds for mirth—
One is nearer God's Heart in a garden
    Than anywhere else on earth.
                    —DOROTHY GURNEY, "The Lord God
                            Planted a Garden"

Oh, Adam was a gardener, and God who made
    him sees
That half a proper gardener's work is done
    upon his knees.
                    —RUDYARD KIPLING, "The Glory of the
                                    Garden"

A weed is no more than a flower in disguise,
Which is seen through at once, if love give a
    man eyes.
                    —JAMES RUSSELL LOWELL, "A Fable for
                                    Critics"

I want death to find me planting my cabbages, but caring little for it, and even less for my imperfect garden. —MICHEL DE MONTAIGNE, *Essays*

What a man needs in gardening is a cast-iron back, with a hinge in it. —CHARLES DUDLEY WARNER, *My Summer in a Garden*

Generations

One generation passeth away, and another generation cometh: but the earth abideth for ever. —BIBLE, *Ecclesiastes* 1:4

As is the generation of leaves, so is that of humanity. The wind scatters the leaves on the ground, but the live timber burgeons with leaves again in the season of spring returning. So one generation of men will grow while another dies. —HOMER, *The Iliad*

Every generation revolts against its fathers and makes friends with its grandfathers. —LEWIS MUMFORD, *The Brown Decades*

> [Claudette Colbert was quoted in *Time* magazine as saying: "Why do grandparents and grandchildren get along so well? They have the same enemy—the mother."]

Each generation imagines itself to be more intelligent than the one that went before it, and wiser than the one that comes after it. —GEORGE ORWELL, *Collected Essays, Journalism, and Letters of George Orwell*

> We think our Fathers Fools, so wise we grow;
> Our Wiser Sons, no doubt, will think us so.
> —ALEXANDER POPE, *An Essay on Criticism*

> Crabbed age and youth cannot live together:
> Youth is full of pleasance, age is full of care.
> —SHAKESPEARE (?), *The Passionate Pilgrim*

Generosity — See CHARITY; GIFTS AND GIVING

Genius and Talent

Whom the gods wish to destroy they first call promising. —CYRIL CONNOLLY, *Enemies of Promise*

Genius is one percent inspiration and ninety-nine percent perspiration. —THOMAS EDISON, quoted in F.L. Dyer's *Edison: His Life and Inventions*

Genius will live and thrive without training, but it does not the less reward the watering-pot and pruning-knife. —MARGARET FULLER, diary entry

Gift, like genius, I often think only means an infinite capacity for taking pains. —JANE ELLICE HOPKINS, *Work Amongst Working Men*

> [This is the wording perhaps most often quoted, but the idea has been voiced by others. Comte de Buffon was quoted in Hérault de Séchelles's *Voyage à Montbard* as saying: "Genius is nothing but a greater aptitude for patience." And Thomas Carlyle wrote in his *Life of Frederick the Great*: " 'Genius' (which means transcendent capacity of taking trouble, first of all)."]

Genius . . . means little more than the faculty of perceiving in an unhabitual way. —WILLIAM JAMES, *The Principles of Psychology*

Everyone has talent. What is rare is the courage to follow the talent to the dark place where it leads. —ERICA JONG, in *The First Ms. Reader*, ed. Francine Klagsbrun

A man of genius makes no mistakes. His errors are volitional and are the portals of discovery. —JAMES JOYCE, *Ulysses*

I think this is the most extraordinary collection of talent, of human knowledge, that has ever been gathered together at the White House—with the possible exception of when Thomas Jefferson dined alone. —JOHN F. KENNEDY, speech (honoring Nobel Prize winners, 1962)

I have so often seen how people come by the name of genius—in the same way, that is, as certain insects come by the name of millipede, not because they have that number of feet, but because most people won't count up to fourteen. —GEORG CHRISTOPH LICHTENBERG, *The Reflections of Lichtenberg*, ed. Norman Allison

Talent is that which is in a man's power; genius is that in whose power a man is. —JAMES RUSSELL LOWELL, *Literary Essays*

Genius does what it must, and Talent does what it can. —OWEN MEREDITH, "Last Words of a Sensitive Second-Rate Poet"

It's a pity one can't imagine what one can't compare to anything. Genius is an African who dreams up snow. —VLADIMIR NABOKOV, *The Gift*

There is no great genius without some touch of madness. —SENECA, *De Tranquillitate Animi*

> [Seneca said he was quoting Aristotle. This consoling thought has also been repeated by many others.]

When a true genius appears in the world, you may know him by this sign, that the dunces are all in confederacy against him. —JONATHAN SWIFT, *Thoughts on Various Subjects*

Ghosts — See THE SUPERNATURAL

Gifts and Giving — See also CHARITY

It is more blessed to give than to receive. —BIBLE, *Acts* 20:35

Every man according as he purposeth in his heart, so let him give; not grudgingly, or of necessity: for God loveth a cheerful giver. —BIBLE, *II Corinthians* 9:7

The manner of giving is worth more than the gift. —PIERRE CORNEILLE, *Le Menteur*

One must be poor to know the luxury of giving. —GEORGE ELIOT, *Middlemarch*

We do not quite forgive a giver. The hand that feeds us is in some danger of being bitten. —RALPH WALDO EMERSON, *Essays*

Nothing costs so much as what is given us. —THOMAS FULLER, *Gnomologia*

Liberality consists less in giving a great deal than in gifts well timed. —LA BRUYÈRE, *Les Caractères*

What is called liberality is often merely the vanity of giving. —LA ROCHEFOUCAULD, *Maxims*

"Presents," I often say, "endear absents." —CHARLES LAMB, *Essays of Elia*

Ever since Eve gave Adam the apple, there has been a misunderstanding between the sexes about gifts. —NAN ROBERTSON, in *New York Times*

> For to the noble mind
> Rich gifts wax poor when givers prove unkind.
> —SHAKESPEARE, *Hamlet*

> Behold, I do not give lectures or a little
>   charity,
> When I give I give myself.
>   —WALT WHITMAN, *Leaves of Grass*

Glory — See also FAME

Who would prefer peace to the glory of hunger and thirst, of wading through mud, and dying in the service of one's country? —JEAN GIRAUDOUX, *Amphitryon 38*

> The boast of heraldry, the pomp of pow'r,
>   And all that beauty, all that wealth e'er gave,
> Awaits alike th' inevitable hour,
>   The paths of glory lead but to the grave.
>   —THOMAS GRAY, "Elegy Written in a
>   Country Churchyard"

Glory is largely a theatrical concept. There is no striving for glory without a vivid awareness of an audience. —ERIC HOFFER, *The True Believer*

There is no road of flowers leading to glory. —JEAN DE LA FONTAINE, *Fables*

To our ashes glory comes too late. —MARTIAL, *Epigrams*

One crowded hour of glorious life is worth an age without a name. —THOMAS OSBERT MORDAUNT, "Verses Written During the War"

> [Quoted by Sir Walter Scott in *Old Mortality*, and often credited to him.]

> Glory is like a circle in the water,
> Which never ceaseth to enlarge itself
> Till by broad spreading it disperse to nought.
> —SHAKESPEARE, *Henry VI, Part I*

Avoid shame, but do not seek glory,—nothing so expensive as glory. —SYDNEY SMITH, quoted in Lady Holland's *Memoir*

How quickly passes away the glory of this world. —THOMAS ÁKEMPIS, *Imitation of Christ*

God — See also PROVIDENCE

We can know what God is not, but we cannot know what He is. —SAINT AUGUSTINE, *De Trinitate*

God is our refuge and strength, a very present help in trouble. —BIBLE, *Psalms* 46:1

I am Alpha and Omega, the beginning and the end, the first and the last. —BIBLE, *Revelation* 22:13

God is love; and he that dwelleth in love dwelleth in God, and God in him. —BIBLE, *I John* 4:16

God is no respecter of persons. —BIBLE, *Acts* 10:34

A God who let us prove his existence would be an idol.
—DIETRICH BONHOEFFER, *No Rusty Swords*

> God is seen God
> In the star, in the stone, in the flesh, in the
>   soul and the clod.
> —ROBERT BROWNING, "Saul"

> God moves in a mysterious way
>   His wonders to perform;
> He plants his footsteps in the sea,
>   And rides upon the storm.
> —WILLIAM COWPER, "Light Shining Out of
>   Darkness"

It is the final proof of God's omnipotence that he need
not exist in order to save us. —PETER DE VRIES, *The
Mackerel Plaza*

God is subtle but he is not malicious. —ALBERT EIN-
STEIN, attributed

> [This is inscribed over a fireplace in Fine Hall at
> Princeton University.]

I, at any rate, am convinced that *He* [God] is not playing at dice. —ALBERT EINSTEIN, letter (1926)

> God, to me, it seems,
> is a verb
> not a noun,
> proper or improper.
> —R. BUCKMINSTER FULLER, *No More
>   Secondhand God*

God will forgive me; it is his trade. —HEINRICH
HEINE, (reportedly said on his deathbed)

An honest god is the noblest work of man. —ROBERT
G. INGERSOLL, *The Gods, and Other Lectures*

[This line is also found in Samuel Butler's *Note-Books*. Both men were parodying Alexander Pope; see under Honesty.]

The Holy One . . . requires the heart. —JUDAH BEN EZEKIEL, in the *Talmud*

[Often translated as "God wants the heart."]

Though the mills of God grind slowly, yet they grind exceeding small. —FRIEDRICH VON LOGAU, "Retribution"

A mighty fortress is our God,
A bulwark never failing.
 —MARTIN LUTHER, "Ein' feste Burg"

Just are the ways of God,
And justifiable to men.
 —JOHN MILTON, *Samson Agonistes*

Man is certainly crazy. He could not make a mite, and he makes gods by the dozen. —MICHEL DE MONTAIGNE, *Essays*

If the triangles made a god, they would give him three sides. —BARON DE MONTESQUIEU, *The Persian Letters*

God is dead: but considering the state Man is in, there will perhaps be caves, for ages yet, in which his shadow will be shown. —FRIEDRICH NIETZSCHE, *The Joyful Wisdom* (also known as *The Gay Science*)

It is convenient that there be gods, and, as it is convenient, let us believe there are. —OVID, *Ars Amatoria*

Had I but served my God with half the zeal
I served my king, he would not in mine age
Have left me naked to mine enemies.
 —SHAKESPEARE, *Henry VIII*

Man proposes, but God disposes. —Thomas à Kempis, *Imitation of Christ*

If God did not exist, it would be necessary to invent him. —Voltaire, "Épître à l'auteur du livre des trois imposteurs"

If God created us in his own image, we have more than reciprocated. —Voltaire, *Le Sottisier*

Goodness

Men have never been good, they are not good and they never will be good. —Karl Barth, *Christian Community*

> He who would do good to another must do it in
>   Minute Particulars:
> General Good is the plea of the scoundrel,
>   hypocrite and flatterer.
>   —William Blake, *Jerusalem*

We know the good, we apprehend it clearly, but we can't bring it to achievement. —Euripides, *Hippolytus*

The Devil himself is good, when he is pleased. —Thomas Fuller, *Gnomologia*

I expect to pass through this world but once. Any good therefore that I can do, or any kindness that I can show to any fellow creature, let me do it now. Let me not defer or neglect it, for I shall not pass this way again. —Stephen Grellet, attributed

The greatest pleasure I know is to do a good action by stealth, and to have it found out by accident. —Charles Lamb, "Table Talk"

Goodness does not more certainly make men happy than happiness makes them good. —Walter Savage Landor, *Imaginary Conversations*

Waste no more time arguing what a good man should be. Be one. —MARCUS AURELIUS, *Meditations*

Good, the more
Communicated, more abundant grows.
—JOHN MILTON, *Paradise Lost*

There is no man so good, who, were he to submit all his thoughts and actions to the laws, would not deserve hanging ten times in his life. —MICHEL DE MONTAIGNE, *Essays*

It is not enough to do good; one must do it the right way. —JOHN MORLEY, *On Compromise*

How far that little candle throws his beams!
So shines a good deed in a naughty world.
—SHAKESPEARE, *The Merchant of Venice*

'Tis only noble to be good.
Kind hearts are more than coronets,
And simple faith than Norman blood.
—ALFRED, LORD TENNYSON, "Lady Clara
Vere de Vere"

To be good is noble; but to show others how to be good is nobler and no trouble. —MARK TWAIN, *Following the Equator*, "Pudd'nhead Wilson's New Calendar"

The best is the enemy of the good. —VOLTAIRE, *Philosophical Dictionary*

Gossip and Rumor

For what do we live, but to make sport for our neighbors, and laugh at them in our turn? —JANE AUSTEN, *Pride and Prejudice*

Love and scandal are the best sweeteners of tea.
—HENRY FIELDING, *Love in Several Masques*

171

A cruel story runs on wheels, and every hand oils the wheels as they run. —OUIDA, *Wisdom, Wit and Pathos*

I lay it down as a fact that if all men knew what others say of them, there would not be four friends in the world. —BLAISE PASCAL, *Pensées*

No one gossips about other people's secret virtues. —BERTRAND RUSSELL, *On Education*

Rumor is not always wrong. —TACITUS, *Life of Agricola*

> Rumor, than which no evil flies more swiftly.
> She flourishes as she flies, gains strength by
>   mere motion.
> Small at first and in fear, she soon rises to
>   heaven,
> Walks upon land and hides her head in the
>   clouds.
>   —VIRGIL, *Aeneid*

There is only one thing in the world worse than being talked about, and that is not being talked about. —OSCAR WILDE, *The Picture of Dorian Gray*

Government

A government of laws and not of men. —JOHN ADAMS, "Novanglus Papers"

[Adams later used this in the Massachusetts Constitution (1780).]

Where the State begins, individual liberty ceases, and vice versa. —MIKHAIL BAKUNIN, *Federalism, Socialism and Anti-Theologism*

Government is a contrivance of human wisdom to provide for human wants. Men have a right that these wants should be provided for by this wisdom. —EDMUND BURKE, *Reflections on the Revolution in France*

Too bad that all the people who know how to run the country are busy driving taxicabs and cutting hair.
—GEORGE BURNS, quoted in *Life*

In the long-run every Government is the exact symbol of its People, with their wisdom and unwisdom.
—THOMAS CARLYLE, *Past and Present*

If the Government is big enough to give you everything you want, it is big enough to take away everything you have. —GERALD R. FORD, quoted in John F. Parker's *If Elected*

> [Barry Goldwater said the same thing in a speech in 1964: "A government that is big enough to give you all you want is big enough to take it all away."]

Which government is best? That which teaches us to govern ourselves. —JOHANN WOLFGANG VON GOETHE, *Proverbs in Prose*

Nothing appears more surprising to those who consider human affairs with a philosophical eye, than the easiness with which the many are governed by the few. —DAVID HUME, *Essays*

It was once said that the moral test of government is how that government treats those who are in the dawn of life, the children; those who are in the twilight of life, the elderly; and those who are in the shadows of life—the sick, the needy and the handicapped. —HUBERT H. HUMPHREY, speech (1977)

Were we directed from Washington when to sow, and when to reap, we should soon want bread. —THOMAS JEFFERSON, *Autobiography*

No man is good enough to govern another man without that other's consent. —ABRAHAM LINCOLN, speech (1854)

It is perfectly true that that government is best which governs least. It is equally true that that government is best which provides most. —WALTER LIPPMANN, *A Preface to Politics*

[See Henry David Thoreau, in this section.]

Every country has the government it deserves. —JOSEPH MARIE DE MAISTRE, letter (1811)

The worst government is the most moral. One composed of cynics is often very tolerant and humane. But when fanatics are on top there is no limit to oppression. —H.L. MENCKEN, *Minority Report: H.L. Mencken's Notebooks*

The great art of governing consists in not letting men grow old in their jobs. —NAPOLEON I, letter (1796)

A little government and a little luck are necessary in life, but only a fool trusts either of them. —P.J. O'ROURKE, quoted in *Quote* magazine

Thou dost not know, my son, with how little wisdom the world is governed. —COUNT AXEL OXENSTIERNA, letter (1648)

[Sometimes attributed to Pope Julius III.]

Government, even in its best state, is but a necessary evil; in its worst state an intolerable one. —THOMAS PAINE, *Common Sense*

Let the people think they govern and they will be governed. —WILLIAM PENN, *Some Fruits of Solitude*

Governments exist to protect the rights of minorities. The loved and the rich need no protection: they have many friends and few enemies. —WENDELL PHILLIPS, speech (1860)

The Government is like a baby's alimentary canal, with a healthy appetite at one end and no responsibility at the other. —RONALD REAGAN, quoted in *New York Times Magazine*

One of the greatest delusions in the world is the hope that the evils in this world are to be cured by legislation. —THOMAS B. REED, speech (1886)

I don't make jokes—I just watch the government and report the facts. —WILL ROGERS, quoted in *Saturday Review*

A government which robs Peter to pay Paul can always depend on the support of Paul. —GEORGE BERNARD SHAW, *Everybody's Political What's What*

I heartily accept the motto,—"That government is best which governs least;" and I should like to see it acted up to more rapidly and systematically. Carried out, it finally amounts to this, which I also believe,—"That government is best which governs not at all."
—HENRY DAVID THOREAU, *Civil Disobedience*

[The "motto" was probably that of *The United States Magazine and Democratic Review.* Its editor, John L. O'Sullivan, had written, in 1837: ". . . all government is evil, and the parent of evil. . . . The best government is that which governs least." The statement is sometimes attributed to Thomas Jefferson, but it has not been found in his writings.]

Gratitude

Next to ingratitude, the most painful thing to bear is gratitude. —HENRY WARD BEECHER, *Proverbs from Plymouth Pulpit*

Revenge is profitable, gratitude is expensive.
—EDWARD GIBBON, *Decline and Fall of the Roman Empire*

There are minds so impatient of inferiority that their gratitude is a species of revenge, and they return benefits, not because recompense is a pleasure, but because obligation is a pain. —SAMUEL JOHNSON, *The Rambler*

The gratitude of most men is nothing but a secret desire to receive greater benefits. —LA ROCHEFOUCAULD, *Maxims*

Gratitude is the memory of the heart. —JEAN BAPTISTE MASSIEU, *Letter to Abbé Sicard*

> A grateful mind
> By owing owes not, but still pays, at once
> Indebted and discharg'd.
> —JOHN MILTON, *Paradise Lost*

Great indebtedness does not make men grateful, but vengeful; and if a little charity is not forgotten, it turns into a gnawing worm. —FRIEDRICH NIETZSCHE, *Thus Spake Zarathustra*

If you pick up a starving dog and make him prosperous, he will not bite you. This is the principal difference between a dog and a man. —MARK TWAIN, *Pudd'nhead Wilson*, "Pudd'nhead Wilson's Calendar"

Great and Small

He that contemneth small things shall fall by little and little. —BIBLE, *Ecclesiasticus* 19:1

No sadder proof can be given by a man of his own littleness than disbelief in great men. —THOMAS CARLYLE, *On Heroes, Hero-Worship and the Heroic in History*

Little drops of water,
  little grains of sand,
Make the mighty ocean
  and the pleasant land.
So the little moments,
  humble though they be,
Make the mighty ages
  of eternity.
      —JULIA A. CARNEY, "Little Things"

It has long been an axiom of mine that the little things are infinitely the most important. —ARTHUR CONAN DOYLE, *The Adventures of Sherlock Holmes*

In small proportions we just beauties see;
And in short measures, life may perfect be.
      —BEN JONSON, "A Part of an Ode . . ."

A toothache will cost a battle, a drizzle cancel an insurrection. —VLADIMIR NABOKOV, *The Eye*

A trifle consoles us because a trifle distresses us. —BLAISE PASCAL, *Pensées*

He who can take no interest in what is small, will take false interest in what is great . . . ; he who cannot make a bank sublime, will make a mountain ridiculous. —JOHN RUSKIN, *Modern Painters*

Trifles make up the happiness or the misery of mortal life. —ALEXANDER SMITH, *Dreamthorp*

Greatness

All rising to great place is by a winding stair. —FRANCIS BACON, *Essays*

Great men are but life-sized. Most of them, indeed, are rather short. —MAX BEERBOHM, *And Even Now*

Great men are not always wise. —BIBLE, *Job* 32:9

Mountains appear more lofty, the nearer they are approached, but great men resemble them not in this particular. —MARGUERITE BLESSINGTON, "Night Thought Book"

They're only truly great who are truly good.
—GEORGE CHAPMAN, *Revenge for Honor*

There is a great man who makes every man feel small. But the real great man is the man who makes every man feel great. —G.K. CHESTERTON, *Charles Dickens*

How dreary—to be—Somebody!
How public—like a Frog—
To tell one's name—the livelong June—
To an admiring Bog!
            —EMILY DICKINSON, "I'm Nobody! Who
                                are you?"

To be great is to be misunderstood. —RALPH WALDO EMERSON, *Essays*, "Self-Reliance"

Not he is great who can alter matter, but he who can alter my state of mind. —RALPH WALDO EMERSON, "The American Scholar"

Great and good are seldom the same man. —THOMAS FULLER, *Gnomologia*

[See George Chapman, in this section, for an opposing view.]

Few great men could pass Personnel. —PAUL GOODMAN, *Growing Up Absurd*

The Great Man is a man who lives a long way off.
—ELBERT HUBBARD, in *The Philistine*

Lives of great men all remind us
We can make our lives sublime.
And, departing, leave behind us
Footprints on the sands of time.
—HENRY WADSWORTH LONGFELLOW, "A
Psalm of Life"

The great man is he who does not lose his child's
heart. —MENCIUS, *Works*

Let us not underestimate the privileges of the *mediocre*. As one climbs *higher*, life becomes ever harder;
the coldness increases, responsibility increases.
—FRIEDRICH NIETZSCHE, *The Antichrist*

But be not afraid of greatness: some are born great,
some achieve greatness and some have greatness
thrust upon 'em. —SHAKESPEARE, *Twelfth Night*

Greed

The bird of paradise alights only upon the hand that
does not grasp. —JOHN BERRY, *Flight of White
Crows*

There is enough in the world for everyone's need, but
not enough for everyone's greed. —FRANK BUCHMAN,
Remaking the World

Nothing is sufficient for the person who finds sufficiency too little. —EPICURUS, in *The Philosophy of
Epicurus* by G.K. Strodach

Avarice and happiness never saw each other, how
then should they become acquainted. —BENJAMIN
FRANKLIN, *Poor Richard's Almanac*

Riches have made more covetous men than covetousness hath made rich men. —THOMAS FULLER, *Gnomologia*

Avarice, the spur of industry. —DAVID HUME, *Essays*

> each generation wastes a little more
> of the future with greed and lust for riches
> —DON MARQUIS, *the lives and times of archy and mehitabel*

> i have noticed
> that when
> chickens quit
> quarrelling over their
> food they often
> find that there is
> enough for all of them
> i wonder if
> it might not
> be the same way
> with the
> human race
> —DON MARQUIS, *the lives and times of archy and mehitabel*

Poverty wants much; but avarice, everything.
—PUBLILIUS SYRUS, *Maxims*

To greed, all nature is insufficient. —SENECA, *Hercules Oetaeus*

> 'T would make one scratch where 't does not
> itch,To see fools live poor to die rich.
> —THOMAS SHADWELL, *Woman Captain*

Grief — See SORROW

Guests — See HOSPITALITY

Guilt

The wicked flee when no man pursueth: but the righteous are bold as a lion. —BIBLE, *Proverbs* 28:1

Guilt: the gift that keeps on giving. —ERMA BOM-BECK, quoted in *Time*

Guilt always hurries towards its complement, punishment: only there does its satisfaction lie. —LAWRENCE DURRELL, *Justine*

True guilt is guilt at the obligation one owes to oneself to be oneself, to actualize oneself. False guilt is guilt felt at not being what other people feel one ought to be or assume that one is. —R.D. LAING, *Self and Others*

> Without guilt
> What is a man? An animal, isn't he?
> A wolf forgiven at his meat,
> A beetle innocent in his copulation.
> —ARCHIBALD MACLEISH, *JB*

Give me six lines written by the most honorable of men, and I will find an excuse in them to hang him. —CARDINAL DE RICHELIEU, *Mirame*

> So full of artless jealousy is guilt,
> It spills itself in fearing to be spilt.
> —SHAKESPEARE, *Hamlet*

Here's the smell of the blood still: all the perfumes of Arabia will not sweeten this little hand. —SHAKE-SPEARE, *Macbeth*

The lady doth protest too much, methinks. —SHAKE-SPEARE, *Hamlet*

Habit

Curious things, habits. People themselves never knew they had them. —AGATHA CHRISTIE, *Witness for the Prosecution*

Habit will reconcile us to everything but change. —CHARLES CALEB COLTON, *Lacon*

Men's natures are alike; it is their habits that separate them. —CONFUCIUS, *Analects*

Habit with him was all the test of truth;
"It must be right: I've done it from my youth."
　　　　　　　—GEORGE CRABBE, *The Borough*

Nothing is in reality either pleasant or unpleasant by nature; but all things become so through habit. —EPICTETUS, *Encheiridion*

Habit is thus the enormous flywheel of society, its most precious conservative agent. It alone is what keeps us all within the bounds of ordinance, and saves the children of fortune from the envious uprisings of the poor. —WILLIAM JAMES, *The Principles of Psychology*

For as good habits of the people require good laws to support them, so laws, to be observed, need good habits on the part of the people. —NICCOLÒ MACHIAVELLI, *The Prince and the Discourses*

Small habits well pursued betimes
May reach the diginity of crimes.
　　　　　　　—HANNAH MORE, *Florio*

Habit is a second nature which prevents us from knowing the first, of which it has neither the cruelties nor the enchantments. —MARCEL PROUST, *Remembrance of Things Past: Cities of the Plain*

Habit is habit, and not to be flung out of the window by any man, but coaxed downstairs a step at a time. —MARK TWAIN, *Pudd'nhead Wilson*, "Pudd'nhead Wilson's Calendar"

To fall into a habit is to begin to cease to be. —MIGUEL DE UNAMUNO, *The Tragic Sense of Life*

Happiness

True happiness is of a retired nature, and an enemy to pomp and noise. —JOSEPH ADDISON, *The Spectator*

Only when a man's life comes to its end in prosperity dare we pronounce him happy. —AESCHYLUS, *Agamemnon*

> [This view was widely held in ancient times. Solon (as quoted by Herodotus in his *Histories*) said: "Call him, however, until he die, not happy but fortunate. . . . In every matter it behooves us to mark well the end: for oftentimes the god gives men a gleam of happiness, and then plunges them into ruin." The thought also occurs in the Bible, in *Ecclesiasticus* 11:28: "Judge none blessed before his death."]

The secret of happiness is to admire without desiring. And that is not happiness. —F.H. BRADLEY, *Aphorisms*

To fill the hour,—that is happiness; to fill the hour, and leave no crevice for a repentance or an approval. —RALPH WALDO EMERSON, *Essays*

To be happy one must have a good stomach and a bad heart. —BERNARD DE FONTENELLE, *Dialogues des morts*

Human felicity is produced not so much by great pieces of good fortune that seldom happen, as by little advantages that occur every day. —BENJAMIN FRANKLIN, *Autobiography*

One feels inclined to say that the intention that man should be "happy" is not included in the plan of "Creation." . . . We are so made that we can derive intense enjoyment only from a contrast and very little from a state of things. —SIGMUND FREUD, *Civilization and its Discontents*

Happiness Makes Up in Height for What It Lacks in Length —ROBERT FROST, (poem title)

Nothing is more fatal to happiness than the remembrance of happiness. —ANDRÉ GIDE, *The Immoralist*

The search for happiness is one of the chief sources of unhappiness. —ERIC HOFFER, *The Passionate State of Mind*

It's pretty hard to tell what does bring happiness. Poverty and wealth have both failed. —KIN HUBBARD, *Abe Martin's Broadcast*

Happiness is like coke—something you get as a by-product in the process of making something else. —ALDOUS HUXLEY, *Point Counter Point*

The happiest people seem to be those who have no particular cause for being happy except that they are so. —WILLIAM RALPH INGE, in *Wit and Wisdom of Dean Inge*, ed. James Marchant

One is never as happy or as unhappy as one thinks. —LA ROCHEFOUCAULD, *Maxims*

> Happiness, to some, elation;
> Is, to others, mere stagnation.
> —AMY LOWELL, "Happiness"

Ask yourself whether you are happy, and you cease to be so. —JOHN STUART MILL, *Autobiography*

No man is happy who does not think himself so. —PUBLILIUS SYRUS, *Maxims*

Happiness is the only sanction of life; where happiness fails, existence remains a mad and lamentable experiment. —GEORGE SANTAYANA, *The Life of Reason*

I were but little happy, if I could say how much.
—SHAKESPEARE, *Much Ado About Nothing*

We have no more right to consume happiness without producing it than to consume wealth without producing it. —GEORGE BERNARD SHAW, *Candida*

A lifetime of happiness! No man alive could bear it: it would be hell on earth. —GEORGE BERNARD SHAW, *Man and Superman*

There are two things to aim at in life: first, to get what you want; and, after that, to enjoy it. Only the wisest of mankind achieve the second. —LOGAN PEARSALL SMITH, *Afterthoughts*

Mankind are always happy for having been happy; so that, if you make them happy now, you make them happy twenty years hence by the memory of it. —SYDNEY SMITH, *Elementary Sketches of Moral Philosophy*

Happiness is an imaginary condition, formerly often attributed by the living to the dead, now usually attributed by adults to children, and by children to adults. —THOMAS SZASZ, *The Second Sin*

Haste

Make haste slowly. —CAESAR AUGUSTUS, quoted by Suetonius in *Lives of the Caesars*

> There's no workman, whatsoever he be,
> That may both work well and hastily.
> —CHAUCER, *The Canterbury Tales*

Whoever is in a hurry shows that the thing he is about is too big for him. —LORD CHESTERFIELD, *Letters to His Son*

No man who is in a hurry is quite civilized. —WILL DURANT, *The Life of Greece*

Nothing is more vulgar than haste. —RALPH WALDO EMERSON, *The Conduct of Life*

Lord Ronald said nothing; he flung himself from the room, flung himself upon his horse and rode madly off in all directions. —STEPHEN LEACOCK, *Nonsense Novels*

Half our life is spent trying to find something to do with the time we have rushed through life trying to save. —WILL ROGERS, *The Autobiography of Will Rogers*

The haste of a fool is the slowest thing in the world. —THOMAS SHADWELL, *A True Widow*

Too swift arrives as tardy as too slow. —SHAKE-SPEARE, *Romeo and Juliet*

Wisely and slow; they stumble that run fast. —SHAKESPEARE, *Romeo and Juliet*

> If it were done when 'tis done, then 'twere well
> It were done quickly.
> > —SHAKESPEARE, *Macbeth*

Hatred and Dislike — See also ANGER

To be loved is to be fortunate, but to be hated is to achieve distinction. —MINNA ANTRIM, *Naked Truth and Veiled Allusions*

> Now Hatred is by far the longest pleasure;
> Men love in haste, but they detest at leisure.
> > —LORD BYRON, *Don Juan*

Love, friendship, respect, do not unite people as much as a common hatred for something. —ANTON CHEKHOV, *Notebooks*

If you hate a person, you hate something in him that is part of yourself. What isn't part of ourselves doesn't disturb us. —HERMANN HESSE, *Demian*

Any kiddie in school can love like a fool,
But hating, my boy, is an art.
—OGDEN NASH, "Plea for Less Malice
Toward Men"

One does not hate as long as one has a low esteem of someone, but only when one esteems him as an equal or a superior. —FRIEDRICH NIETZSCHE, *Beyond Good and Evil*

Any man who hates dogs and babies can't be all bad. —LEO ROSTEN, speech (at a dinner honoring W.C. Fields, 1939)
[This seems to be the basis for the quotation often attributed to Fields: "Anyone who hates children and dogs can't be all bad."]

Hatred, as well as love, renders its votaries credulous. —JEAN-JACQUES ROUSSEAU, *Confessions*

I do desire we may be better strangers. —SHAKESPEARE, *As You Like It*

Health and Fitness

Health indeed is a precious thing, to recover and preserve which we undergo any misery, drink bitter potions, freely give our goods: restore a man to his health, his purse lies open to thee. —ROBERT BURTON, *The Anatomy of Melancholy*

The trouble about always trying to preserve the health of the body is that it is so difficult to do without destroying the health of the mind. —G.K. CHESTERTON, *Come to Think of It*

Those who think they have not time for bodily exercise will sooner or later have to find time for illness.
—EDWARD STANLEY, EARL OF DERBY, speech (1873)

Better to hunt in fields, for health unbought,
Than fee the doctor for a nauseous draught.
The wise, for cure, on exercise depend;
God never made his work for man to mend.
    —JOHN DRYDEN, "Epistle to John Driden
                            of Chesterton"

Early to bed and early to rise, makes a man healthy, wealthy, and wise. —BENJAMIN FRANKLIN, *Poor Richard's Almanac*

[James Thurber's variant in *Fables for Our Time*: "Early to rise and early to bed makes a male healthy and wealthy and dead."]

You should pray for a sound mind in a sound body. (*Orandum est ut sit mens sana in corpore sano.*)
—JUVENAL, *Satires*

It is a wearisome illness to preserve one's health by too strict a regimen. —LA ROCHEFOUCAULD, *Maxims*

A sound mind in a sound body, is a short but full description of a happy state in this world. He that has these two, has little more to wish for; and he that wants either of them, will be little the better for anything else. —JOHN LOCKE, *Some Thoughts Concerning Education*

Joy and Temperance and Repose
Slam the door on the doctor's nose.
    —HENRY WADSWORTH LONGFELLOW, "The
                            Best Medicines"

Life is not merely being alive, but being well.
—MARTIAL, *Epigrams*

It is better to lose health like a spendthrift than to waste it like a miser. —ROBERT LOUIS STEVENSON, *Virginibus Puerisque*

The beneficent effects of the regular quarter-hour's exercise before breakfast is more than offset by the mental wear and tear involved in getting out of bed fifteen minutes earlier than one otherwise would. — SIMEON STRUNSKY, *The Patient Observer*

Our body is a machine for living. It is organized for that, it is its nature. Let life go on in it unhindered and let it defend itself, it will do more than if you paralyze it by encumbering it with remedies. —LEO TOLSTOY, *War and Peace*

The Heart and Emotion

The heart is deceitful above all things, and desperately wicked: who can know it? —BIBLE, *Jeremiah* 17:9

Where your treasure is, there will your heart be also. —BIBLE, *Matthew* 6:21

Seeing's believing, but feeling's the truth. —THOMAS FULLER, *Gnomologia*

All the knowledge I possess everyone else can acquire, but my heart is all my own. —JOHANN WOLFGANG VON GOETHE, *The Sorrows of Young Werther*

There are moments in life, when the heart is
  so full of emotion
That if by chance it be shaken, or into its
  depths like a pebble
Drops some careless word, it overflows, and
  its secret,
Spilt on the ground like water, can never be
  gathered together.
    —HENRY WADSWORTH LONGFELLOW, *The Courtship of Miles Standish*

Pity me that the heart is slow to learn
What the swift mind beholds at every turn.
　　　—EDNA ST. VINCENT MILLAY, "Pity me not
　　　　　　because the light of day"

The heart has its reasons which reason knows nothing of. —BLAISE PASCAL, *Pensées*

The heart is a small thing, but desireth great matters. It is not sufficient for a kite's dinner, yet the whole world is not sufficient for it. —FRANCIS QUARLES, *Emblems*

It is only with the heart that one can see rightly; what is essential is invisible to the eye. —ANTOINE DE SAINT-EXUPÉRY, *The Little Prince*

My heart is a lonely hunter that hunts on a lonely hill. —WILLIAM SHARP, "The Lonely Hunter"

[Carson McCullers used this as the basis for the title of a novel: *The Heart Is a Lonely Hunter*.]

In matters of the heart, nothing is true except the improbable. —MADAME DE STAËL, letter (1810)

Now that my ladder's gone
I must lie down where all the ladders start
In the foul rag and bone shop of the heart.
　　　—W.B. YEATS, "The Circus Animals'
　　　　　　Desertion"

Heaven, Hell, and the Hereafter

The chief problem about death, incidentally, is the fear that there may be no afterlife. . . . Also, there is the fear that there is an afterlife but no one will know where it's being held. —WOODY ALLEN, *Without Feathers*

If it's heaven for climate, it's hell for company. —JAMES M. BARRIE, *The Little Minister*

CLOV: Do you believe in the life to come?
HAMM: Mine was always that.
—SAMUEL BECKETT, *Endgame*

Hell, madame, is to love no longer. —GEORGES BER
NANOS, *The Diary of a Country Priest*

Hell is oneself,
Hell is alone, the other figures in it
Merely projections.
—T.S. ELIOT, *The Cocktail Party*

Hell is full of good meanings and wishings.
—GEORGE HERBERT, *Jacula Prudentum*

[The proverb "Hell is paved with good intentions"
appeared in 1670 in John Ray's *English Proverbs*.]

Work and pray, live on hay,
You'll get pie in the sky when you die.
—JOE HILL, "The Preacher and the
Slave"

Many might go to heaven with half the labor they go
to hell. —BEN JONSON, *Timber*

There is wishful thinking in Hell as well as on Earth.
—C.S. LEWIS, *The Screwtape Letters*

Probably no invention came more easily to man than
Heaven. —GEORG CHRISTOPH LICHTENBERG, *Aphorisms*

Hell hath no limits, nor is circumscribed
In one self place, for where we are is hell,
And where hell is there must we ever be.
—CHRISTOPHER MARLOWE, *Doctor Faustus*

Long is the way
And hard, that out of Hell leads up to light.
—JOHN MILTON, *Paradise Lost*

Which way I fly is Hell; myself am Hell;
And in the lowest deep a lower deep
Still threat'ning to devour me opens wide,
To which the Hell I suffer seems a Heav'n.
—JOHN MILTON, *Paradise Lost*

Earth has no sorrow that Heaven cannot heal.
—THOMAS MOORE, "Come, Ye Disconsolate"

The way to Heaven out of all places is of like length
and distance. —THOMAS MORE, *Utopia*

The infliction of cruelty with a good conscience is a
delight to moralists. That is why they invented Hell.
—BERTRAND RUSSELL, *Sceptical Essays*

Men have feverishly conceived a heaven only to find
it insipid, and a hell to find it ridiculous. —GEORGE
SANTAYANA, *The Life of Reason*

Hell is other people. —JEAN-PAUL SARTRE, *No Exit*

If you go to Heaven without being naturally qualified
for it, you will not enjoy yourself there. —GEORGE
BERNARD SHAW, *Man and Superman*

Hell is a city much like London—
A populous and smoky city.
—PERCY BYSSHE SHELLEY, "Peter Bell the
Third"

The descent to Avernus is easy. —VIRGIL, *Aeneid*

The human mind is inspired enough when it comes
to inventing horrors; it is when it tries to invent a
Heaven that it shows itself cloddish. —EVELYN
WAUGH, *Put Out More Flags*

Help

You can only help one of your luckless
brothers
By trampling down a dozen others.
—BERTOLT BRECHT, *The Good Woman of
Setzuan*

If I can stop one Heart from breaking
I shall not live in vain
If I can ease one life the Aching
Or cool one Pain

Or help one fainting Robin
Unto his Nest again
I shall not live in Vain.
  —EMILY DICKINSON, "If I can stop one
          Heart from breaking"

Down in their hearts, wise men know this truth: the only way to help yourself is to help others. —ELBERT HUBBARD, in *The Philistine*

Don't shout for help at night. You may wake your neighbors. —STANISLAW LEC, *Unkempt Thoughts*

Perhaps everything terrible is in its deepest being something helpless that wants help from us.
—RAINER MARIA RILKE, *Letters to a Young Poet*

'Tis not enough to help the feeble up,
But to support him after.
          —SHAKESPEARE, *Timon of Athens*

The Hereafter — See HEAVEN, HELL, AND THE HERE-AFTER

Heroism

No hero is immortal till he dies. —W.H. AUDEN, "A Short Ode to a Philologist"

ANDREA: Unhappy the land that has no heroes! . . .
GALILEO: No, unhappy the land that needs heroes.
          —BERTOLT BRECHT, *Life of Galileo*

The real hero is always a hero by mistake; he dreams of being an honest coward like everybody else.
—UMBERTO ECO, *Travels in Hyperreality*

  [John F. Kennedy, when asked how he had become

a war hero, replied: "It was involuntary. They sank my boat."—quoted by Arthur M. Schlesinger, Jr., in *A Thousand Days*.]

Every hero becomes a bore at last. —RALPH WALDO EMERSON, *Representative Men*

Show me a hero and I will write you a tragedy. —F. SCOTT FITZGERALD, *The Crack-Up*, ed. Edmund Wilson

A hero cannot be a hero unless in an heroic world. —NATHANIEL HAWTHORNE, *Journals*

Heroes are created by popular demand, sometimes out of the scantiest materials, or none at all. —GERALD W. JOHNSON, *American Heroes and Hero-Worship*

Heroism, the Caucasian mountaineers say, is endurance for one moment more. —GEORGE F. KENNAN, letter (1921)

> See the conquering hero comes!
> Sound the trumpets, beat the drums!
> —THOMAS MORELL, *Judas Maccabaeus*

This thing of being a hero, about the main thing to do is to know when to die. Prolonged life has ruined more men than it ever made. —WILL ROGERS, *The Autobiography of Will Rogers*

History — See also THE PAST

Man is a history-making creature who can neither repeat his past nor leave it behind. —W.H. AUDEN, *The Dyer's Hand*

Happy is the nation without a history. —CESARE BECCARIA, *Treatise of Crimes and of Punishment*
 [Thomas Carlyle expressed a similar sentiment in

Life of Frederick the Great: "Happy the people whose annals are blank in history books!"]

HISTORY, *n.* An account mostly false, of events mostly unimportant, which are brought about by rulers mostly knaves, and soldiers mostly fools.
—AMBROSE BIERCE, *The Devil's Dictionary*

It has been said that though God cannot alter the past, historians can; it is perhaps because they can be useful to Him in this respect that He tolerates their existence. —SAMUEL BUTLER (d 1902), *Erewhon Revisited*

History is the essence of innumerable biographies.
—THOMAS CARLYLE, *Critical and Miscellaneous Essays*

To be ignorant of what occurred before you were born is to remain always a child. For what is the worth of human life, unless it is woven into the life of our ancestors by the records of history? —CICERO, *Orator*

History is more or less bunk. It's tradition. We don't want tradition. We want to live in the present and the only history that is worth a tinker's damn is the history we make today. —HENRY FORD, quoted in *Chicago Tribune*

History never looks like history when you are living through it. It always looks confusing and messy, and it always feels uncomfortable. —JOHN W. GARDNER, *No Easy Victories*

History . . . is indeed little more than the register of the crimes, follies, and misfortunes of mankind.
—EDWARD GIBBON, *Decline and Fall of the Roman Empire*

[Voltaire had expressed the same view in *L'Ingénu*:

195

"History is no more than the portrayal of crimes and misfortunes."]

There is nothing to be learned from history anymore. We're in science fiction now. —ALLEN GINSBERG, quoted in Christopher Butler's *After the Wake*

What experience and history teach is this—that people and governments never have learned anything from history, or acted on principles deduced from it. —G.W.F. HEGEL, *Philosophy of History*

[George Bernard Shaw, in *Man and Superman*, "The Revolutionist's Handbook," expressed the notion in these words: "If history repeats itself, and the unexpected always happens, how incapable must Man be of learning from experience!"]

History, Stephen said, is a nightmare from which I am trying to awake. —JAMES JOYCE, *Ulysses*

Hegel remarks somewhere that all great world-historic facts and personages appear, so to speak, twice. He forgot to add: the first time as tragedy, the second time as farce. —KARL MARX, "The Eighteenth Brumaire of Louis Napoleon"

We have need of history in its entirety, not to fall back into it, but to see if we can escape from it. —JOSÉ ORTEGA Y GASSET, *The Revolt of the Masses*

"Who controls the past," ran the Party slogan, "controls the future: who controls the present controls the past." —GEORGE ORWELL, *1984*

A historian is a prophet in reverse. —FRIEDRICH VON SCHLEGEL, in *Athenaeum*

Holidays

I have often thought, says Sir Roger, it happens very well that Christmas should fall out in the middle of winter. —JOSEPH ADDISON, *The Spectator*

Yes, Virginia, there is a Santa Claus. He exists as certainly as love and generosity and devotion exist.
—FRANCIS P. CHURCH, editorial in *New York Sun*

(Thanksgiving) 'Twas founded be th' Puritans to give thanks f'r bein' presarved fr'm th' Indyans, an' . . . we keep it to give thanks we are presarved fr'm th' Puritans. —FINLEY PETER DUNNE, *Mr. Dooley's Opinions*

Holidays
Have no pity.
   —EUGENIO MONTALE, "Eastbourne"

'Twas the night before Christmas, when all
 through the house
Not a creature was stirring—not even a mouse;
The stockings were hung by the chimney with
 care,
In hopes that St. Nicholas soon would be there.
  —CLEMENT C. MOORE, "A Visit from St.
           Nicholas"

Heap on more wood!—the wind is chill;
But let it whistle as it will,
We'll keep our Christmas merry still.
   —SIR WALTER SCOTT, *Marmion*

Ring out the old, ring in the new,
 Ring, happy bells, across the snow: The year
 is going, let him go;
Ring out the false, ring in the true.
  —ALFRED, LORD TENNYSON, *In Memoriam*

At Christmas play, and make good cheer,
For Christmas comes but once a year.
  —THOMAS TUSSER, *Five Hundred Points*
      of Good Husbandry

April 1. This is the day upon which we are reminded of what we are on the other three hundred and sixty-four. —MARK TWAIN, *Pudd'nhead Wilson*, "Pudd'nhead Wilson's Calendar"

To perceive Christmas through its wrapping becomes more difficult with every year. —E.B. WHITE, *The Second Tree from the Corner*

Home

A man's house is his castle. —EDWARD COKE, *The Third Part of the Institutes of the Laws of England*

A man builds a fine house; and now he has a master, and a task for life: he is to furnish, watch, show it, and keep it in repair, the rest of his days. —RALPH WALDO EMERSON, *Society and Solitude*

> Home is the place where, when you have to go
>   there,
> They have to take you in.
> > —ROBERT FROST, "The Death
> >   of the Hired Man"

It takes a heap o' livin' in a house t' make it home. —EDGAR A. GUEST, "Home"

> The stately homes of England!
>   How beautiful they stand,
> Amidst their tall ancestral trees,
> O'er all the pleasant land!
> > —FELICIA DOROTHEA HEMANS,
> >   "The Homes of England"

[Virginia Woolf offered a less exalted view in *The Common Reader*: "Those comfortably padded lunatic asylums which are known, euphemistically, as the stately homes of England."]

> Where we love is home,
> Home that our feet may leave, but not our
>   hearts.
> > —OLIVER WENDELL HOLMES, SR.,
> >   "Homesick in Heaven"

The happiness of the domestic fireside is the first boon of Heaven; and it is well it is so, since it is that which is the lot of the mass of mankind. —THOMAS JEFFERSON, letter (1813)

Home is the girl's prison and the woman's workhouse. —GEORGE BERNARD SHAW, *Man and Superman*, "The Revolutionist's Handbook"

You Can't Go Home Again. —THOMAS WOLFE, (title of novel)

Honesty

He that resolves to deal with none but honest men must leave off dealing. —THOMAS FULLER, *Gnomologia*

It is difficult but not impossible to conduct strictly honest business. . . . What is true is that honesty is incompatible with the amassing of a large fortune. —MOHANDAS K. GANDHI, *Non-Violence in Peace and War*

Honesty is praised and starves. —JUVENAL, *Satires*

What is more arrogant than honesty? —URSULA K. LE GUIN, *The Left Hand of Darkness*

It is annoying to be honest to no purpose. —OVID, *Epistulae ex Ponto*

An honest man's the noblest work of God. —ALEXANDER POPE, *An Essay on Man*

Ay, sir; to be honest, as this world goes, is to be one man picked out of ten thousand. —SHAKESPEARE, *Hamlet*

"Honesty is the best policy," but he who acts on that principle is not an honest man. —RICHARD WHATELY, *Thoughts and Apothegms*

Honor

Honor is like a rugged island without a shore; once you have left it, you cannot return. —NICOLAS BOILEAU, *Satires*

Honor is a luxury for aristocrats, but it is a necessity for hall porters. —G.K. CHESTERTON, *Heretics*

The louder he talked of his honor, the faster we counted our spoons. —RALPH WALDO EMERSON, *Conduct of Life*

There is nothing left to me but honor, and my life, which is saved. —FRANCIS I OF FRANCE, letter (to his mother after the Battle of Pavia, 1525)
[Often quoted as "All is lost save honor."]

Hold it the greatest sin to prefer existence to honor, and for the sake of life to lose the reasons for living. —JUVENAL, *Satires*

> I could not love thee, dear, so much,
> Loved I not honor more.
>   —RICHARD LOVELACE, "To Luscasta, on
>   Going to the Wars"

The difference between a moral man and a man of honor is that the latter regrets a discreditable act, even when it has worked and he has not been caught. —H.L. MENCKEN, *Prejudices*

> Honor and shame from no condition rise;
> Act well your part, there all the honor lies.
>   —ALEXANDER POPE, *An Essay on Man*

Without money honor is nothing but a malady. —JEAN RACINE, *Les Plaideurs*

Set honor in one eye and death i' the other
And I will look on both indifferently;
For let the gods so speed me as I love
The name of honor more than I fear death.
> —SHAKESPEARE, *Julius Caesar*

Honor wears different coats to different eyes. —BARBARA TUCHMAN, *The Guns of August*

Hope

Hope is a waking dream. —ARISTOTLE, quoted by Diogenes Laertius in *Lives of the Philosophers*

[This has also been attributed to Pindar and Plato.]

Hope is a good breakfast, but it is a bad supper.
—FRANCIS BACON, *Apophthegms*

Hope is a risk that must be run. —GEORGES BERNANOS, *Last Essays*

Hope deferred maketh the heart sick. —BIBLE, *Proverbs* 13:12

Hope! of all ills that men endure,
The only cheap and universal cure.
> —ABRAHAM COWLEY, *The Mistress*

"Hope" is the thing with feathers—
That perches in the soul—
And sings the tune without the words—
And never stops—at all—
> —EMILY DICKINSON, " 'Hope' is the thing
> with feathers"

If it were not for Hopes, the Heart would break.
—THOMAS FULLER, *Gnomologia*

Hope is the poor man's bread. —GEORGE HERBERT, *Jacula Prudentum*

I suppose it can be truthfully said that Hope is the only universal liar who never loses his reputation for veracity. —ROBERT G. INGERSOLL, speech (1892)

Hope is itself a species of happiness, and, perhaps, the chief happiness which this world affords. —SAMUEL JOHNSON, quoted in James Boswell's *The Life of Samuel Johnson*

The natural flights of the human mind are not from pleasure to pleasure, but from hope to hope. —SAMUEL JOHNSON, *The Rambler*

Hope has as many lives as a cat or a king. —HENRY WADSWORTH LONGFELLOW, *Hyperion*

Hope is the worst of evils, for it prolongs the torment of man. —FRIEDRICH NIETZSCHE, *Human, All-too-Human*

Things which you don't hope happen more frequently than things which you do hope. —PLAUTUS, *Mostellaria*

> Hope springs eternal in the human breast;
> Man never is, but always to be blest.
> —ALEXANDER POPE, *An Essay on Man*

More are taken in by hope than by cunning. —MARQUIS DE VAUVENARGUES, *Reflections and Maxims*

Hospitality

What is there more kindly than the feeling between host and guest? —AESCHYLUS, *The Libation Bearers*

When hospitality becomes an art it loses its very soul. —MAX BEERBOHM, *And Even Now*

Let brotherly love continue.

Be not forgetful to entertain strangers: for thereby some have entertained angels unawares. —BIBLE, *Hebrews* 13:1–2

Fish and guests in three days are stale. —JOHN LYLY, *Euphues*

> [This three day limit on hospitality dates to ancient times. It is used by Plautus in *Miles Gloriosus*: "No guest is so welcome in a friend's house that he will not become a nuisance after three days." The rule is probably best known in the words of Benjamin Franklin in *Poor Richard's Almanac*: "Fish and guests stink in three days."]

> For I, who hold sage Homer's rule the best,
> Welcome the coming, speed the going guest.
> —ALEXANDER POPE, *Imitations of Horace*

[Pope here repeated the phrasing he had used in an earlier translation of Homer's *The Odyssey*:

> True friendship's laws are by this rule express'd,
> Welcome the coming, speed the parting guest.]

> Unbidden guests
> Are often welcomest when they are gone.
> —SHAKESPEARE, *Henry VI, Part I*

A hundred thousand welcomes. I could weep
And I could laugh, I am light and heavy.
Welcome.

> —SHAKESPEARE, *Coriolanus*

Humans and Human Nature — See also MEN; MEN AND WOMEN; WOMEN

Drinking when we are not thirsty and making love all year round, madam; that is all there is to distinguish us from other animals. —PIERRE-AUGUSTIN CARON DE BEAUMARCHAIS, *The Marriage of Figaro*

For Mercy has a human heart;
Pity, a human face;
And Love, the human form divine;
And Peace, the human dress.
—WILLIAM BLAKE, *Songs of Innocence*
"The Divine Image"

Cruelty has a human heart,
And jealousy a human face—
Terror, the human form divine,
And secrecy, the human dress.
—WILLIAM BLAKE, *Songs of Experience*
"A Divine Image"

Everyone is as God made him, and often a great deal worse. —MIGUEL DE CERVANTES, *Don Quixote de la Mancha*

A wonderful fact to reflect upon, that every human creature is constituted to be that profound secret and mystery to every other. —CHARLES DICKENS, *A Tale of Two Cities*

What is man, when you come to think upon him, but a minutely set, ingenious machine for turning, with infinite artfulness, the red wine of Shiraz into urine? —ISAK DINESEN, *Seven Gothic Tales*

In spite of everything I still believe that people are really good at heart. —ANNE FRANK, diary entry (1944) (*Diary of a Young Girl*)

Man is the only animal that laughs and weeps; for he is the only animal that is struck with the difference between what things are, and what they ought to be. —WILLIAM HAZLITT, *Lectures on the English Comic Writers*

No arts; no letters; no society; and which is worst of all, continual fear and danger of violent death; and the life of man, solitary, poor, nasty, brutish, and short. —THOMAS HOBBES, *Leviathan*

[Hobbes was describing life in a state of nature.]

Man, biologically considered, and whatever else he may be in the bargain, is simply the most formidable of all the beasts of prey, and, indeed, the only one that preys systematically on its own species. —WILLIAM JAMES, in *Atlantic*

Limited in his nature, infinite in his desires, man is a fallen god who remembers the heavens.
—ALPHONSE DE LAMARTINE, *Méditations poétiques*

Man would be *other*wise. That is the essence of the specifically human. —ANTONIO MACHADO, *Juan de Mairena*

A human being . . . an ingenious assembly of portable plumbing. —CHRISTOPHER MORLEY, *Human Being*

Man is but a reed, the most feeble thing in nature, but he is a thinking reed. —BLAISE PASCAL, *Pensées*

All human evil comes from a single cause, man's inability to sit still in a room. —BLAISE PASCAL, *Pensées*

Man is a biped without feathers. —PLATO, *Politicus*

Man is no man, but a wolf. —PLAUTUS, *Asinaria*

[Often quoted as "Man is a wolf to man."]

Man is the only animal that knows nothing, and can learn nothing without being taught. —PLINY THE ELDER, *Natural History*

Nothing is more wretched or more proud than man.
—PLINY THE ELDER, *Natural History*

> Great lord of all things, yet a prey to all;
> Sole judge of truth, in endless error hurled;
> The glory, jest and riddle of the world!
> —ALEXANDER POPE, *An Essay on Man*

Man is the measure of all things. —PROTAGORAS, attributed

The more I see of men, the more I admire dogs.
—(MADAME) JEANNE-MARIE ROLAND, attributed

> [Also attributed to Madame de Sévigné and to Ouida.]

> How beauteous mankind is! O brave new
>   world,
> That has such people in 't!
> —SHAKESPEARE, *The Tempest*

> We are such stuff
> As dreams are made on, and our little life
> Is rounded with a sleep.
> —SHAKESPEARE, *The Tempest*

There are many wonderful things, but none is more wonderful than man. —SOPHOCLES, *Antigone*

I am a man; and nothing human is foreign to me.
—TERENCE, *Heauton Timoroumenos*

Man is a rational animal who always loses his temper when he is called upon to act in accordance with the dictates of reason. —OSCAR WILDE, *Intentions*, "The Critic as Artist"

Humility — See also MODESTY

Blessed are the meek: for they shall inherit the earth.
—BIBLE, *Matthew* 5:5

> [Also in the Old Testament, in Psalms 37:11: "The meek shall inherit the earth."]

"I am well aware that I am the umblest person going," said Uriah Heep, modestly; "let the other be where he may. My mother is likewise a very umble person. We live in a numble abode, Master Copperfield, but have much to be thankful for." —CHARLES DICKENS, *David Copperfield*

The meek shall inherit the earth, but not the mineral rights. —J. PAUL GETTY, quoted in Robert Lenzner's *The Great Getty*

[See also The Bible, in this section.]

You've no idea what a poor opinion I have of myself— and how little I deserve it. —W.S. GILBERT, *Ruddigore*

Plenty of people want to be pious, but no one yearns to be humble. —LA ROCHEFOUCAULD, *Maxims*

One may be humble out of pride. —MICHEL DE MONTAIGNE, *Essays*

Humility is a virtue all preach, none practice, and yet everybody is content to hear. The master thinks it good doctrine for his servant, the laity for the clergy, and the clergy for the laity. —JOHN SELDEN, *Table Talk*

Humor and Wit

Men will confess to treason, murder, arson, false teeth, or a wig. How many of them will own up to a lack of humor? —FRANK MOORE COLBY, *The Colby Essays*

A difference of taste in jokes is a great strain on the affections. —GEORGE ELIOT, *Daniel Deronda*

Humor is an affirmation of dignity, a declaration of man's superiority to all that befalls him. —ROMAIN GARY, *Promise at Dawn*

Impropriety is the soul of wit. —W. SOMERSET MAUGHAM, *The Moon and Sixpence*

Everybody likes a kidder, but nobody lends him money. —ARTHUR MILLER, *Death of a Salesman*

> Satire should, like a polished razor keen,
> Wound with a touch that's scarcely felt or
> seen.
> —LADY MARY WORTLEY MONTAGU, *To the Imitator of the First Satire of Horace*

Humor brings insight and tolerance. Irony brings a deeper and less friendly understanding. —AGNES REPPLIER, *In Pursuit of Laughter*

Everything is funny as long as it is happening to somebody else. —WILL ROGERS, *Illiterate Digest*

There's no possibility of being witty without a little ill-nature; the malice of a good thing is the barb that makes it stick. —RICHARD BRINSLEY SHERIDAN, *The School for Scandal*

Wit consists in seeing the resemblance between things which differ, and the difference between things which are alike. —MADAME DE STAËL, *De l'Allemagne*

Satire is a sort of glass, wherein beholders do generally discover everybody's face but their own. —JONATHAN SWIFT, *The Battle of the Books*

Humor is emotional chaos remembered in tranquillity. —JAMES THURBER, in *New York Post*

> [Thurber's allusion here is to Wordsworth's description of poetry. See William Wordsworth, under Poetry and Poets.]

The secret source of Humor itself is not joy but sorrow. There is no humor in heaven. —MARK TWAIN, *Following the Equator*, "Pudd'nhead Wilson's New Calendar"

I love such mirth as does not make friends ashamed to look upon one another next morning. —IZAAK WALTON, *The Compleat Angler*

Hunger — See FOOD AND EATING; POVERTY

Husbands — See MARRIAGE

Hypocrisy

What makes it so plausible to assume that hypocrisy is the vice of vices is that integrity can indeed exist under the cover of all other vices except this one. Only crime and the criminal, it is true, confront us with the perplexity of radical evil; but only the hypocrite is really rotten to the core. —HANNAH ARENDT, *On Revolution*

The true hypocrite is the one who ceases to perceive his deception, the one who lies with sincerity. —ANDRÉ GIDE, *Journal of "The Counterfeiters"*

The only vice that cannot be forgiven is hypocrisy. The repentance of a hypocrite is itself hypocrisy. —WILLIAM HAZLITT, *Characteristics*

Man is the only animal that learns by being hypocritical. He pretends to be polite and then, eventually, he *becomes* polite. —JEAN KERR, *Finishing Touches*

Hypocrisy is the homage that vice pays to virtue. —LA ROCHEFOUCAULD, *Maxims*

A hypocrite is a person who—but who isn't? —DON MARQUIS, attributed

> For neither Man nor Angel can discern
> Hypocrisy, the only evil that walks
> Invisible, except to God alone.
>   —JOHN MILTON, *Paradise Lost*

We have, in fact, two kinds of morality side by side: one which we preach but do not practice, and another which we practice but seldom preach.
—BERTRAND RUSSELL, *Sceptical Essays*

One may smile, and smile, and be a villain. —SHAKE-SPEARE, *Hamlet*

A Christian is a man who feels
Repentance on a Sunday
For what he did on Saturday
And is going to do on Monday.
—THOMAS RUSSELL YBARRA,
"The Christian"

Ideals and Idealism

No one regards what is before his feet; we all gaze at the stars. —QUINTUS ENNIUS, *Iphigenia*, quoted in Cicero's *De Divinatione*

Idealism is the noble toga that political gentlemen drape over their will to power. —ALDOUS HUXLEY, quoted in *New York Herald Tribune*

Every form of addiction is bad, no matter whether the narcotic be alcohol or morphine or idealism. —CARL JUNG, *Memories, Dreams, Reflections*

If a man hasn't discovered something he will die for, he isn't fit to live. —MARTIN LUTHER KING, JR., speech (1963)

An idealist is one who, on noticing that a rose smells better than a cabbage, concludes that it will also make better soup. —H.L. MENCKEN, *A Mencken Chrestomathy*

People are willing to devise and praise Utopias but not to live in them. —DAVID PRYCE-JONES, in *The Times* (London)

We are all in the gutter, but some of us are looking at the stars. —OSCAR WILDE, *Lady Windermere's Fan*

Ideas

Nothing is more dangerous than an idea, when you have only one idea. —ALAIN, *Libres-propos*

Every man with an idea has at least two or three followers. —BROOKS ATKINSON, *Once Around the Sun*

One of the greatest pains to human nature is the pain of a new idea. —WALTER BAGEHOT, *Physics and Politics*

The wise only possess ideas . . . the greater part of mankind are possessed by them. —SAMUEL TAYLOR COLERIDGE, *Defoe*

No idea is so antiquated that it was not once modern. No idea is so modern that it will not someday be antiquated. —ELLEN GLASGOW, speech (1936)

An idea that is not dangerous is unworthy of being called an idea at all. —ELBERT HUBBARD, *Roycroft Dictionary and Book of Epigrams*

One can resist the invasion of armies; one cannot resist the invasion of ideas. —VICTOR HUGO, *Histoire d'un crime*

> [Often quoted in forms that correspond only loosely to Hugo's original words, for example: "No army can withstand the strength of an idea whose time has come."]

An idea, to be suggestive, must come to the individual with the force of a revelation. —WILLIAM JAMES, *The Varieties of Religious Experience*

The ideas of economists and political philosophers, both when they are right and when they are wrong, are more powerful than is commonly understood. Indeed the world is ruled by little else. Practical men, who believe themselves to be quite exempt from any intellectual influences, are usually the slaves of some defunct economist. —JOHN MAYNARD KEYNES, *The General Theory of Employment, Interest and Money*

An idea isn't responsible for the people who believe in it. —DON MARQUIS, in *New York Sun*

General notions are generally wrong. —LADY MARY WORTLEY MONTAGU, letter (to her husband, 1710)

For an idea ever to be fashionable is ominous, since it must afterwards be always old-fashioned.
—GEORGE SANTAYANA, *Winds of Doctrine*

Idleness and Laziness

It has been said that idleness is the parent of mischief, which is very true; but mischief itself is merely an attempt to escape from the dreary vacuum of idleness. —GEORGE BORROW, *Lavengro*

It is impossible to enjoy idling thoroughly unless one has plenty of work to do. —JEROME K. JEROME, *The Idle Thoughts of an Idle Fellow*

If you are idle, be not solitary; if you are solitary, be not idle. —SAMUEL JOHNSON, letter (to James Boswell, 1779)

> [Johnson was offering a variation on the advice Robert Burton gave for avoiding melancholy in *The Anatomy of Melancholy*: "Be not solitary, be not idle."]

Every man is, or hopes to be, an idler. —SAMUEL JOHNSON, *The Idler*

Lazy people are always wanting to do something.
—MARQUIS DE VAUVENARGUES, *Reflections and Maxims*

For Satan finds some mischief still
For idle hands to do.
       —ISAAC WATTS, *Divine Songs for Children*

To do nothing at all is the most difficult thing in the world, the most difficult and the most intellectual.
—OSCAR WILDE, *Intentions*, "The Critic as Artist"

Ignorance and Stupidity

If the blind lead the blind, both shall fall into the ditch.   —BIBLE, *Matthew* 15:14

It iz better tew know nothing than tew know what ain't so. —JOSH BILLINGS, *Encyclopedia of Proverbial Philosophy*

Ignorance is not innocence but sin. —ROBERT BROWNING, "The Inn Album"

Stupidity's the deliberate cultivation of ignorance.
—WILLIAM GADDIS, *Carpenter's Gothic*

   . . . where ignorance is bliss,
   'Tis folly to be wise.
             —THOMAS GRAY, "Ode on a Distant
                    Prospect of Eton College"

Nothing in all the world is more dangerous than sincere ignorance and conscientious stupidity. —MARTIN LUTHER KING, JR., *Strength to Love*

Our knowledge can only be finite, while our ignorance must necessarily be infinite. —KARL POPPER, lecture (1960)

You know everybody is ignorant, only on different subjects. —WILL ROGERS, in *New York Times*

> Against stupidity the very gods
> Themselves contend in vain.
>   —FRIEDRICH VON SCHILLER, *Joan of Arc*

Illness —

I reckon being ill as one of the great pleasures of life, provided one is not too ill and is not obliged to work till one is better. —SAMUEL BUTLER (d 1902), *The Way of All Flesh*

Epidemics have often been more influential than statesmen and soldiers in shaping the course of political history, and diseases may also color the moods of civilizations. —RENÉ DUBOS AND JEAN DUBOS, *The White Plague*

If you start to think about your physical or moral condition, you usually find that you are sick. —JOHANN WOLFGANG VON GOETHE, *Proverbs in Prose*

How sickness enlarges the dimension of a man's self to himself! —CHARLES LAMB, *Last Essays of Elia*

Falling ill is not something that happens to us, it is a choice we make as a result of things happening to us. —JONATHAN MILLER, *The Body in Question*

Illness is the night-side of life, a more onerous citizenship. Everyone who is born holds dual citizenship, in the kingdom of the well and in the kingdom of the sick. Although we all prefer to use only the good passport, sooner or later each of us is obliged, at least for a spell, to identify ourselves as citizens of that other place. —SUSAN SONTAG, in *New York Review of Books*

Illusion —

Beware that you do not lose the substance by grasping at the shadow. —AESOP, *Fables*

But time strips our illusions of their hue,
And one by one in turn, some grand mistake
Casts off its bright skin yearly like the snake.
—LORD BYRON, *Don Juan*

I do not know whether I was then a man dreaming I was a butterfly, or whether I am now a butterfly dreaming I am a man. —CHUANG-TZU, *Chuang-tzu*

Every age is fed on illusions, lest men should renounce life early and the human race come to an end. —JOSEPH CONRAD, *Victory*

Rob the average man of his life-illusion and you rob him also of his happiness. —HENRIK IBSEN, *The Wild Duck*

All that we see or seem
Is but a dream within a dream.
—EDGAR ALLAN POE, "A Dream Within a
Dream"

Don't part with your illusions. When they are gone, you may still exist, but you have ceased to live.
—MARK TWAIN, *Pudd'nhead Wilson*, "Pudd'nhead Wilson's Calendar"

Imagination

What is now proved was once only imagin'd. —WILLIAM BLAKE, *The Marriage of Heaven and Hell*

Imagination, which is the Eldorado of the poet and of the novel-writer, often proves the most pernicious gift to the individuals who compose the talkers instead of the writers in society. —MARGUERITE BLESSINGTON, *The Repealers*

The function of the imagination is not to make strange things settled, so much as to make settled things strange. —G.K. CHESTERTON, *The Defendant*

215

To make a prairie it takes a clover and one bee,
One clover, and a bee,
And revery.
The revery alone will do,
If bees are few.
　　　—EMILY DICKINSON, "To make a prairie it
　　　　　　takes a clover and one bee"

Imagination is more important than knowledge.
—ALBERT EINSTEIN, *On Science*

Were it not for imagination, Sir, a man would be as
happy in the arms of a chambermaid as of a Duchess.
—SAMUEL JOHNSON, quoted in James Boswell's *The
Life of Samuel Johnson*

Heard melodies are sweet, but those unheard
　Are sweeter.
　　　—JOHN KEATS, "Ode on a Grecian Urn"

Safe upon the solid rock the ugly houses stand:
Come and see my shining palace built upon
　　the sand!
　　　—EDNA ST. VINCENT MILLAY, "Second Fig"

The lunatic, the lover and the poet
Are of imagination all compact.
　　　—SHAKESPEARE, *A Midsummer Night's
　　　　　　　　Dream*

We say God and the imagination are one . . .
How high that highest candle lights the dark.
　　　—WALLACE STEVENS, "Final Soliloquy of
　　　　　　the Interior Paramour"

Skill without imagination is craftsmanship and gives
us many useful objects such as wickerwork picnic
baskets. Imagination without skill gives us modern
art. —TOM STOPPARD, *Artist Descending a Stair-
case*

Imitation

Imitation is the sincerest flattery. —CHARLES CALEB COLTON, *Lacon*

When people are free to do as they please, they usually imitate each other. —ERIC HOFFER, *The Passionate State of Mind*

No man ever yet became great by imitation. —SAMUEL JOHNSON, *The Rambler*

To do just the opposite is also a form of imitation. —GEORG CHRISTOPH LICHTENBERG, *Aphorisms*

Immature artists imitate. Mature artists steal. —LIONEL TRILLING, in *Esquire*
> [T.S. Eliot had said this of poets, in *The Sacred Wood*: "Immature poets imitate; mature poets steal; bad poets deface what they take, and good poets make it into something better.]

With the exception of the instinct of self-preservation, the propensity for emulation is probably the strongest and most alert and persistent of the economic motives proper. —THORSTEIN VEBLEN, *The Theory of the Leisure Class*

Most people are other people. Their thoughts are someone else's opinions, their lives a mimicry, their passions a quotation. —OSCAR WILDE, *De Profundis*

Immortality

I don't want to achieve immortality through my work. . . . I want to achieve it through not dying. —WOODY ALLEN, quoted in *Woody Allen and his Comedy* by Eric Lax

The belief in immortality rests not very much on the hope of going on. Few of us want to do that, but we would like very much to begin again. —HEYWOOD BROUN, *Pieces of Hate*

Someone has somewhere commented on the fact that millions long for immortality who don't know what to do with themselves on a rainy Sunday afternoon. —SUSAN ERTZ, *Anger in the Sky*

It must require an inordinate share of vanity and presumption, too, after enjoying so much that is good and beautiful on earth, to ask the Lord for immortality in addition to it all. —HEINRICH HEINE, *City of Lucca*

Man is the only animal that contemplates death, and also the only animal that shows any sign of doubt of its finality. —WILLIAM ERNEST HOCKING, *The Meaning of Immortality in Human Experience*

Our hope of immortality does not come from any religions, but nearly all religions come from that hope. —ROBERT G. INGERSOLL, quoted in *Chicago Times*

We feel and know that we are eternal. —BENEDICT DE SPINOZA, *Ethics*

> Still seems it strange, that thou shouldst live
>   forever?
> Is it less strange, that thou shouldst live at all?
> This is a miracle; and that no more.
>   —EDWARD YOUNG, *Night Thoughts on
>   Life, Death, and Immortality*

All men think all men mortal, but themselves.
            —EDWARD YOUNG, *Night Thoughts on
                Life, Death, and Immortality*

Indecision

We are always getting ready to live, but never living. —RALPH WALDO EMERSON, *Journals*

Then indecision brings its own delays,
And days are lost lamenting o'er lost days.
—JOHANN WOLFGANG VON GOETHE, *Faust*

There is no more miserable human being than one in whom nothing is habitual but indecision. —WILLIAM JAMES, *The Principles of Psychology*

He who hesitates is sometimes saved. —JAMES THURBER, *The James Thurber Carnival*

Independence — See FREEDOM AND LIBERTY; SELF-RELIANCE

Indifference — See APATHY AND INDIFFERENCE

Individuality

The universal does not attract us until housed in an individual. —RALPH WALDO EMERSON, *The Method of Nature*

We fancy men are individuals; so are pumpkins; but every pumpkin in the field goes through every point of pumpkin history. —RALPH WALDO EMERSON, *Essays*

Men are born equal but they are also born different. —ERICH FROMM, *Escape from Freedom*

When we lose the right to be different, we lose the privilege to be free. —CHARLES EVANS HUGHES, speech (1925)

The strongest man in the world is he who stands most alone. —HENRIK IBSEN, *An Enemy of the People*

Whatever crushes individuality is despotism, by whatever name it may be called. —JOHN STUART MILL, *On Liberty*

There never were in the world two opinions alike, no more than two hairs or two grains; the most universal quality is diversity. —MICHEL DE MONTAIGNE, *Essays*

If a man does not keep pace with his companions, perhaps it is because he hears a different drummer. Let him step to the music which he hears, however measured or far away. —HENRY DAVID THOREAU, *Walden*

Indulgence — See PLEASURE AND INDULGENCE

Infidelity

> What men call gallantry, and gods adultery,
> Is much more common where the climate's
>   sultry.
> —LORD BYRON, Don Juan

Where there's Marriage without Love, there will be Love without Marriage. —BENJAMIN FRANKLIN, *Poor Richard's Almanac*

> Die for adultery! No:
> The wren goes to't, and the small gilded fly
> Does lecher in my sight.
> —SHAKESPEARE, King Lear

Initiative — See AMBITION; BOLDNESS AND ENTERPRISE

Injury

The injuries we do and those we suffer are seldom weighed in the same scales. —AESOP, *Fables*

An injury engraves itself on metal; a benefit is written on the waves. —JEAN BERTAUT, attributed

[See Shakespeare, under Reputation, for a similar thought.]

Take away your opinion, and then there is taken away the complaint, "I have been harmed." Take away the complaint, "I have been harmed," and the harm is taken away. —MARCUS AURELIUS, *Meditations*

Whom they have injured they also hate. —SENECA, *Epistulae ad Lucilium*

[Similarly: "It is human nature to hate those whom you have injured"—Tacitus: *Life of Agricola*.]

He who injured you was either stronger or weaker. If weaker, spare him; if stronger, spare yourself. —SENECA, *De Ira*

Innocence

Unto the pure all things are pure. —BIBLE, *Titus* 1:15

No, it is not only our fate but our business to lose innocence, and once we have lost that, it is futile to attempt a picnic in Eden. —ELIZABETH BOWEN, *Orion III*

To vice, innocence must always seem only a superior kind of chicanery. —OUIDA, *Wisdom, Wit and Pathos*

True, conscious Honor is to feel no sin,
He's armed without that's innocent within;
Be this thy Screen, and this thy Wall of Brass.
　　—ALEXANDER POPE, *Imitations of Horace*

Whoever blushes is already guilty; true innocence is ashamed of nothing. —JEAN-JACQUES ROUSSEAU, *Émile*

The innocent and the beautiful
Have no enemy but time.
　　—W.B. YEATS, "In Memory of Eva Gore-
　　　　Booth and Con Markiewicz"

221

Insanity — See MENTAL DISORDER

Inspiration

Thy word is a lamp unto my feet, and a light unto my path. —BIBLE, *Psalms* 119:105

No one was ever great without some portion of divine inspiration. —CICERO, *De Natura Deorum*

> [The last two words are sometimes rendered as "divine afflatus," from the Latin *adflatu divino*.]

> O! for a Muse of fire, that would ascend
> The brightest heaven of invention!
> —SHAKESPEARE, *Henry V*

> Biting my truant pen, beating myself for spite:
> "Fool," said my Muse to me, "look in thy heart,
> and write!"
> —PHILIP SIDNEY, *Astrophel and Stella*

> Why does my Muse only speak when she is
> unhappy?
> She does not, I only listen when I am unhappy
> When I am happy I live and despise writing
> For my Muse this cannot but be dispiriting.
> —STEVIE SMITH, "My Muse"

Just as appetite comes by eating, so work brings inspiration, if inspiration is not discernible at the beginning. —IGOR STRAVINSKY, *An Autobiography*

Insults and Abuse

One may be continually abusive without saying any thing just; but one cannot be always laughing at a man without now and then stumbling on something witty. —JANE AUSTEN, *Pride and Prejudice*

An injury is much sooner forgotten than an insult.
—LORD CHESTERFIELD, *Letters to His Son*

It is not he who reviles or strikes you who insults you, but your opinion that these things are insulting.
—EPICTETUS, *Encheiridion*

The way to procure insults is to submit to them.
—WILLIAM HAZLITT, *Characteristics*

It is often better not to see an insult than to avenge it. —SENECA, *De Ira*

If a man's character is to be abused, say what you will, there's nobody like a relation to do the business.
—WILLIAM MAKEPEACE THACKERAY, *Vanity Fair*

Intelligence and Intellectuals

Cleverness is serviceable for everything, sufficient for nothing. —HENRI-FRÉDÉRIC AMIEL, *Journal intime*

> To the man-in-the-street, who, I'm sorry to say,
> Is a keen observer of life,
> The word "Intellectual" suggests straight away
> A man who's untrue to his wife.
> —W.H. AUDEN, *New Year Letter*

Since it is seldom clear whether intellectual activity denotes a superior mode of being or a vital deficiency, opinion swings between considering intellect a privilege and seeing it as a handicap. —JACQUES BARZUN, *The House of Intellect*

Intellectuals are people who believe that ideas are of more importance than values. That is to say, their own ideas and other people's values. —GERALD BRENAN, *Thoughts in a Dry Season*

An intellectual is someone whose mind watches itself. —ALBERT CAMUS, *Notebooks*

It is not enough to have a good mind. The main thing is to use it well. —RENÉ DESCARTES, *Discourse on Method*

No one is satisfied with his fortune, nor dissatisfied with his intellect. —ANTOINETTE DESHOULIÈRES (epigram)

The test of a first-rate intelligence is the ability to hold two opposed ideas in the mind at the same time, and still retain the ability to function. —F. SCOTT FITZGERALD, *The Crack-Up*, ed. Edmund Wilson

The greatest intelligence is precisely the one that suffers most from its own limitations. —ANDRÉ GIDE, *The Counterfeiters*

A highbrow is the kind of person who looks at a sausage and thinks of Picasso. —A.P. HERBERT, *The Highbrow*

Intelligence barred . . . quarrelling, sulking, anger, silences of withdrawal, accusations and tears. Above all, intelligence forbids tears. —DORIS LESSING, "To Room Nineteen"

The greater intellect one has, the more originality one finds in men. Ordinary persons find no difference between men. —BLAISE PASCAL, *Pensées*

Intolerance — See PREJUDICE AND INTOLERANCE

Invention and Discovery

Eureka! (I have found it!) —ARCHIMEDES, quoted by Vitruvius Pollio in *De Architectura*

> [Archimedes' reputed exclamation upon discovering a method of determining the purity of gold.]

And if there had been more of the world,
They would have reached it.
            —LUÍS DE CAMÕES, quoted by Daniel J.
                Boorstin in *The Discoverers*

I don't think necessity is the mother of invention—invention, in my opinion, arises directly from idleness, possibly also from laziness. To save oneself trouble. —AGATHA CHRISTIE, *An Autobiography*

Invention breeds invention. —RALPH WALDO EMERSON, *Society and Solitude*

One doesn't discover new lands without consenting to lose sight of the shore for a very long time. —ANDRÉ GIDE, *The Counterfeiters*

> Then felt I like some watcher of the skies
>   When a new planet swims into his ken;
> Or like stout Cortez when with eagle eyes
>   He star'd at the Pacific—and all his men
> Look'd at each other with a wild surmise—
>   Silent, upon a peak in Darien.
>   —JOHN KEATS, "On First Looking into
>   Chapman's Homer"

Discovery consists of seeing what everybody has seen and thinking what nobody has thought. —ALBERT SZENT-GYÖRGYI, in *The Scientist Speculates*, ed. Irving Good

Name the greatest of all the inventors: Accident. —MARK TWAIN, *Notebooks*

Ireland and the Irish

> Now Ireland has her madness and her weather
>   still,
> For poetry makes nothing happen.
>   —W.H. AUDEN, "In Memory of W.B.
>   Yeats"

The Irish are a *fair people*;—they never speak well of one another. —SAMUEL JOHNSON, quoted in James Boswell's *The Life of Samuel Johnson*

The Irish don't know what they want and are prepared to fight to the death to get it. —SIDNEY LITTLEWOOD, speech (1961)

> The Irish say Your trouble is their
> trouble and your
> joy their joy? I wish
> I could believe it;
> I am troubled, I'm dissatisfied, I'm Irish.
>   —MARIANNE MOORE, "Spenser's Ireland"

> Romantic Ireland's dead and gone,
> It's with O'Leary in the grave.
>   —W.B. YEATS, "September, 1913"

Jealousy and Envy

The dullard's envy of brilliant men is always assuaged by the suspicion that they will come to a bad end. —MAX BEERBOHM, *Zuleika Dobson*

Jealousy is cruel as the grave: the coals thereof are coals of fire. —BIBLE, *Song of Solomon* 8:6

The ear of jealousy heareth all things. —BIBLE, *Wisdom of Solomon* 1:10

Every other sin hath some pleasure annexed to it, or will admit of an excuse: envy alone wants both. —ROBERT BURTON, *The Anatomy of Melancholy*

It is not love that is blind, but jealousy. —LAWRENCE DURRELL, *Justine*

Anger and jealousy can no more bear to lose sight of their objects than love. —GEORGE ELIOT, *The Mill on the Floss*

Jealousy: that dragon which slays love under the pretense of keeping it alive. —HAVELOCK ELLIS, *On Life and Sex: Essays of Love and Virtue*

Nothing sharpens sight like envy. —THOMAS FULLER, *Gnomologia*

Whoever envies another confesses his superiority. —SAMUEL JOHNSON, *The Rambler*

Jealousy is all the fun you think they had . . . —ERICA JONG, *How to Save Your Own Life*

Jealousy is always born with love, but does not always die with it. —LA ROCHEFOUCAULD, *Maxims*

To jealousy, nothing is more frightful than laughter. —FRANÇOISE SAGAN, *La Chamade*

> O! beware, my lord, of jealousy;
> It is the green-eyed monster which doth mock
> The meat it feeds on.
> —SHAKESPEARE, *Othello*

> Trifles light as air
> Are to the jealous confirmations strong
> As proofs of holy writ.
> —SHAKESPEARE, *Othello*

Whenever a friend succeeds, a little something in me dies. —GORE VIDAL, in *Sunday Times Magazine* (London)

Jews — See RELIGION

Journalism — See NEWS AND NEWSPAPERS

Joy — See CHEERFULNESS; HAPPINESS

Judgment

Judge not, that ye be not judged. —BIBLE, *Matthew* 7:1

Feeling without judgment is a washy draught indeed; but judgment untempered by feeling is too bitter and husky a morsel for human deglutition. —CHARLOTTE BRONTË, *Jane Eyre*

> And diff'ring judgments serve but to declare
> That truth lies somewhere, if we knew but
> where.
> > —WILLIAM COWPER, "Hope"

Everyone complains of his memory, and no one complains of his judgment. —LA ROCHEFOUCAULD, *Maxims*

He that judges without informing himself to the utmost that he is capable, cannot acquit himself of judging amiss. —JOHN LOCKE, *An Essay Concerning Human Understanding*

We praise or blame as one or the other affords more opportunity for exhibiting our power of judgment. —FRIEDRICH NIETZSCHE, *Human, All-too-Human*

> 'Tis with our judgments as our watches, none
> Go just alike, yet each believes his own.
> > —ALEXANDER POPE, *An Essay on
> > Criticism*

The number of those who undergo the fatigue of judging for themselves is very small indeed. —RICHARD BRINSLEY SHERIDAN, *The Critic*

Justice — See also EQUALITY

It is better that ten guilty persons escape than that one innocent suffer. —WILLIAM BLACKSTONE, *Commentaries on the Laws of England*

> [Voltaire had made a similar statement (in *Zadig*): "It is better to risk saving a guilty person than to condemn an innocent one."]

For justice, though she's painted blind,
Is to the weaker side inclined.
   —SAMUEL BUTLER (d 1680), *Hudibras*

"There's the King's Messenger. He's in prison now, being punished: and the trial doesn't even begin till next Wednesday: and of course the crime comes last of all."

 "Suppose he never commits the crime?" said Alice.

"That would be all the better, wouldn't it?"
   —LEWIS CARROLL, *Through the Looking-Glass*

Justice shines by its own light. —CICERO, *De Officiis*

There is no such thing as justice—in or out of court.
—CLARENCE DARROW, quoted in *New York Times*

Justice is always violent to the party offending, for every man is innocent in his own eyes. —DANIEL DEFOE, "The Shortest Way With The Dissenters"

I say that justice is truth in action. —BENJAMIN DISRAELI, speech (1851)

Justice is the means by which established injustices are sanctioned. —ANATOLE FRANCE, *Crainquebille*

A jury consists of twelve persons chosen to decide who has the better lawyer. —ROBERT FROST, attributed

Justice should not only be done, but should manifestly and undoubtedly be seen to be done. —GORDON HEWART, judicial opinion (1924)

Injustice anywhere is a threat to justice everywhere.
—MARTIN LUTHER KING, JR., "Letter from Birmingham Jail"

 [This open letter was widely reprinted after its first publication in April 1963.]

Injustice is relatively easy to bear; what stings is justice. —H.L. MENCKEN, *Prejudices*

Justice is lame as well as blind, amongst us.
—THOMAS OTWAY, *Venice Preserved*

Justice without force is powerless; force without justice is tyrannical. —BLAISE PASCAL, *Pensées*

Mankind censure injustice, fearing that they may be the victims of it and not because they shrink from committing it. —PLATO, *The Republic*

The judge is condemned when the criminal is acquitted. —PUBLILIUS SYRUS, *Maxims*

We love justice greatly, and just men but little.
—JOSEPH ROUX, *Meditations of a Parish Priest*

Use every man after his desert, and who should 'scape whipping? —SHAKESPEARE, *Hamlet*

There is a point beyond which even justice becomes unjust. —SOPHOCLES, *Electra*

Kindness

No act of kindness, no matter how small, is ever wasted. —AESOP, *Fables*

Kindness is ever the begetter of kindness. —SOPHOCLES, *Ajax*

> So many gods, so many creeds,
>   So many paths that wind and wind,
>   While just the art of being kind
> Is all the sad world needs.
>   —ELLA WHEELER WILCOX, "The
>   World's Need"

One can always be kind to people one cares nothing about. —OSCAR WILDE, *The Picture of Dorian Gray*

> . . . that best portion of a good man's life.
> His little, nameless, unremembered acts
> Of kindness and of love.
> > —WILLIAM WORDSWORTH, "Lines Com-
> > posed a Few Miles above Tintern Abbey"

Kings — See LEADERS AND RULERS

Kissing

What of soul was left, I wonder, when the kissing had to stop? —ROBERT BROWNING, "A Toccata of Galuppi's"

Oh what lies there are in kisses! —HEINRICH HEINE, *In den Küssen, welche Lüge*

The sound of a kiss is not so loud as that of a cannon, but its echo lasts a great deal longer. —OLIVER WENDELL HOLMES, SR., *The Professor at the Breakfast-Table*

> Drink to me only with thine eyes,
> And I will pledge with mine;
> Or leave a kiss but in the cup
> And I'll not look for wine.
> > —BEN JONSON, "To Celia"

Sweet Helen, make me immortal with a kiss.
—CHRISTOPHER MARLOWE, *Doctor Faustus*

A kiss can be a comma, a question mark or an exclamation point. That's basic spelling that every woman ought to know. —MISTINGUETT, in *Theatre Arts*

> A kiss, when all is said, what is it?
> An oath that's given closer than before;

A promise more precise; the sealing of
Confessions that till then were barely
   breathed;
A rosy dot placed on the i in loving;
A secret that's confided to a mouth
And not to ears.
     —EDMOND ROSTAND, *Cyrano de Bergerac*

Dear as remember'd kisses after death,
And sweet as those by hopeless fancy feign'd
On lips that are for others.
     —ALFRED, LORD TENNYSON, *The Princess*

Knowledge and Learning — See also EDUCATION;
TEACHERS AND TEACHING

Well, knowledge is a fine thing, and mother Eve thought so; but she smarted so severely for hers, that most of her daughters have been afraid of it since.
—ABIGAIL ADAMS, letter (1791)

What one knows is, in youth, of little moment; they know enough who know how to learn. —HENRY ADAMS, *The Education of Henry Adams*

Learning teacheth more in one year than experience in twenty. —ROGER ASCHAM, *The Scholemaster*

Knowledge is the conformity of the object and the intellect. —AVERROËS, *Destructio Destructionum*

For knowledge, too, is itself power. —FRANCIS BACON, *Meditationes Sacrae*

When you know a thing, to hold that you know it, and when you do not know a thing, to allow that you do not know it: this is knowledge. —CONFUCIUS, *Analects*

We shall not cease from exploration
And the end of all our exploring
Will be to arrive where we started
And know the place for the first time.
   —T.S. ELIOT, *Four Quartets*: "Little
        Gidding"

Whoso neglects learning in his youth,
Loses the past and is dead for the future.
      —EURIPIDES (fragment)

That which any one has been long learning unwillingly,
he unlearns with proportionable eagerness and haste.
—WILLIAM HAZLITT, "On Personal Character"

If a little knowledge is dangerous, where is the man
who has so much as to be out of danger? —THOMAS
HENRY HUXLEY, *On Elemental Instruction in Physiology*

All knowledge is of itself of some value. There is nothing so minute or inconsiderable that I would not
rather know it than not. —SAMUEL JOHNSON, quoted
in James Boswell's *The Life of Samuel Johnson*

All wish to know, but none want to pay the fee.
—JUVENAL, *Satires*

That is what learning is. You suddenly understand
something you've understood all your life, but in a
new way. —DORIS LESSING, *The Four-Gated City*

A little learning is a dangerous thing;
Drink deep, or taste not the Pierian spring:
There shallow Draughts intoxicate the Brain,
And drinking largely sobers us again.
    —ALEXANDER POPE, *An Essay on
        Criticism*

[The first line is often misquoted as "A little knowledge is a dangerous thing." See T.H. Huxley, in this
section.]

The desire of knowledge, like the thirst of riches, increases ever with the acquisition of it. —LAURENCE STERNE, *Tristram Shandy*

Language

"When *I* use a word," Humpty Dumpty said in rather a scornful tone, "it means just what I choose it to mean—neither more nor less."

"The question is," said Alice, "whether you *can* make words mean so many different things."

"The question is," said Humpty Dumpty, "which is to be master—that's all."
    —LEWIS CARROLL, *Through the Looking-Glass*

All slang is metaphor, and all metaphor is poetry. —G.K. CHESTERTON, *The Defendant*

Words, as is well known, are great foes of reality. —JOSEPH CONRAD, *Under Western Eyes*

Write with the learned, pronounce with the vulgar. —BENJAMIN FRANKLIN, *Poor Richard's Almanac*

Thanks to words, we have been able to rise above the brutes; and thanks to words, we have often sunk to the level of the demons. —ALDOUS HUXLEY, *Adonis and the Alphabet*

It's a damn poor mind that can think of only one way to spell a word! —ANDREW JACKSON, quoted in an advertisement (1982)

Language is the dress of thought. —SAMUEL JOHNSON, *The Lives of the Eminent English Poets: Cowley*

   [Similarly expressed by Lord Chesterfield, in a letter in 1750: "Words are the dress of thoughts; which should no more be presented in rags, tatters, and dirt than your person should."]

234

Words are, of course, the most powerful drug used by mankind. —RUDYARD KIPLING, speech (1923)

"Correct" spelling, indeed, is one of the arts that are far more esteemed by schoolma'ams than by practical men, neck-deep in the heat and agony of the world. —H.L. MENCKEN, *The American Language*

The greater part of the world's troubles are due to questions of grammar. —MICHEL DE MONTAIGNE, *Essays*

> [Edmund Burke expressed a similar thought, in a letter written sometime around 1795: "A very great part of the mischiefs that vex this world arise from words."]

Those that will combat use and custom by the strict rules of grammar do but jest. —MICHEL DE MONTAIGNE, *Essays*

Slang is a language that rolls up its sleeves, spits on its hands, and goes to work. —CARL SANDBURG, quoted in *New York Times*

England and America are two countries separated by the same language. —GEORGE BERNARD SHAW, quoted in *Reader's Digest*

Man is a creature who lives not upon bread alone, but principally by catchwords. —ROBERT LOUIS STEVENSON, *Virginibus Puerisque*

When I read some of the rules for speaking and writing the English language correctly, . . . I think—
> Any fool can make a rule
> And every fool will mind it.
> —HENRY DAVID THOREAU, *Journal*

The difference between the *almost right* word and the *right* word is really a large matter—'tis the difference between the lightning-bug and the lightning.
—MARK TWAIN, in *The Art of Authorship*, ed. George Bainton

Why care for grammar as long as we are good?
—ARTEMUS WARD, *Artemus Ward in London*

. . . English is an almost grammarless language.
—RICHARD GRANT WHITE, *Words and Their Uses*

The limits of my language mean the limits of my world. —LUDWIG WITTGENSTEIN, *Tractatus Logico-Philosophicus*

Laughter and Smiles

Laffing iz the sensation ov pheeling good all over, and showing it principally in one spot. —JOSH BILLINGS, *Josh Billing's Comical Lexicon*

There is nothing sillier than a silly laugh. —CATUL-LUS, *Carmina*

The most wasted day of all is that in which we have not laughed. —SÉBASTIEN-ROCH NICOLAS CHAM-FORT, *Maximes et pensées*

In my mind there is nothing so illiberal, and so ill-bred, as audible laughter. . . . I am neither of a melancholy, nor a cynical disposition, and am as willing and as apt to be pleased as anybody; but I am sure that since I have had the full use of my reason, nobody has ever heard me laugh. —LORD CHESTER-FIELD, *Letters to His Son*

What was significant about the laughter . . . was not just the fact that it provides internal exercise for a person . . .—a form of jogging for the innards—but that it creates a mood in which the other positive emotions can be put to work, too. —NORMAN COUSINS, *Anatomy of an Illness*

Men show their characters in nothing more clearly than in what they think laughable. —JOHANN WOLFGANG VON GOETHE, *Maxims and Reflections*

Laughter is nothing else but sudden glory arising from some sudden conception of some eminency in ourselves, by comparison with the infirmity of others, or with our own formerly. —THOMAS HOBBES, *On Human Nature*

We must laugh before we are happy for fear of dying without having laughed at all. —LA BRUYÈRE, *Les Caractères*

A smile is the chosen vehicle of all ambiguities. —HERMAN MELVILLE, *Pierre*

There's daggers in men's smiles. —SHAKESPEARE, *Macbeth*

I have a great desire to make people smile—not laugh, but smile. Laughter is too aggressive. People bare their teeth. —MURIEL SPARK, quoted in *The Times* (London)

Law and Lawyers

Law is a Bottomless-Pit, it is a Cormorant, a Harpy, that devours everything. —JOHN ARBUTHNOT, *The History of John Bull*

One Law for the Lion and Ox is Oppression. —WILLIAM BLAKE, *The Marriage of Heaven and Hell*

If there were no bad people, there would be no good lawyers. —CHARLES DICKENS, *The Old Curiosity Shop*

"If the law supposes that," said Mr. Bumble, . . . "the law is a ass—a idiot. If that's the eye of the law, the law is a bachelor; and the worst I wish the law is, that his eye may be opened by experience—by experience." —CHARLES DICKENS, *Oliver Twist*

. . . the majestic equality of the law, which forbids the rich as well as the poor to sleep under bridges, to beg in the streets, and to steal bread. —ANATOLE FRANCE, *The Red Lily*

Fragile as reason is and limited as law is as the institutionalized medium of reason, that's all we have standing between us and the tyranny of mere will and the cruelty of unbridled, undisciplined feeling. —FELIX FRANKFURTER, *Felix Frankfurter Reminisces*

Laws too gentle are seldom obeyed; too severe, seldom executed. —BENJAMIN FRANKLIN, *Poor Richard's Almanac*

All laws are an attempt to domesticate the natural ferocity of the species. —JOHN W. GARDNER, in *San Francisco Examiner & Chronicle*

It will be of little avail to the people that the laws are made by men of their own choice if the laws be so voluminous that they cannot be read, or so incoherent that they cannot be understood. —ALEXANDER HAMILTON, *The Federalist*

There are not enough jails, not enough policemen, not enough courts to enforce a law not supported by the people. —HUBERT H. HUMPHREY, speech (1965)

Lawyers [are] operators of the toll bridge across which anyone in search of justice has to pass.
—JANE BRYANT QUINN, in *Newsweek*

Ignorance of the law excuses no man; not that all men know the law, but because 'tis an excuse every man will plead, and no man can tell how to confute him. —JOHN SELDEN, *Table Talk*

Laws do not persuade because they threaten. —SENECA, *Epistulae ad Lucilium*

The first thing we do, let's kill all the lawyers.
—SHAKESPEARE, *Henry VI, Part II*

Laws are like spiders' webs: if some light or powerless thing falls into them, it is caught, but a bigger one can break through and get away. —SOLON, quoted by Diogenes Laertius in *Lives of the Philosophers*

[Anacharsis was quoted by Plutarch in *Parallel Lives* making a similar statement: "Laws are like spiders' webs; they hold the weak and delicate who are caught in their meshes, but are torn to pieces by the rich and powerful." The image of law as a web was also taken up by later writers. Jonathan Swift, for example, wrote in his *Essay on the Faculties of the Mind*: "Laws are like cobwebs, which may catch small flies, but let wasps and hornets break through."]

Laziness — See IDLENESS AND LAZINESS

Leaders and Rulers — See also TYRANNY

He who is to be a good ruler must have first been ruled. —ARISTOTLE, *Politics*

It is a miserable state of mind to have few things to desire and many things to fear; and yet that commonly is the case of kings. —FRANCIS BACON, *Essays*

I would rather be right than be President. —HENRY CLAY, speech (1850)

> I am monarch of all I survey,
> My right there is none to dispute;
> From the center all round to the sea,
> I am lord of the fowl and the brute.
> > —WILLIAM COWPER, "Verses Supposed to
> > be Written by Alexander Selkirk"

> In enterprise of martial kind
> When there was any fighting,
> He led his reg'ment from behind
> He found it less exciting.
> > —W.S. GILBERT, *The Gondoliers*

When a man assumes a public trust, he should consider himself as public property. —THOMAS JEFFERSON, attributed

A President's hardest task is not to *do* what is right, but to *know* what is right. —LYNDON B. JOHNSON, speech (1965)

> A leader is best
> When people barely know that he exists,
> Not so good when people obey and acclaim him,
> Worst when they despise him.
> > —LAO-TZU, *The Way of Life*

I have to follow them, I am their leader. —ALEXANDRE-AUGUSTE LEDRU-ROLLIN, attributed

> [Ledru-Rollin was a leader in the Revolution of 1848 in France.]

The final test of a leader is that he leaves behind him in other men the conviction and the will to carry on. —WALTER LIPPMANN, in *New York Herald Tribune*

I am the state! (*L'état, c'est moi!*) —LOUIS XIV OF FRANCE, attributed

The first method for estimating the intelligence of a ruler is to look at the men he has around him. —NICCOLÒ MACHIAVELLI, *The Prince*

The real leader has no need to lead—he is content to point the way. —HENRY MILLER, *The Wisdom of the Heart*

A leader is a dealer in hope. —NAPOLEON I, attributed

When the President does it, that means that it is not illegal. —RICHARD M. NIXON, television interview (with David Frost)

Contrary to the unsophisticated suggestions of melodrama, to rule is not so much a question of the heavy hand as of the firm seat. —JOSÉ ORTEGA Y GASSET, *The Revolt of the Masses*

The person who knows "how" will always have a job. The person who knows "why" will always be his boss. —DIANE RAVITCH, speech (1985)

It is impossible to reign innocently. —LOUIS DE SAINT-JUST, speech (1793)
> [This comment was made at the sentencing of Louis XVI to death. The following year Saint-Just was himself sentenced to death.]

The first art of a monarch is the power to endure hatred. —SENECA, *Hercules Furens*

Uneasy lies the head that wears a crown. —SHAKESPEARE, *Henry IV, Part II*

All kings is mostly rapscallions. —MARK TWAIN, *Huckleberry Finn*

Learning — See KNOWLEDGE AND LEARNING

Leisure

The wisdom of a learned man cometh by opportunity of leisure: and he that hath little business shall become wise. —BIBLE, *Ecclesiasticus* 38:24

We are closer to the ants than to the butterflies. Very few people can endure much leisure. —GERALD BRENAN, *Thoughts in a Dry Season*

> When a man's busy, why leisure
> Strikes him as wonderful pleasure:
> 'Faith, and at leisure once is he?
> Straightway he wants to be busy.
> —ROBERT BROWNING, "The Glove"

> What is this life if, full of care,
> We have no time to stand and stare.
> —W.H. DAVIES, "Leisure"

Increased means and increased leisure are the two civilizers of man. —BENJAMIN DISRAELI, speech (1872)

You will soon break the bow if you keep it always stretched. —PHAEDRUS, *Fables*

To be able to fill leisure intelligently is the last product of civilization, and at present very few people have reached this level. —BERTRAND RUSSELL, *The Conquest of Happiness*

> If all the year were playing holidays,
> To sport would be as tedious as to work.
> —SHAKESPEARE, *Henry IV, Part I*

Lending — See BORROWING AND LENDING

Liberals and Conservatives

CONSERVATIVE, *n.* A statesman who is enamored of existing evils, as distinguished from the Liberal, who wishes to replace them with others. —AMBROSE BIERCE, *The Devil's Dictionary*

The healthy stomach is nothing if not conservative. Few radicals have good digestions. —SAMUEL BUTLER (*d* 1902), *Note-Books*

All conservatism is based upon the idea that if you leave things alone you leave them as they are. But you do not. If you leave a thing alone you leave it to a torrent of change. —G.K. CHESTERTON, *Orthodoxy*

A conservative government is an organized hypocrisy. —BENJAMIN DISRAELI, speech (1845)

Men are conservatives when they are least vigorous, or when they are most luxurious. They are conservatives after dinner, or before taking their rest; when they are sick, or aged. In the morning, or when their intellect or their conscience has been aroused; when they hear music, or when they read poetry, they are radicals. —RALPH WALDO EMERSON, lecture (1844)

There is always a certain meanness in the argument of conservatism, joined with a certain superiority in its fact. —RALPH WALDO EMERSON, *The Conservative*

To be absolutely honest, what I feel really bad about is that I don't feel worse. There's the ineffectual liberal's problem in a nutshell. —MICHAEL FRAYN, in *The Observer*

> I never dared be radical when young
> For fear it would make me conservative when
>   old.
>   —ROBERT FROST, "Precaution"

A liberal is a man who is willing to spend somebody else's money. —CARTER GLASS, quoted in *New York Times*

I do not know which makes a man more conservative—to know nothing but the present, or nothing but the past. —JOHN MAYNARD KEYNES, *The End of Laissez-Faire*

Liberalism . . . is the supreme form of generosity. . . . It announces the determination to share existence with the enemy; more than that, with an enemy which is weak. —JOSÉ ORTEGA Y GASSET, *The Revolt of the Masses*

A radical is a man with both feet firmly planted—in the air; a conservative is a man with two perfectly good legs who, however, has never learned to walk forward; . . . a liberal is a man who uses his legs and his hands at the behest—at the command—of his head. —FRANKLIN D. ROOSEVELT, radio address (1939)

Liberty — See FREEDOM AND LIBERTY

Life

Life is a long lesson in humility. —JAMES M. BARRIE, *The Little Minister*

If it were possible to talk to the unborn, one could never explain to them how it feels to be alive, for life is washed in the speechless real. —JACQUES BARZUN, *The House of Intellect*

Is life worth living? This is a question for an embryo, not for a man. —SAMUEL BUTLER (d 1902), *Note-Books*

Life is the art of drawing sufficient conclusions from insufficient premises. —SAMUEL BUTLER (d 1902), *Note-Books*

Life is one long process of getting tired. —SAMUEL BUTLER (d 1902), *Note-Books*

Life is an incurable disease. —ABRAHAM COWLEY, "To Dr. Scarborough"

> Birth, and copulation, and death.
> That's all the facts when you come to brass
>   tacks.
> —T.S. ELIOT, *Sweeney Agonistes*

Life is made up of marble and mud. —NATHANIEL HAWTHORNE, *The House of Seven Gables*

Life is short, art long, opportunity fleeting, experience treacherous, judgment difficult. —HIPPOCRATES, *Aphorisms*

> [The quotation is often given in Latin, as *Ars longa, vita brevis*. Many others have taken up this idea, such as Chaucer in *The Parliament of Fowls*:
> "The life so short, the craft so long to learn,
> The effort so hard, so keen the conquering."
> See also Longfellow, under Transience.]

Life is just one damned thing after another.
—ELBERT HUBBARD, *A Thousand and One Epigrams*

> [Frequently attributed to Frank Ward O'Malley. See Edna St. Vincent Millay's response, in this section.]

Live all you can; it's a mistake not to. It doesn't so much matter what you do in particular, so long as you have your life. If you haven't had that, what *have* you had? —HENRY JAMES, *The Ambassadors*

As far as we can discern, the sole purpose of human existence is to kindle a light in the darkness of mere being. —CARL JUNG, *Memories, Dreams, Reflections*

Life can only be understood backwards; but it must be lived forwards. —SØREN KIERKEGAARD, *Life*

When life is miserable it is painful to endure it; when it is happy it is horrible to lose it; both come to the same thing. Life is something to do when you can't get to sleep. —LA BRUYÈRE, *Les Caractères*

We are always beginning to live, but are never living. —MARCUS MANILIUS, *Astronomica*

> [Emerson found the situation unchanged. He wrote in his journal in 1834: "We are always getting ready to live, but never living."]

It is not true that life is one damn thing after another—it's one damn thing over and over. —EDNA ST. VINCENT MILLAY, letter (1930)

Life is a foreign language: all men mispronounce it. —CHRISTOPHER MORLEY, *Thunder on the Left*

> Oh, life is a glorious cycle of song,
> A medley of extemporanea;
> And love is a thing that can never go wrong;
> And I am Marie of Roumania.
> —DOROTHY PARKER, "Comment"

Life is short, but its ills make it seem long. —PUBLILIUS SYRUS, *Maxims*

There are no classes in life for beginners; right away you are always asked to deal with what is most difficult. —RAINER MARIA RILKE, *The Notebooks of Malte Laurids Brigge*

There is no cure for birth and death save to enjoy the interval. —GEORGE SANTAYANA, *Soliloquies in England*

Life is as tedious as a twice-told tale
Vexing the dull ear of a drowsy man.
　　　　　　　　　—SHAKESPEARE, *King John*

Life's but a walking shadow, a poor player
That struts and frets his hour upon the stage
And then is heard no more: it is a tale
Told by an idiot, full of sound and fury,
Signifying nothing.
　　　　　　　　　—SHAKESPEARE, *Macbeth*

All the world's a stage,
And all the men and women merely players;
They have their exits and their entrances;
And one man in his time plays many parts,
His acts being seven ages.
　　　　　　　　　—SHAKESPEARE, *As You Like It*

The shortness of life cannot dissuade us from its pleasures, nor console us for its pains. —MARQUIS DE VAUVENARGUES, *Reflections and Maxims*

Life is an offensive, directed against the repetitious mechanism of the Universe. —ALFRED NORTH WHITEHEAD, *Adventures of Ideas*

I spent the afternoon musing on Life. If you come to think of it, what a queer thing Life is! So unlike anything else, don't you know, if you see what I mean. —P.G. WODEHOUSE, *My Man Jeeves*

Literature — See BOOKS AND READING; WRITING AND WRITERS

Logic — See REASON AND LOGIC

Loneliness — See SOLITUDE AND LONELINESS

Loss

'Tis better to have loved and lost, than never to have lost at all. —SAMUEL BUTLER (d 1902), *The Way of All Flesh*

[For the original lines by Tennyson, see under Love.]

By an image we hold on to our lost treasures, but it is the wrenching loss that forms the image, composes, binds the bouquet. —COLETTE, *Mes Apprentissages*

> For 'tis a truth well known to most,
> That whatsoever thing is lost
> We seek it, ere it come to light,
> In every cranny but the right.
> —WILLIAM COWPER, "The Retired Cat"

There are occasions when it is undoubtedly better to incur loss than to make gain. —PLAUTUS, *The Captives*

> He that is robb'd, not wanting what is stol'n,
> Let him not know't, and he's not robb'd at all.
> —SHAKESPEARE, *Othello*

[Publilius Syrus wrote in his *Maxims*: "The loss which is unknown is no loss at all."]

> Wise men ne'er sit and wail their loss,
> But cheerly seek how to redress their harms.
> —SHAKESPEARE, *Henry VI, Part III*

> Praising what is lost
> Makes the remembrance dear.
> —SHAKESPEARE, *All's Well That Ends Well*

> And the stately ships go on
>   To their haven under the hill;
> But O for the touch of a vanish'd hand,
>   And the sound of a voice that is still!
> —ALFRED, LORD TENNYSON,
>   "Break, Break, Break"

A coin, sleeve-button or a collar-button dropped in a bedroom will hide itself and be hard to find. A handkerchief in bed *can't* be found. —MARK TWAIN, *Notebooks*

Love

It is impossible to love and to be wise. —FRANCIS BACON, *Essays*

[Many have made this observation. As early as the first century B.C. Publilius Syrus in his *Maxims* said: "A god could hardly love and be wise."]

One hour of right-down love
Is worth an age of dully living on.
                    —APHRA BEHN, *The Rover*

Love ceases to be a pleasure, when it ceases to be a secret. —APHRA BEHN, *The Lover's Watch*

Better is a dinner of herbs where love is, than a stalled ox and hatred therewith. —BIBLE, *Proverbs* 15:17

Set me as a seal upon thy heart, as a seal upon thine arm: for love is strong as death. —BIBLE, *Song of Solomon* 8:6

There is no fear in love; but perfect love casteth out fear. —BIBLE, *I John* 4:18

Love seeketh not Itself to please,
Nor for itself hath any care,
But for another gives it ease,
And builds a Heaven in Hell's despair.
. . . .
Love seeketh only Self to please,
To bind another to Its delight,
Joys in another's loss of ease,
And builds a Hell in Heaven's despite.
            —WILLIAM BLAKE, "The Clod and the
                              Pebble"

To fall in love is to create a religion that has a fallible god. —JORGE LUIS BORGES, *Other Inquisitions*

> How do I love thee? Let me count the ways.
> I love thee to the depth and breadth and
>   height
> My soul can reach.
>   —ELIZABETH BARRETT BROWNING, *Sonnets*
>   *from the Portuguese*

> God be thanked, the meanest of his creatures
> Boasts two soul-sides, one to face the world
>   with,
> One to show a woman when he loves her!
>   —ROBERT BROWNING, "One Word More"

> O my luve's like a red, red rose,
>   That's newly sprung in June:
> O my luve's like the melodie
>   That's sweetly play'd in tune.
>   —ROBERT BURNS, "A Red, Red Rose"

O what a heaven is love! O what a hell! —THOMAS DEKKER, *The Honest Whore*

> Love all love of other sights controls,
> And makes one little room an everywhere.
>   —JOHN DONNE, "The Good Morrow"

> I am two fools, I know,
> For loving, and for saying so
> In whining Poetry.
>   —JOHN DONNE, "The Triple Fool"

> For, Heaven be thank'd, we live in such an
>   age,
> When no man dies for love, but on the stage.
>   —JOHN DRYDEN, *Mithridates*

All mankind love a lover. —RALPH WALDO EMERSON, *Essays*

250

A Book of Verses underneath the Bough,
A Jug of Wine, a Loaf of Bread—and Thou
Beside me singing in the Wilderness—
Oh, Wilderness were Paradise enow!
      —EDWARD FITZGERALD, *The Rubáiyát of*
                Omar Khayyám

It seems that it is madder never to abandon oneself, than often to be infatuated; better to be wounded, a captive, and a slave, than always to walk in armor.
—MARGARET FULLER, *Summer on the Lakes*

For, you see, each day I love you more,
Today more than yesterday and less than
    tomorrow.
        —ROSEMONDE GÉRARD, "L'éternelle
                chanson"

Two souls with but a single thought,
Two hearts that beat as one.
        —FRIEDRICH HALM, *Ingomar the*
                Barbarian

A lover without indiscretion is no lover at all.
—THOMAS HARDY, *The Hand of Ethelberta*

Love and a cough cannot be hid. —GEORGE HERBERT, *Jacula Prudentum*

At the beginning and at the end of love the two lovers are embarrassed to find themselves alone. —LA BRUYÈRE, *Les Caractères*

If we judge of love by its usual effects, it resembles hatred more than friendship. —LA ROCHEFOUCAULD, *Maxims*

It is with true love as it is with ghosts; everyone talks of it, but few have seen it. —LA ROCHEFOUCAULD, *Maxims*

It is love, not reason, that is stronger than death.
—THOMAS MANN, *The Magic Mountain*

[See also The Bible, *Song of Solomon*, in this section.]

Who ever loved that loved not at first sight? —CHRISTOPHER MARLOWE, *Hero and Leander*

[This was quoted by Shakespeare in *As You Like It*.]

Come live with me, and be my love;
And we will all the pleasures prove
That valleys, groves, hills, and fields,
Woods or steepy mountain yields.
> —CHRISTOPHER MARLOWE, "The
> Passionate Shepherd to His Love"

[John Donne wrote some very similar lines in "The Bait":
Come live with me, and be my love,
And we will some new pleasures prove
Of golden sands, and crystal brooks,
With silken lines, and silver hooks.]

Love is a kind of warfare. —OVID, *Ars Amatoria*

At the touch of love everyone becomes a poet.
—PLATO, *Symposium*

Life has taught us that love does not consist in gazing at each other but in looking outward together in the same direction. —ANTOINE DE SAINT-EXUPÉRY, *Wind, Sand, and Stars*

There is only one happiness in life, to love and be loved. —GEORGE SAND, letter (1862)

If thou remember'st not the slightest folly
That ever love did make thee run into,
Thou hast not loved.
> —SHAKESPEARE, *As You Like It*

The course of true love never did run smooth.
—SHAKESPEARE, *A Midsummer Night's Dream*

> Let me not to the marriage of true minds
> Admit impediments. Love is not love
> Which alters when it alteration finds
> Or bends with the remover to remove.
> O, no! it is an ever-fixèd mark
> That looks on tempests and is never shaken.
> —SHAKESPEARE, *Sonnet XVI*

> Shall I compare thee to a summer's day?
> Thou art more lovely and more temperate.
> —SHAKESPEARE, *Sonnet XVIII*

All's fair in love and war. —FRANCIS EDWARD SMEDLEY, *Frank Fairleigh*

[Smedley seems to have been the first to use this wording, but the idea was not new. Francis Beaumont and John Fletcher earlier wrote in *The Lovers' Progress*:

> All stratagems
> In love, and that the sharpest war, are
> lawful."

And Susannah Centlivre wrote in *Love at a Venture*: "All policy's allowed in war and love."]

> One word
> Frees us of all the weight and pain of life:
> That word is love.
> —SOPHOCLES, *Oedipus at Colonus*

> 'Tis better to have loved and lost
> Than never to have loved at all.
> —ALFRED, LORD TENNYSON, *In Memoriam*

[See also Samuel Butler's parody, under Loss.]

Love is the child of illusion and the parent of disillusion. —MIGUEL DE UNAMUNO, *The Tragic Sense of Life*

Love conquers all things; let us too surrender to Love.
—Virgil, *Eclogues*

> Yet each man kills the thing he loves,
>   By each let this be heard,
> Some do it with a bitter look,
>   Some with a flattering word.
> The coward does it with a kiss,
>   The brave man with a sword!
>   —Oscar Wilde, *The Ballad of*
>   *Reading Gaol*

Loyalty — See FAITHFULNESS AND LOYALTY

Luck — See also FORTUNE AND CHANCE

Of course I believe in luck. How otherwise to explain the success of some people you detest? —Jean Cocteau, quoted in *Look*

Luck is a mighty queer thing. All you know about it for certain is that it's bound to change. —Bret Harte, *The Outcasts of Poker Flat*

I am a great believer in luck, and I find the harder I work the more I have of it. —Stephen Leacock, *Literary Lapses*

> You can take it as understood
> That your luck changes only if it's good.
>   —Ogden Nash, "Roulette Us Be Gay"

Luck is not something you can mention in the presence of self-made men. —E.B. White, *One Man's Meat*

Lying and Liars

Young as he was, his instinct told him that the best liar is he who makes the smallest amount of lying go the longest way. —Samuel Butler (d 1902), *The Way of All Flesh*

The great masses of the people . . . will more easily fall victims to a great lie than to a small one. —ADOLF HITLER, *Mein Kampf*

Sin has many tools, but a lie is the handle which fits them all. —OLIVER WENDELL HOLMES, SR., *The Autocrat of the Breakfast-Table*

A liar needs a good memory. —QUINTILIAN, *De Institutione Oratoria*

[The point has also been made by others, including Montaigne, (*Essays*): "He who is not sure of his memory should not undertake the trade of lying," and by F.M. Knowles, in *A Cheerful Year Book*: "There is nothing so pathetic as a forgetful liar."]

A little inaccuracy sometimes saves tons of explanation. —SAKI, *The Square Egg*

A lie is an abomination unto the Lord, and a very present help in trouble. —ADLAI E. STEVENSON, speech (1951)

[Stevenson was probably not the originator of this jumbled Biblical quotation (combining Proverbs 12:22 and Psalms 46:1). It seems to have been around for some time before he used it.]

The cruelest lies are often told in silence. —ROBERT LOUIS STEVENSON, *Virginibus Puerisque*

One of the most striking differences between a cat and a lie is that a cat has only nine lives. —MARK TWAIN, *Pudd'nhead Wilson*, "Pudd'nhead Wilson's Calendar"

Machines — See TECHNOLOGY

Madness — See MENTAL DISORDER

Majorities — See also MINORITIES

One with the law is a majority. —CALVIN COOLIDGE, speech (1920)

A majority is always the best repartee. —BENJAMIN DISRAELI, *Tancred*

The majority has the *might*—more's the pity—but it hasn't the *right*. . . . The minority is always right. —HENRIK IBSEN, *An Enemy of the People*

One, on God's side, is a majority. —WENDELL PHILLIPS, speech (1859)

> [Thomas B. Reed commented in a speech in 1885: "One, with God, is always a majority, but many a martyr has been burned at the stake while the votes were being counted."]

Any man more right than his neighbors constitutes a majority of one. —HENRY DAVID THOREAU, *Civil Disobedience*

Hain't we got all the fools in town on our side? And ain't that a big enough majority in any town? —MARK TWAIN, *The Adventures of Huckleberry Finn*

Mankind — See HUMANS AND HUMAN NATURE

Manners

Good manners are the settled medium of social, as specie is of commercial, life; returns are equally expected for both. —LORD CHESTERFIELD, *Letters to His Son*

> [Samuel Johnson said of Lord Chesterfield's letters to his son, "They teach the morals of a whore, and the manners of a dancing master." (quoted in James Boswell's *The Life of Samuel Johnson*). Johnson was himself considered by many to be rather uncouth.]

Good manners are made up of petty sacrifices. —RALPH WALDO EMERSON, *Letters and Social Aims*

Life is not so short but that there is always time enough for courtesy. —RALPH WALDO EMERSON, *Letters and Social Aims*

More tears have been shed over men's lack of manners than their lack of morals. —HELEN HATHAWAY, *Manners for Men*

In truth, politeness is artificial good humor, it covers the natural want of it, and ends by rendering habitual a substitute nearly equivalent to the real virtue. —THOMAS JEFFERSON, letter (1808)

Tact is after all a kind of mind reading. —SARAH ORNE JEWETT, *The Country of the Pointed Firs and Other Stories*

There can be no defense like elaborate courtesy. —E.V. LUCAS, *Reading, Writing, and Remembering*

At a dinner party one should eat wisely but not too well, and talk well but not too wisely. —W. SOMERSET MAUGHAM, *A Writer's Notebook*

Civility costs nothing and buys everything. —LADY MARY WORTLEY MONTAGU, letter (1756)

Politeness is the art of choosing among one's real thoughts. —ABEL STEVENS, *Life of Mme. de Staël*

Good breeding consists in concealing how much we think of ourselves and how little we think of the other person. —MARK TWAIN, *Notebooks*

Politeness is organized indifference. —PAUL VALÉRY, *Tel quel*

Marriage

It is a truth universally acknowledged, that a single man in possession of a good fortune, must be in want of a wife. —JANE AUSTEN, *Pride and Prejudice*

257

It is better to marry than to burn. —BIBLE, *I Corinthians* 7:9

One was never married, and that's his hell; another is, and that's his plague. —ROBERT BURTON, *The Anatomy of Melancholy*

Wedlock—the deep, deep peace of the double bed after the hurly-burly of the chaise-longue. —MRS. PATRICK CAMPBELL, quoted in Ralph G. Martin's *Jennie*

> Wife and servant are the same,
> But only differ in the name:
> For when that fatal knot is tied,
> Which nothing, nothing can divide:
> When she the word *obey* has said,
> And man by law supreme has made,
> Then all that's kind is laid aside,
> And nothing left but state and pride.
> —LADY MARY CHUDLEIGH, "To the Ladies"

> SHARPER: Thus grief still treads upon the
>   heels of pleasure:
> Marry'd in haste, we may repent at leisure.
> SETTER: Some by experience find those words
>   misplac'd:
> At leisure marry'd, they repent in haste.
> —WILLIAM CONGREVE, *The Old Bachelor*

And all the young ladies said . . . that to be sure a love-match was the only thing for happiness, where the parties could anyway afford it. —MARIA EDGEWORTH, *Castle Rackrent*

Marriage has many pains, but celibacy has no pleasures. —SAMUEL JOHNSON, *Rasselas*

> [Others have noted a similar contrast; for example, Thomas Love Peacock, in *Melincourt*, said: "Marriage may often be a stormy lake, but celibacy is almost always a muddy horsepond."]

A gentleman who had been very unhappy in marriage, married immediately after his wife died: Johnson said, it was the triumph of hope over experience.
—SAMUEL JOHNSON, quoted in James Boswell's *The Life of Samuel Johnson*

Sometimes it was worth all the disadvantages of marriage just to have that: one friend in an indifferent world. —ERICA JONG, *Fear of Flying*

There are few women so perfect that their husbands do not regret having married them at least once a day. —LA BRUYÈRE, *Les Caractères*

> So they were married—to be the more
>   together—
> And found they were never again so much
>   together,
> Divided by the morning tea,
> By the evening paper,
> By children and tradesmen's bills.
>   —LOUIS MACNEICE, "Les Sylphides"

Marriage may be compared to a cage: the birds outside despair to get in and those within despair to get out. —MICHEL DE MONTAIGNE, *Essays*

It doesn't much signify whom one marries, for one is sure to find next morning that it was someone else.
—SAMUEL ROGERS, *Table Talk*

Marriage is popular because it combines the maximum of temptation with the maximum of opportunity. —GEORGE BERNARD SHAW, *Man and Superman*, "The Revolutionist's Handbook"

When two people are under the influence of the most violent, most insane, most delusive, and most transient of passions, they are required to swear that they will remain in that excited, abnormal, and exhausting condition continuously until death do them part.
—GEORGE BERNARD SHAW, *Getting Married*

Marriage is the only adventure open to the timid.
—VOLTAIRE, *Pensées d'un Philosophe*

Men marry because they are tired; women because they are curious. Both are disappointed. —OSCAR WILDE, *A Woman of No Importance*

Marriage is a bribe to make a housekeeper think she's a householder. —THORNTON WILDER, *The Merchant of Yonkers*

Mathematics

There is no royal road to geometry. —EUCLID (said to Ptolemy I), quoted in Proclus, *Commentary on Euclid*

One has to be able to count, if only so that at fifty one doesn't marry a girl of twenty. —MAXIM GORKY, *The Zykovs*

The knowledge of numbers is one of the chief distinctions between us and the brutes. —LADY MARY WORTLEY MONTAGU, letter (1753)

Mathematics may be defined as the subject in which we never know what we are talking about, nor whether what we are saying is true. —BERTRAND RUSSELL, *Mysticism and Logic*

Mathematics . . . possesses not only truth, but supreme beauty—a beauty cold and austere, like that of sculpture. —BERTRAND RUSSELL, *The Study of Mathematics*

What would life be without arithmetic, but a scene of horrors? —SYDNEY SMITH, letter (1835)

Maturity

When I was a child, I spake as a child, I understood as a child, I thought as a child: but when I became a man, I put away childish things. —BIBLE, *I Corinthians* 13:11

Grown up, and that is a terribly hard thing to do. It is much easier to skip it and go from one childhood to another. —F. SCOTT FITZGERALD, *The Crack-Up*, ed. Edmund Wilson

Youth condemns; maturity condones. —AMY LOWELL, *Tendencies in Modern American Poetry*

Man's maturity: to have regained the seriousness that he had as a child at play. —FRIEDRICH NIETZSCHE, *Beyond Good and Evil*

To be adult is to be alone. —JEAN ROSTAND, *A Biologist's Thoughts*

One's prime is elusive. You little girls, when you grow up, must be on the alert to recognize your prime at whatever time of your life it may occur. You must live it to the full. —MURIEL SPARK, *The Prime of Miss Jean Brodie*

The mark of the immature man is that he wants to die nobly for a cause, while the mark of the mature man is that he wants to live humbly for one. —WILHELM STEKEL, quoted by J.D. Salinger in *The Catcher in the Rye*

Maturity is a high price to pay for growing up. —TOM STOPPARD, *Where Are They Now?*

> When I can look Life in the eyes,
> Grown calm and very coldly wise,
> Life will have given me the Truth,
> And taken in exchange—my youth.
> —SARA TEASDALE, "Wisdom"

Maxims and Proverbs

Proverbs are short sayings drawn from long experience. —MIGUEL DE CERVANTES, *Don Quixote de la Mancha*

Proverbs may not improperly be called the philosophy of the common people. —JAMES HOWELL, *Proverbs*

Nothing ever becomes real till it is experienced—even a proverb is no proverb to you till your life has illustrated it. —JOHN KEATS, letter (1819)

Nothing is so useless as a general maxim. —THOMAS BABINGTON MACAULAY, *Literary Essays contributed to the Edinburgh Review*

The platitude turned on its head is still a platitude. —NORMAN MAILER, *Advertisements for Myself*

A proverb is one man's wit and all men's wisdom. —JOHN RUSSELL, quoted in James Mackintosh's *Memoirs*

Almost every wise saying has an opposite one, no less wise, to balance it. —GEORGE SANTAYANA, *Little Essays*

Medicine and Doctors — See also HEALTH AND FITNESS; ILLNESS

[It is infinitely better to transplant a heart] than to bury it so it can be devoured by worms. —CHRISTIAAN BARNARD, quoted in *Time*

I find the medicine worse than the malady. —FRANCIS BEAUMONT AND JOHN FLETCHER, *Love's Cure*

> [This sentiment is far older than these 17th-century playwrights. It is found in the *Maxims* of Publilius Syrus, written in the first century B.C.: "There are some remedies worse than the disease."]

> Physicians of the Utmost Fame
> Were called at once; but when they came
> They answered, as they took their Fees,
> "There is no Cure for this Disease."
> —HILAIRE BELLOC, "Henry King"

Physician, heal thyself. —BIBLE, *Luke* 4:23

Medicine, the only profession that labors incessantly to destroy the reason for its own existence. —JAMES BRYCE, speech (1914)

> Surgeons must be very careful
> When they take the knife!
> Underneath their fine incisions
> Stirs the Culprit—*Life!*
> > —EMILY DICKINSON, "Surgeons must be
> > very careful"

God heals, and the doctor takes the fee. —BENJAMIN FRANKLIN, *Poor Richard's Almanac*

> [Similarly: "God heals, and the physician hath the thanks."—George Herbert, *Outlandish Proverbs*.]

Extreme remedies are very appropriate for extreme diseases. —HIPPOCRATES, *Aphorisms*

One of the most difficult things to contend with in a hospital is the assumption on the part of the staff that because you have lost your gall bladder you have also lost your mind. —JEAN KERR, *Please Don't Eat the Daisies*

As long as men are liable to die and are desirous to live, a physician will be made fun of, but he will be well paid. —LA BRUYÈRE, *Les Caractères*

Poisons and medicine are oftentimes the same substance given with different intents. —PETER MERE LATHAM, *General Remarks on the Practice of Medicine*

The desire to take medicine is perhaps the greatest feature which distinguishes man from animals.
—WILLIAM OSLER, *Science and Immortality*

Cur'd yesterday of my disease,
I died last night of my physician.
—MATTHEW PRIOR, "The Remedy Worse
than the Disease"

There are worse occupations in this world than feeling a woman's pulse. —LAURENCE STERNE, *A Sentimental Journey*

Formerly, when religion was strong and science weak, men mistook magic for medicine; now, when science is strong and religion weak, men mistake medicine for magic. —THOMAS SZASZ, *The Second Sin*

The great secret of doctors, known only to their wives, but still hidden from the public, is that most things get better by themselves; most things, in fact, are better in the morning. —LEWIS THOMAS, in *New York Times Magazine*

It should be the function of medicine to help people die young as late in life as possible. —ERNST WYNDER, quoted in *New York Times*

Memory

Memories are hunting horns
Whose sound dies on the wind.
—GUILLAUME APOLLINAIRE,
"Cors de chasse"

And we forget because we must
And not because we will.
—MATTHEW ARNOLD, "Absence"

Not the power to remember, but its very opposite, the power to forget, is a necessary condition for our existence. —SHOLEM ASCH, *The Nazarene*

If any one faculty of our nature may be called *more* wonderful than the rest, I do think it is memory. . . . The memory is sometimes so retentive, so serviceable, so obedient—at others, so bewildered and so weak—and at others again, so tyrannic, so beyond control!— We are to be sure a miracle every way—but our powers of recollecting and of forgetting, do seem peculiarly past finding out. —JANE AUSTEN, *Mansfield Park*

God gave us memory so that we might have roses in December. —JAMES M. BARRIE, speech (1922)

"The horror of that moment," the King went on, "I shall *never, never* forget!"
"You will, though," the Queen said, "if you don't make a memorandum of it."
  —LEWIS CARROLL, *Through the Looking-Glass*

Memory is the thing you forget with. —ALEXANDER CHASE, *Perspectives*

There is no greater sorrow than to recall happiness in times of misery. —DANTE, *Inferno*

O Memory, thou fond deceiver,
  Still importunate and vain,
To former joys recurring ever,
  And turning all the past to pain.
  —OLIVER GOLDSMITH, *The Captivity*

To endeavor to forget anyone is a certain way of thinking of nothing else. —LA BRUYÈRE, *Les Caractères*

"I did this," says my memory. "I cannot have done this," says my pride, remaining inexorable. Eventually, my memory yields. —FRIEDRICH NIETZSCHE, *Beyond Good and Evil*

The richness of life lies in memories we have forgotten. —CESARE PAVESE, diary entry (*The Burning Brand: Diaries 1935–50*)

Time, which changes people, does not alter the image we have retained of them. —MARCEL PROUST, *Remembrance of Things Past: The Past Recaptured*

> Better by far you should forget and smile
> Than that you should remember and be sad.
> —CHRISTINA ROSSETTI, "Remember"

Things that were hard to bear are sweet to remember. —SENECA, *Hercules Furens*

> Music, when soft voices die,
> Vibrates in the memory;
> Odors, when sweet violets sicken,
> Live within the sense they quicken.
> —PERCY BYSSHE SHELLEY, "To—"

Men

If there is anything disagreeable going on men are always sure to get out of it. —JANE AUSTEN, *Persuasion*

Men build bridges and throw railroads across deserts, and yet they contend successfully that the job of sewing on a button is beyond them. Accordingly, they don't have to sew buttons. —HEYWOOD BROUN, *Seeing Things at Night*

> Men are but children of a larger growth;
> Our appetites as apt to change as theirs,
> And full as craving too, and full as vain.
> —JOHN DRYDEN, *All for Love*

Men's men: gentle or simple, they're much of a muchness. —GEORGE ELIOT, *Daniel Deronda*

The male stereotype makes masculinity not just a fact of biology but something that must be proved and re-proved, a continual quest for an ever-receding Holy Grail. —MARC FEIGEN FASTEAU, *The Male Machine*

What a piece of work is a man! How noble in reason! how infinite in faculty! in form and moving how express and admirable! in action how like an angel! in apprehension how like a god! the beauty of the world! the paragon of animals! And yet, to me, what is this quintessence of dust? man delights not me— no, nor women neither. —SHAKESPEARE, *Hamlet*

Sigh no more, ladies, sigh no more,
   Men were deceivers ever,
One foot in sea and one on shore,
   To one thing constant never.
     —SHAKESPEARE, *Much Ado About Nothing*

His life was gentle, and the elements
So mix'd in him that Nature might stand up
And say to all the world, "This was a man!"
     —SHAKESPEARE, *Julius Caesar*

A man who has no office to go to—I don't care who he is—is a trial of which you can have no conception. —GEORGE BERNARD SHAW, *The Irrational Knot*

It is funny the two things most men are proudest of is the thing that any man can do and doing does in the same way, that is being drunk and being the father of their son. —GERTRUDE STEIN, *Everybody's Autobiography*

It's not the men in my life that counts—it's the life in my men. —MAE WEST, in the film *I'm No Angel*

Men and Women

In the new code of laws which I suppose it will be necessary for you to make, I desire you would remember the ladies and be more generous and favorable to them than your ancestors. Do not put such unlimited power into the hands of the husbands. Remember, all men would be tyrants if they could. —ABIGAIL ADAMS, letter (to John Adams, 1776)

In passing, also, I would like to say that the first time Adam had a chance he laid the blame on woman. —NANCY ASTOR, *My Two Countries*

There is more difference within the sexes than between them. —IVY COMPTON-BURNETT, *Mother and Son*

I'm not denyin' the women are foolish: God Almighty made 'em to match the men. —GEORGE ELIOT, *Adam Bede*

I should like to know what is the proper function of women, if it is not to make reasons for husbands to stay at home, and still stronger reasons for bachelors to go out. —GEORGE ELIOT, *The Mill on the Floss*

The same passions in man and woman nonetheless differ in tempo; hence man and woman do not cease misunderstanding one another. —FRIEDRICH NIETZSCHE, *Beyond Good and Evil*

I can't live either without you or with you. —OVID, *Amores*

> Woman wants monogamy;
> Man delights in novelty.
> Love is woman's moon and sun;
> Man has other forms of fun. . . .
> With this the gist and sum of it,
> What earthly good can come of it?
> —DOROTHY PARKER, "General Review of
> the Sex Situation"

> Men, some to bus'ness, some to pleasure take;
> But ev'ry woman is at heart a rake.
> —ALEXANDER POPE, *Moral Essays*

In our civilization, men are afraid that they will not be men enough and women are afraid that they might be considered only women. —THEODORE REIK, quoted in *Esquire*

Now, we are becoming the men we wanted to marry. —GLORIA STEINEM, speech (1981)

'Tis strange what a man may do, and a woman yet think him an angel. —WILLIAM MAKEPEACE THACKERAY, *Henry Esmond*

In politics if you want anything said, ask a man. If you want anything done, ask a woman. —MARGARET THATCHER, quoted in *People*

That . . . man . . . says women can't have as much rights as men, 'cause Christ wasn't a woman. . . . Where did your Christ come from? . . . From God and a woman. Man had nothing to do with him. —SOJOURNER TRUTH, speech (1851)

God created man and, finding him not sufficiently alone, gave him a companion to make him feel his solitude more keenly. —PAUL VALÉRY, *Tel quel*

LORD ILLINGWORTH: The Book of Life begins with a man and a woman in a garden.
MRS. ALLONBY: It ends with Revelations.
　　　　　　　—OSCAR WILDE, *A Woman of No Importance*

Women have served all these centuries as looking-glasses possessing the magic and delicious power of reflecting the figure of man at twice its natural size. —VIRGINIA WOOLF, *A Room of One's Own*

Mental Illness

There is a pleasure sure,
In being mad, which none but madmen know!
　　　　　—JOHN DRYDEN, *The Spanish Friar*

Whom the gods wish to destroy, they first make mad.
—EURIPIDES (fragment)

[This became a proverbial saying.]

Neurosis is always a substitute for legitimate suffering. —CARL JUNG, attributed

Insanity is the exception in individuals. In groups, parties, peoples, and times it is the rule. —FRIEDRICH NIETZSCHE, *Beyond Good and Evil*

All the greatest things we know have come to us from neurotics. It is they and they only who have founded religions and created great works of art. Never will the world be conscious of how much it owes to them, nor above all of what they have suffered in order to bestow their gifts on it. —MARCEL PROUST, *Remembrance of Things Past: The Guermantes Way*

Though this be madness, yet there is method in't.
—SHAKESPEARE, *Hamlet*

I am but mad north-north-west: when the wind is southerly I know a hawk from a handsaw. —SHAKESPEARE, *Hamlet*

If you talk to God, you are praying; if God talks to you, you have schizophrenia. —THOMAS SZASZ, *The Second Sin*

Neurosis is the way of avoiding non-being by avoiding being. —PAUL TILLICH, *The Courage To Be*

Mercy and Compassion — See also SYMPATHY AND PITY

We hand folks over to God's mercy, and show none ourselves. —GEORGE ELIOT, *Adam Bede*

Thwackum was for doing justice and leaving mercy to heaven. —HENRY FIELDING, *Tom Jones*

The quality of mercy is not strain'd,
It droppeth as the gentle rain from heaven
Upon the place beneath: it is twice bless'd;
It blesseth him that gives and him that takes.
—SHAKESPEARE, *The Merchant of Venice*

Nothing emboldens sin so much as mercy. —SHAKE-
SPEARE, *Timon of Athens*

Worse than idle is compassion
If it ends in tears and sighs.
—WILLIAM WORDSWORTH, "The Armenian
Lady's Love"

Middle Age — See AGE AND AGING

Military — See also WAR; WAR AND PEACE

No nation ever had an army large enough to guarantee
it against attack in time of peace or insure it victory in
time of war. —CALVIN COOLIDGE, speech (1925)

In the councils of government we must guard against
the acquisition of unwarranted influence, whether
sought or unsought, by the military-industrial complex. The potential for the disastrous rise of mis-
placed power exists and will persist. —DWIGHT D.
EISENHOWER, speech (farewell address, 1961)

[This is the earliest known use of the term "military-industrial complex."]

I am the very model of a modern Major-General;
I've information vegetable, animal and mineral;
I know the Kings of England, and I quote the
    fights historical,
From Marathon to Waterloo, in order
    categorical.
—W.S. GILBERT, *The Pirates of Penzance*

Guns will make us powerful; butter will only make us
fat. —HERMANN GÖRING, speech (1936)

Every man thinks meanly of himself for not having been a soldier. —SAMUEL JOHNSON, quoted in James Boswell's *The Life of Samuel Johnson*

> For it's Tommy this, an' Tommy that, an'
> "Chuck him out, the brute!"
> But it's "Savior of 'is country" when the guns
> begin to shoot.
> —RUDYARD KIPLING, "Tommy"
>
> ["Tommy Atkins"—a name used for a private in the British army.]

An army marches on its stomach. —NAPOLEON I, attributed

> [Also sometimes attributed to Frederick the Great.]

Soldiers generally win battles; generals get credit for them. —NAPOLEON I, attributed

> Our God and soldiers we alike adore
> Ev'n at the brink of danger; not before:
> After deliverance, both alike requited,
> Our God's forgotten, and our soldiers slighted.
> —FRANCIS QUARLES, *Emblems*

Fortune is always on the side of the big battalions. —MARIE DE SÉVIGNÉ, letter (1673)

> [Variations on this statement include Roger de Bussy-Rabutin's "God is generally for the big squadrons against the small ones" (in a letter in 1677), and Voltaire's "It is said that God is always on the side of the big battalions" (in a letter in 1770). See also Tacitus, under Strength.]

>   Then a soldier,
> Full of strange oaths and bearded like the pard,
> Jealous in honor, sudden and quick in quarrel,
> Seeking the bubble reputation
> Even in the cannon's mouth.
> —SHAKESPEARE, *As You Like It*

Dead battles, like dead generals, hold the military mind in their dead grip, and Germans, no less than other peoples, prepare for the last war. —BARBARA TUCHMAN, *The Guns of August*

When I reflect upon the characters and attainments of some of the General officers of this army . . . on whom I am to rely . . . I tremble: and, as Lord Chesterfield said of the Generals of his day, "I only hope that when the enemy reads the list of their names he trembles as I do." —ARTHUR WELLESLEY, DUKE OF WELLINGTON, military dispatch (1810)

The battle of Waterloo was won on the playing fields of Eton. —ARTHUR WELLESLEY, DUKE OF WELLINGTON, attributed

[Although this has traditionally been attributed to the Duke of Wellington, it appears unlikely that he ever actually said it.]

The Mind

I cannot escape the objection that there is no state of mind, however simple, that does not change every moment. —HENRI BERGSON, *Introduction to Metaphysics*

BRAIN, *n.* An apparatus with which we think that we think. —AMBROSE BIERCE, *The Devil's Dictionary*

The march of the human mind is slow. —EDMUND BURKE, speech (1775)

The empires of the future are the empires of the mind. —WINSTON CHURCHILL, speech (1944)

The mind of man is capable of anything—because everything is in it, all the past as well as all the future. —JOSEPH CONRAD, *Heart of Darkness*

My mind to me a kingdom is;
  Such present joys therein I find
That it excels all other bliss
  That earth affords or grows by kind.
                    —EDWARD DYER, "My Mind to Me a
                                      Kingdom Is"

The voice of the intellect is a soft one, but it does not rest until it has gained a hearing. —SIGMUND FREUD, *The Future of an Illusion*

The mind is like a sheet of white paper in this, that the impressions it receives the oftenest, and retains the longest, are black ones. —JULIUS C. HARE AND AUGUSTUS W. HARE, *Guesses at Truth*

There is an unseemly exposure of the mind, as well as of the body. —WILLIAM HAZLITT, *Sketches and Essays*

Little minds are interested in the extraordinary; great minds in the commonplace. —ELBERT HUBBARD, *Roycroft Dictionary and Book of Epigrams*

Such as are your habitual thoughts, such also will be the character of your mind; for the soul is dyed by the thoughts. —MARCUS AURELIUS, *Meditations*

The mind is its own place, and in itself
Can make a Heaven of Hell, a Hell of Heaven.
                    —JOHN MILTON, *Paradise Lost*

The mind is a dangerous weapon, even to the possessor, if he knows not discreetly how to use it. —MICHEL DE MONTAIGNE, *Essays*

An improper mind is a perpetual feast. —LOGAN PEARSALL SMITH, *Afterthoughts*

Mind is the great lever of all things; human thought is the process by which human ends are ultimately answered. —DANIEL WEBSTER, speech (1825)

Minorities — See also MAJORITIES

Every new opinion, at its starting, is precisely in a minority of one. —THOMAS CARLYLE, *On Heroes, Hero-Worship and the Heroic in History*

Shall we judge a country by the majority, or by the minority? By the minority, surely. —RALPH WALDO EMERSON, *The Conduct of Life*

How a minority,
Reaching a majority,
Seizing authority,
Hates a minority!
         —LEONARD H. ROBBINS, attributed

Misery — See DESPAIR; SORROW; UNHAPPINESS

Misfortune — See ADVERSITY

Mistakes — See ERROR

Mobs — See CROWDS

Moderation and Abstinence

To many, total abstinence is easier than perfect moderation. —SAINT AUGUSTINE, *On the Good of Marriage*

Moderation is the silken string running through the pearl chain of all virtues. —JOSEPH HALL, *Christian Moderation*

We never repent of having eaten too little. —THOMAS JEFFERSON, "A Decalogue of Canons for observation in practical life" (in letter, 1825)

Moderation is a virtue only in those who are thought to have an alternative. —HENRY A. KISSINGER, quoted in *The Observer*

Men have made a virtue of moderation to limit the ambition of the great, and to console people of mediocrity for their want of fortune and of merit. —LA ROCHEFOUCAULD, *Maxims*

Moderation in temper, is always a virtue; but moderation in principle, is a species of vice. —THOMAS PAINE, *Letter Addressed to the Addressers of the Late Proclamation*

The people who are regarded as moral luminaries are those who forego ordinary pleasures themselves and find compensation in interfering with the pleasures of others. —BERTRAND RUSSELL, *Sceptical Essays*

Nothing in excess. —SOLON, quoted by Diogenes Laertius in *Lives of the Philosophers*

> [This has been attributed to others, as well, including Thales of Miletus and Socrates. It was inscribed on the temple of Apollo at Delphi.]

Modern Times

More than any other time in history, mankind faces a crossroads. One path leads to despair and utter hopelessness. The other, to total extinction. Let us pray we have the wisdom to choose correctly. —WOODY ALLEN, *Side Effects*

I saw the best minds of my generation destroyed by madness, starving hysterical naked. —ALLEN GINSBERG, *Howl*

Never before has man had such capacity to control his own environment, to end thirst and hunger, to conquer poverty and disease, to banish illiteracy and massive human misery. We have the power to make this the best generation of mankind in the history of the world or to make it the last. —JOHN F. KENNEDY, speech (1963)

The means by which we live have outdistanced the ends for which we live. Our scientific power has outrun our spiritual power. We have guided missiles and misguided men. —MARTIN LUTHER KING, JR., *Strength to Love*

We live in a moment of history where change is so speeded up that we begin to see the present only when it is already disappearing. —R.D. LAING, *The Politics of Experience*

The horror of the Twentieth Century was the size of each new event, and the paucity of its reverberation. —NORMAN MAILER, *Of a Fire on the Moon*

Human history becomes more and more a race between education and catastrophe. —H.G. WELLS, *The Outline of History*

Modesty

Modesty is the only sure bait when you angle for praise. —LORD CHESTERFIELD, *Letters to His Son*

A modest man is usually admired—if people ever hear of him. —EDGAR WATSON HOWE, *Ventures in Common Sense*

When anyone remains modest, not after praise but after blame, then his modesty is real. —JEAN PAUL RICHTER, *Hesperus*

With people of only moderate ability modesty is mere honesty; but with those who possess great talent it is hypocrisy. —ARTHUR SCHOPENHAUER, *Parerga and Paralipomena*

Monarchs — See LEADERS AND RULERS

Money

Money is like muck, not good except it be spread. —FRANCIS BACON, *Essays*

Money, it turned out, was exactly like sex, you thought of nothing else if you didn't have it and thought of other things if you did. —JAMES BALDWIN, *Nobody Knows My Name*

Money speaks sense in a language all nations understand. —APHRA BEHN, *The Rover*

> I'm tired of Love: I'm still more tired of Rhyme.
> But Money gives me pleasure all the time.
> —HILAIRE BELLOC, "Fatigued"

A feast is made for laughter, and wine maketh merry: but money answereth all things. —BIBLE, *Ecclesiastes* 10:19

The love of money is the root of all evil. —BIBLE, *I Timothy* 6:10

Those who have some means think that the most important thing in the world is love. The poor know that it is money. —GERALD BRENAN, *Thoughts in a Dry Season*

> What makes all doctrines plain and clear?
> About two hundred pounds a year.
> And that which was prov'd true before,
> Prove false again? Two hundred more.
> —SAMUEL BUTLER (d 1680), *Hudibras*

It has been said that the love of money is the root of all evil. The want of money is so quite as truly. —SAMUEL BUTLER (d 1902), *Erewhon*
[See The Bible, *Timothy*, above.]

Ready money *is* Aladdin's lamp. —LORD BYRON, *Don Juan*

Annual income twenty pounds, annual expenditure nineteen nineteen and six, result happiness. Annual income twenty pounds, annual expenditure twenty pounds ought and six, result misery. —CHARLES DICKENS, *David Copperfield*

A billion here, a billion there, and pretty soon you're talking big money. —EVERETT M. DIRKSEN, widely attributed

[Written evidence for this often-repeated comment, attributed to Senator Dirksen, has not been found.]

Never ask of money spent
Where the spender thinks it went.
Nobody was ever meant
To remember or invent
What he did with every cent.
   —ROBERT FROST, "The Hardship of
           Accounting"

Money is a singular thing. It ranks with love as man's greatest source of joy. And with death as his greatest source of anxiety. —JOHN KENNETH GALBRAITH, *The Age of Uncertainty*

The Almighty Dollar, that great object of universal devotion throughout our land. —WASHINGTON IRVING, "The Creole Village"

There are few ways in which a man can be more innocently employed than in getting money. —SAMUEL JOHNSON, quoted in James Boswell's *The Life of Samuel Johnson*

It is better that a man should tyrannize over his bank balance than over his fellow citizens. —JOHN MAYNARD KEYNES, *The General Theory of Employment, Interest and Money*

Money is like a sixth sense without which you cannot make a complete use of the other five. —W. SOMERSET MAUGHAM, *Of Human Bondage*

Money couldn't buy friends but you got a better class of enemy. —SPIKE MILLIGAN, *Puckoon*

[This quotation is possibly not original with Milligan, for it has been attributed to other sources as well.]

I finally know what distinguishes man from the other beasts: financial worries. —JULES RENARD, *The Journal of Jules Renard*, ed. Louise Bogan and Elizabeth Roget

Never invest your money in anything that eats or needs repainting. —BILLY ROSE, in *New York Post*

There are few sorrows, however poignant, in which a good income is of no avail. —LOGAN PEARSALL SMITH, *Afterthoughts*

There was a time when a fool and his money were soon parted, but now it happens to everybody. —ADLAI E. STEVENSON, quoted in Bill Adler's *The Stevenson Wit*

There are two times in a man's life when he should not speculate: when he can't afford it, and when he can. —MARK TWAIN, *Following the Equator*, "Pudd'nhead Wilson's New Calendar"

Months of the Year — See SEASONS

The Moon — See SKY AND SPACE

Morality and Ethics

It is easier to fight for one's principles than to live up to them. —ALFRED ADLER, quoted in *Alfred Adler* by Phyllis Bottome

[See also Adlai E. Stevenson, in this section]

No morality can be founded on authority, even if the authority were divine. —A.J. AYER, *Essay on Humanism*

The greatest happiness of the greatest number is the foundation of morals and legislation. —JEREMY BENTHAM, *The Commonplace Book*

[This basic tenet of Utilitarianism had been formulated by others, as Bentham himself acknowledged. Francis Hutcheson had written in *Inquiry into the Original of Our Ideas of Beauty and Virtue*: "That action is best which procures the greatest happiness for the greatest numbers."]

The propriety of some persons seems to consist in having improper thoughts about their neighbors. —F.H. BRADLEY, *Aphorisms*

I know only that what is moral is what you feel good after and what is immoral is what you feel bad after. —ERNEST HEMINGWAY, *Death in the Afternoon*

Let's find out what everyone is doing,
And then stop everyone from doing it.
—A.P. HERBERT, "Let's Stop Somebody from Doing Something!"

An ethical person ought to do more than he's required to do and less than he's allowed to do. —MICHAEL JOSEPHSON, quoted in Bill Moyers' *World of Ideas*

Morality is not really the doctrine of how to make ourselves happy but of how we are to be *worthy* of happiness. —IMMANUEL KANT, *Critique of Practical Reason*

There is . . . but one categorical imperative, namely, this: *Act only on that maxim whereby thou canst at the same time will that it should become a universal law.* —IMMANUEL KANT, *Fundamental Principles of the Metaphysic of Morals*

It is an open question whether any behavior based on fear of eternal punishment can be regarded as ethical or should be regarded as merely cowardly. —MARGARET MEAD, in *Redbook*

Puritanism—The haunting fear that someone, somewhere, may be happy. —H.L. MENCKEN, *A Mencken Chrestomathy*

Morality is the herd-instinct in the individual. —FRIEDRICH NIETZSCHE, *The Joyful Wisdom* (also known as *The Gay Science*)

There are no moral phenomena, only a moral interpretation of phenomena. —FRIEDRICH NIETZSCHE, *Beyond Good and Evil*

As soon as one is unhappy one becomes moral. —MARCEL PROUST, *Remembrance of Things Past: Within a Budding Grove*

It is often easier to fight for principles than to live up to them. —ADLAI E. STEVENSON, speech (1952)

If your morals make you dreary, depend upon it, they are wrong. —ROBERT LOUIS STEVENSON, *Across the Plains*

All those men have their price. —ROBERT WALPOLE, quoted in William Coxe's *Memoirs of Sir Robert Walpole*

> [Probably the basis for the quotation often attributed to Walpole, "Every man has his price."]

Mortality — See DEATH; See also IMMORTALITY

Mothers — See PARENTS AND PARENTHOOD

Murder — See CRIME

Music

> Music, the greatest good that mortals know,
> And all of heaven we have below.
> —JOSEPH ADDISON, "Song for St. Cecilia's Day"

Nothing is capable of being well set to music that is not nonsense. —JOSEPH ADDISON, *The Spectator*

No opera plot can be sensible, for in sensible situations people do not sing. —W.H. AUDEN, in *Time*

Music is a higher revelation than all wisdom and philosophy. —LUDWIG VAN BEETHOVEN, quoted in A.W. Thayer's *Life of Beethoven*

> Music has charms to soothe a savage breast,
> To soften rocks, or bend a knotted oak.
> —WILLIAM CONGREVE, *The Mourning Bride*

[Often quoted erroneously as "to soothe the savage beast."]

Extraordinary how potent cheap music is. —NOËL COWARD, *Private Lives*

Opera is when a guy gets stabbed in the back and, instead of bleeding, he sings. —ED GARDNER, on the radio show *Duffy's Tavern*

When people hear good music, it makes them homesick for something they never had, and never will have. —EDGAR WATSON HOWE, *Country Town Sayings*

After silence, that which comes nearest to expressing the inexpressible is music. —ALDOUS HUXLEY, *Music at Night*

Melody is a form of remembrance. . . . It must have a quality of inevitability in our ears. —GIAN CARLO MENOTTI, quoted in *Time*

Is it not strange that sheeps' guts should hale souls out of men's bodies? —SHAKESPEARE, *Much Ado About Nothing*

> If music be the food of love, play on;
> Give me excess of it, that, surfeiting,
>   The appetite may sicken, and so die.
> > —SHAKESPEARE, *Twelfth Night*

Hell is full of musical amateurs: music is the brandy of the damned. —GEORGE BERNARD SHAW, *Man and Superman*

> Just as my fingers on the keys
> Make music, so the selfsame sounds
> On my spirit make a music, too.
>
> Music is feeling, then, not sound.
> > —WALLACE STEVENS, "Peter Quince at
> > > the Clavier"

Music is, by its very nature, essentially powerless to *express* anything at all . . . music expresses itself. —IGOR STRAVINSKY, quoted in *Esquire*

Names

The glory and the nothing of a name. —LORD BYRON, "Churchill's Grave"

A nickname is the hardest stone that the devil can throw at a man. —WILLIAM HAZLITT, *Sketches and Essays*

The name of a man is a numbing blow from which he never recovers. —MARSHALL MCLUHAN, *Understanding Media*

Each planet, each plant, each butterfly, each moth, each beetle, becomes doubly real to you when you know its name. Lucky indeed are those who from their earliest childhood have heard all these things named. —JOHN COWPER POWYS, *The Meaning of Culture*

What's in a name? that which we call a rose
By any other name would smell as sweet.
                    —SHAKESPEARE, *Romeo and Juliet*

Narcissism — See CONCEIT, EGOTISM, AND VANITY

Nationalism — See PATRIOTISM AND NATIONALISM

Nations

A thousand years scarce serve to form a state;
An hour may lay it in the dust.
                    —LORD BYRON, *Childe Harold's
                                        Pilgrimage*

The history of every country begins in the heart of a man or a woman. —WILLA CATHER, *O Pioneers!*

A nation never falls but by suicide. —RALPH WALDO EMERSON, *Journals*

Men may be linked in friendship. Nations are linked only by interests. —ROLF HOCHHUTH, *The Soldiers*

[Charles de Gaulle held the same view. *US News & World Report* quoted him as saying: "No nation has friends—only interests."]

The nations which have put mankind and posterity most in their debt have been small states—Israel, Athens, Florence, Elizabethan England. —WILLIAM RALPH INGE, in *Wit and Wisdom of Dean Inge*, ed. James Marchant

The great nations have always acted like gangsters, and the small nations like prostitutes. —STANLEY KUBRICK, quoted in *The Guardian*

Borders are scratched across the hearts of men
By strangers with a calm, judicial pen,
And when the borders bleed we watch with
        dread
The lines of ink along the map turn red.
                    —MARYA MANNES, "Gaza Strip"

To have common glories in the past, a common will in the present; to have done great things together; to wish to do greater; these are the essential conditions which make up a people. —ERNEST RENAN, quoted by José Ortega y Gasset in *The Revolt of the Masses*

Great nations write their autobiographies in three manuscripts—the book of their deeds, the book of their words, and the book of their art. Not one of these books can be understood unless we read the two others; but of the three the only quite trustworthy one is the last. —JOHN RUSKIN, *St. Mark's Rest: The History of Venice*

No nation is fit to sit in judgment upon any other nation. —WOODROW WILSON, speech (1915)

Nature — See also THE ENVIRONMENT

Nature, to be commanded, must be obeyed. —FRANCIS BACON, *Novum Organum*

As well expect Nature to answer to your human values as to come into your house and sit in a chair. The economy of nature, its checks and balances, its measurements of competing life—all this is its great marvel and has an ethic of its own. —HENRY BESTON, *The Outermost House*

Speak to the earth, and it shall teach thee. —BIBLE, *Job* 12:8

> To see a World in a Grain of Sand
> And a Heaven in a Wild Flower,
> Hold Infinity in the palm of your hand
> And Eternity in an hour.
> —WILLIAM BLAKE, "Auguries of Innocence"

All things are artificial, for nature is the art of God. —THOMAS BROWNE, *Religio Medici*

You could cover the whole world with asphalt, but sooner or later green grass would break through.
—ILYA EHRENBURG, quoted in *New York Times Book Review*

Why should we fear to be crushed by savage elements, we who are made up of the same elements?
—RALPH WALDO EMERSON, *The Conduct of Life*

You may drive out Nature with a pitchfork, yet she will always hurry back. —HORACE, *Epistles*

To a person uninstructed in natural history, his country or sea-side stroll is a walk through a gallery filled with wonderful works of art, nine-tenths of which have their faces turned to the wall. —THOMAS HENRY HUXLEY, "On the Educational Value of the Natural History Sciences"

The whole of nature, as has been said, is a conjugation of the verb to eat, in the active and passive.
—WILLIAM RALPH INGE, *Outspoken Essays*

In nature there are neither rewards nor punishments—there are consequences. —ROBERT G. INGERSOLL, *Some Reasons Why*

Never does nature say one thing and wisdom another. —JUVENAL, *Satires*

> Accuse not Nature, she hath done her part;
> Do thou but thine.
> —JOHN MILTON, *Paradise Lost*

It is far from easy to determine whether she [Nature] has proved to man a kind parent or a merciless stepmother. —PLINY THE ELDER, *Natural History*

Nature abhors a vacuum. —FRANÇOIS RABELAIS, *Gargantua and Pantagruel*

Pile the bodies high at Austerlitz and Waterloo.
Shovel them under and let me work—
I am the grass; I cover all.
     —CARL SANDBURG, "Grass"

One touch of nature makes the whole world kin.
—SHAKESPEARE, *Troilus and Cressida*

In nature, there is less death and destruction than
death and transmutation. —EDWIN WAY TEALE, *Circle of the Seasons*

Nature, red in tooth and claw. —ALFRED, LORD TENNYSON, *In Memoriam*

I chatter, chatter, as I flow,
To join the brimming river,
For men may come and men may go,
But I go on forever.
    —ALFRED, LORD TENNYSON, "The Brook"

Nature is ruthless when it comes to matching the
quantity of life in any given place to the quantity of
nourishment available. —KURT VONNEGUT, quoted
in *Countryside*

Sometimes I think that a vacuum is a hell of a lot
better than some of the stuff that nature replaces it
with. —TENNESSEE WILLIAMS, *Cat on a Hot Tin Roof*

[See Rabelais, in this section.]

Nature never did betray
The heart that loved her.
    —WILLIAM WORDSWORTH, "Lines Composed a Few Miles Above Tintern Abbey"

Necessity

Necessity has no law. —SAINT AUGUSTINE, *Soliloquia Animae ad Deum*

[See also Publilius Syrus, in this section.]

We do what we must, and call it by the best names.
—RALPH WALDO EMERSON, *The Conduct of Life*

Necessity never made a good bargain. —BENJAMIN FRANKLIN, *Poor Richard's Almanac*

Necessity is not a fact but an interpretation.
—FRIEDRICH NIETZSCHE, *The Will to Power*

Necessity is the plea for every infringement of human freedom. It is the argument of tyrants; it is the creed of slaves. —WILLIAM PITT, speech (1783)

Necessity gives the law, but does not itself submit to it. —PUBLILIUS SYRUS, *Maxims*

Teach thy necessity to reason thus;
There is no virtue like necessity.
—SHAKESPEARE, *Richard II*

[The proverb "to make a virtue of necessity" predated Shakespeare. It appears to have originated in Roman times.]

Necessity delivers us from the embarrassment of choice. —MARQUIS DE VAUVENARGUES, *Reflections and Maxims*

Negotiation — See DIPLOMACY

Neighbors

You may talk of the tyranny of Nero and Tiberius; but the real tyranny is the tyranny of your next-door neighbor. —WALTER BAGEHOT, in *National Review*

Thou shalt love thy neighbor as thyself. —BIBLE, *Leviticus* 19:18

[Quoted in the New Testament, Matthew 22:39.]

My apple trees will never get across
And eat the cones under his pines, I tell him.
He only says, "Good fences make good
    neighbors."
                —ROBERT FROST, "Mending Wall"

[See George Herbert, below, for an earlier formulation of this idea.]

Love your neighbor, yet pull not down your hedge.
—GEORGE HERBERT, *Jacula Prudentum*

It is easier to love humanity as a whole than to love one's neighbor. —ERIC HOFFER, in *New York Times Magazine*

It is your concern when the wall next door is on fire.
—HORACE, *Epistles*

Neurosis — See MENTAL DISORDER

Newness — See NOVELTY

News and Newspapers — See also FREEDOM OF SPEECH AND THE PRESS

When a dog bites a man, that is not news, because it happens so often. But if a man bites a dog, that is news. —JOHN B. BOGART, quoted in Frank M. O'Brien's *The Story of the Sun*

[This is also attributed to Charles A. Dana, editor of the *New York Sun*. Bogart was city editor of the *Sun*.]

Journalism largely consists in saying "Lord Jones Dead" to people who never knew that Lord Jones was alive. —G.K. CHESTERTON, *The Wisdom of Father Brown*

The more abhorrent a news item the more comforting it was to be the recipient, since the fact that it had happened elsewhere proved that it had not happened here, was not happening here, and would therefore never happen here. —JOHN FOWLES, *The Ebony Tower*

Were it left to me to decide whether we should have a government without newspapers, or newspapers without a government, I should not hesitate a moment to prefer the latter. But I should mean that every man should receive those papers and be capable of reading them. —THOMAS JEFFERSON, letter (1787)

People everywhere confuse what they read in newspapers with news. —A.J. LIEBLING, in *New Yorker*

Once a newspaper touches a story, the facts are lost forever, even to the protagonists. —NORMAN MAILER, *The Presidential Papers*

A good newspaper, I suppose, is a nation talking to itself. —ARTHUR MILLER, quoted in *The Observer*

If it's far away, it's news, but if it's close at home, it's sociology. —JAMES RESTON, quoted in *Wall Street Journal*

The nature of bad news infects the teller. —SHAKESPEARE, *Antony and Cleopatra*

Nobody likes the bringer of bad news. —SOPHOCLES, *Antigone*

How many beautiful trees gave their lives that today's scandal should, without delay, reach a million readers! —EDWIN WAY TEALE, *Circle of the Seasons*

Journalism—an ability to meet the challenge of filling the space. —REBECCA WEST, in *New York Herald Tribune*

Night — See TIMES OF DAY

Nonviolence — See PEACE AND NONVIOLENCE

Nostalgia

> Backward, turn backward, O Time, in your
>   flight,
> Make me a child again, just for to-night!
> —ELIZABETH CHASE AKERS, "Rock Me to
>   Sleep, Mother"

In every age "the good old days" were a myth. No one ever thought they were good at the time. For every age has consisted of crises that seemed intolerable to the people who lived through them. —BROOKS ATKINSON, *Once Around the Sun*

Nostalgia is a seductive liar. —GEORGE BALL, in *Newsweek*

It is one of the paradoxes of American literature that our writers are forever looking back with love and nostalgia at lives they couldn't wait to leave. —ANATOLE BROYARD, in *New York Times*

Oh, the good times when we were so unhappy. —ALEXANDRE DUMAS, PÈRE, *Le Chevalier d'Harmental*

They spend their time mostly looking forward to the past. —JOHN OSBORNE, *Look Back in Anger*

Reminiscences make one feel so deliciously aged and sad. —GEORGE BERNARD SHAW, *The Irrational Knot*

> Deep as love,
> Deep as first love, and wild with all regret;
> O Death in Life, the days that are no more!
> —ALFRED, LORD TENNYSON, *The Princess*

Novelty

He that will not apply new remedies must expect new evils, for time is the greatest innovator. —FRANCIS BACON, *Essays*

There is nothing new except what has been forgotten. —MADEMOISELLE BERTIN, attributed

[Mlle. Bertin was Marie Antoinette's milliner.]

The thing that hath been, it is that which shall be; and that which is done is that which shall be done: and there is no new thing under the sun. —BIBLE, *Ecclesiastes* 1:9

By nature, men love newfangledness. —CHAUCER, *The Canterbury Tales*

Nothing quite new is perfect. —CICERO, *Brutus*

[This has also been translated as "Nothing is brought to perfection on its first invention."]

Even in slight things the experience of the new is rarely without some stirring of foreboding. —ERIC HOFFER, *The Ordeal of Change*

There are three things which the public will always clamor for, sooner or later: namely, Novelty, novelty, novelty. —THOMAS HOOD, announcement for *Comic Annual*

Obedience

Obedience is in a way the mother of all virtues. —SAINT AUGUSTINE, *On the Good of Marriage*

"She still seems to me in her own way a person born to command," said Luce. . . .

"I wonder if anyone is born to obey," said Isabel.

"That may be why people command rather badly, that they have no suitable material to work on." —IVY COMPTON-BURNETT, *Parents and Children*

Come when you're called
And do as you're bid;
Shut the door after you
And you'll never be chid.
　　　　　—MARIA EDGEWORTH, *The Contrast*

Let thy Child's first Lesson be Obedience, and the second will be what thou wilt. —BENJAMIN FRANKLIN, *Poor Richard's Almanac*

The man who does something under orders is not unhappy; he is unhappy who does something against his will. —SENECA, *Epistulae ad Lucilium*

　. . . obedience,
Bane of all genius, virtue, freedom, truth,
Makes slaves of men, and, of the human frame,
A mechanized automaton.
　　　　　—PERCY BYSSHE SHELLEY, "Queen Mab"

Theirs not to make reply,
Theirs not to reason why,
Theirs but to do and die.
　　　　　—ALFRED, LORD TENNYSON, "The Charge
　　　　　　　　　　of the Light Brigade"

Observation

Every scene, even the commonest, is wonderful, if only one can detach oneself, casting off all memory of use and custom and behold it, as it were, for the first time. —ARNOLD BENNETT, quoted in *Reader's Digest*

You can observe a lot just by watching. —YOGI BERRA, attributed

[Berra was explaining why he was competent to be manager of the Yankees despite his lack of managerial experience.]

Where the telescope ends, the microscope begins. Which of the two has the grander view? —VICTOR HUGO, *Les Misérables*

I am a camera with its shutter open, quite passive, recording, not thinking. —CHRISTOPHER ISHERWOOD, *Goodby to Berlin*

Ocean — See THE SEA

Old Age — See AGE AND AGING

Opinion

Some men are just as sure of the truth of their opinions as are others of what they know. —ARISTOTLE, *Nichomachean Ethics*

> Public opinion is no more than this:
> What people think that other people think.
> > —ALFRED AUSTIN, *Prince Lucifer*

The man who never alters his opinion is like standing water, and breeds reptiles of the mind. —WILLIAM BLAKE, *The Marriage of Heaven and Hell*

> Men get opinions as boys learn to spell,
> By reiteration chiefly.
> > —ELIZABETH BARRETT BROWNING, *Aurora Leigh*

The world is not run by thought, nor by imagination, but by opinion. —ELIZABETH DREW, *The Modern Novel*

The only sin which we never forgive in each other is difference of opinion. —RALPH WALDO EMERSON, *Society and Solitude*

They that approve a private opinion, call it opinion; but they that mislike it, heresy: and yet heresy signifies no more than private opinion. —THOMAS HOBBES, *Leviathan*

Those who never retract their opinions love themselves more than they love truth. —JOSEPH JOUBERT, *Pensées*

New opinions are always suspected, and usually opposed, without any other reason but because they are not already common. —JOHN LOCKE, *An Essay Concerning Human Understanding*

Men are never so good or so bad as their opinions. —JAMES MACKINTOSH, *Progress of Ethical Philosophy*

> Some praise at Morning what they blame at
>   Night;
> But always think the last Opinion right.
>   —ALEXANDER POPE, *An Essay on*
>   *Criticism*

A government can be no better than the public opinion which sustains it. —FRANKLIN D. ROOSEVELT, speech (1936)

So many men, so many opinions. —TERENCE, *Phormio*

It were not best that we should all think alike; it is difference of opinion that makes horse races. —MARK TWAIN, *Pudd'nhead Wilson*, "Pudd'nhead Wilson's Calendar"

Opportunity

A wise man will make more opportunities than he finds. —FRANCIS BACON, *Essays*

The right man is the one who seizes the moment. —JOHANN WOLFGANG VON GOETHE, *Faust*

Opportunities flit by while we sit regretting the chances we have lost, and the happiness that comes to us we heed not, because of the happiness that is gone. —JEROME K. JEROME, *The Idle Thoughts of an Idle Fellow*

Opportunities are usually disguised as hard work, so most people don't recognize them. —ANN LANDERS, attributed

While we stop to think, we often miss our opportunity. —PUBLILIUS SYRUS, *Maxims*

> There is a tide in the affairs of men,
> Which, taken at the flood, leads on to fortune;
> Omitted, all the voyage of their life
> Is bound in shallows and in miseries.
> —SHAKESPEARE, *Julius Caesar*

> [Lord Byron offered a variation of this in *Don Juan*:
> There is a tide in the affairs of women,
> Which, taken at the flood, leads—God knows
> where.]

Opportunities are seldom labeled. —JOHN A. SHEDD, *Salt from My Attic*

Oppression — See TYRANNY

Optimism and Pessimism

Pessimism, when you get used to it, is just as agreeable as optimism. —ARNOLD BENNETT, *Things that Have Interested Me*

The optimist proclaims that we live in the best of all possible worlds; and the pessimist fears this is true. —JAMES BRANCH CABELL, *The Silver Stallion*

I came to the conclusion that the optimist thought everything good except the pessimist, and that the pessimist thought everything bad, except himself. —G.K. CHESTERTON, *Orthodoxy*

The place where optimism most flourishes is the lunatic asylum. —HAVELOCK ELLIS, *The Dance of Life*

Two men look out through the same bars:
One sees the mud, and one the stars.
                    —FREDERICK LANGBRIDGE, *A Cluster of
                                        Quiet Thoughts*

If we see light at the end of the tunnel,
It's the light of the oncoming train.
                    —ROBERT LOWELL, "Since 1939"

an optimist is a guy
that has never had
much experience
            —DON MARQUIS, *archy and mehitabel*

Rosiness is not a worse windowpane than gloomy gray when viewing the world. —GRACE PALEY, *Enormous Changes at the Last Minute*

I am an optimist, unrepentant and militant. After all, in order not to be a fool an optimist must know how sad a place the world can be. It is only the pessimist who finds this out anew every day. —PETER USTINOV, *Dear Me*

All is for the best in the best of possible worlds. —VOLTAIRE, *Candide*

Order and Efficiency

Chaos often breeds life, when order breeds habit. —HENRY ADAMS, *The Education of Henry Adams*

The human understanding, from its peculiar nature, easily supposes a greater degree of order and equality in things than it really finds. —FRANCIS BACON, *Novum Organum*

I must Create a System or be enslav'd by another Man's. —WILLIAM BLAKE, *Jerusalem*

Good order is the foundation of all good things. —EDMUND BURKE, *Reflections on the Revolution in France*

In my youth I stressed freedom, and in my old age I stress order. I have made the great discovery that liberty is a product of order. —WILL DURANT, quoted in *Time*

It is a rare life that remains orderly even in private. —MICHEL DE MONTAIGNE, *Essays*

A place for everything, and everything in its place. —SAMUEL SMILES, *Thrift*

Have a place for everything and keep the thing somewhere else. This is not advice, it is merely custom. —MARK TWAIN, *Notebooks*

The Ordinary

Men are seldom more commonplace than on supreme occasions. —SAMUEL BUTLER (*d* 1902), *Note-Books*

> And God, who studies each separate soul,
> Out of commonplace lives makes his beautiful
>   whole.
>   —SUSAN COOLIDGE, "Commonplace"

If we had a keen vision of all that is ordinary in human life, it would be like hearing the grass grow or the squirrel's heart beat, and we should die of that roar which is the other side of silence. —GEORGE ELIOT, *Middlemarch*

If your daily life seems poor, do not blame it; blame yourself, tell yourself that you are not poet enough to call forth its riches. —RAINER MARIA RILKE, *Letters to a Young Poet*

It requires a very unusual mind to undertake the analysis of the obvious. —ALFRED NORTH WHITEHEAD, *Science and the Modern World*

Originality

No bird has ever uttered note
That was not in some first bird's throat;
Since Eden's freshness and man's fall
No rose has been original.
　　　—THOMAS BAILEY ALDRICH, "Originality"

The merit of *originality* is not novelty; it is sincerity. The believing man is the original man; whatsoever he believes, he believes it for himself, not for another. —THOMAS CARLYLE, *On Heroes, Hero-Worship and the Heroic in History*

The original writer is not he who does not imitate others, but he who can be imitated by none. —FRANÇOIS-RENÉ DE CHATEAUBRIAND, *The Genius of Christianity*

A thought is often original, though you have uttered it a hundred times. —OLIVER WENDELL HOLMES, SR., *The Autocrat of the Breakfast-Table*

Originality, I fear, is too often only undetected and frequently unconscious plagiarism. —WILLIAM RALPH INGE, in *Wit and Wisdom of Dean Inge*, ed. James Marchant

All good things which exist are the fruits of originality. —JOHN STUART MILL, *On Liberty*

Originality does not consist in saying what no one has ever said before, but in saying exactly what you think yourself. —JAMES FITZJAMES STEPHEN, attributed

In fact, nothing is said that has not been said before. —TERENCE, *Eunuchus*

[This too has been said by others: Robert Burton, in *The Anatomy of Melancholy*, wrote: "We can say nothing but what hath been said." And La Bruyère said: "We come too late to say anything which has not been said already"—*Les Caractères*. Burton had a consoling thought, adding ". . . he that comes last is commonly best."]

What a good thing Adam had. When he said a good thing he knew nobody had said it before. —MARK TWAIN, *Notebooks*

Pain and Suffering

About suffering they were never wrong,
The Old Masters: how well they understood
Its human position; how it takes place
While someone else is eating or opening a
    window or just walking dully along.
      —W.H. AUDEN, "Musée des Beaux Arts"

Pain—has an Element of Blank—
It cannot recollect
When it begun—or if there were
A time when it was not—.
      —EMILY DICKINSON, "Pain—has an
                Element of Blank"

Physical pain however great ends in itself and falls away like dry husks from the mind, whilst moral discords and nervous horrors sear the soul. —ALICE JAMES, diary entry (1892)

Those who do not feel pain seldom think that it is felt. —SAMUEL JOHNSON, *The Rambler*

Although the world is full of suffering, it is full also of the overcoming of it. —HELEN KELLER, *Optimism*

Know how sublime a thing it is
To suffer and be strong.
—HENRY WADSWORTH LONGFELLOW, "The
Light of Stars"

It is not true that suffering ennobles the character; happiness does that sometimes, but suffering, for the most part, makes men petty and vindictive. —W. SOMERSET MAUGHAM, *The Moon and Sixpence*

If you want to live your whole life free from
pain
You must become either a god or else a
corpse.
Consider other men's troubles; that will
comfort yours.
—MENANDER (fragment)

No pain, no palm; no thorns, no throne; no gall, no glory; no cross, no crown. —WILLIAM PENN, *No Cross, No Crown*

[See also John Ray in note at Adlai E. Stevenson, under Achievement.]

Who breathes, must suffer, and who thinks,
must mourn;
And he alone is bless'd, who ne'er was born.
—MATTHEW PRIOR, *Solomon on the Vanity
of the World*

There is no real evil in life, except great pain; all the rest is imaginary, and depends on the light in which we view things. —MARIE DE SÉVIGNÉ, letter (c. 1680)

For there was never yet philosopher
That could endure the toothache patiently.
—SHAKESPEARE, *Much Ado About Nothing*

One must, in one's life, make a choice between boredom and suffering. —MADAME DE STAËL, letter (1800)

Nothing begins and nothing ends
   That is not paid with moan;
For we are born in other's pain,
   And perish in our own.
         —FRANCIS THOMPSON, "Daisy"

Suffering is permanent, obscure and dark,
And shares the nature of infinity.
       —WILLIAM WORDSWORTH, *The Borderers*

Painting — See ART AND ARTISTS

Parents and Parenthood

The joys of parents are secret: and so are their griefs and fears. —FRANCIS BACON, *Essays*

What the mother sings to the cradle goes all the way down to the coffin. —HENRY WARD BEECHER, *Proverbs from Plymouth Pulpit*

If you have never been hated by your child, you have never been a parent. —BETTE DAVIS, *The Lonely Life*

Who of us is mature enough for offspring before the offspring themselves arrive? The value of marriage is not that adults produce children but that children produce adults. —PETER DE VRIES, *Tunnel of Love*

There are times when parenthood seems nothing but feeding the mouth that bites you. —PETER DE VRIES, *Tunnel of Love*

Where yet was ever found a mother,
Who'd give her booby for another?
         —JOHN GAY, *Fables*

LEONTINE. An only son, sir, might expect more indulgence.
CROAKER. An only father, sir, might expect more obedience.
      —OLIVER GOLDSMITH, *The Good-Natured Man*

> Children aren't happy with nothing to ignore,
> And that's what parents were created for.
> —OGDEN NASH, "The Parent"

Parents—especially stepparents—are sometimes a bit of a disappointment to their children. They don't fulfill the promise of their early years. —ANTHONY POWELL, *A Dance to the Music of Time: A Buyer's Market*

No matter how old a mother is she watches her middle-aged children for signs of improvement. —FLORIDA SCOTT-MAXWELL, *The Measure of My Days*

It is a wise father that knows his own child. —SHAKESPEARE, *The Merchant of Venice*

You know more than you think you do. —BENJAMIN SPOCK, *Baby and Child Care*

Parenthood remains the greatest single preserve of the amateur. —ALVIN TOFFLER, *Future Shock*

I have found the best way to give advice to your children is to find out what they want and then advise them to do it. —HARRY S TRUMAN, television interview (interviewed by his daughter, Margaret)

> For the hand that rocks the cradle
> Is the hand that rules the world.
> —WILLIAM ROSS WALLACE, "What Rules
> the World"

Children begin by loving their parents. After a time they judge them. Rarely, if ever, do they forgive them. —OSCAR WILDE, *A Woman of No Importance*

There are no illegitimate children—only illegitimate parents. —LEON R. YANKWICH, judicial opinion (1928)

Parting

"It is never good dwelling on good-byes," she said, "it

is not the being together that it prolongs, it is the parting." —ELIZABETH BIBESCO, *The Fir and the Palm*

> Parting is all we know of heaven,
> And all we need of hell.
> —EMILY DICKINSON, "My life closed twice
> before its close"

> They who go
> Feel not the pain of parting; it is they
> Who stay behind that suffer.
> —HENRY WADSWORTH LONGFELLOW,
> *Michael Angelo*

Every parting gives a foretaste of death; every coming together again a foretaste of the resurrection. —ARTHUR SCHOPENHAUER, *Parerga and Paralipomena*

> Good night, good night! parting is such sweet
> sorrow,
> That I shall say good night till it be morrow.
> —SHAKESPEARE, *Romeo and Juliet*

Passion

The man who is master of his passions is Reason's slave. —CYRIL CONNOLLY, quoted in *Turnstile One*

One declaims endlessly against the passions; one imputes all of man's suffering to them. One forgets that they are also the source of all his pleasures. —DENIS DIDEROT, *Pensées philosophiques*

Man is only truly great when he acts from the passions. —BENJAMIN DISRAELI, *Coningsby*

Passion, though a bad regulator, is a powerful spring. —RALPH WALDO EMERSON, *The Conduct of Life*

Nothing great in the world has been accomplished without passion. —G.W.F. HEGEL, *Philosophy of History*

Bee to the blossom, moth to the flame;
Each to his passion; what's in a name?
>—HELEN HUNT JACKSON, "Vanity of
>Vanities"

A man who has not passed through the inferno of his passions has never overcome them. —CARL JUNG, *Memories, Dreams, Reflections*

If we resist our passions, it is more from their weakness than from our strength. —LA ROCHEFOUCAULD, *Maxims*

The will to overcome a passion is in the end merely the will of another or several other passions. —FRIEDRICH NIETZSCHE, *Beyond Good and Evil*

The natural man has only two primal passions, to get and to beget. —WILLIAM OSLER, *Science and Immortality*

>Give me that man
That is not passion's slave, and I will wear him
In my heart's core, ay, in my heart of heart,
As I do thee.
>—SHAKESPEARE, *Hamlet*

The Past — See also HISTORY

This only is denied even to God: the power to undo the past. —AGATHON, quoted by Aristotle in *Nicomachean Ethics*

So we beat on, boats against the current, borne back ceaselessly into the past. —F. SCOTT FITZGERALD, *The Great Gatsby*

The past is a foreign country: they do things differently there. —L.P. HARTLEY, *The Go-Between*

Why doesn't the past decently bury itself, instead of sitting waiting to be admired by the present? —D.H. LAWRENCE, *St. Mawr*

I tell you the past is a bucket of ashes. —CARL SANDBURG, "Prairie"

Progress, far from consisting in change, depends on retentiveness. . . . Those who cannot remember the past are condemned to repeat it. —GEORGE SANTAYANA, *The Life of Reason*

What's past is prologue. —SHAKESPEARE, *The Tempest*

The past is the only dead thing that smells sweet. —EDWARD THOMAS, "Early One Morning"

One point has already been proved: Everything that happened once can happen again. —JACOBO TIMERMAN, *Prisoner Without a Name, Cell Without a Number*

But where are the snows of yesteryear? —FRANÇOIS VILLON, "Ballade of the Ladies of Bygone Times"

Patience

Patience is a flatterer, sir—and an ass, sir. —APHRA BEHN, *The Feigned Curtezans*

PATIENCE, *n.* A minor form of despair, disguised as a virtue. —AMBROSE BIERCE, *The Devil's Dictionary*

He preacheth patience that never knew pain. —HENRY GEORGE BOHN, *Handbook of Proverbs*

307

Ah, "All things come to those who wait,"
(I say these words to make me glad),
But something answers, soft and sad,
"They come, but often come too late."
— VIOLET FANE, "Tout vient à qui sait
attendre"

Job was not so miserable in his sufferings, as happy in his patience. — THOMAS FULLER, *Gnomologia*

Patience, that blending of moral courage with physical timidity. — THOMAS HARDY, *Tess of the D'Ubervilles*

They also serve who only stand and wait. — JOHN MILTON, "On His Blindness"

Everything comes in time to those who can wait.
— FRANÇOIS RABELAIS, *Gargantua and Pantagruel*

[This saying also occurs in the works of others, including Longfellow and Disraeli. Thomas Edison gave it a different twist (in *Golden Book*): "Everything comes to him that hustles while he waits." See also Violet Fane, in this section.]

Patience is bitter, but its fruit is sweet. — JEAN-JACQUES ROUSSEAU, *Émile*

How poor are they that have not patience!
What wound did ever heal but by degrees?
— SHAKESPEARE, *Othello*

Patriotism and Nationalism

Patriotism is a lively sense of collective responsibility. Nationalism is a silly cock crowing on its own dunghill. — RICHARD ALDINGTON, *The Colonel's Daughter*

No man can be a patriot on an empty stomach.
— WILLIAM COWPER BRANN, in *The Iconoclast*

"My country, right or wrong," is a thing that no patriot would think of saying except in a desperate case. It is like saying, "My mother, drunk or sober." —G.K. CHESTERTON, *The Defendant*

Patriotism is when love of your own people comes first; nationalism, when hate for people other than your own comes first. —CHARLES DE GAULLE, quoted in *Life*

Our country! In her intercourse with foreign nations, may she always be in the right; but our country, right or wrong. —STEPHEN DECATUR, said in making a toast (1816)

Nationalism is an infantile disease. It is the measles of mankind. —ALBERT EINSTEIN, attributed

I only regret that I have but one life to lose for my country. —NATHAN HALE, said before being hanged by the British as a spy (Sept. 22, 1776)

Sweet and glorious it is to die for one's country. —HORACE, *Odes*

[Ernest Hemingway commented in *Esquire*: "They wrote in the old days that it is sweet and fitting to die for one's country. But in modern war there is nothing sweet nor fitting in your dying. You will die like a dog for no good reason."]

Patriotism is the last refuge of a scoundrel. —SAMUEL JOHNSON, quoted in James Boswell's *The Life of Samuel Johnson*

And so, my fellow Americans: ask not what your country can do for you—ask what you can do for your country. My fellow citizens of the world: ask not what America will do for you, but what together we can do for the freedom of man. —JOHN F. KENNEDY, speech (inaugural address, 1961)

[As with many memorable quotes, Kennedy's words echoed earlier speakers. Oliver Wendell

Holmes, Jr. had said in 1884: ". . . it is now the moment when . . . we pause . . . to recall what our country has done for each of us, and to ask ourselves what we can do for our country in return."]

Patriotism is often an arbitrary veneration of real estate above principles. —GEORGE JEAN NATHAN, *Testament of a Critic*

> Breathes there the man, with soul so dead,
> Who never to himself hath said,
>   This is my own, my native land?
>   —SIR WALTER SCOTT, *The Lay of the Last Minstrel*

Peace — See PEACE AND NONVIOLENCE; WAR AND PEACE

Peace and Nonviolence

The lion and the calf shall lie down together but the calf won't get much sleep. —WOODY ALLEN, *Without Feathers*

[The reference here is to The Bible, *Isaiah* 11:6; see in this section.]

They shall beat their swords into plough-shares, and their spears into pruning-hooks: nation shall not lift up sword against nation, neither shall they learn war any more. —BIBLE, *Isaiah* 2:4

The wolf also shall dwell with the lamb, and the leopard shall lie down with the kid; and the calf and the young lion and the fatling together; and a little child shall lead them. —BIBLE, *Isaiah* 11:6

Resist not evil: but whosoever shall smite thee on thy right cheek, turn to him the other also. —BIBLE, *Matthew* 5:39

Blessed are the peace-makers: for they shall be called the children of God. —BIBLE, *Matthew* 5:9

Lord Salisbury and myself have brought you back peace—but a peace I hope with honor. —BENJAMIN DISRAELI, speech (1878)

[The phrase "peace with honor" is probably better known from its use by Neville Chamberlain in a speech in 1938 after the Munich Conference: "This is the second time in our history that there has come back from Germany . . . peace with honor. I believe it is peace for our time."]

"Peace upon earth!" was said. We sing it,
And pay a million priests to bring it.
After two thousand years of mass
We've got as far as poison-gas.
          —THOMAS HARDY, "Christmas: 1924"

Peace is not an absence of war, it is a virtue, a state of mind, a disposition for benevolence, confidence, justice. —BENEDICT DE SPINOZA, *Theological-Political Treatise*

Only a peace between equals can last. Only a peace the very principle of which is equality and a common participation in a common benefit. —WOODROW WILSON, speech (1917)

The People

The voice of the people is the voice of God. (*Vox populi, vox dei.*) —ALCUIN, letter (to Charlemagne, c. 800)

[These words have often been quoted, but Alcuin was himself quoting what other people said rather than expressing his own sentiments. The larger context: "Nor should we listen to those who say, 'The voice of the people is the voice of God,' for the turbulence of the mob is always close to insanity." Alexander Pope wrote in his *Imitations of Horace*:
    The People's voice is odd;
    It is, and it is not, the voice of God.]

The public! How many fools does it take to make a public? —SÉBASTIEN-ROCH NICOLAS CHAMFORT, *Maximes et Pensées*

> Nor is the people's judgment always true:
> The most may err as grossly as the few.
> —JOHN DRYDEN, *Absalom and Achitophel*

All the world over, I will back the masses against the classes. —WILLIAM EWART GLADSTONE, speech (1886)

You [the people] are a many-headed beast. —HORACE, *Epistles*

Two things only it [the public] anxiously desires— bread and circus games. —JUVENAL, *Satires*

Why should there not be a patient confidence in the ultimate justice of the people? Is there any better or equal hope in the world? —ABRAHAM LINCOLN, speech (first inaugural address, 1861)

No one in this world, so far as I know—and I have searched the records for years, and employed agents to help me—has ever lost money by underestimating the intelligence of the great masses of the plain people. —H.L. MENCKEN, in *Chicago Tribune*

> [This seems likely to be the basis for the quotation often attributed to Mencken: "No one ever went broke underestimating the intelligence of the American people."]

> I am the people—the mob—the crowd—the
>   mass.
> Do you know that all the great work of the
>   world is done through me?
>   —CARL SANDBURG, "I Am the People,
>   the Mob"

Peoples and Places

> And this is good old Boston,
> The home of the bean and the cod,
> Where the Lowells talk only to Cabots,
> And the Cabots talk only to God.
> —JOHN COLLINS BOSSIDY, toast, given at
> Holy Cross College alumni dinner (1910)

England is a paradise for women and hell for horses; Italy is a paradise for horses, hell for women, as the diverb goes. —ROBERT BURTON, *The Anatomy of Melancholy*

Venice is like eating an entire box of chocolate liqueurs in one go. —TRUMAN CAPOTE, quoted in *The Observer*

I cannot forecast to you the action of Russia. It is a riddle wrapped in a mystery inside an enigma. —WINSTON CHURCHILL, speech (1939)

India is a geographical term. It is no more a united nation than the Equator. —WINSTON CHURCHILL, speech (1931)

On the whole, I'd rather be in Philadelphia. —W.C. FIELDS, attributed

[Fields supposedly suggested this statement, often associated with him, as his epitaph.]

New York . . . that unnatural city where every one is an exile, none more so than the American. —CHARLOTTE PERKINS GILMAN, *The Living of Charlotte Perkins Gilman*

If you are lucky enough to have lived in Paris as a young man, then wherever you go for the rest of your life, it stays with you, for Paris is a moveable feast. —ERNEST HEMINGWAY, *A Moveable Feast*

Well, little old Noisyville-on-the-Subway is good enough for me. —O. HENRY, *Strictly Business*

How appallingly thorough these Germans always managed to be, how emphatic! In sex no less than in war, in scholarship, in science. Diving deeper than anyone else and coming up muddier. —ALDOUS HUXLEY, *Time Must Have a Stop*

When a man is tired of London, he is tired of life; for there is in London all that life can afford. —SAMUEL JOHNSON, quoted in James Boswell's *The Life of Samuel Johnson*

Washington was a city of Southern efficiency and Northern charm. —JOHN F. KENNEDY, quoted in William Manchester's *Portrait of a President*

> Oh, East is East, and West is West, and never
>   the twain shall meet,
> Till Earth and Sky stand presently at God's
>   great Judgment Seat.
>   —RUDYARD KIPLING, "The Ballad of East
>   and West"

> On the road to Mandalay,
> Where the flyin'-fishes play,
> An' the dawn comes up like thunder outer
>   China 'crost the Bay!
>   —RUDYARD KIPLING, "Mandalay"

The most serious charge which can be brought against New England is not Puritanism but February. —JOSEPH WOOD KRUTCH, *The Twelve Seasons*

There is always something new out of Africa. —PLINY THE ELDER, *Natural History*

> Hog Butcher for the World,
> Tool Maker, Stacker of Wheat,
> Player with Railroads and the Nation's Freight
>   Handler;
> Stormy, husky, brawling,
> City of the Big Shoulders.
>   —CARL SANDBURG, "Chicago"

What was the use of my having come from Oakland it was not natural to have come from there yes write about it if I like or anything if I like but not there, there is no there there. —GERTRUDE STEIN, *Everybody's Autobiography*

There must be something in the Japanese character that saves them from the despair Americans feel in similar throes of consuming. The American, gorging himself on merchandise, develops a sense of guilty self-consciousness; if the Japanese have these doubts they do not show them. Perhaps hesitation is not part of the national character, or perhaps the ones who hesitate are trampled by the crowds of shoppers—that natural selection that capitalist society practices against the reflective. —PAUL THEROUX, *The Great Railway Bazaar*

When the missionaries came to Africa they had the Bible and we had the land. They said "let us pray." We closed our eyes. When we opened them, we had the Bible and they had the land. —DESMOND TUTU, quoted in *The Observer*

I fear the Greeks even when they bring gifts. —VIRGIL, *Aeneid*

In Italy for thirty years under the Borgias they had warfare, terror, murder, bloodshed—they produced Michelangelo, Leonardo da Vinci and the Renaissance. In Switzerland they had brotherly love, five hundred years of democracy and peace and what did that produce . . . ? The cuckoo clock. —ORSON WELLES, in the film *The Third Man*

> [These words were apparently Welles' own, added by him to the filmscript by Graham Greene.]

Perception

If the doors of perception were cleansed everything would appear to man as it is, infinite. —WILLIAM BLAKE, *The Marriage of Heaven and Hell*

The eye altering, alters all. —WILLIAM BLAKE, "The Mental Traveller"

> 'Tis distance lends enchantment to the view,
> And robes the mountain in its azure hue.
> —THOMAS CAMPBELL, *Pleasures of Hope*

In every object there is inexhaustible meaning; the eye sees in it what the eye brings means of seeing. —THOMAS CARLYLE, *The French Revolution*

> "I see nobody on the road," said Alice.
> "I only wish *I* had such eyes," the King remarked in a fretful tone."To be able to see Nobody! And at that distance too! Why, it's as much as *I* can do to see real people, by this light!"
> —LEWIS CARROLL, *Through the Looking-Glass*

It is the mind which creates the world about us, and even though we stand side by side in the same meadow, my eyes will never see what is beheld by yours, my heart will never stir to the emotions with which yours is touched. —GEORGE GISSING, *The Private Papers of Henry Ryecroft*

> All seems infected that th'infected spy,
> As all looks yellow to the jaundic'd eye.
> —ALEXANDER POPE, *An Essay on Criticism*

Every man takes the limits of his own field of vision for the limits of the world. —ARTHUR SCHOPENHAUER, *Parerga and Paralipomena*

Perseverance and Effort

> Resolve must be the firmer, spirit the bolder,
> Courage the greater, as our strength grows less.
> —ANONYMOUS, "The Battle of Maldon"

Where I am, I don't know, I'll never know, in the silence you don't know, you must go on, I can't go on, I'll go on. —SAMUEL BECKETT, *The Unnamable*

I have nothing to offer but blood, toil, tears and sweat. —WINSTON CHURCHILL, speech (1940)

. . . we shall not flag or fail. We shall go on to the end. We shall fight in France, we shall fight on the seas and oceans, we shall fight with growing confidence and growing strength in the air, we shall defend our island, whatever the cost may be. We shall fight on the beaches, we shall fight on the landing grounds, we shall fight in the fields and in the streets, we shall fight in the hills; we shall never surrender. —WINSTON CHURCHILL, speech (1940)

> To persevere, trusting in what hopes he has,
> is courage in a man.
> —EURIPIDES, *Heracles*

If at first you don't succeed, try, try again. Then quit. No use being a damn fool about it. —W.C. FIELDS, quoted in John Robert Colombo's *Popcorn in Paradise*

> If at first you don't succeed,
> Try, try again.
> —WILLIAM EDWARD HICKSON, "Try and
> Try Again"

[See W.C. Fields' advice, above.]

God is with those who persevere. —KORAN, ch. VIII

'Tis known by the name of perseverance in a good cause,—and of obstinacy in a bad one. —LAURENCE STERNE, *Tristram Shandy*

Personality — See CHARACTER AND PERSONALITY

Persuasion

If you would convince others, seem open to conviction yourself. —LORD CHESTERFIELD, *Letters to His Son*

> Charming women can true converts make,
> We love the precepts for the teacher's sake.
> —GEORGE FARQUHAR, *The Constant Couple*

By persuading others, we convince ourselves. —JUNIUS, in *Public Advertiser* (London)

["Junius" was the pseudonym of an unidentified writer of letters addressed to the *Public Advertiser*.]

> His tongue
> Dropt manna, and could make the worse appear
> The better reason.
> —JOHN MILTON, *Paradise Lost*

You have not converted a man because you have silenced him. —JOHN MORLEY, *On Compromise*

It is impossible to persuade a man who does not disagree, but smiles. —MURIEL SPARK, *The Prime of Miss Jean Brodie*

Pessimism — See OPTIMISM AND PESSIMISM

Pets — See ANIMALS

Philanthropy — See CHARITY; GIFTS AND GIVING

Philosophy

Metaphysics is the finding of bad reasons for what we believe upon instinct; but to find these reasons is no less an instinct. —F.H. BRADLEY, *Appearance and Reality*

I would say of metaphysicians what Scaliger said of the Basques: they are said to understand each other, but I do not believe it. —SÉBASTIEN-ROCH NICOLAS CHAMFORT, *Maximes et Pensées*

[The person referred to is Joseph Justus Scaliger, a 16th-century French scholar. Others have also remarked on the unintelligibility of metaphysicians: "When he to whom one speaks does not understand, and he who speaks himself does not understand, that is metaphysics."—Voltaire: *Philosophical Dictionary*; "Metaphysics is almost always an attempt to prove the incredible by an appeal to the unintelligible."—H.L. Mencken: *Minority Report: H.L. Mencken's Notebooks*.]

There is nothing so absurd but some philosopher has said it. —CICERO, *De Divinatione*

[René Descartes expressed the same sentiment, in his *Discourse on Method*: "There is nothing so strange or so unbelievable that it has not been said by one philosopher or another."]

You can't do without philosophy, since everything has its hidden meaning which we must know. —MAXIM GORKY, *The Zykovs*

> Do not all charms fly
> At the mere touch of cold philosphy?
> . . . .
> Philosophy will clip an Angel's wings,
> Conquer all mysteries by rule and line,
> Empty the haunted air, and gnomed mine—
> Unweave a rainbow.
>
> —JOHN KEATS, "Lamia"

Wonder is the foundation of all philosophy, inquiry the progress, ignorance the end. —MICHEL DE MONTAIGNE, *Essays*

To teach how to live without certainty, and yet without being paralyzed by hesitation, is perhaps the chief thing that philosophy, in our age, can still do for those who study it. —BERTRAND RUSSELL, *A History of Western Philosophy*

The safest general characterization of the European philosophical tradition is that it consists of a series of footnotes to Plato. —ALFRED NORTH WHITEHEAD, *Process and Reality*

Philosophy begins in wonder. And, at the end, when philosophic thought has done its best, the wonder remains. —ALFRED NORTH WHITEHEAD, *Modes of Thought*

Philosophy is not a theory but an activity. —LUDWIG WITTGENSTEIN, *Tractatus Logico-Philosophicus*

Photography

The virtue of the camera is not the power it has to transform the photographer into an artist, but the impulse it gives him to keep on looking. —BROOKS ATKINSON, *Once Around the Sun*

The camera cannot lie, but it can be an accessory to untruth. —HAROLD EVANS, *Pictures on a Page*

The camera is an instrument that teaches people how to see without a camera. —DOROTHEA LANGE, quoted in *Los Angeles Times*

The camera makes everyone a tourist in other people's reality, and eventually in one's own. —SUSAN SONTAG, in *New York Review of Books*

Pity — See SYMPATHY AND PITY

Places — See PEOPLES AND PLACES

Plagiarism — See IMITATION; WRITING AND WRITERS

Plans

The finest plans have always been spoiled by the littleness of them that should carry them out. Even emperors can't do it all by themselves. —BERTOLT BRECHT, *Mother Courage*

You can never plan the future by the past.
—EDMUND BURKE, letter (1791)
  [Compare Patrick Henry's comment, under Experience.]

Make no little plans; they have no magic to stir men's blood. —DANIEL H. BURNHAM, quoted in Charles Moore's *Daniel H. Burnham*

  The best laid schemes o' mice an' men
    Gang aft a-gley,
  An' lea'e us nought but grief an' pain
    For promis'd joy.
              —ROBERT BURNS, "To a Mouse"

The more human beings proceed by plan the more effectively they may be hit by accident. —FRIEDRICH DÜRRENMATT, *The Physicists*

It is a bad plan that admits of no modification.
—PUBLILIUS SYRUS, *Maxims*

If anyone counts upon one day ahead or even more, he does not think. For there can be no tomorrow until we have safely passed the day that is with us still.
—SOPHOCLES, *The Women of Trachis*

Pleasure and Indulgence

One half of the world cannot understand the pleasures of the other. —JANE AUSTEN, *Emma*

A man hath no better thing under the sun, than to eat, and to drink, and to be merry. —BIBLE, *Ecclesiastes* 8:15

> But pleasures are like poppies spread,
> You seize the flow'r, its bloom is shed.
> —ROBERT BURNS, "Tam O'Shanter"

> Though sages may pour out their wisdom's
>   treasure,
> There is no sterner moralist than Pleasure.
> —LORD BYRON, *Don Juan*

No man is a hypocrite in his pleasures. —SAMUEL JOHNSON, quoted in James Boswell's *The Life of Samuel Johnson*

Nothing is more hopeless than a scheme of merriment. —SAMUEL JOHNSON, *The Idler*

Most men pursue pleasure with such breathless haste that they hurry past it. —SØREN KIERKEGAARD, *Either/Or: A Fragment of Life*

Give us the luxuries of life, and we will dispense with its necessaries. —JOHN LOTHROP MOTLEY, quoted by Oliver Wendell Holmes, Sr. in *The Autocrat of the Breakfast-Table*

[A similar saying is attributed to Frank Lloyd Wright: "Give me the luxuries of life and I will willingly do without the necessities."]

All the things I really like to do are either illegal, immoral, or fattening. —ALEXANDER WOOLLCOTT, attributed

Poetry and Poets

It's a sad fact about our culture that a poet can earn much more money writing or talking about his art than he can by practicing it. —W.H. AUDEN, *The Dyer's Hand*

> I
> have nothing to say and I am saying it
> and that is poetry.
> —JOHN CAGE, "45' for a Speaker"

I wish our clever young poets would remember my homely definitions of prose and poetry; that is, prose—words in their best order; poetry—the best words in the best order. —SAMUEL TAYLOR COLE- RIDGE, *Table Talk*

Poetry's unnat'ral; no man ever talked poetry 'cept a beadle on boxin' day. —CHARLES DICKENS, *Pickwick Papers*

Genuine poetry can communicate before it is under- stood. —T.S. ELIOT, *Dante*

Poetry is either something that lives like fire inside you—like music to the musician . . .—or else it is nothing, an empty, formalized bore around which pedants can endlessly drone their notes and expla- nations. —F. SCOTT FITZGERALD, letter (1940)

Poetry should surprise by a fine excess, and not by singularity; it should strike the reader as a wording of his own highest thoughts, and appear almost a remembrance. —JOHN KEATS, letter (1818)

When power leads man toward arrogance, poetry reminds him of his limitations. When power narrows the areas of man's concern, poetry reminds him of the richness and diversity of his existence. When power corrupts, poetry cleanses. —JOHN F. KEN- NEDY, speech (1963)

323

A poem should not mean
But be.
—ARCHIBALD MACLEISH, "Ars poetica"

The courage of the poet is to keep ajar the door that leads into madness. —CHRISTOPHER MORLEY, *Inward Ho!*

Poetry is adolescence fermented and thus preserved. —JOSÉ ORTEGA Y GASSET, in *Partisan Review*

Poetry . . . is the revelation of a feeling that the poet believes to be interior and personal—which the reader recognizes as his own. —SALVATORE QUASIMODO, speech (1960)

Poetry "is the suggestion, by the imagination, of noble grounds for the noble emotions." —JOHN RUSKIN, *Modern Painters*

Poetry is the opening and closing of a door, leaving those who look through to guess about what is seen during a moment. —CARL SANDBURG, *Good Morning, America*

A poet is a nightingale, who sits in darkness and sings to cheer its own solitude with sweet sounds. —PERCY BYSSHE SHELLEY, *A Defense of Poetry*

The poet makes silk dresses out of worms. —WALLACE STEVENS, *Opus Posthumous*

The poet is the priest of the invisible. —WALLACE STEVENS, *Opus Posthumous*

A poet's pleasure is to withhold a little of his meaning, to intensify by mystification. He unzips the veil from beauty, but does not remove it. —E.B. WHITE, *One Man's Meat*

Poetry is the spontaneous overflow of powerful feelings: it takes its origin from emotion recollected in tranquillity. —WILLIAM WORDSWORTH, *Lyrical Ballads*

We make out of the quarrel with others, rhetoric, but of the quarrel with ourselves, poetry. —W.B. YEATS, *Essays*

Politics and Politicians

The trouble with this country is that there are too many politicians who believe, with a conviction based on experience, that you can fool all of the people all of the time. —FRANKLIN P. ADAMS, *Nods and Becks*

    [See also Lincoln, under Deception and Fraud.]

Politics, as a practice, whatever its professions, has always been the systematic organization of hatreds. —HENRY ADAMS, *The Education of Henry Adams*

Man is by nature a political animal. —ARISTOTLE, *Politics*

Politics is the art of the possible. —OTTO VON BISMARCK, attributed

    [See John Kenneth Galbraith's comment in this section.]

Politics are usually the executive expression of human immaturity. —VERA BRITTAIN, *Rebel Passion*

I have come to the conclusion that politics are too serious a matter to be left to the politicians.
—CHARLES DE GAULLE, quoted by Clement Attlee in *A Prime Minister Remembers*, by Francis Williams)

    [See also Clemenceau, under War.]

Since a politician never believes what he says, he is surprised when others believe him. —CHARLES DE GAULLE, quoted in *Newsweek*

An election is coming. Universal peace is declared, and the foxes have a sincere interest in prolonging the lives of the poultry. —GEORGE ELIOT, *Felix Holt*

Politics is not the art of the possible. It consists in choosing between the disastrous and the unpalatable. —JOHN KENNETH GALBRAITH, *Ambassador's Journal*

We'd all like to vote for the best man, but he's never a candidate. —KIN HUBBARD, *The Best of Kin Hubbard*

Politicians are the same all over. They promise to build a bridge even where there is no river. —NIKITA KHRUSHCHEV, comment made to American reporters

Politics is war without bloodshed while war is politics with bloodshed. —MAO TSE-TUNG, lecture (1938)

> did you ever
> notice that when
> a politician
> does get an idea
> he usually
> gets it all wrong
> —DON MARQUIS, *archys life of mehitabel*

Ideas are great arrows, but there has to be a bow. And politics is the bow of idealism. —BILL MOYERS, in *Time*

Politics I supposed to be the second-oldest profession. I have come to realize that it bears a very close resemblance to the first. —RONALD REAGAN, quoted in *Los Angeles Herald-Examiner*

All politics are based on the indifference of the majority. —JAMES RESTON, in *New York Times*

I will not accept if nominated, and will not serve if elected. —GEN. WILLIAM T. SHERMAN, telegram (responding to the suggestion he run for President, 1884)

Politics is perhaps the only profession for which no preparation is thought necessary. —ROBERT LOUIS STEVENSON, *Familiar Studies of Men and Books*

A politician is a man who understands government, and it takes a politician to run a government. A statesman is a politician who's been dead ten or fifteen years. —HARRY S TRUMAN, quoted in *New York World Telegram and Sun*

Politics is the art of preventing people from taking part in affairs which properly concern them. —PAUL VALÉRY, *Tel quel*

Politics makes strange bedfellows. —CHARLES DUDLEY WARNER, *My Summer in a Garden*

Poor — See POVERTY; RICH AND POOR

Population and Birth Control

I was ever of the opinion, that the honest man who married, and brought up a large family, did more service than he who continued single, and only talked of population. —OLIVER GOLDSMITH, *The Vicar of Wakefield*

It is now quite lawful for a Catholic woman to avoid pregnancy by a resort to mathematics, though she is still forbidden to resort to physics and chemistry. —H.L. MENCKEN, *Notebooks*

We want far better reasons for having children than not knowing how to prevent them. —DORA RUSSELL, *Hypatia*

No woman can call herself free who does not own and control her body. No woman can call herself free until she can choose consciously whether she will or will not be a mother. —MARGARET SANGER, in *Parade*

We have been God-like in our planned breeding of our domesticated plants and animals, but we have been rabbit-like in our unplanned breeding of ourselves. —ARNOLD TOYNBEE, quoted in *National Observer*

Possessions and Property

The goal of all inanimate objects is to resist man and ultimately to defeat him. —RUSSELL BAKER, in *New York Times*

Property has its duties as well as its rights. —THOMAS DRUMMOND, letter (1838)

No land is bad, but land is worse. If a man owns land, the land owns him. Now let him leave home, if he dare. —THOMAS DRUMMOND, letter (1838)

What we call real estate—the solid ground to build a house on—is the broad foundation on which nearly all the guilt of this world rests. —NATHANIEL HAWTHORNE, *The House of Seven Gables*

Property is the fruit of labor—property is desirable—is a positive good in the world. That some should be rich, shows that others may become rich, and hence is just encouragement to industry and enterprise. —ABRAHAM LINCOLN, speech (1864)

Property is theft. —PIERRE-JOSEPH PROUDHON, *What Is Property?*

Without that sense of security which property gives, the land would still be uncultivated. —FRANÇOIS QUESNAY, *Maximes*

328

For it so falls out
That what we have we prize not to the worth
Whiles we enjoy it, but being lack'd and lost,
Why, then we rack the value, then we find
The virtue that possession would not show us
Whiles it was ours.
    —SHAKESPEARE, *Much Ado About Nothing*

The want of a thing is perplexing enough, but the possession of it is intolerable. —JOHN VANBRUGH, *The Confederacy*

From the respect paid to property flow, as from a poisoned fountain, most of the evils and vices which render this world such a dreary scene to the contemplative mind. —MARY WOLLSTONECRAFT, *A Vindication of the Rights of Woman*

Give a man the secure possession of a bleak rock, and he will turn it into a garden; give him a nine years' lease of a garden, and he will convert it into a desert. . . . The magic of property turns sand into gold. —ARTHUR YOUNG, *Travels in France*

Poverty — See also RICH AND POOR

Anyone who has ever struggled with poverty knows how extremely expensive it is to be poor. —JAMES BALDWIN, *Nobody Knows My Name*

For the poor always ye have with you. —BIBLE, *John* 12:8

Poverty makes you wise but it's a curse. —BERTOLT BRECHT, *The Threepenny Opera*

There is no scandal like rags, nor any crime so shameful as poverty. —GEORGE FARQUHAR, *The Beaux' Stratagem*

I used to think I was poor. Then they told me I wasn't poor, I was needy. They told me it was self-defeating to think of myself as needy, I was deprived. Then they told me underprivileged was overused. I was disadvantaged. I still don't have a dime. But I have a great vocabulary. —JULES FEIFFER, cartoon

For every talent that poverty has stimulated it has blighted a hundred. —JOHN W. GARDNER, *Excellence*

People who are much too sensitive to demand of cripples that they run races ask of the poor that they get up and act just like everyone else in society. —MICHAEL HARRINGTON, *The Other America*

I want there to be no peasant in my kingdom so poor that he cannot have a chicken in his pot every Sunday. —HENRI IV, OF FRANCE (HENRY OF NAVARRE), attributed

All the arguments which are brought to represent poverty as no evil, show it to be evidently a great evil. You never find people laboring to convince you that you may live very happily upon a plentiful fortune. —SAMUEL JOHNSON, quoted in James Boswell's *The Life of Samuel Johnson*

A decent provision for the poor, is the true test of civilization. —SAMUEL JOHNSON, quoted in James Boswell's *The Life of Samuel Johnson*

If a free society cannot help the many who are poor, it cannot save the few who are rich. —JOHN F. KENNEDY, speech (inaugural address, 1961)

A hungry man is not a free man. —ADLAI E. STEVENSON, speech (1952)

When poverty is more disgraceful than even vice, is not morality cut to the quick? —MARY WOLLSTONECRAFT, *A Vindication of the Rights of Woman*

Power

Power tends to corrupt, and absolute power corrupts absolutely. Great men are almost always bad men. . . . There is no worse heresy than that the office sanctifies the holder of it. —LORD ACTON, letter (1887)

> [Lord Acton's words are the most frequently quoted, but he was not the first to make this observation. See William Pitt, in this section.]

I am more and more convinced that man is a dangerous creature; and that power, whether vested in many or a few, is ever grasping, and like the grave, cries "Give, give!" —ABIGAIL ADAMS, letter (to John Adams, 1775)

It is a strange desire to seek power and to lose liberty, or to seek power over others and to lose power over a man's self. —FRANCIS BACON, *Essays*

The greater the power, the more dangerous the abuse. —EDMUND BURKE, speech (1771)

To know the pains of power, we must go to those who have it; to know its pleasures, we must go to those who are seeking it: the pains of power are real, its pleasures imaginary. —CHARLES CALEB COLTON, *Lacon*

Our sense of power is more vivid when we break a man's spirit than when we win his heart. —ERIC HOFFER, *The Passionate State of Mind*

The only prize much cared for by the powerful is power. The prize of the general is not a bigger tent, but command. —OLIVER WENDELL HOLMES, JR., in *Collected Legal Papers*

Power is the great aphrodisiac. —HENRY A. KISSINGER, quoted in *New York Times*

> [This is sometimes quoted as "Power is the ultimate aphrodisiac."]

Power never takes a back step—only in the face of more power. —MALCOLM X, *Malcolm X Speaks*

Every Communist must grasp the truth: "Political power grows out of the barrel of a gun." —MAO TSE-TUNG, speech (1938)

> To reign is worth ambition though in hell:
> Better to reign in hell, than serve in heav'n.
> —JOHN MILTON, *Paradise Lost*

Unlimited power is apt to corrupt the minds of those who possess it. —WILLIAM PITT, speech (1770)

> Power, like a desolating pestilence,
> Pollutes whate'er it touches.
> —PERCY BYSSHE SHELLEY, *Queen Mab*

Praise and Flattery

There is no such whetstone, to sharpen a good wit and encourage a will to learning, as is praise.
—ROGER ASCHAM, *The Scholemaster*

Praise out of season, or tactlessly bestowed, can freeze the heart as much as blame. —PEARL S. BUCK, *To My Daughters, With Love*

The advantage of doing one's praising to oneself is that one can lay it on so thick and exactly in the right places. —SAMUEL BUTLER (d 1902), *The Way of All Flesh*

The praise of a fool is incense to the wisest of us.
—BENJAMIN DISRAELI, *Vivian Grey*

Praise makes good men better and bad men worse.
—THOMAS FULLER, *Gnomologia*

Praising all alike, is praising none. —JOHN GAY, *Epistles*

A compliment is something like a kiss through a veil. —VICTOR HUGO, *Les Misérables*

The refusal of praise is a desire to be praised twice. —LA ROCHEFOUCAULD, *Maxims*

Praise undeserv'd is scandal in disguise. —ALEXANDER POPE, *Imitations of Horace*

> [Pope was quoting—with a variation—a line from "To the Celebrated Beauties of the British Court," written by someone identified only as Broadhurst: "Praise undeserv'd is satire in disguise."]

I will praise any man that will praise me. —SHAKESPEARE, *Antony and Cleopatra*

> But when I tell him he hates flatterers,
> He says he does, being then most flattered.
> —SHAKESPEARE, *Julius Caesar*

What really flatters a man is that you think him worth flattering. —GEORGE BERNARD SHAW, *John Bull's Other Island*

Praise is the best diet for us, after all. —SYDNEY SMITH, quoted in Lady Holland's *Memoir*

Among the smaller duties of life I hardly know any one more important than that of not praising where praise is not due. —SYDNEY SMITH, *Elementary Sketches of Moral Philosophy*

None are more taken in by flattery than the proud, who wish to be the first and are not. —BENEDICT DE SPINOZA, *Ethics*

Flattery is all right—if you don't inhale. —ADLAI E. STEVENSON, speech (1961)

'Tis an old maxim in the schools,
That flattery's the food of fools;
Yet now and then your men of wit
Will condescend to take a bit.
—JONATHAN SWIFT, "Cadenus and
Vanessa"

Prayer

The wish to pray is a prayer in itself. —GEORGES
BERNANOS, *The Diary of a Country Priest*

But when ye pray, use not vain repetitions, as the
heathen do: for they think that they shall be heard
for their much speaking. Be not ye therefore like unto
them: for your Father knoweth what things ye have
need of before ye ask him. —BIBLE, *Matthew* 6:7–8

PRAY, *v.* To ask that the laws of the universe be
annulled in behalf of a single petitioner, confessedly
unworthy. —AMBROSE BIERCE, *The Devil's Dictionary*

Being mortal, never pray for an untroubled life;
But ask the gods to give you an enduring heart.
—MENANDER (fragment)

There are few men who durst publish to the world the
prayers they make to God. —MICHEL DE MONTAIGNE,
Essays

My words fly up, my thoughts remain below:
Words without thoughts never to heaven go.
—SHAKESPEARE, *Hamlet*

If thou shouldst never see my face again,
Pray for my soul. More things are wrought by
prayer
Than this world dreams of.
—ALFRED, LORD TENNYSON, *The Idylls of
the King*

Whatever a man prays for, he prays for a miracle. Every prayer reduces itself to this: "Great God, grant that twice two be not four." —IVAN TURGENEV, *Prayer*

Prediction

Your sons and your daughters shall prophesy, your old men shall dream dreams, your young men shall see visions. —BIBLE, *Joel* 2:28

A prophet is not without honor, save in his own country, and in his own house. —BIBLE, *Matthew* 13:57

A hopeful disposition is not the sole qualification to be a prophet. —WINSTON CHURCHILL, speech (1927)

Among all forms of mistake, prophecy is the most gratuitous. —GEORGE ELIOT, *Middlemarch*

The best of seers is he who guesses well. —EURIPIDES (fragment)

The best Qualification of a Prophet is to have a good Memory. —GEORGE SAVILE, *The Complete Works of George Savile*

Prejudice and Intolerance — See also RACE AND ETHNIC HERITAGE

Prejudices, it is well known, are most difficult to eradicate from the heart whose soil has never been loosened or fertilized by education; they grow there, firm as weeds among stones. —CHARLOTTE BRONTË, *Jane Eyre*

Bigotry may be roughly defined as the anger of men who have no opinions. —G.K. CHESTERTON, *Heretics*

There are only two ways to be quite unprejudiced and impartial. One is to be completely ignorant. The other is to be completely indifferent. Bias and prejudice are attitudes to be kept in hand, not attitudes to be avoided. —CHARLES P. CURTIS, *A Commonplace Book*

Prejudices are the props of civilization. —ANDRÉ GIDE, *The Counterfeiters*

Without the aid of prejudice and custom, I should not be able to find my way across the room. —WILLIAM HAZLITT, *Sketches and Essays*

Intolerance itself is a form of egoism, and to condemn egoism intolerantly is to share it. —GEORGE SANTAYANA, *Winds of Doctrine*

Passion and prejudice govern the world; only under the name of reason. —JOHN WESLEY, letter (1770)

[William Hazlitt wrote in his *Sketches and Essays*: "Prejudice is never easy unless it can pass itself off for reason."]

The Present

Happy the man, and happy he alone,
  He, who can call today his own;
  He who, secure within, can say:
"Tomorrow do thy worst, for I have liv'd
    today."
      —JOHN DRYDEN, translation of Horace's
                      Odes

Today's today. Tomorrow, we may be
ourselves gone down the drain of Eternity.
            —EURIPIDES, *Alcestis*

Seize the day, put no trust in the morrow. —HORACE, *Odes*

[The first part is often quoted in Latin: *Carpe diem.*]

The present is the necessary product of all the past,

the necessary cause of all the future. —ROBERT G. INGERSOLL, lecture (1899)

No mind is much employed upon the present: recollection and anticipation fill up almost all our moments. —SAMUEL JOHNSON, *Rasselas*

To live in the past or in the future may be less satisfying than to live in the present, but it can never be as disillusioning. —R.D. LAING, *Self and Others*

The word *now* is like a bomb through the window, and it ticks. —ARTHUR MILLER, *After the Fall*

The only living life is in the past and future . . . the present is an interlude . . . strange interlude in which we call on past and future to bear witness we are living! —EUGENE O'NEILL, *Strange Interlude*

Past and to come seems best; things present worst. —SHAKESPEARE, *Henry IV, Part II*

Presidents — See LEADERS AND RULERS

Press — See FREEDOM OF SPEECH AND THE PRESS; See also NEWS AND NEWSPAPERS

Pride and Self-Respect

Pride goeth before destruction, and a haughty spirit before a fall. —BIBLE, *Proverbs* 16:18
[This has now become "Pride goeth before a fall."]

He saw a cottage with a double coach house,
   A cottage of gentility;
And the Devil did grin, for his darling sin
   Is pride that apes humility.
               —SAMUEL TAYLOR COLERIDGE,
                 "The Devil's Thoughts"

[Robert Southey, who may have collaborated with Coleridge on this, later wrote an expanded version, called "The Devil's Walk," in which the original last two lines became:

>And he owned with a grin
>That his favorite sin
>Is pride that apes humility.]

There is a paradox in pride: it makes some men ridiculous, but prevents others from becoming so.
—CHARLES CALEB COLTON, *Lacon*

Wounded vanity knows when it is mortally hurt; and limps off the field, piteous, all disguises thrown away. But pride carries its banner to the last; and fast as it is driven from one field unfurls it in another, never admitting that there is a shade less honor in the second field than in the first, or in the third than in the second. —HELEN HUNT JACKSON, *Ramona*

Self-respect—The secure feeling that no one, as yet, is suspicious. —H.L. MENCKEN, *A Mencken Chrestomathy*

No one can make you feel inferior without your consent. —ELEANOR ROOSEVELT, *This Is My Story*

Nobody holds a good opinion of a man who has a low opinion of himself. —ANTHONY TROLLOPE, *Orley Farm*

Privacy

"If everybody minded their own business," the Duchess said in a hoarse growl, "the world would go round a deal faster than it does." —LEWIS CARROLL, *Alice's Adventures in Wonderland*

The personal life of every individual is based on secrecy, and perhaps it is partly for that reason that civilized man is so nervously anxious that personal privacy should be respected. —ANTON CHEKHOV, "The Lady with the Dog"

I'm Nobody! Who are you?
Are you—Nobody—Too?
Then there's a pair of us?
Don't tell! they'd advertise—you know!
    —EMILY DICKINSON, "I'm Nobody! Who
                                    are you?"

Let there be space in your togetherness. —KAHLIL
GIBRAN, *The Prophet*

Civilization is the progress toward a society of privacy. The savage's whole existence is public, ruled by the laws of his tribe. Civilization is the process of setting man free from men. —AYN RAND, *The Fountainhead*

The state has no business in the bedrooms of the nation. —PIERRE ELLIOTT TRUDEAU, quoted in *The Globe and Mail* (Toronto)

Problems

Almost anything is easier to get into than to get out of. —AGNES ALLEN, attributed, in *Omni*

What we're saying today is that you're either part of the solution or you're part of the problem. —ELDRIDGE CLEAVER, speech (1968)

Everything has two handles, one by which it may be borne, the other by which it may not. —EPICTETUS, *Encheiridion*

Problems are only opportunities in work clothes. —HENRY J. KAISER, attributed

All progress is precarious, and the solution of one problem brings us face to face with another problem. —MARTIN LUTHER KING, JR., *Strength to Love*

There is always an easy solution to every human problem—neat, plausible, and wrong. —H.L. MENCKEN, *Prejudices*

Unrest of spirit is a mark of life; one problem after another presents itself and in the solving of them we can find our greatest pleasure. —KARL MENNINGER, in *New York Herald Tribune*

Procrastination

No idleness, no laziness, no procrastination; never put off till tomorrow what you can do today. —LORD CHESTERFIELD, *Letters to His Son*

> [Chesterfield did not claim to be the originator of this advice, which also appears in Benjamin Franklin's *Poor Richard's Almanac* but no doubt predates both men. It has proved irresistible to parodists. William Brighty Rands wrote in "Lilliput Levee":
>> Never do today what you can
>> Put off till tomorrow.
> Aaron Burr said (as quoted by James Parton in *Life of Aaron Burr*): "'Never do today what you can as well do tomorrow,' because something may occur to make you regret your premature action."]

It is an undoubted truth, that the less one has to do, the less time one finds to do it in. One yawns, one procrastinates, one can do it when one will, and therefore one seldom does it at all. —LORD CHESTERFIELD, *Letters to His Son*

> [Perhaps an early version of Parkinson's Law. See C. Northcote Parkinson, under Work.]

Delay is preferable to error. —THOMAS JEFFERSON, letter (to George Washington, 1792)

> procrastination is the
> art of keeping
> up with yesterday.
>> —DON MARQUIS, *archy and mehitabel*

Procrastination is the thief of time. —EDWARD YOUNG, *Night Thoughts on Life, Death, and Immortality*

[See Oscar Wilde, under Punctuality, for a sly rephrasing.]

Progress

Progress, man's distinctive mark alone,
Not God's, and not the beasts': God is, they are,
Man partly is and wholly hopes to be.
> —ROBERT BROWNING, "A Death in the
> Desert"

All progress is based upon a universal innate desire on the part of every organism to live beyond its income. —SAMUEL BUTLER (*d* 1902), *Note-Books*

"A slow sort of country!" said the Queen."Now, *here*, you see, it takes all the running *you* can do, to keep in the same place. If you want to get somewhere else, you must run at least twice as fast as that."
> —LEWIS CARROLL, *Through the Looking-Glass*

What we call "Progress" is the exchange of one nuisance for another nuisance. —HAVELOCK ELLIS, *Impressions and Comments*

All that is human must retrograde if it does not advance. —EDWARD GIBBON, *The Decline and Fall of the Roman Empire*

Is it progress if a cannibal uses knife and fork?
—STANISLAW LEC, *Unkempt Thoughts*

Every step of progress the world has made has been from scaffold to scaffold, and from stake to stake.
—WENDELL PHILLIPS, speech (1851)

Man's "progress" is but a gradual discovery that his questions have no meaning. —ANTOINE DE SAINT-EXUPÉRY, *The Wisdom of the Sands*

The reasonable man adapts himself to the world: the unreasonable one persists in trying to adapt the world to himself. Therefore all progress depends on the unreasonable man. —GEORGE BERNARD SHAW, *Man and Superman*, "The Revolutionist's Handbook"

Scientific progress makes moral progress a necessity; for if man's power is increased, the checks that restrain him from abusing it must be strengthened. —MADAME DE STAËL, *The Influence of Literature upon Society*

"Progress" affects few. Only revolution can affect many. —ALICE WALKER, in *MS.*

Property — See POSSESSIONS AND PROPERTY

Prophecy — See PREDICTION

Proverbs — See MAXIMS AND PROVERBS

Providence — See also GOD

To put one's trust in God is only a longer way of saying that one will chance it. —SAMUEL BUTLER (*d* 1902), *Note-Books*

> There's a divinity that shapes our ends,
> Rough-hew them how we will.
> —SHAKESPEARE, *Hamlet*

Prudence and Foresight

Put your trust in God, my boys, and keep your powder dry! —VALENTINE BLACKER, "Oliver [Cromwell]'s Advice"

> [This is frequently attributed to Oliver Cromwell, but Blacker may well have been the source of the connection with Cromwell.]

For those that fly may fight again,
Which he can never do that's slain.
— SAMUEL BUTLER (d 1680), *Hudibras*

[The idea was an ancient one, repeated by various Greek and Roman authors, including Menander and Tertullian.]

'Tis the part of a wise man to keep himself today for tomorrow, and not venture all his eggs in one basket.
— MIGUEL DE CERVANTES, *Don Quixote de la Mancha*

Chi Wen Tze always thought three times before acting. Twice would have been enough. — CONFUCIUS, *Analects*

For want of a nail the shoe is lost, for want of a shoe the horse is lost, for want of a horse the rider is lost.
— GEORGE HERBERT, *Jacula Prudentum*

[Benjamin Franklin included this in *Poor Richard's Almanac.*]

There is a homely adage which runs: "Speak softly and carry a big stick; you will go far." — THEODORE ROOSEVELT, speech (1901)

In baiting a mouse-trap with cheese, always leave room for the mouse. — SAKI, *The Square Egg*

The better part of valor is discretion. — SHAKE-SPEARE, *Henry IV, Part I*

Put all your eggs in the one basket and—WATCH THAT BASKET. — MARK TWAIN, *Pudd'nhead Wilson*, "Pudd'nhead Wilson's Calendar"

Psychiatry and Psychology

Of course, Behaviorism "works." So does torture. Give me a no-nonsense, down-to-earth behaviorist, a few drugs, and simple electrical appliances, and in six months I will have him reciting the Athanasian Creed in public. — W.H. AUDEN, *A Certain World*

Psychiatry's chief contribution to philosophy is the discovery that the toilet is the seat of the soul.
—ALEXANDER CHASE, *Perspectives*

It might be said of psychoanalysis that if you give it your little finger it will soon have your whole hand.
—SIGMUND FREUD, *Introductory Lectures on Psychoanalysis*

The man who once cursed his fate, now curses himself—and pays his psychoanalyst. —JOHN W. GARDNER, *No Easy Victories*

Anybody who goes to a psychiatrist ought to have his head examined. —SAMUEL GOLDWYN, attributed

> [As with many remarks attributed to Samuel Goldwyn, there does not seem to be any direct evidence that he ever said this.]

Fortunately analysis is not the only way to resolve inner conflicts. Life itself still remains a very effective therapist. —KAREN HORNEY, *Our Inner Conflicts*

> Psychology which explains everything
> explains nothing,
> and we are still in doubt.
> —MARIANNE MOORE, "Marriage"

A psychiatrist is a man who goes to the Folies-Bergère and looks at the audience. —MERVYN STOCKWOOD, quoted in *The Observer*

The purpose of psychology is to give us a completely different idea of the things we know best. —PAUL VALÉRY, *Tel quel*

Punctuality

Five minutes! Zounds! I have been five minutes too late all my lifetime! —HANNAH COWLEY, *The Belle's Stratagem*

Punctuality is the politeness of kings. —LOUIS XVIII
OF FRANCE, attributed

Punctuality is the virtue of the bored. —EVELYN
WAUGH, diary entry (*Diaries of Evelyn Waugh*)

He was always late on principle, his principle being
that punctuality is the thief of time. —OSCAR WILDE,
The Picture of Dorian Gray

    [Compare Edward Young, under Procrastination.]

Punishment

No punishment has ever possessed enough power of
deterrence to prevent the commission of crimes. On
the contrary, whatever the punishment, once a spe-
cific crime has appeared for the first time, its reap-
pearance is more likely than its initial emergence
could ever have been. —HANNAH ARENDT, *Eichmann
in Jerusalem*

All punishment is mischief. All punishment in itself
is evil. —JEREMY BENTHAM, *Introduction to Principles of Morals and Legislation*

And if any mischief follow, then thou shalt give life
for life, Eye for eye, tooth for tooth, hand for hand,
foot for foot,
Burning for burning, wound for wound, stripe for
stripe. —BIBLE, *Exodus* 21:23–25

    [This concept of retribution was in the earlier (c.
    2100 B.C.) Code of Hammurabi: "If a man destroy
    the eye of another man, they shall destroy his eye."]

He that spareth the rod hateth his son: but he that
loveth him chasteneth him betimes. —BIBLE, *Proverbs* 13:24

Let the punishment match the offense. —CICERO, *De
Legibus*

My object all sublime
I shall achieve in time—
To let the punishment fit the crime—
The punishment fit the crime.
                    —W.S. GILBERT, *The Mikado*

[See also Cicero, above.]

The refined punishments of the spiritual mode are usually much more indecent and dangerous than a good smack. —D.H. LAWRENCE, *Fantasia of the Unconscious*

Distrust all in whom the impulse to punish is powerful! —FRIEDRICH NIETZSCHE, *Thus Spake Zarathustra*

It is a smaller thing to suffer punishment than to have deserved it. —OVID, *Epistulae ex Ponto*

Men are not hanged for stealing horses, but that horses may not be stolen. —GEORGE SAVILE, *Political, Moral, and Miscellaneous Thoughts and Reflections*

Whipping and abuse are like laudanum: You have to double the dose as the sensibilities decline. —HARRIET BEECHER STOWE, *Uncle Tom's Cabin*

I'm all for bringing back the birch, but only between consenting adults. —GORE VIDAL, television interview (1973)

Men simply copied the realities of their hearts when they built prisons. —RICHARD WRIGHT, *The Outsider*

Purpose

Competence is a narrow ideal. Competence makes the trains run on time but doesn't know where they're going. —GEORGE BUSH, speech (accepting nomination for president, 1988)

"Would you tell me, please, which way I ought to go from here?"

"That depends a good deal on where you want to get to," said the [Cheshire] Cat.

"I don't much care where—" said Alice.

"Then it doesn't matter which way you go," said the Cat.

—LEWIS CARROLL, *Alice's Adventures in Wonderland*

The last temptation is the greatest treason:
To do the right deed for the wrong reason.
—T.S. ELIOT, *Murder in the Cathedral*

In the name of noble purposes men have committed unspeakable acts of cruelty against one another.
—J. WILLIAM FULBRIGHT, speech (1963)

I find the great thing in this world is not so much where we stand, as in what direction we are moving.
—OLIVER WENDELL HOLMES, SR., *The Autocrat of the Breakfast-Table*

Constantly to seek the purpose of life is one of the odd escapes of man. If he finds what he seeks it will not be worth that pebble on the path. —KRISHNAMURTI, "The Only Revolution: California"

The trouble with our age is that it is all signpost and no destination. —LOUIS KRONENBERGER, *Company Manners*

Because it's there. —GEORGE MALLORY, quoted in *New York Times* (answering the question of why he wanted to climb Mount Everest)

The great and glorious masterpiece of man is to know how to live to purpose. —MICHEL DE MONTAIGNE, *Essays*

Life is lost at finding itself all alone. Mere egoism is a labyrinth. . . . Really to live is to be directed towards something, to progress towards a goal. —JOSÉ ORTEGA Y GASSET, *The Revolt of the Masses*

Nothing contributes so much to tranquilize the mind as a steady purpose—a point on which the soul may fix its intellectual eye. —MARY SHELLEY, *Frankenstein*

Quarrels — See ARGUMENTS AND CONTROVERSY

Questions

To ask the hard question is simple. —W.H. AUDEN, "The Question"

Examinations are formidable even to the best prepared, for the greatest fool may ask more than the wisest man can answer. —CHARLES CALEB COLTON, *Lacon*

Questioning is not the mode of conversation among gentlemen. —SAMUEL JOHNSON, quoted in James Boswell's *The Life of Samuel Johnson*

> I keep six honest serving-men
> (They taught me all I knew);
> Their names are What and Why and When
> And How and Where And Who.
> > —RUDYARD KIPLING, "The Elephant
> > Child"

It is not every question that deserves an answer.
—PUBLILIUS SYRUS, *Maxims*

It is better to ask some of the questions than to know all the answers. —JAMES THURBER, *The James Thurber Carnival*

No question is ever settled
  Until it is settled right.
           —ELLA WHEELER WILCOX, "Settle the
                      Question Right"

[Also attributed—though not in verse form—to
Abraham Lincoln.]

Quotations

The surest way to make a monkey of a man is to quote
him. —ROBERT BENCHLEY, *My Ten Years in a Quandary*

It is a good thing for an uneducated man to read
books of quotations. —WINSTON CHURCHILL, *My
Early Life*

I hate quotations. Tell me what you know. —RALPH
WALDO EMERSON, *Journals*

[Emerson seems to have felt some ambivalence; see
the following quote.]

Next to the originator of a good sentence is the first
quoter of it. —RALPH WALDO EMERSON, *Letters and
Social Aims*

Though old the thought and oft expressed,
  'Tis his at last who says it best.
           —JAMES RUSSELL LOWELL, "For an
                      Autograph"

I quote others only in order the better to express
myself. —MICHEL DE MONTAIGNE, *Essays*

I shall never be ashamed of citing a bad author if the
line is good. —SENECA, *De Tranquillitate Animi*

Famous remarks are very seldom quoted correctly.
—SIMEON STRUNSKY, *No Mean City*

Some for renown, on scraps of learning dote,
And think they grow immortal as they quote.
—EDWARD YOUNG, *Love of Fame*

Race and Ethnic Heritage — See also EQUALITY;
PREJUDICE AND INTOLERANCE

It is not healthy when a nation lives within a nation,
as colored Americans are living inside America. A
nation cannot live confident of its tomorrow if its ref-
ugees are among its citizens. —PEARL S. BUCK, *What
America Means to Me*

The conquest of the earth, which mostly means the
taking it away from those who have a different com-
plexion or slightly flatter noses than ourselves, is not
a pretty thing when you look into it too much.
—JOSEPH CONRAD, *Heart of Darkness*

The white man's happiness cannot be purchased by
the black man's misery. —FREDERICK DOUGLASS, in
The North Star

The problem of the twentieth century is the problem
of the color line. —W.E.B. DU BOIS, *The Souls of
Black Folk*

When people like me, they tell me it is in spite of my
color. When they dislike me, they point out that it is
not because of my color. —FRANTZ FANON, *Black
Skin, White Masks*

The so-called white races are really pinko-grey.
—E.M. FORSTER, *A Passage to India*

"It's powerful," he said.
"What?"
"That one drop of Negro blood—because just *one*
drop of black blood makes a man colored. *One* drop—
you are a Negro!"
—LANGSTON HUGHES, *Simple Takes a Wife*

No one has been barred on account of his race from fighting or dying for America—there are no "white" or "colored" signs on the foxholes or graveyards of battle. —JOHN F. KENNEDY, message to Congress (on proposed Civil Rights bill, 1963)

After all, there is but one race—humanity. —GEORGE MOORE, *The Bending of the Bough*

Why should I mourn at the untimely fate of my people? Tribe follows tribe, and nation follows nation, like the waves of the sea. It is the order of nature, and regret is useless. Your time of decay may be distant, but it will surely come, for even the White Man whose God walked and talked with him as friend with friend, cannot be exempt from the common destiny. We may be brothers after all. We will see. —CHIEF SEATTLE, "My People" (a reply to Washington Territory Governor Isaac Stevens' offer in 1854 to purchase land)

Radio — See TELEVISION AND RADIO

Rain — See WEATHER

Reading — See BOOKS AND READING

Reality

Reality only reveals itself when it is illuminated by a ray of poetry. —GEORGES BRAQUE, quoted in *The Times* (London)

Everything is a dangerous drug except reality, which is unendurable. —CYRIL CONNOLLY, *The Unquiet Grave*

He who confronts the paradoxical exposes himself to reality. —FRIEDRICH DÜRRENMATT, *The Physicists*

> . . . human kind
> cannot bear very much reality.
> —T.S. ELIOT, *Four Quartets*: "Burnt
> Norton"

There is no reality except the one contained within us. That is why so many people live such an unreal life. They take the images outside them for reality and never allow the world within to assert itself. —HERMANN HESSE, *Demian*

The horror no less than the charm of real life consists precisely in the recurrent actualization of the inconceivable. —ALDOUS HUXLEY, *Themes and Variations*

No, no there is nothing in the world that can be imagined in advance, not the slightest thing. Everything is made up of so many unique particulars that are impossible to foresee. In imagination, we pass over them in our haste and don't notice that they're missing. But realities are slow and indescribably detailed. —RAINER MARIA RILKE, *The Notebooks of Malte Laurids Brigge*

Reason and Logic

Every man's reason is every man's oracle: this oracle is best consulted in the silence of retirement. —HENRY ST. JOHN, VISCOUNT BOLINGBROKE, *Letters on the Use and Study of History*

"Contrariwise," continued Tweedledee, "if it was so, it might be; and if it were so, it would be; but as it isn't, it ain't. That's logic." —LEWIS CARROLL, *Through the Looking-Glass*

Man has such a predilection for systems and abstract deductions that he is ready to distort the truth intentionally, he is ready to deny the evidence of his senses only to justify his logic. —FYODOR DOSTOYEVSKY, *Notes from Underground*

I'll not listen to reason. . . . Reason always means what someone else has got to say. —ELIZABETH GASKELL, *Cranford*

There was only one catch and that was Catch-22, which specified that a concern for one's own safety in the face of dangers that were real and immediate was the process of a rational mind. Orr was crazy and could be grounded. All he had to do was ask; and as soon as he did, he would no longer be crazy and would have to fly more missions. Orr would be crazy to fly more missions and sane if he didn't, but if he was sane he had to fly them. If he flew them he was crazy and didn't have to; but if he didn't want to he was sane and had to. —JOSEPH HELLER, *Catch-22*

Human beings are the only creatures who are able to behave irrationally in the name of reason. —ASHLEY MONTAGU, quoted in *New York Times*

The last function of reason is to recognize that there are an infinity of things which surpass it. —BLAISE PASCAL, *Pensées*

Logic is one thing, the human animal another. You can quite easily propose a logical solution to something and at the same time hope in your heart of hearts it won't work out. —LUIGI PIRANDELLO, *The Pleasure of Honesty*

> Who reasons wisely is not therefore wise;
> His pride in reasoning, not in acting, lies.
> —ALEXANDER POPE, *Moral Essays*

The man who listens to Reason is lost: Reason enslaves all whose minds are not strong enough to master her. —GEORGE BERNARD SHAW, *Man and Superman*, "The Revolutionist's Handbook"

A mind all logic is like a knife all blade. It makes the hand bleed that uses it. —RABINDRANATH TAGORE, *Stray Birds*

Rebellion — See REVOLUTION AND REBELLION

Reform and Reformers

Every reform, however necessary, will by weak minds be carried to an excess which will itself need reforming. —SAMUEL TAYLOR COLERIDGE, *Biographia Literaria*

A man that'd expict to thrain lobsters to fly in a year is called a loonytic; but a man that thinks men can be tu-rrned into angels be an iliction is called a ray-former an' remains at large. —FINLEY PETER DUNNE, *Mr. Dooley's Opinions*

Reform must come from within, not from without. You cannot legislate for virtue. —JAMES CARDINAL GIBBONS, speech (1909)

Those who are fond of setting things to rights, have no great objection to seeing them wrong. —WILLIAM HAZLITT, *Characteristics*

A man should never put on his best trousers when he goes out to battle for freedom and truth. —HENRIK IBSEN, *An Enemy of the People*

Unless the reformer can invent something which substitutes attractive virtues for attractive vices, he will fail. —WALTER LIPPMANN, *A Preface to Politics*

The men with the muck-rakes are often indispensible to the well-being of society; but only if they know when to stop raking the muck. —THEODORE ROOSEVELT, speech (1906)

Reformers who are always compromising, have not yet grasped the idea that truth is the only safe ground to stand upon. —ELIZABETH CADY STANTON, *The Woman's Bible*

If anything ail a man, so that he does not perform his functions, if he have a pain in his bowels even,—for that is the seat of sympathy,—he forthwith sets about reforming the world. —HENRY DAVID THOREAU, *Walden*

Nothing so needs reforming as other people's habits. —MARK TWAIN, *Pudd'nhead Wilson*, "Pudd'nhead Wilson's Calendar"

A reformer is a guy who rides through a sewer in a glass-bottomed boat. —JAMES ("JIMMY") WALKER, speech (1928)

Regret

We might have been—These are but common
    words,
And yet they make the sum of life's bewailing.
            —LETITIA ELIZABETH LANDON, "Three
            Extracts from the Diary of a Week"

When to the sessions of sweet silent thought
I summon up remembrance of things past,
I sigh the lack of many a thing I sought,
And with old woes new wail my dear time's
    waste.
            —SHAKESPEARE, *Sonnet XXX*

            What 'twas weak to do
'Tis weaker to lament, once being done.
            —PERCY BYSSHE SHELLEY, *The Cenci*

The bitterest tears shed over graves are for words left unsaid and deeds left undone. —HARRIET BEECHER STOWE, *Little Foxes*

Make the most of your regrets. . . . To regret deeply is to live afresh. —HENRY DAVID THOREAU, *Journal*

For of all sad words of tongue or pen,
The saddest are these: "It might have been!"
—JOHN GREENLEAF WHITTIER,
"Maud Muller"

Relatives — See FAMILY

Religion

You don't have to be dowdy to be a Christian.
—TAMMY FAYE BAKKER, quoted in *Newsweek*

Religion is to mysticism what popularization is to science. —HENRI BERGSON, *The Two Sources of Morality and Religion*

HEATHEN, *n.* A benighted creature who has the folly to worship something that he can see and feel.
—AMBROSE BIERCE, *The Devil's Dictionary*

Religion converts despair, which destroys, into resignation, which submits. —MARGUERITE BLESSINGTON, *Commonplace Book*

Every day people are straying away from the church and going back to God. —LENNY BRUCE, in *The Essential Lenny Bruce*

If Jesus Christ were to come today, people would not even crucify him. They would ask him to dinner, and hear what he had to say, and make fun of it.
—THOMAS CARLYLE, quoted in D.A. Wilson's *Carlyle at his Zenith*

The Christian ideal has not been tried and found wanting. It has been found difficult; and left untried.
—G.K. CHESTERTON, *What's Wrong with the World*

Men will wrangle for religion, write for it, fight for it, die for it; anything but live for it. —CHARLES CALEB COLTON, *Lacon*

Yes, I am a Jew, and when the ancestors of the right honorable gentleman were brutal savages in an unknown island, mine were priests in the temple of Solomon. —BENJAMIN DISRAELI, attributed

[Disraeli was responding to an opponent in Parliament. A similar statement is attributed to U.S. Senator Judah P. Benjamin, in reply to another senator: "The gentleman will please remember that when his half-civilized ancestors were hunting wild boar in the forests of Silesia, mine were the princes of the earth."]

Science without religion is lame, religion without science is blind. —ALBERT EINSTEIN, *Out of My Later Years*

The religions we call false were once true. —RALPH WALDO EMERSON, *Essays*

I would rather live in a world where my life is surrounded by mystery than live in a world so small that my mind could comprehend it. —HARRY EMERSON FOSDICK, *Riverside Sermons*

Without philosophy man cannot know what he makes; without religion he cannot know why. —ERIC GILL, quoted in *Christian Science Monitor*

Religion either makes men wise and virtuous, or it makes them set up false pretenses to both. . . . Religion is, in grosser minds, an enemy to self-knowledge. —WILLIAM HAZLITT, "On Religious Hypocrisy"

No man with any sense of humor, ever founded a religion. —ROBERT G. INGERSOLL, *Prose-Poems and Selections*

I count religion but a childish toy,
And hold there is no sin but ignorance.
—CHRISTOPHER MARLOWE, *The Jew of Malta*

Religion is the sigh of the oppressed creature, the feelings of a heartless world, just as it is the spirit of unspiritual conditions. It is the opium of the people. —KARL MARX, "Toward the Critique of the Hegelian Philosophy of Right"

The two great European narcotics, alcohol and Christianity. —FRIEDRICH NIETZSCHE, *Twilight of the Idols*

Christianity has made of death a terror which was unknown to the gay calmness of the Pagan. —OUIDA, "The Failure of Christianity"

There is only one religion, though there are a hundred versions of it. —GEORGE BERNARD SHAW, *Arms and the Man*

Every man is his own doctor of divinity in the last resort. —ROBERT LOUIS STEVENSON, *An Inland Voyage*

Heresy is the lifeblood of religions. It is faith that begets heretics. There are no heresies in a dead religion. —ANDRÉ SUARÈS, *Péguy*

We have just enough religion to make us hate, but not enough to make us love one another. —JONATHAN SWIFT, *Thoughts on Various Subjects*

Whatever you do, crush the infamy. —VOLTAIRE, letter (1762)

[The phrase "*écrasez l'infâme*" recurs in Voltaire's letters. Voltaire said that the infamy he meant was superstition, but many have interpreted it as referring to clericalism or organized religion.]

Repentance and Remorse

Joy shall be in heaven over one sinner that repenteth, more than over ninety and nine just persons which need no repentance. —BIBLE, *Luke* 15:7

Repentance is but want of power to sin. —JOHN DRYDEN, *Palamon and Arcite*

> There are people who are very resourceful
> At being remorseful,
> And who apparently feel that the best way to
>   make friends
> Is to do something terrible and then make
>   amends.
>   —OGDEN NASH, "Hearts of Gold"

One man's remorse is another man's reminiscence. —OGDEN NASH, "A Clean Conscience Never Relaxes"

Remorse goes to sleep when we are in the enjoyment of prosperity, but makes itself felt in adversity. —JEAN-JACQUES ROUSSEAU, *Confessions*

Repentance for past crimes is just and easy; but sin-no-more's a task too hard for mortals. —JOHN VANBRUGH, *The Relapse*

Reputation — See also CHARACTER AND PERSONALITY

> Let us honor if we can
> The vertical man,
> Though we value none
> But the horizontal one.
>   —W.H. AUDEN, "Shorts"

A good name is rather to be chosen than great riches. —BIBLE, *Proverbs* 22:1

Posterity is as likely to be wrong as anybody else. —HEYWOOD BROUN, *Sitting on the World*

He that hath the name to be an early riser may sleep till noon. —JAMES HOWELL, *Proverbs*

Be it true or false, what is said about men often has as much influence upon their lives, and especially upon their destinies, as what they do. —VICTOR HUGO, *Les Misérables*

There is a report that Piso is dead; it is a great loss; he was an honest man, who deserved to live longer; he was intelligent and agreeable, resolute and courageous, to be depended upon, generous and faithful. Add: provided he is really dead. —LA BRUYÈRE, *Les Caractères*

How strangely men act. They will not praise those who are living at the same time and living with themselves; but to be themselves praised by posterity, by those whom they have never seen or ever will see, this they set much value on. —MARCUS AURELIUS, *Meditations*

> Men's evil manners live in brass; their virtues
> We write in water.
> > —SHAKESPEARE, *Henry VIII*

> Good name in man and woman, dear my
>   lord,
> Is the immediate jewel of their souls;
> Who steals my purse steals trash; 'tis
>   something, nothing;
> 'Twas mine, 'tis his, and has been slave to
>   thousands;
> But he that filches from me my good name
> Robs me of that which not enriches him
> And makes me poor indeed.
> > —SHAKESPEARE, *Othello*

Reputation is an idle and most false imposition; oft got without merit, and lost without deserving.
—SHAKESPEARE, *Othello*

Resignation

It's over, and can't be helped, and that's one consolation, as they always says in Turkey, ven they cuts the wrong man's head off. —CHARLES DICKENS, *Pickwick Papers*

> Teach us to care and not to care
> Teach us to sit still.
> —T.S. ELIOT, *Ash-Wednesday*

Seek not that the things which happen should happen as you wish; but wish the things which happen to be as they are, and you will have a tranquil flow of life. —EPICTETUS, *Encheiridion*

What is called resignation is confirmed desperation. —HENRY DAVID THOREAU, *Walden*

A calm despair, without angry convulsions and without reproaches toward heaven, is wisdom itself. —ALFRED DE VIGNY, *Journal d'un poète*

Resolution — See DETERMINATION

Responsibility — See DUTY AND RESPONSIBILITY

Rest

We combat obstacles in order to get repose, and, when got, the repose is insupportable. —HENRY ADAMS, *The Education of Henry Adams*

> Absence of occupation is not rest,
> A mind quite vacant is a mind distress'd.
> —WILLIAM COWPER, *Retirement*

Too much rest becomes a pain. —HOMER, *The Odyssey*

Our foster-nurse of nature is repose. —SHAKE-SPEARE, *King Lear*

> Sleep after toil, port after stormy seas,
> Ease after war, death after life does greatly
>   please.
> > —EDMUND SPENSER, *The Faerie Queen*

Repose is a good thing, but boredom is its brother. —VOLTAIRE, attributed

Results — See CONSEQUENCES

Retirement — See also SOLITUDE AND LONELINESS

> Retired is being tired twice, I've thought,
> First tired of working,
> Then tired of not.
> > —RICHARD ARMOUR, *Going Like Sixty*

Cessation of work is not accompanied by cessation of expenses. —CATO THE ELDER, *De Agri Cultura*

Few men of action have been able to make a graceful exit at the appropriate time. —MALCOLM MUGGER-IDGE, *Chronicles of Wasted Time*

Nothing is more usual than the sight of old people who yearn for retirement: and nothing is so rare than those who have retired and do not regret it. —CHARLES DE SAINT-ÉVREMOND, quoted by Simone de Beauvoir in *The Coming of Age*

Revenge

Men regard it as their right to return evil for evil—and, if they cannot, feel they have lost their liberty. —ARISTOTLE, *Nichomachean Ethics*

A man that studieth revenge keeps his own wounds green, which otherwise would heal and do well. —FRANCIS BACON, *Essays*

Vengeance is mine; I will repay, saith the Lord.
—BIBLE, *Romans* 12:19

Living well is the best revenge. —GEORGE HERBERT,
Jacula Prudentum

The best way of avenging yourself is not to become
like the wrongdoer. —MARCUS AURELIUS, *Meditations*

> Revenge, at first though sweet,
> Bitter ere long back on itself recoils.
> > —JOHN MILTON, *Paradise Lost*

> Vengeance to God alone belongs;
> But, when I think on all my wrongs,
> My blood is liquid flame!
> > —SIR WALTER SCOTT, *Marmion*

> Heat not a furnace for your foe so hot
> That it do singe yourself.
> > —SHAKESPEARE, *Henry VIII*

Revolution and Rebellion

It is well known that the most radical revolutionary
will become a conservative on the day after the revolution. —HANNAH ARENDT, in *New Yorker*

Revolutions are not about trifles, but they spring
from trifles. —ARISTOTLE, *Politics*

What is a rebel? A man who says no. —ALBERT
CAMUS, *The Rebel*

A revolution is not a bed of roses . . . a revolution is
a struggle to the death between the future and the
past. —FIDEL CASTRO, speech (1961)

No one can go on being a rebel too long without turning into an autocrat. —LAWRENCE DURRELL, *The
Alexandria Quartet: Balthazar*

All successful revolutions are the kicking in of a rotten door. The violence of revolutions is the violence of men who charge into a vacuum. —JOHN KENNETH GALBRAITH, *The Age of Uncertainty*

The tree of liberty must be refreshed from time to time with the blood of patriots and tyrants. It is its natural manure. —THOMAS JEFFERSON, letter (1787)

A little rebellion, now and then, is a good thing, and as necessary in the political world as storms in the physical. —THOMAS JEFFERSON, letter (to James Madison, 1787)

Those who make peaceful revolution impossible will make violent revolution inevitable. —JOHN F. KENNEDY, speech (1962)

Revolutions are the locomotives of history. —NIKITA KHRUSHCHEV, speech (1957)

When smashing monuments, save the pedestals— they always come in handy. —STANISLAW LEC, *Unkempt Thoughts*

Revolution is not a dinner party, nor an essay, nor a painting, nor a piece of embroidery; it cannot be advanced softly, gradually, carefully, considerately, respectfully, politely, plainly and modestly. —MAO TSE-TUNG, quoted in *Time*

Let the ruling classes tremble at a Communist revolution. The proletarians have nothing to lose but their chains. They have a world to win. Workers of the world, unite! —KARL MARX AND FRIEDRICH ENGELS, *The Communist Manifesto*

Revolution is not the uprising against pre-existing order, but the setting up of a new order contradictory to the traditional one. —JOSÉ ORTEGA Y GASSET, *The Revolt of the Masses*

When the people contend for their liberty, they seldom get anything by their victory but new masters.
—GEORGE SAVILE, *Political, Moral, and Miscellaneous Thoughts and Reflections*

Revolutions have never lightened the burden of tyranny: they have only shifted it to another shoulder.
—GEORGE BERNARD SHAW, *Man and Superman*, "The Revolutionist's Handbook"

Rich and Poor — See also POVERTY; WEALTH

There are only two families in the world, as a grandmother of mine used to say: the haves and the have-nots. —MIGUEL DE CERVANTES, *Don Quixote de la Mancha*

If rich, it is easy enough to conceal our wealth but, if poor, it is not quite so easy to conceal our poverty. We shall find it is less difficult to hide a thousand guineas, than one hole in our coat. —CHARLES CALEB COLTON, *Lacon*

Let them eat cake. —MARIE-ANTOINETTE, attributed
[Although this is traditionally attributed to Marie-Antoinette, the saying actually occurs in Jean-Jacques Rousseau's *Confessions*, written before Marie-Antoinette's arrival in France. Rousseau describes the remark as "the thoughtless saying of a great princess."]

It is an unfortunate human failing that a full pocketbook often groans more loudly than an empty stomach. —FRANKLIN D. ROOSEVELT, speech (1940)

Through tatter'd clothes small vices do
    appear;
Robes and furr'd gowns hide all.
                —SHAKESPEARE, *King Lear*

Rights

Men their rights and nothing more; women their rights and nothing less. —SUSAN B. ANTHONY, *The Revolution*

America did not invent human rights. In a very real sense . . . human rights invented America. —JIMMY CARTER, speech (farewell address, 1981)

A right is not what someone gives you; it's what no one can take from you. —RAMSEY CLARK, in *New York Times*

"Freedom from fear" could be said to sum up the whole philosophy of human rights. —DAG HAMMARSKJÖLD, speech (1956)

I am the inferior of any man whose rights I trample under foot. —ROBERT G. INGERSOLL, "Liberty"

Most people, no doubt, when they espouse human rights, make their own mental reservations about the proper application of the word *human*. —SUZANNE LA FOLLETTE, *Concerning Women*

As a man is said to have a right to his property, he may be equally said to have a property in his rights. —JAMES MADISON, in *National Gazette*

As if it harm'd me, giving others the same chances and rights as myself—as if it were not indispensable to my own rights that others possess the same. —WALT WHITMAN, "Thought"

Risk — See BOLDNESS AND ENTERPRISE; DANGER; GAMES AND GAMBLING

Rivalry — See COMPETITION

Robbery — See CRIME

Romance — See FLIRTATION AND ROMANCE

Rulers — See LEADERS AND RULERS

Rumor — See GOSSIP AND RUMOR

Safety — See SECURITY

Sailing — See SHIPS AND SAILING

Satire — See HUMOR AND WIT

Scandal — See GOSSIP AND RUMOR

Science — See also TECHNOLOGY

In teaching man, experimental science results in lessening his pride more and more by proving to him every day that primary causes, like the objective reality of things, will be hidden from him forever and that he can only know relations. —CLAUDE BERNARD, *Introduction à la médecine expérimentale*

We have grasped the mystery of the atom and rejected the Sermon on the Mount. —GEN. OMAR BRADLEY, speech (1948)

That is the essence of science: ask an impertinent question, and you are on the way to a pertinent answer. —JACOB BRONOWSKI, *The Ascent of Man*

The First Clarke Law states, "If an elderly but distinguished scientist says that something is possible he is almost certainly right, but if he says that it is impossible he is very probably wrong." —ARTHUR C. CLARKE, quoted in *New Yorker*

In science the credit goes to the man who convinces the world, not to the man to whom the idea first occurs. —FRANCIS DARWIN, in *Eugenics Review*

What Art was to the ancient world, Science is to the modern; the distinctive faculty. In the minds of men, the useful has succeeded to the beautiful. —BENJAMIN DISRAELI, *Coningsby*

The whole of science is nothing more than a refinement of everyday thinking. —ALBERT EINSTEIN, *Out of My Later Years*

The great tragedy of Science—the slaying of a beautiful hypothesis by an ugly fact. —THOMAS HENRY HUXLEY, *Collected Essays*

I am sorry to say that there is too much point to the wisecrack that life is extinct on other planets because their scientists were more advanced than ours. —JOHN F. KENNEDY, speech (1959)

It is a good morning exercise for a research scientist to discard a pet hypothesis every day before breakfast. It keeps him young. —KONRAD LORENZ, *On Aggression*

In some sort of crude sense which no vulgarity, no humor, no overstatement can quite extinguish, the physicists have known sin; and this is a knowledge which they cannot lose. —J. ROBERT OPPENHEIMER, lecture (1947)

Scientific discovery and scientific knowledge have been achieved only by those who have gone in pursuit of it without any practical purpose whatsoever in view. —MAX PLANCK, *Where is Science Going?*

Science is built up of facts, as a house is built of stones; but an accumulation of facts is no more a science than a heap of stones is a house. —JULES-HENRI POINCARÉ, *Science and Hypothesis*

The simplest schoolboy is now familiar with truths for which Archimedes would have sacrificed his life.
—ERNEST RENAN, *Souvenirs d'enfance et de jeunesse*

Science tells us what we can know, but what we can know is little, and if we forget how much we cannot know we become insensitive to many things of very great importance. —BERTRAND RUSSELL, *A History of Western Philosophy*

People must understand that science is inherently neither a potential for good nor for evil. It is a potential to be harnessed by man to do his bidding.
—GLENN T. SEABORG, interview (Associated Press, 1964)

Man has wrested from nature the power to make the world a desert or to make the deserts bloom. There is no evil in the atom; only in men's souls. —ADLAI E. STEVENSON, speech (1952)

True science teaches, above all, to doubt and to be ignorant. —MIGUEL DE UNAMUNO, *The Tragic Sense of Life*

The Sea

They that go down to the sea in ships, that do business in great waters;
These see the works of the Lord, and his wonders in the deep. —BIBLE, *Psalms* 107: 23–24

In its mysterious past it [the sea] encompasses all the dim origins of life and receives in the end, after, it may be, many transmutations, the dead husks of that same life. For all at last return to the sea—to Oceanus, the ocean river, like the everflowing stream of time, the beginning and the end. —RACHEL CARSON, *The Sea Around Us*

Water, water, every where,
And all the boards did shrink;
Water, water, every where,
Nor any drop to drink.
　　　　—SAMUEL TAYLOR COLERIDGE, *The Rime
　　　　　　　　of the Ancient Mariner*

The sea has never been friendly to man. At most it has been the accomplice of human restlesness.
—JOSEPH CONRAD, *The Mirror of the Sea*

There is nothing so desperately monotonous as the sea, and I no longer wonder at the cruelty of pirates.
—JAMES RUSSELL LOWELL, *Fireside Travels*

I must down to the seas again, to the lonely
　　sea and the sky,
And all I ask is a tall ship and a star to steer
　　her by,
And the wheel's kick and wind's song and the
　　white sail's shaking,
And a gray mist on the sea's face and a gray
　　dawn breaking.
　　　　　—JOHN MASEFIELD, "Sea Fever"

There is one knows not what sweet mystery about this sea, whose gently awful stirrings seem to speak of some hidden soul beneath. —HERMAN MELVILLE, *Moby Dick*

The sea hates a coward. —EUGENE O'NEILL, *Mourning becomes Electra*

Break, break, break,
　　On thy cold gray stones, O sea!
And I would that my tongue could utter
　　The thoughts that arise in me.
　　　　　　—ALFRED, LORD TENNYSON,
　　　　　　　"Break, Break, Break"

Seasons

Rise up, my love, my fair one, and come away.
For lo, the winter is past, the rain is over and gone;
The flowers appear on the earth; the time of the singing
of birds is come, and the voice of the turtle is heard in
our land. —BIBLE, *Song of Solomon* 2:10–12

["Turtle" here refers to a turtledove.]

The year's at the spring
And day's at the morn;
Morning's at seven;
The hill-side's dew-pearled;
The lark's on the wing;
The snail's on the thorn;
God's in his heaven—
All's right with the world!
          —ROBERT BROWNING, *Pippa Passes*

The melancholy days are come, the saddest of
    the year,
Of wailing winds, and naked woods, and
    meadows brown and sere.
     —WILLIAM CULLEN BRYANT, "The Death of
                 the Flowers"

The scarlet of the maples can shake me like a cry
Of bugles going by.
And my lonely spirit thrills
To see the frosty asters like a smoke upon the
    hills.
        —BLISS CARMAN, "A Vagabond Song"

Fallen leaves lying on the grass in the November sun
bring more happiness than the daffodils. —CYRIL
CONNOLLY, *The Unquiet Grave*

There's a certain Slant of light,
Winter Afternoons—
That oppresses, like the Heft
Of Cathedral Tunes.
        —EMILY DICKINSON, "There's a certain
                Slant of light"

371

April is the cruellest month, breeding
Lilacs out of the dead land, mixing
Memory and desire, stirring
Dull roots with spring rain.
> —T.S. ELIOT, *The Waste Land*

The sun was warm but the wind was chill.
You know how it is with an April day
When the sun is out and the wind is still,
You're one month on in the middle of May.
But if you so much as dare to speak,
A cloud comes over the sunlit arch,
A wind comes off a frozen peak,
And you're two months back in the middle of
    March.
> —ROBERT FROST, "Two Tramps
> in Mud Time"

Summer afternoon—summer afternoon; to me those
have always been the two most beautiful words in the
English language. —HENRY JAMES, quoted in Edith
Wharton's *A Backward Glance*

Hard is the heart that loveth nought
In May.
> —GUILLAUME DE LORRIS AND JEAN DE
> MEUN, *The Romaunt of the Rose*
> translated by Chaucer, c. 1370

And what is so rare as a day in June?
Then, if ever, come perfect days.
> —JAMES RUSSELL LOWELL, *The Vision of
> Sir Launfal*

    April
Comes like an idiot, babbling and strewing
    flowers.
> —EDNA ST. VINCENT MILLAY, "Spring"

In those vernal seasons of the year, when the air is calm and pleasant, it were an injury and sullenness against Nature not to go out and see her riches, and partake in her rejoicing with heaven and earth.
—JOHN MILTON, *Of Education*

Spring makes everything young again, save man.
—JEAN PAUL RICHTER, *Hesperus*

> O, it sets my heart a-clickin' like the tickin' of
>   a clock,
> When the frost is on the punkin and the
>   fodder's in the shock.
> > —JAMES WHITCOMB RILEY, "When the
> > Frost Is on the Punkin"

>   O Wind,
> If Winter comes, can Spring be far behind?
> > —PERCY BYSSHE SHELLEY, "Ode to the
> > West Wind"

In the spring a young man's fancy lightly turns to thoughts of love. —ALFRED, LORD TENNYSON, "Locksley Hall"

> April, April,
> Laugh thy girlish laughter;
> Then, the moment after,
> Weep thy girlish tears!
> > —WILLIAM WATSON, "April"

Secrets

None are so fond of secrets as those who do not mean to keep them; such persons covet secrets as a spendthrift covets money, for the purpose of circulation.
—CHARLES CALEB COLTON, *Lacon*

I know that's a secret, for it's whispered everywhere.
—WILLIAM CONGREVE, *Love for Love*

Three may keep a secret, if two of them are dead.
—BENJAMIN FRANKLIN, *Poor Richard's Almanac*

Three may keep counsel, if two be away. —JOHN
HEYWOOD, *Proverbs*

> [This proverb occurs in varying forms in the works
> of other authors, including Shakespeare in *Romeo
> and Juliet*: "Two may keep counsel, putting one
> away." See also Benjamin Franklin, above.]

How can we expect another to keep our secret if we
have been unable to keep it ourselves? —LA ROCHE-
FOUCAULD, *Maxims*

Shy and unready men are great betrayers of secrets:
for there are few wants more urgent for the moment
than the want of something to say. —HENRY TAYLOR,
The Statesman

Security

Those who would give up essential Liberty, to purchase a little temporary Safety, deserve neither Liberty nor Safety. —BENJAMIN FRANKLIN, in *The
Papers of Ben Franklin*, ed. L.W. Labaree

Security is mostly a superstition. It does not exist in
nature, nor do the children of men as a whole experience it. . . . Avoiding danger is no safer in the long
run than outright exposure. . . . Life is either a daring adventure or nothing. —HELEN KELLER, *The
Open Door*

There is no security on this earth; there is only
opportunity. —GEN. DOUGLAS MACARTHUR, quoted
in Courtney Whitney's *MacArthur: His Rendezvous
with History*

We must plan for freedom, and not only for security,
if for no other reason than that only freedom can
make security secure. —KARL POPPER, *The Open
Society and Its Enemies*

A ship in harbor is safe, but that is not what ships are built for. —JOHN A. SHEDD, *Salt from My Attic*

The desire for safety stands against every great and noble enterprise. —TACITUS, *Annals*

The Self

> Resolve to be thyself; and know that he,
> Who finds himself, loses his misery!
> —MATTHEW ARNOLD, "Self-Dependence"

The arch-flatterer, with whom all the petty flatterers have intelligence, is a man's self. —FRANCIS BACON, *Essays*

The Ideal is in thyself, the impediment too is in thyself. —THOMAS CARLYLE, *Sartor Resartus*

One may understand the cosmos, but never the ego; the self is more distant than any star. —G.K. CHESTERTON, *Orthodoxy*

We are all serving a life-sentence in the dungeon of self. —CYRIL CONNOLLY, *The Unquiet Grave*

As accidental as my life may be, or as that random humor is, which governs it, I know nothing, after all, so real or substantial as myself. —ANTHONY ASHLEY COOPER, EARL OF SHAFTESBURY, *Characteristics*

Everybody has his own theater, in which he is manager, actor, prompter, playwright, sceneshifter, boxkeeper, doorkeeper, all in one, and audience into the bargain. —JULIUS C. HARE AND AUGUSTUS W. HARE, *Guesses at Truth*

No man would, I think, exchange his existence with any other man, however fortunate. We had as lief not be, as not be ourselves. —WILLIAM HAZLITT, *Table Talk*

If I am not for myself, who is for me? And if I am only for myself, what am I? If not now, when? —HILLEL, in the *Talmud*

There is no such thing as an isolated man or woman; we are each of us made up of a cluster of appurtenances. What do you call one's self? Where does it begin? Where does it end? It overflows into everything that belongs to us—and then it flows back again. —HENRY JAMES, *The Portrait of a Lady*

A man never speaks of himself without losing something. What he says in his disfavor is always believed, but when he commends himself, he arouses mistrust. —MICHEL DE MONTAIGNE, *Essays*

> This above all: to thine own self be true,
> And it must follow, as the night the day,
> Thou canst not then be false to any man.
> > —SHAKESPEARE, *Hamlet*

> Our remedies oft in ourselves do lie,
> Which we ascribe to heaven.
> > —SHAKESPEARE, *All's Well*
> > *That Ends Well*

People often say that this or that person has not yet found himself. But the self is not something one finds, it is something one creates. —THOMAS SZASZ, *The Second Sin*

> I celebrate myself, and sing myself,
> And what I assume you shall assume,
> For every atom belonging to me as good
> > belongs to you.
> > —WALT WHITMAN, *Leaves of Grass*

> I have said that the soul is not more than the body,
> And I have said that the body is not more than the
> > soul,
> And nothing, not God, is greater to one than one's
> > self is.
> > —WALT WHITMAN, *Leaves of Grass*

Self-Condemnation

We confess our bad qualities to others out of fear of appearing naive or ridiculous by not being aware of them. —GERALD BRENAN, *Thoughts in a Dry Season*

All censure of a man's self is oblique praise. It is in order to show how much he can spare. It has all the invidiousness of self-praise, and all the reproach of falsehood. —SAMUEL JOHNSON, quoted in James Boswell's *The Life of Samuel Johnson*

Whoever despises himself still esteems the despiser within himself. —FRIEDRICH NIETZSCHE, *Beyond Good and Evil*

Too liberal self-accusations are generally but so many traps for acquittal with applause. —SAMUEL RICHARDSON, *Pamela*

Self-Confidence — See CONFIDENCE

Self-Control

He that is slow to anger is better than the mighty; and he that ruleth his spirit, than he that taketh a city. —BIBLE, *Proverbs* 16:32

> If you can keep your head when all about you
> Are losing theirs and blaming it on you;
> If you can trust yourself when all men doubt
>   you,
> But make allowance for their doubting too; . . .
> If you can meet with Triumph and Disaster
> And treat those two impostors just the same . . .
> Yours is the Earth and everything that's in it.
>   —RUDYARD KIPLING, "If—"

[See Jean Kerr's comment, under Crisis and Upheaval.]

He who conquers others is strong;
He who conquers himself is mighty.
—LAO-TZU, *The Way of Life*

He that would govern others, first should be
Master of himself.
—PHILIP MASSINGER, *The Bondman*

He is most powerful who has power over himself.
—SENECA, *Epistulae ad Lucilium*

Self-reverence, self-knowledge, self-control,
These three alone lead life to sovereign power.
—ALFRED, LORD TENNYSON, "Oenone"

Self-Deception — See SELF-KNOWLEDGE AND SELF-DECEPTION

Self-Improvement

Every day, in every way, I am getting better and better. —ÉMILE COUÉ, widely promoted formula for self-healing by autosuggestion

There's only one corner of the universe you can be certain of improving, and that's your own self.
—ALDOUS HUXLEY, *Time Must Have a Stop*

At thirty man suspects himself a fool;
Knows it at forty, and reforms his plan;
At fifty chides his infamous delay,
Pushes his prudent purpose to resolve;
In all the magnanimity of thought
Resolves; and re-resolves; then dies the same.
—EDWARD YOUNG, *Night Thoughts on Life, Death, and Immortality*

Self-Interest

Self-interest is but the survival of the animal in us. Humanity only begins for man with self-surrender.
—HENRI-FRÉDÉRIC AMIEL, *Journal intime*

Men are not against you; they are merely for themselves. —GENE FOWLER, *Skyline*

The least pain in our little finger gives us more concern and uneasiness than the destruction of millions of our fellow beings. —WILLIAM HAZLITT, "American Literature—Dr. Channing"

Self-interest speaks all sorts of tongues, and plays all sorts of roles, even that of disinterestedness. —LA ROCHEFOUCAULD, *Maxims*

Even wisdom has to yield to self-interest. —PINDAR, *Pythian Odes*

It is not from the benevolence of the butcher, the brewer, or the baker that we expect our dinner, but from their regard to their own interest. —ADAM SMITH, *The Wealth of Nations*

"That is well said," replied Candide, "but we must cultivate our garden." —VOLTAIRE, *Candide*

Self-Knowledge and Self-Deception

To know one's self is wisdom, but not to know one's neighbors is genius. —MINNA ANTRIM, *Naked Truth and Veiled Allusions*

> O wad some Pow'r the giftie gie us
> To see oursels as others see us!
> —ROBERT BURNS, "To a Louse"

Nothing is easier than self-deceit. For what each man wishes, that he also believes to be true.
—DEMOSTHENES, *Third Olynthiac*

He who knows others is learned;
He who knows himself is wise.
—LAO-TZU, *Tao-te Ching*

I have often wondered how it is that every man loves himself more than all the rest of men, but yet sets less value on his own opinion of himself than on the opinion of others. —MARCUS AURELIUS, *Meditations*

This 'Know Yourself' is a silly proverb in some
    ways;
To know the man next door is a much more
    useful rule.
—MENANDER (fragment)

["Know thyself" was inscribed on the temple of Apollo at Delphi.]

Know then thyself, presume not God to scan;
The proper study of mankind is man.
—ALEXANDER POPE, *An Essay on Man*

Nature never deceives us; it is always we who deceive ourselves. —JEAN-JACQUES ROUSSEAU, *Émile*

The unexamined life is not worth living. —SOCRATES, quoted in Plato's *Apology*

Only the shallow know themselves. —OSCAR WILDE, *Phrases and Philosophies for the Use of the Young*

Self-Love — See CONCEIT, EGOTISM, AND VANITY

Self-Reliance

The gods help them that help themselves. —AESOP, *Fables*

[This proverb appears, with slight variations, in the works of La Fontaine, George Herbert, Algernon Sidney, Benjamin Franklin, and others. See also Sophocles, in this section.]

No bird soars too high, if he soars with his own wings.
—WILLIAM BLAKE, *The Marriage of Heaven and Hell*

Every man is the architect of his own fortune. —
APPIUS CLAUDIUS CAECUS, quoted by Sallust,
"Speech to Caesar on the State"

Whoever then wishes to be free, let him neither wish
for anything nor avoid anything which depends on
others. If he does not observe this rule, he must be a
slave. —EPICTETUS, *Encheiridion*

If you'd have it done, Go: if not, Send. —BENJAMIN
FRANKLIN, *Poor Richard's Almanac*

Heaven never helps the men who will not act.
—SOPHOCLES (fragment)

Self-Respect — See PRIDE AND SELF-RESPECT

Self-Righteousness

He that is without sin among you, let him first cast a
stone at her. —BIBLE, *John* 8:7

> [Sometimes misquoted as "let him cast the first
> stone." This comes from the story of a woman
> caught in adultery, which is traditionally placed at
> the beginning of the eighth chapter of John, but
> which some 20th century translations omit alto-
> gether.]

Opposition may become sweet to a man when he has
christened it persecution. —GEORGE ELIOT, *Janet's
Repentance*

Human beings are perhaps never more frightening
than when they are convinced beyond doubt that
they are right. —LAURENS VAN DER POST, *The Lost
World of the Kalahari*

Moral indignation is jealousy with a halo. —H.G. WELLS, *The Wife of Sir Isaac Harman*

Self-Sacrifice

It is a far, far better thing that I do, than I have ever done; it is a far, far better rest that I go to, than I have ever known. —CHARLES DICKENS, *A Tale of Two Cities*

> [The thoughts of Sydney Carton as he awaits execution.]

Self-sacrifice is the real miracle out of which all the reported miracles grew. —RALPH WALDO EMERSON, *Society and Solitude*

How much easier is self-sacrifice than self-realization! —ERIC HOFFER, in *New York Times Magazine*

Whoever has really sacrificed anything, knows that he wanted and got something in return. —FRIEDRICH NIETZSCHE, *Beyond Good and Evil*

Self-sacrifice enables us to sacrifice other people without blushing. —GEORGE BERNARD SHAW, *Man and Superman*, "The Revolutionist's Handbook"

> Too long a sacrifice
> Can make a stone of the heart.
> —W.B. YEATS, "Easter 1916"

Selling — See BUYING AND SELLING

Sense — See WISDOM AND SENSE

The Senses

The ear tends to be lazy, craves the familiar, and is shocked by the unexpected: the eye, on the other hand, tends to be impatient, craves the novel and is bored by repetition. —W.H. AUDEN, *The Dyer's Hand*

The sanitary and mechanical age we are now entering makes up for the mercy it grants to our sense of smell by the ferocity with which it assails our sense of hearing. —HAVELOCK ELLIS, *Impressions and Comments*

Moral qualities rule the world, but at short distances, the senses are despotic. —RALPH WALDO EMERSON, *Essays*

Men trust their ears less than their eyes. —HERODOTUS, *Histories*

Nothing awakens a reminiscence like an odor.
—VICTOR HUGO, *Les Misérables*

. . . people earnestly seeking what they do not want, while they neglect the real blessings in their possession, I mean the innocent gratification of their senses, which is all we can properly call our own.
—LADY MARY WORTLEY MONTAGU, letter (1761)

Sex

Is sex dirty? Only if it's done right. —WOODY ALLEN, *Everything You Always Wanted to Know about Sex* (film)

Give me chastity and continence—but not yet.
—SAINT AUGUSTINE, *Confessions*

Sex-appeal is the keynote of our whole civilization.
—HENRI BERGSON, *The Two Sources of Morality and Religion*

> Licence my roving hands, and let them go,
> Before, behind, between, above, below.
> O my America! my new-found-land.
> > —JOHN DONNE, "To his Mistress
> > going to Bed"

But did thee feel the earth move? —ERNEST HEMING-
WAY, *For Whom the Bell Tolls*

"Bed," as the Italian proverb succinctly puts it, "is
the poor man's opera." —ALDOUS HUXLEY, *Heaven
and Hell*

. . . and his heart was going like mad and yes I said
yes I will Yes. —JAMES JOYCE, *Ulysses*

There is nothing like desire for preventing the thing
one says from bearing any resemblance to what one
has in one's mind. —MARCEL PROUST, *Remembrance of Things Past: The Guermantes Way*

Is it not strange that desire should so many years
outlive performance? —SHAKESPEARE, *Henry IV,
Part II*

Shame

Shame is Pride's cloak. —WILLIAM BLAKE, *The Marriage of Heaven and Hell*

Whilst shame keeps its watch, virtue is not wholly
extinguished in the heart. —EDMUND BURKE,
Reflections on the Revolution in France

We are ashamed of everything that is real about us;
ashamed of ourselves, of our relatives, of our
incomes, of our accents, of our opinions, of our experience, just as we are ashamed of our naked skins.
—GEORGE BERNARD SHAW, *Man and Superman*

The more things a man is ashamed of, the more
respectable he is. —GEORGE BERNARD SHAW, *Man
and Superman*

I never wonder to see men wicked, but I often wonder
to see them not ashamed. —JONATHAN SWIFT,
Thoughts on Various Subjects

Man is the only animal that blushes. Or needs to.
—MARK TWAIN, *Following the Equator*, "Pudd'nhead Wilson's New Calendar"

Ships and Sailing

No man will be a sailor who has contrivance enough to get himself into a jail; for being in a ship is being in a jail, with the chance of being drowned. —SAMUEL JOHNSON, quoted in James Boswell's *The Life of Samuel Johnson*

> [Robert Burton had made the same comparison in *The Anatomy of Melancholy*: "What is a ship but a prison?"]

Don't give up the ship! —CAPT. JAMES LAWRENCE, attributed

> [Lawrence is said to have uttered these words after being fatally wounded during a battle with a British ship in 1813. These words have also been attributed to Captain James Mugford, who was mortally wounded in a battle with the British in 1776. Oliver Hazard Perry had the words inscribed on a flag that he flew on his ship during the battle of Lake Erie in 1813.]

Sickness — See ILLNESS

Silence

Even a fool, when he holdeth his peace, is counted wise. —BIBLE, *Proverbs* 17:28

> [A very similar idea is found in the *Maxims* of Publilius Syrus: "Let a fool hold his tongue and he will pass for a sage."]

There is no such thing as an empty space or an empty time. There is always something to see, something to hear. In fact, try as we may to make a silence, we cannot. —JOHN CAGE, *Silence*

Speech is of Time, Silence is of Eternity. —THOMAS CARLYLE, *Sartor Resartus*

Blessed is the man who, having nothing to say, abstains from giving us wordy evidence of the fact. —GEORGE ELIOT, *Impressions of Theophrastus Such*

> The deepest feeling always shows itself in
> silence;
> not in silence, but restraint.
> —MARIANNE MOORE, "Silence"

I often regret that I have spoken; never that I have been silent. —PUBLILIUS SYRUS, *Maxims*

The world would be happier if men had the same capacity to be silent that they have to speak. —BENEDICT DE SPINOZA, *Ethics*

Silence may be as variously shaded as speech. —EDITH WHARTON, *The Reef*

What can be said at all can be said clearly; and whereof one cannot speak thereof one must be silent. —LUDWIG WITTGENSTEIN, *Tractatus Logico-Philosophicus*

Simplicity

Less is more. —ROBERT BROWNING, "Andrea del Sarto"

> [A favorite saying of the architect Ludwig Mies van der Rohe. The architect Robert Venturi's comment: "Less is a bore."—quoted in *Time*]

> Far from the madding crowd's ignoble strife,
> Their sober wishes never learned to stray;
> Along the cool, sequestered vale of life
> They kept the noiseless tenor of their way.
> —THOMAS GRAY, "Elegy Written in a
> Country Churchyard"

Teach us Delight in simple things,
And Mirth that has no bitter springs.
　　　　　　　—RUDYARD KIPLING, "The
　　　　　　　　　　　　Children's Song"

Manifest plainness,
Embrace simplicity,
Reduce selfishness,
Have few desires.
　　　　　　—LAO-TZU, *The Way of Life*

Our life is frittered away by detail. . . . Simplify, simplify. —HENRY DAVID THOREAU, *Walden*

The guiding motto in the life of every natural philosopher should be, Seek simplicity and distrust it.
—ALFRED NORTH WHITEHEAD, *The Concept of Nature*

Sin — See VICE AND SIN; See also EVIL

Sincerity — See CANDOR AND SINCERITY

Skepticism — See DOUBT AND SKEPTICISM

Skill — See ABILITY

Sky and Space

That's one small step for a man, and one giant leap for mankind. —NEIL ARMSTRONG, statement, on being the first person to set foot on the moon (1969)

> [The message was originally heard without the word "a" before "man," and was reported that way. Armstrong later made the correction.]

The heavens declare the glory of God; and the firmament sheweth his handy work. —BIBLE, *Psalms* 19:1

And that inverted Bowl they call the Sky,
Whereunder crawling coop'd we live and die,
    Lift not your hands to *It* for help—for it
As impotently moves as you or I.
        —EDWARD FITZGERALD, *The Rubáiyát of*
                Omar Khayyám

The moon is nothing
But a circumambulating aphrodisiac
Divinely subsidized to provoke the world
Into a rising birth-rate.
        —CHRISTOPHER FRY, *The Lady's Not for*
                Burning

Space isn't remote at all. It's only an hour's drive
away if your car could go straight upwards. —FRED
HOYLE, quoted in *The Observer*

Silently one by one, in the infinite meadows of
    heaven,
Blossomed the lovely stars, the forget-me-nots
    of the angels.
        —HENRY WADSWORTH LONGFELLOW,
                Evangeline

The moon was a ghostly galleon tossed upon cloudy
seas. —ALFRED NOYES, "The Highwayman"

                Heaven's ebon vault,
Studded with stars unutterably bright,
Through which the moon's unclouded
        grandeur rolls,
Seems like a canopy which love has spread
To curtain her sleeping world.
        —PERCY BYSSHE SHELLEY, "Queen Mab"

The unquiet republic of the maze
Of planets, struggling fierce towards heaven's
    free wilderness.
        —PERCY BYSSHE SHELLEY, *Prometheus*
                Unbound

With how sad steps, O Moon, thou climb'st the
    skies!
How silently, and with how wan a face!
        —PHILIP SIDNEY, *Astrophel and Stella*

My heart leaps up when I behold
  A rainbow in the sky:
So was it when my life began;
So is it now I am a man:
So be it when I shall grow old,
  Or let me die!
        —WILLIAM WORDSWORTH, "My Heart
                        Leaps Up"

Sleep

Death, so called, is a thing which makes men
    weep,
And yet a third of life is passed in sleep.
        —LORD BYRON, *Don Juan*

Laugh and the world laughs with you, snore and you
sleep alone. —MRS. PATRICK CAMPBELL, letter (to
George Bernard Shaw, 1912)

[See Ella Wheeler Wilcox, under Sorrow.]

Blessings on him who invented sleep, the cloak that
covers all human thoughts, the food that satisfies
hunger, the drink that quenches thirst, the fire that
warms cold, the cold that moderates heat, and,
lastly, the common currency that buys all things, the
balance and weight that equalizes the shepherd and
the king, the simpleton and the sage. —MIGUEL DE
CERVANTES, *Don Quixote de la Mancha*

Oh sleep! it is a gentle thing,
Beloved from pole to pole.
        —SAMUEL TAYLOR COLERIDGE, *The Rime*
                of the Ancient Mariner

. . . that provisional tomb where the living exile sighs, weeps, fights and succumbs, and is born again, remembering nothing, with the day. —COLETTE, *The Cat*

The pillow is a silent Sibyl, and it is better to sleep on things beforehand than lie awake about them afterwards. —BALTASAR GRACIÁN, *The Art of Worldly Wisdom*

There she encountered Sleep, the brother of Death. —HOMER, *The Iliad*

> [The comparison of sleep to death has been made by many writers. Thomas Browne wrote in *Religio Medici*: "We term sleep a death . . . by which we may be literally said to die daily; in fine, so like death, I dare not trust it without my prayers."]

One must have all the virtues to sleep well. Shall I bear false witness? Shall I commit adultery? Shall I covet my neighbor's maid? All that would go ill with good sleep. —FRIEDRICH NIETZSCHE, *Thus Spake Zarathustra*

He sleeps well who knows not that he sleeps ill. —PUBLILIUS SYRUS, *Maxims*

> Methought I heard a voice cry "Sleep no more!
> Macbeth does murder sleep," the innocent
>   sleep,
> Sleep that knits up the ravell'd sleave of care,
> The death of each day's life, sore labor's bath,
> Balm of hurt minds, great nature's second
>   course,
> Chief nourisher in life's feast.
>   —SHAKESPEARE, *Macbeth*

Small — See GREAT AND SMALL

Smiles — See LAUGHTER AND SMILES

Smoking

The believing we do something when we do nothing is the first illusion of tobacco. —RALPH WALDO EMERSON, *Journals*

A custom loathsome to the eye, hateful to the nose, harmful to the brain, dangerous to the lungs, and in the black, stinking fume thereof, nearest resembling the horrible Stygian smoke of the pit that is bottomless. —JAMES I, *A Counterblaste to Tobacco*

A woman is only a woman, but a good cigar is a smoke. —RUDYARD KIPLING, "The Betrothed"

> For thy sake, Tobacco, I
> Would do any thing but die.
> —CHARLES LAMB, *A Farewell to Tobacco*

Snobbery

The true snob never rests; there is always a higher goal to attain, and there are, by the same token, always more and more people to look down upon. —RUSSELL LYNES, in *Harper's*

I sent the club a wire stating, PLEASE ACCEPT MY RESIGNATION. I DON'T WANT TO BELONG TO ANY CLUB THAT WILL ACCEPT ME AS A MEMBER. —GROUCHO MARX, *Groucho and Me*

> He'd have the best, and that was none too good;
>   No barrier could hold, before his terms.
> He lies below, correct in cypress wood,
>   And entertains the most exclusive worms.
>   —DOROTHY PARKER, "Tombstones in the
>   Starlight" (The Very Rich Man)

His hatred of snobs was a derivative of his snobbishness, but made the simpletons (in other words, everyone) believe that he was immune from snobbishness. —MARCEL PROUST, *Remembrance of Things Past: The Guermantes Way*

Laughter would be bereaved if snobbery died.
—PETER USTINOV, quoted in *The Observer*

Snow — See WEATHER

Socialism — See COMMUNISM AND SOCIALISM

Society — See also COMPANIONSHIP

He who is unable to live in society, or who has no need because he is sufficient for himself, must be either a beast or a god. —ARISTOTLE, *Politics*

Men was formed for society, and is neither capable of living alone, nor has the courage to do it. —WILLIAM BLACKSTONE, *Commentaries on the Laws of England*

Society is a masked ball, where every one hides his real character, and reveals it in hiding. —RALPH WALDO EMERSON, *The Conduct of Life*

Men would not live long in society were they not the dupes of one another. —LA ROCHEFOUCAULD, *Maxims*

Human society *is* always, whether it will or no, aristocratic by its very essence, to the extreme that it is a society in the measure that it is aristocratic, and ceases to be such when it ceases to be aristocratic.
—JOSÉ ORTEGA Y GASSET, *The Revolt of the Masses*

Go very light on the vices, such as carrying on in society. The social ramble ain't restful. —SATCHEL PAIGE, "Formula for Staying Young"
[See also Paige, under Age and Aging.]

Man is a social animal. —SENECA, *De Beneficiis*

Society is no comfort
To one not sociable.
—SHAKESPEARE, *Cymbeline*

GERALD: I suppose society is wonderfully delight-ful!

LORD ILLINGWORTH: To be in it is merely a bore. But to be out of it simply a tragedy.
> —OSCAR WILDE, *A Woman of No Importance*

Soldiers — See MILITARY

Solitude and Loneliness

> Alone, alone, all all alone,
> Alone on a wide wide sea!
> And never a saint took pity on
> My soul in agony.
> > —SAMUEL TAYLOR COLERIDGE, *The Rime of the Ancient Mariner*

There are days when solitude is a heady wine that intoxicates you with freedom, others when it is a bitter tonic, and still others when it is a poison that makes you beat your head against the wall.
—COLETTE, *Earthly Paradise*

We live, as we dream—alone. —JOSEPH CONRAD, *Heart of Darkness*

> I have been one acquainted with the night.
> I have walked out in rain—and back in rain.
> I have outwalked the furthest city light.
> > —ROBERT FROST, "Acquainted with the Night"

I want to be alone. —GRETA GARBO, in the film *Grand Hotel*

> Full many a flower is born to blush unseen,
> And waste its sweetness on the desert air.
> > —THOMAS GRAY, "Elegy Written in a Country Churchyard"

Solitude is as needful to the imagination as society is wholesome for the character. —JAMES RUSSELL LOWELL, *Among My Books*

Solitude gives birth to the original in us, to beauty unfamiliar and perilous—to poetry. But also, it gives birth to the opposite: to the perverse, the illicit, the absurd. —THOMAS MANN, *Death in Venice*

It is good to be solitary, for solitude is difficult; that something is difficult must be a reason the more for us to do it. —RAINER MARIA RILKE, *Letters to a Young Poet*

Solitude vivifies; isolation kills. —JOSEPH ROUX, *Meditations of a Parish Priest*

One can acquire everything in solitude, except character. —STENDHAL, *On Love*

I never found the companion that was so companionable as solitude. —HENRY DAVID THOREAU, *Walden*

Loneliness is the ultimate poverty. —ABIGAIL VAN BUREN, "Dear Abby" column

We're all of us sentenced to solitary confinement inside our own skins, for life! —TENNESSEE WILLIAMS, *Orpheus Descending*

Loneliness . . . is and always has been the central and inevitable experience of every man. —THOMAS WOLFE, *You Can't Go Home Again*

Sorrow

> I tell you, hopeless grief is passionless;
> That only men incredulous of despair,
> Half-taught in anguish, through the midnight
>   air
> Beat upward to God's throne in loud access
> Of shrieking and reproach.
>   —ELIZABETH BARRETT BROWNING, "Grief"

Sorrow never comes too late. —THOMAS GRAY, "Ode on a Distant Prospect of Eton College"

> Into each life some rain must fall,
> Some days must be dark and dreary.
> > —HENRY WADSWORTH LONGFELLOW, "The
> > Rainy Day"

Sorrow is tranquillity remembered in emotion. —DOROTHY PARKER, "Sentiment"

> [This is a switch on Wordsworth's definition of poetry; see William Wordsworth, under Poetry and Poets. For another variation, see James Thurber, under Humor and Wit.]

Happiness is beneficial for the body but it is grief that develops the powers of the mind. —MARCEL PROUST, *Remembrance of Things Past: The Past Recaptured*

> When sorrows come, they come not single
> > spies,
> But in battalions.
> > —SHAKESPEARE, *Hamlet*

> We look before and after,
>   And pine for what is not;
> Our sincerest laughter
>   With some pain is fraught;
> Our sweetest songs are those that tell of
>   saddest thought.
> > —PERCY BYSSHE SHELLEY, "To a Skylark"

> Laugh and the world laughs with you;
>   Weep, and you weep alone;
> For the sad old earth must borrow its mirth,
>   But has trouble enough of its own.
> > —ELLA WHEELER WILCOX, "Solitude"

The Soul

For what is a man profited, if he shall gain the whole world, and lose his own soul? —BIBLE, *Matthew* 16:26

Build thee more stately mansions, O my soul,
As the swift seasons roll!
Leave thy low-vaulted past!
      —OLIVER WENDELL HOLMES, SR., "The
            Chambered Nautilus"

Life is real! Life is earnest!
And the grave is not its goal;
Dust thou art, to dust returnest,
Was not spoken of the soul.
      —HENRY WADSWORTH LONGFELLOW, "A
            Psalm of Life"

Most people sell their souls and live with a good conscience on the proceeds. —LOGAN PEARSALL SMITH, *Afterthoughts*

An aged man is but a paltry thing,
A tattered coat upon a stick, unless
Soul clap its hands and sing, and louder sing
For every tatter in its mortal dress.
      —W.B. YEATS, "Sailing to Byzantium"

Space — See SKY AND SPACE; See also TECHNOLOGY

Speech and Speakers

Speech is too often not . . . the art of concealing Thought; but of quite stifling and suspending Thought. —THOMAS CARLYLE, *Sartor Resartus*

"Then you should say what you mean," the March Hare went on.
"I do," Alice hastily replied; "at least—at least I mean what I say—that's the same thing, you know."
"Not the same thing a bit!" said the Hatter. "Why, you might just as well say that 'I see what I eat' is the same thing as 'I eat what I see'!"
      —LEWIS CARROLL, *Alice's Adventures in*
            Wonderland

I have never accepted what many people have kindly said—namely, that I inspired the nation. . . . It was the nation and the race dwelling all round the globe that had the lion's heart. I had the luck to be called upon to give the roar. —WINSTON CHURCHILL, speech (marking his 80th birthday, 1954)

A word is dead
When it is said,
Some say.
I say it just
Begins to live
That day.
        —EMILY DICKINSON, "A word is dead"

The true use of speech is not so much to express our wants as to conceal them. —OLIVER GOLDSMITH, *The Bee*

People do not seem to talk for the sake of expressing their opinions, but to maintain an opinion for the sake of talking. —WILLIAM HAZLITT, *Table Talk*

The tongue of man is a twisty thing, there are plenty of words there of every kind. —HOMER, *The Iliad*

The word once spoken flies beyond recall. —HORACE, *Epistles*

A sharp tongue is the only edge tool that grows keener with constant use. —WASHINGTON IRVING, "Rip Van Winkle"

Speech is civilization itself. The word, even the most contradictious word, preserves contact—it is silence which isolates. —THOMAS MANN, *The Magic Mountain*

Good Heavens! For more than forty years I have been speaking prose without knowing it. —MOLIÈRE, *Le Bourgeois gentilhomme*

What orators lack in depth they make up to you in length. —BARON DE MONTESQUIEU, *Letters*

Speech is a mirror of the soul: as a man speaks, so is he. —PUBLILIUS SYRUS, *Maxims*

Spirit — See COURAGE; THE SOUL; THE SUPERNATURAL

Sports

It's just a job. Grass grows, birds fly, waves pound the sand. I beat people up. —MUHAMMAD ALI, quoted in *New York Times*

In America, it is sport that is the opiate of the masses. —RUSSELL BAKER, in *New York Times*

[See Karl Marx, under Religion.]

Whoever wants to know the heart and mind of America had better learn baseball, the rules and realities of the game—and do it by watching first some high-school or small-town teams. —JACQUES BARZUN, *God's Country and Mine*

Sports do not build character. They reveal it. —HAYWOOD HALE BROUN, quoted in James A. Michener's *Sports in America*

Nice guys finish last. —LEO DUROCHER, attributed

[There is some disagreement as to whether Durocher said precisely this. He did, however, use it as the title of his 1975 autobiography.]

Pro football is like nuclear warfare. There are no winners, only survivors. —FRANK GIFFORD, quoted in *Sports Illustrated*

He can run, but he can't hide. —JOE LOUIS, quoted in *New York Herald Tribune*

[Louis was commenting on his upcoming fight with Billy Conn.]

Many Continentals think life is a game; the English think cricket is a game. —GEORGE MIKES, *How to be an Alien*

Serious sport has nothing to do with fair play. It is bound up with hatred, jealousy, boastfulness, disregard of all rules and sadistic pleasure in witnessing violence. In other words, it is war minus the shooting. —GEORGE ORWELL, *Shooting an Elephant*

> Oh, somewhere in this favored land the sun is
>   shining bright;
> The band is playing somewhere, and
>   somewhere hearts are light,
> And somewhere men are laughing, and little
>   children shout;
> But there is no joy in Mudville—mighty Casey
>   has struck out.
>   —ERNEST L. THAYER, "Casey at Bat"

The English country gentleman galloping after a fox—the unspeakable in full pursuit of the uneatable. —OSCAR WILDE, *A Woman of No Importance*

Spring — See SEASONS

Statistics

Statistics are like alienists—they will testify for either side. —FIORELLO H. LA GUARDIA, in *Liberty*

He uses statistics as a drunken man uses lampposts—for support rather than illumination. —ANDREW LANG, attributed

There are two kinds of statistics, the kind you look up and the kind you make up. —REX STOUT, *Death of a Doxy*

Every moment dies a man,
   Every moment one is born.
       —ALFRED, LORD TENNYSON, "The
            Vision of Sin"

[The mathematician Charles Babbage offered an
emendation in a letter to Tennyson:
   Every moment dies a man,
   Every moment 1$\frac{1}{16}$ is born."]

. . . the remark attributed to Disraeli . . . : "There are
three kinds of lies: lies, damned lies, and statistics."
—MARK TWAIN, *Autobiography*

[This remark has been attributed to others as well.]

Stealing — See CRIME

Strength

It is as easy for the strong man to be strong, as it is
for the weak to be weak. —RALPH WALDO EMERSON,
Essays, "Self-Reliance"

Beyond his strength no man can fight, although he
be eager. —HOMER, *The Iliad*

It is excellent
To have a giant's strength; but it is tyrannous
To use it like a giant.
      —SHAKESPEARE, *Measure for Measure*

The gods are on the side of the stronger. —TACITUS,
Histories

My strength is as the strength of ten,
   Because my heart is pure.
      —ALFRED, LORD TENNYSON, "Sir Galahad"

Study — See EDUCATION; KNOWLEDGE AND LEARNING

Stupidity — See IGNORANCE AND STUPIDITY; See also FOOLS AND FOOLISHNESS

Style

The style is the man himself. —COMTE DE BUFFON, *Discours sur le style*

Take care of the sense, and the sounds will take care of themselves. —LEWIS CARROLL, *Alice's Adventures in Wonderland*

> [See Lord Chesterfield, under Thrift, for the statement this was based on.]

After all, it is STYLE alone by which posterity will judge of a great work, for an author can have nothing truly his own but his style. —ISAAC D'ISRAELI, *Literary Miscellanies*

Self-plagiarism is style. —ALFRED HITCHCOCK, quoted in *The Observer*

Unless one is a genius, it is best to aim at being intelligible. —ANTHONY HOPE, *The Dolly Dialogues*

An old tutor of a college said to one of his pupils: "Read over your compositions, and wherever you meet with a passage which you think is particularly fine, strike it out." —SAMUEL JOHNSON, quoted in James Boswell's *The Life of Samuel Johnson*

When we see a natural style, we are quite surprised and delighted, for we expected to see an author and we find a man. —BLAISE PASCAL, *Pensées*

Proper words in proper places, make the true definition of a style. —JONATHAN SWIFT, letter (1720)

Style is the dress of thought; a modest dress,
Neat, but not gaudy, will true critics please.
—SAMUEL WESLEY, "An Epistle to a
Friend Concerning Poetry"

[Lord Chesterfield wrote in a letter in 1749: "Style is the dress of thoughts." See also Samuel Johnson, under Language, for a similar idea.]

Success and Failure — See also VICTORY AND DEFEAT

'Tis not in mortals to command success,
But we'll do more, Sempronius; we'll deserve it.
—JOSEPH ADDISON, *Cato*

The toughest thing about success is that you've got to keep on being a success. —IRVING BERLIN, quoted in *Theatre Arts*

All men that are ruined, are ruined on the side of their natural propensities. —EDMUND BURKE, *Letters on a Regicide Peace*

Success is counted sweetest
By those who ne'er succeed.
—EMILY DICKINSON, "Success is counted
sweetest"

Nothing succeeds like success. —ALEXANDRE DUMAS, PÈRE, *Ange Pitou*

[A French proverb. See under Excess for Oscar Wilde's version.]

Success is relative:
It is what we can make of the mess we have
made of things.
—T.S. ELIOT, *Family Reunion*

Along with success comes a reputation for wisdom.
—EURIPIDES, *Hippolytus*

Half the failures in life arise from pulling in one's horse as he is leaping. —JULIUS C. HARE AND AUGUSTUS HARE, *Guesses at Truth*

> There's dignity in suffering—
> Nobility in pain—
> But failure is a salted wound
> That burns and burns again.
> —MARGERY ELDREDGE HOWELL,
> "Wormwood"

A failure is a man who has blundered, but is not able to cash in the experience. —ELBERT HUBBARD, *Roycroft Dictionary and Book of Epigrams*

There is the greatest practical benefit in making a few failures early in life. —THOMAS HENRY HUXLEY, *Critiques and Addresses*

. . . the moral flabbiness born of the exclusive worship of the bitch-goddess *Success*. That—with the squalid cash interpretation put on the word success—is our national disease. —WILLIAM JAMES, letter (to H.G. Wells, 1906)

There are only two ways of getting on in the world—either by one's own industry, or by the stupidity of others. —LA BRUYÈRE, *Les Caractères*

I have always observed that to succeed in the world one should seem a fool, but be wise. —BARON DE MONTESQUIEU, *Pensées diverses*

The success of most things depends upon knowing how long it will take to succeed. —BARON DE MONTESQUIEU, *Pensées diverses*

There is only one success—to be able to spend your life in your own way. —CHRISTOPHER MORLEY, *Where the Blue Begins*

Success has always been the worst of liars. —FRIEDRICH NIETZSCHE, *Beyond Good and Evil*

Sadness usually results from one of the following causes—either when a man does not succeed, or is ashamed of his success. —SENECA, *De Tranquillitate Animi*

I cannot give you the formula for success, but I can give you the formula for failure—which is: Try to please everybody. —HERBERT BAYARD SWOPE, speech (1950)

Suffering — See PAIN AND SUFFERING

Suicide

There is but one truly serious philosophical problem, and that is suicide. Judging whether life is or is not worth living amounts to answering the fundamental question of philosophy. —ALBERT CAMUS, *The Myth of Sisyphus*

There are many who dare not kill themselves for fear of what the neighbors will say. —CYRIL CONNOLLY, *The Unquiet Grave*

A suicide kills two people, Maggie, that's what it's for! —ARTHUR MILLER, *After the Fall*

The thought of suicide is a great consolation; one can get through many a bad night with it. —FRIEDRICH NIETZSCHE, *Beyond Good and Evil*

> Razors pain you;
> Rivers are damp;
> Acids stain you;
> And drugs cause cramp.
> Guns aren't lawful;
> Nooses give;
> Gas smells awful;
> You might as well live.
>   —DOROTHY PARKER, "Résumé"

We cannot tear out a single page of our life, but we can throw the whole book in the fire. —GEORGE SAND, *Mauprat*

To be, or not to be: that is the question:
Whether 'tis nobler in the mind to suffer
The slings and arrows of outrageous fortune,
Or to take arms against a sea of troubles,
And by opposing end them?
                            —SHAKESPEARE, *Hamlet*

Summer — See SEASONS

The Supernatural

When the first baby laughed for the first time, the laugh broke into a thousand pieces and they all went skipping about, and that was the beginning of fairies. —JAMES M. BARRIE, *Peter Pan*

Religion
Has made an honest woman of the
        supernatural.
            —CHRISTOPHER FRY, *The Lady's Not for
                                        Burning*

Millions of spiritual Creatures walk the Earth
Unseen, both when we wake, and when we
        sleep.
            —JOHN MILTON, *Paradise Lost*

There are more things in heaven and earth,
        Horatio,
Than are dreamt of in your philosophy.
                    —SHAKESPEARE, *Hamlet*

Ah, yes, superstition: it would appear to be cowardice in face of the supernatural. —THEOPHRASTUS, *The Characters*

Sympathy and Pity — See also MERCY AND COMPASSION

One cannot weep for the entire world. It is beyond human strength. One must choose. —JEAN ANOUILH, *Cécile*

Everybody in the world ought to be sorry for everybody else. We all have our little private hell. —BETTINA VON HUTTEN, *The Halo*

> No one is so accursed by fate,
> No one so utterly desolate
>   But some heart, though unknown,
>   Responds unto his own.
>   —HENRY WADSWORTH LONGFELLOW,
>   "Endymion"

> there is always
> a comforting thought
> in time of trouble when
> it is not our trouble.
>   —DON MARQUIS, *archy does his part*

To be unhappy is only half the misfortune—to be pitied—is misery complete. —ARTHUR SCHNITZLER, *Anatol: Questioning Fate*

Only when the sense of the pain of others begins—does man begin. —YEVGENY YEVTUSHENKO, quoted in *Quote* magazine

Tact — See DIPLOMACY; MANNERS

Talent — See GENIUS AND TALENT

Talking — See CONVERSATION

Taste

Good taste is better than bad taste, but bad taste is better than no taste. —ARNOLD BENNETT, in *Evening Standard*

Bad taste is simply saying the truth before it should be said. —MEL BROOKS, quoted in John Robert Colombo's *Popcorn in Paradise*

What is food to one, is to others bitter poison.
—LUCRETIUS, *De Rerum Natura*
[This is an early version of the proverb "One man's meat is another's poison."]

The kind of people who always go on about whether a thing is in good taste invariably have very bad taste. —JOE ORTON, quoted in *Behind the Scenes*

Taste . . . is the only morality. . . . Tell me what you like, and I'll tell you what you are. —JOHN RUSKIN, *The Crown of Wild Olive*

The play, I remember, pleased not the million; 'twas caviar to the general. —SHAKESPEARE, *Hamlet*

Do not do unto others as you would that they should do unto you. Their tastes may not be the same.
—GEORGE BERNARD SHAW, *Man and Superman*, "The Revolutionist's Handbook"

Every great and original writer, in proportion as he is great and original, must himself create the taste by which he is to be relished. —WILLIAM WORDSWORTH, letter (1807)

Taxes

To tax and to please, no more than to love and to be wise, is not given to men. —EDMUND BURKE, speech (1774)

The art of taxation consists in so plucking the goose as to obtain the largest possible amount of feathers with the smallest possible amount of hissing. —JEAN BAPTISTE COLBERT, attributed
[Colbert was Minister of Finance under Louis XIV.]

Of all debts men are least willing to pay the taxes. What a satire is this on government! Everywhere they think they get their money's worth, except for these.
—RALPH WALDO EMERSON, *Essays*

Taxes are what we pay for civilized society. —OLIVER WENDELL HOLMES, JR., judicial opinion (1904)

Taxation without representation is tyranny.
—JAMES OTIS, attributed

The Income Tax has made more Liars out of the American people than Golf has. —WILL ROGERS, *Illiterate Digest*

Teachers and Teaching — See also EDUCATION

A teacher affects eternity; he can never tell where his influence stops. —HENRY ADAMS, *The Education of Henry Adams*

And gladly would he learn, and gladly teach.
—CHAUCER, *The Canterbury Tales*

Who dares to teach must never cease to learn.
—JOHN COTTON DANA, motto composed for Kean College, New Jersey

The whole art of teaching is only the art of awakening the natural curiosity of young minds for the purpose of satisfying it afterwards. —ANATOLE FRANCE, *The Crime of Sylvestre Bonnard*

Men must be taught as if you taught them
    not,
And things proposed as things forgot.
                —ALEXANDER POPE, *An Essay on
                            Criticism*

He who can, does. He who cannot, teaches.
—GEORGE BERNARD SHAW, *Man and Superman*, "The Revolutionist's Handbook"

Technology — See also COMPUTERS; SCIENCE

Any sufficiently advanced technology is indistinguishable from magic. —ARTHUR C. CLARKE, *The Lost Worlds of 2001*

The first rule of intelligent tinkering is to save all the parts. —PAUL EHRLICH, in *Saturday Review*

   [Ehrlich credits this to Aldo Leopold, although the quotation is generally associated with Ehrlich.]

The machine unmakes the man. Now that the machine is so perfect, the engineer is nobody.
—RALPH WALDO EMERSON, *Society and Solitude*

Technology . . . the knack of so arranging the world that we need not experience it. —MAX FRISCH, *Homo Faber*

If there is technological advance without social advance, there is, almost automatically, an increase in human misery. —MICHAEL HARRINGTON, *The Other America*

One machine can do the work of fifty ordinary men. No machine can do the work of one extraordinary man. —ELBERT HUBBARD, in *The Philistine*

Electronic calculators can solve problems which the man who made them cannot solve; but no government-subsidized commission of engineers and physicists could create a worm. —JOSEPH WOOD KRUTCH, *The Twelve Seasons*

By his very success in inventing labor-saving devices modern man has manufactured an abyss of boredom that only the privileged classes in earlier civilizations have ever fathomed. —LEWIS MUMFORD, *The Conduct of Life*

One has to look out for engineers—they begin with sewing machines and end up with the atomic bomb. —MARCEL PAGNOL, *Critique des critiques*

Machines are worshipped because they are beautiful, and valued because they confer power; they are hated because they are hideous, and loathed because they impose slavery. —BERTRAND RUSSELL, *Sceptical Essays*

Technology . . . is a queer thing; it brings you great gifts with one hand, and it stabs you in the back with the other. —C.P. SNOW, quoted in *New York Times*

Teenagers — See ADOLESCENCE; YOUTH

Television and Radio

TV—a clever contraction derived from the words Terrible Vaudeville. . . . It is our latest medium—we call it a medium because nothing is well done. —GOODMAN ACE, letter (to Groucho Marx, 1953)

> [Ernie Kovacs has been credited with a similar comment on television: "A medium, so called because it is neither rare nor well done."]

Television is the first truly democratic culture—the first culture available to everyone and entirely governed by what the people want. The most terrifying thing is what people do want. —CLIVE BARNES, in *New York Times*

Some television programs are so much chewing gum for the eyes. —JOHN MASON BROWN, attributed

> [Sometimes attributed to Frank Lloyd Wright.]

It is a medium of entertainment which permits millions of people to listen to the same joke at the same time, and yet remain lonesome. —T.S. ELIOT, quoted in *New York Post*

There is no medical proof that television causes brain damage. . . . In fact, TV is probably the least physically harmful of all the narcotics known to man. — CHRISTOPHER LEHMANN-HAUPT, in *New York Times*

Television brought the brutality of war into the comfort of the living room. Vietnam was lost in the living rooms of America—not on the battlefields of Vietnam. —MARSHALL MCLUHAN, quoted in *Montreal Gazette*

When television is good, nothing . . . is better. But when television is bad, nothing is worse. I invite you to sit down in front of your television set when your station goes on the air . . . and keep your eyes glued to that set until the station signs off. I can assure you that you will observe a vast wasteland. —NEWTON MINOW, speech (1961)

I hate television. I hate it as much as peanuts. But I can't stop eating peanuts. —ORSON WELLES, in *New York Herald Tribune*

Temptation

Watch and pray, that ye enter not into temptation: the spirit indeed is willing, but the flesh is weak. —BIBLE, *Matthew* 26:41

There is not any memory with less satisfaction in it than the memory of some temptation we resisted. —JAMES BRANCH CABELL, *Jurgen*

No temptation can ever be measured by the value of its object. —COLETTE, *Earthly Paradise*

The best way to get the better of temptation is just to yield to it. —CLEMENTINA STIRLING GRAHAM, *Mystifications*

[An idea better known in the words of Oscar Wilde: "The only way to get rid of a temptation is to yield

411

to it. Resist it, and your soul grows sick with longing for the things it has forbidden to itself.—*The Picture of Dorian Gray.*]

"You oughtn't to yield to temptation."
"Well, somebody must, or the thing becomes absurd," said I.
—ANTHONY HOPE, *The Dolly Dialogues*

There are several good protections against temptations, but the surest is cowardice. —MARK TWAIN, *Following the Equator*, "Pudd'nhead Wilson's New Calendar"

Theater and Film, Actors and Acting

For an actress to be a success she must have the face of Venus, the brains of Minerva, the grace of Terpsichore, the memory of Macaulay, the figure of Juno, and the hide of a rhinoceros. —ETHEL BARRYMORE, quoted in George Jean Nathan's *The Theatre in the Fifties*

In the theater the audience wants to be surprised—but by things that they expect. —TRISTAN BERNARD, *Contes, repliques et bon mots*

An actor's a guy who, if you ain't talking about him, ain't listening. —MARLON BRANDO, quoted in *The Observer*

Photography is truth. The cinema is truth twenty-four times per second. —JEAN-LUC GODARD, *La Petit Soldat* (film)

Why should people go out and pay to see bad movies when they can stay at home and see bad television for nothing? —SAMUEL GOLDWYN, quoted in *The Observer*

The words "Kiss Kiss Bang Bang" which I saw on an Italian movie poster, are perhaps the briefest statement imaginable of the basic appeal of movies.
—PAULINE KAEL, *Kiss Kiss Bang Bang*

Movies are so rarely great art that if we cannot appreciate great *trash* we have very little reason to be interested in them. —PAULINE KAEL, quoted in John Robert Colombo's *Popcorn in Paradise*

The structure of a play is always the story of how the birds came home to roost. —ARTHUR MILLER, in *Harper's*

Acting is a masochistic form of exhibitionism. It is not quite the occupation of an adult. —LAURENCE OLIVIER, quoted in *Time*

Acting is merely the art of keeping a large group of people from coughing. —RALPH RICHARDSON, quoted in *Time*

A movie star is not an artist, he is an art object. —RICHARD SCHICKEL, quoted in John Robert Colombo's *Popcorn in Paradise*

The play's the thing
Wherein I'll catch the conscience of the king.
        —SHAKESPEARE, *Hamlet*

Speak the speech, I pray you, as I pronounced it to you, trippingly on the tongue: but if you mouth it, as many of your players do, I had as lief the town-crier spoke my lines. —SHAKESPEARE, *Hamlet*

The bad end unhappily, the good unluckily. That is what tragedy means. —TOM STOPPARD, *Rosencrantz and Guildenstern are Dead*

I wouldn't say when you've seen one Western you've seen the lot; but when you've seen the lot you get the feeling you've seen one. —KATHARINE WHITEHORN, *Sunday Best*

Theft — See CRIME

Thought

The people who say: "You are what you eat" have always seemed addled to me. In my opinion, you are what you think, and if you don't think, you can eat all the meat in Kansas City and still be nothing but a vegetable. —RUSSELL BAKER, *The Rescue of Miss Yaskell*

I think, therefore I am. (*Cogito, ergo sum.*) —RENÉ DESCARTES, *Discourse on Method*

What was once thought can never be unthought.
—FRIEDRICH DÜRRENMATT, *The Physicists*

If a man sits down to think, he is immediately asked if he has the headache. —RALPH WALDO EMERSON, *Journals*

A great many people think they are thinking when they are merely rearranging their prejudices.
—WILLIAM JAMES, attributed

The thoughts that come often unsought, and, as it were, drop into the mind, are commonly the most valuable of any we have. —JOHN LOCKE, letter (1699)

My thought is *me*: that's why I can't stop. I exist because I think. . . and I can't stop myself from thinking. —JEAN-PAUL SARTRE, *Nausea*

There is nothing either good or bad, but thinking makes it so. —SHAKESPEARE, *Hamlet*

Yond Cassius has a lean and hungry look;
He thinks too much: such men are dangerous.
—SHAKESPEARE, *Julius Caesar*

Man's great misfortune is that he has no organ, no kind of eyelid or brake, to mask or block a thought, or all thought, when he wants to. —PAUL VALÉRY, *Tel quel*

The grinding of the intellect is for most people as painful as a dentist's drill. —LEONARD WOOLF, quoted in *The Observer*

Thrift

I knew once a very covetous, sordid fellow, who used to say, "Take care of the pence, for the pounds will take care of themselves." —LORD CHESTERFIELD, *Letters to His Son*

> [The fellow was William Lowndes, a former secretary of the (British) treasury. The quote is sometimes given as ". . . and the pounds. . . ." See also Lewis Carroll's variation, under Style.]

Everybody is always in favor of general economy and particular expenditure. —ANTHONY EDEN, quoted in *The Observer*

Economy is going without something you do want in case you should, some day, want something you probably won't want. —ANTHONY HOPE, *The Dolly Dialogues*

People want economy and they will pay any price to get it. —LEE IACOCCA, quoted in *New York Times*

I would rather have my people laugh at my economies than weep for my extravagance. —OSCAR II OF SWEDEN, attributed

Let us all be happy, and live within our means, even if we have to borrer the money to do it with. —ARTE-MUS WARD, *Artemus Ward in London*

To recommend thrift to the poor is both grotesque and insulting. It is like advising a man who is starving to eat less. —OSCAR WILDE, *The Soul of Man under Socialism*

Time

Well, time wounds all heels. —JANE ACE, quoted by Goodman Ace in *The Fine Art of Hypochondria*

Time is a great teacher, but unfortunately it kills all its pupils. —HECTOR BERLIOZ, quoted in *Almanach des lettres françaises*

To every thing there is a season, and a time to every purpose under the heaven. —BIBLE, *Ecclesiastes* 3:1

Time ripens all things. No man is born wise.
—MIGUEL DE CERVANTES, *Don Quixote de la Mancha*

Take care of the minutes, for the hours will take care of themselves. —LORD CHESTERFIELD, *Letters to His Son*
[See also Lord Chesterfield, under Thrift.]

Time is a Test of Trouble—
But not a Remedy—
If such it prove, it prove too
There was no Malady—.
—EMILY DICKINSON, "They say that 'Time assuages' "

Time goes, you say? Ah no!
Alas, Time stays, *we* go.
—AUSTIN DOBSON, "The Paradox of Time"

Time present and time past
Are both perhaps present in time future,
And time future contained in time past.
    —T.S. ELIOT, *Four Quartets*:
       "Burnt Norton"

They [the days] come and go like muffled and veiled figures sent from a distant friendly party; but they say nothing, and if we do not use the gifts they bring, they carry them as silently away. —RALPH WALDO EMERSON, *Society and Solitude*

Time will reveal everything. It is a babbler, and speaks even when not asked. —EURIPIDES (fragment)

Dost thou love life? Then do not squander time; for that's the stuff life is made of. —BENJAMIN FRANKLIN, *Poor Richard's Almanac*

Remember that time is money. —BENJAMIN FRANKLIN, *Advice to a Young Tradesman*

Time is change; we measure its passing by how much things alter. —NADINE GORDIMER, *The Late Bourgeois World*

Time flies over us, but leaves its shadow behind.
 —NATHANIEL HAWTHORNE, *The Marble Faun*

Those who make the worst use of their time most complain of its shortness. —LA BRUYÈRE, *Les Caractères*

We kill time; time buries us. —JOAQUIM MARIA MACHADO DE ASSIS, *Epitaph for a Small Winner*

Time is a great legalizer, even in the field of morals.
—H.L. MENCKEN, *A Book of Prefaces*

Death and taxes and childbirth! There's never any convenient time for any of them. —MARGARET MITCHELL, *Gone with the Wind*

Time makes more converts than reason. —THOMAS PAINE, *Common Sense*

Time heals griefs and quarrels, for we change and are no longer the same persons. —BLAISE PASCAL, *Pensées*

Time is at once the most valuable and the most perishable of all our possessions. —JOHN RANDOLPH, quoted by William Cabell Bruce in *John Randolph of Roanoke*

> Ah! the clock is always slow;
> It is later than you think.
> —ROBERT W. SERVICE, "It Is Later Than
> You Think"

> Tomorrow, and tomorrow, and tomorrow,
> Creeps in this petty pace from day to day
> To the last syllable of recorded time,
> And all our yesterdays have lighted fools
> The way to dusty death.
> —SHAKESPEARE, *Macbeth*

> Come what come may
> Time and the hour runs through the roughest
> day.
> —SHAKESPEARE, *Macbeth*

> Time turns the old days to derision,
> Our loves into corpses or wives;
> And marriage and death and division
> Make barren our lives.
> —ALGERNON CHARLES SWINBURNE,
> "Dolores"

As if you could kill time without injuring eternity. —HENRY DAVID THOREAU, *Walden*

Time speeds away irretrievably. —VIRGIL, *Georgics*

> The bell strikes one. We take no note of time
> But from its loss.
> > —EDWARD YOUNG, *Night Thoughts on
> > Life, Death, and Immortality*

Times of Day

Weeping may endure for a night, but joy cometh in the morning. —BIBLE, *Psalms* 30:5

> The night has a thousand eyes,
>   And the day but one;
> Yet the light of the bright world dies,
> With the dying sun.
> > —FRANCIS WILLIAM BOURDILLON, "Light"

> > > The night
> Shows stars and women in a better light.
> > —LORD BYRON, *Don Juan*

> Awake! for Morning in the Bowl of Night
> Has flung the Stone that puts the Stars to
>   Flight:
> And Lo! the Hunter of the East has caught
> The Sultan's Turret in a Noose of Light.
> > —EDWARD FITZGERALD, *The Rubáiyát of
> > Omar Khayyám*

> And the night shall be filled with music,
>   And the cares that infest the day,
> Shall fold their tents, like the Arabs,
>   And as silently steal away.
> > —HENRY WADSWORTH LONGFELLOW, "The
> > Day Is Done"

Night hath a thousand eyes. —JOHN LYLY, *The Maides Metamorphosis*

[See also F. W. Bourdillon, in this section.]

Sweet is the breath of morn, her rising sweet,
With charm of earliest birds.
—JOHN MILTON, *Paradise Lost*

Three o'clock is always too late or too early for anything you want to do. —JEAN-PAUL SARTRE, *Nausea*

'Tis now the very witching time of night,
When churchyards yawn and hell itself
    breathes out
Contagion to this world.
—SHAKESPEARE, *Hamlet*

Come into the garden, Maud,
  For the black bat, night, has flown.
—ALFRED, LORD TENNYSON, *Maud*

For what human ill does not dawn seem to be an alleviation? —THORNTON WILDER, *The Bridge of San Luis Rey*

Tolerance

Toleration is good for all, or it is good for none.
—EDMUND BURKE, speech (1773)

More and more people care about religious tolerance as fewer and fewer care about religion. —ALEXANDER CHASE, *Perspectives*

It does me no injury for my neighbor to say there are twenty gods, or no God. —THOMAS JEFFERSON, *Notes on the State of Virginia*

It is easy to be tolerant when you do not care.
—CLEMENT F. ROGERS, *Verify Your References*

Though all society is founded on intolerance, all improvement is founded on tolerance. —GEORGE BERNARD SHAW, *Saint Joan*

So long as a man rides his HOBBY-HORSE peaceably and quietly along the King's highway, and neither compels you or me to get up behind him,—pray, Sir, what have either you or I to do with it? —LAURENCE STERNE, *Tristram Shandy*

Trade — See BUSINESS

Tradition — See CUSTOM AND TRADITION

Transience

Vanity of vanities, saith the Preacher, vanity of vanities; all is vanity.
What profit hath a man of all his labor which he taketh under the sun?
One generation passeth away, and another generation cometh: but the earth abideth for ever.
—BIBLE, *Ecclesiastes* 1:2–4

Loveliest of lovely things are they,
On earth, that soonest pass away.
—WILLIAM CULLEN BRYANT, "A Scene on
the Bank of the Hudson"

Oh threats of Hell and Hopes of Paradise!
One thing at least is certain—*This* Life flies;
One thing is certain and the rest is Lies;
The Flower that once has blown forever dies.
—EDWARD FITZGERALD, *The Rubáiyát of
Omar Khayyám*

Gather ye rosebuds while ye may,
Old Time is still a-flying,
And this same flower that smiles today
Tomorrow will be dying.
—ROBERT HERRICK, "To the Virgins to
Make Much of Time"

421

Art is long, and Time is fleeting,
  And our hearts, though stout and brave,
Still, like muffled drums, are beating
  Funeral marches to the grave.
         —HENRY WADSWORTH LONGFELLOW, "A
                    Psalm of Life"

Everything is only for a day, both that which remembers and that which is remembered. —MARCUS AURELIUS, *Meditations*

But at my back I always hear
Time's wingèd chariot hurrying near;
And yonder all before us lie
Deserts of vast eternity.
         —ANDREW MARVELL, "To His Coy
                    Mistress"

My candle burns at both ends;
  It will not last the night;
But ah, my foes, and oh, my friends—
  It gives a lovely light!
         —EDNA ST. VINCENT MILLAY, "First Fig"

Beauty is but a flower
Which wrinkles will devour;
Brightness falls from the air.
         —THOMAS NASHE, "In a Time of
                    Pestilence"

Travel

The time to enjoy a European trip is about three weeks after unpacking. —GEORGE ADE, *Forty Modern Fables*

Traveling is the ruin of all happiness. There's no looking at a building here, after seeing Italy. —FANNY BURNEY, *Cecilia*

Travel can be one of the most rewarding forms of introspection. —LAWRENCE DURRELL, *Bitter Lemons*

A man who has not been in Italy is always conscious of an inferiority. —SAMUEL JOHNSON, quoted in James Boswell's *The Life of Samuel Johnson*

Thanks to the interstate highway system, it is now possible to travel across the country from coast to coast without seeing anything. —CHARLES KURALT, *On the Road*

Travelers are always discoverers, especially those who travel by air. There are no signposts in the sky to show a man has passed that way before. There are no channels marked. The flier breaks each second into new uncharted seas. —ANNE MORROW LINDBERGH, *North to the Orient*

A man travels the world in search of what he needs and returns home to find it. —GEORGE MOORE, *The Brook Kerith*

For my part, I travel not to go anywhere, but to go. I travel for travel's sake. The great affair is to move.
 —ROBERT LOUIS STEVENSON, *Travels with a Donkey*

> I cannot rest from travel; I will drink
> Life to the lees.
> —ALFRED, LORD TENNYSON, "Ulysses"

Travel is glamorous only in retrospect. —PAUL THEROUX, quoted in *The Observer*

Extensive traveling induces a feeling of encapsulation; and travel, so broadening at first, contracts the mind. —PAUL THEROUX, *The Great Railway Bazaar*

Treason — See BETRAYAL

Trees — See FLOWERS AND TREES

Trifles — See GREAT AND SMALL

Troubles — See ADVERSITY; PROBLEMS

Trust

Thrust ivrybody—but cut th' ca-ards. —FINLEY
PETER DUNNE, *Mr. Dooley's Philosophy*

Trust men and they will be true to you; treat them
greatly and they will show themselves great.
—RALPH WALDO EMERSON, *Essays*

It is better to suffer wrong than to do it, and happier
to be sometimes cheated than not to trust. —SAMUEL
JOHNSON, *The Rambler*

It is more shameful to mistrust one's friends than to
be deceived by them. —LA ROCHEFOUCAULD, *Maxims*

In long experience I find that a man who trusts
nobody is apt to be the kind of man nobody trusts.
—HAROLD MACMILLAN, quoted in *New York Herald
Tribune*

> As contagion
> of sickness makes sickness,
>
> contagion of trust can make trust.
> —MARIANNE MOORE, "In Distrust of Merits"

Truth

The truth is often a terrible weapon of aggression. It
is possible to lie, and even to murder, for the truth.
—ALFRED ADLER, *Problems of Neurosis*

Ye shall know the truth, and the truth shall make you
free. —BIBLE, *John* 8:32

As scarce as truth is, the supply has always been in
excess of the demand. —JOSH BILLINGS, *Affurisms
from Josh Billings: His Sayings*

> A truth that's told with bad intent
> Beats all the lies you can invent.
> —WILLIAM BLAKE, "Auguries of
> Innocence"

Truth exists, only falsehood has to be invented.
—GEORGES BRAQUE, *Pensées sur l'art*

> 'T is strange,—but true; for Truth is always
>   strange—
> Stranger than fiction: if it could be told,
> How much would novels gain by the exchange!
> —LORD BYRON, *Don Juan*

In wartime, truth is so precious that she should always be attended by a bodyguard of lies. —WINSTON CHURCHILL, quoted in *Time*

When you have eliminated the impossible, whatever remains, *however improbable,* must be the truth. —ARTHUR CONAN DOYLE, *The Sign of Four*

It is the customary fate of new truths to begin as heresies and to end as superstitions. —THOMAS HENRY HUXLEY, *The Coming of Age of The Origin of Species*

There are no new truths, but only truths that have not been recognized by those who have perceived them without noticing. A truth is something that everyone can be shown to know and to have known, as people say, all along. —MARY MCCARTHY, *On the Contrary*

It takes two to speak the truth—one to speak, and another to hear. —HENRY DAVID THOREAU, *A Week on the Concord and Merrimack Rivers*

I never give them hell. I just tell the truth, and they think it is hell. —HARRY S TRUMAN, quoted in *Look*

There are truths which are not for all men, nor for all times. —VOLTAIRE, letter (1761)

There is nothing so powerful as truth,—and often nothing so strange. —DANIEL WEBSTER, speech (1830)

[See also Lord Byron, in this section.]

There are no whole truths; all truths are half-truths. It is trying to treat them as whole truths that plays the devil. —ALFRED NORTH WHITEHEAD, *Dialogues*

Tyranny

Any excuse will serve a tyrant. —AESOP, *Fables*

Under conditions of tyranny it is far easier to act than to think. —HANNAH ARENDT, quoted in W.H. Auden's *A Certain World*

Dictators ride to and fro upon tigers which they dare not dismount. And the tigers are getting hungry. —WINSTON CHURCHILL, *While England Slept*
> [There is a Chinese proverb, "He who rides a tiger is afraid to dismount."]

> Nature has left this tincture in the blood,
> That all men would be tyrants if they could.
> —DANIEL DEFOE, *The Kentish Petition*

Wherever Law ends, Tyranny begins. —JOHN LOCKE, *Second Treatise of Government*
> [Also said by William Pitt, in a speech in 1770: ". . . where laws end, tyranny begins."]

If you want a picture of the future, imagine a boot stamping on a human face—forever. —GEORGE ORWELL, *1984*

BIG BROTHER IS WATCHING YOU. —GEORGE ORWELL, *1984*

Tyranny is always better organized than freedom. —CHARLES PÉGUY, *Basic Verities*

426

Understanding

The human understanding is like a false mirror, which, receiving rays irregularly, distorts and discolors the nature of things by mingling its own nature with it. —FRANCIS BACON, *Novum Organum*

We see through a glass, darkly. —BIBLE, *I Corinthians* 13:12

Get wisdom: and with all thy getting get understanding. —BIBLE, *Proverbs* 4:7

A moment's insight is sometimes worth a life's experience. —OLIVER WENDELL HOLMES, SR., *The Professor at the Breakfast-Table*

The brain is like a muscle. When we think well, we feel good. Understanding is a kind of ecstasy. —CARL SAGAN, *Broca's Brain*

To understand everything makes one very indulgent. —MADAME DE STAËL, *Corinne*

   [This is probably the source of the quotation "To understand everything is to forgive everything," commonly attributed to Madame de Staël.]

Unhappiness — See also SORROW

A moment of time may make us unhappy forever. —JOHN GAY, *The Beggar's Opera*

Men who are unhappy, like men who sleep badly, are always proud of the fact. —BERTRAND RUSSELL, *The Conquest of Happiness*

Misery acquaints a man with strange bed-fellows. —SHAKESPEARE, *The Tempest*

The secret of being miserable is to have leisure to bother about whether you are happy or not. The cure for it is occupation. —GEORGE BERNARD SHAW, *Parents and Children*

Noble deeds and hot baths are the best cures for depression. —DODIE SMITH, *I Capture the Castle*

If misery loves company, misery has company enough. —HENRY DAVID THOREAU, *Journal*

United States — See AMERICA AND AMERICANS

Unity

If a house be divided against itself, that house cannot stand. —BIBLE, *Mark 3:25*

> [This is well known in the form quoted by Abraham Lincoln in a speech in 1858: "A house divided against itself cannot stand. I believe this government cannot endure permanently half slave and half free."]

When bad men combine, the good must associate; else they will fall, one by one, an unpitied sacrifice in a contemptible struggle. —EDMUND BURKE, *Thoughts on the Cause of the Present Discontents*

All for one, one for all, that is our device. —ALEXANDRE DUMAS, PÈRE, *The Three Musketeers*

Only connect! That was the whole of her sermon. Only connect the prose and the passion, and both will be exalted, and human love will be seen at its height. Live in fragments no longer. Only connect, and the beast and the monk, robbed of the isolation that is life to either, will die. —E.M. FORSTER, *Howards End*

We must all hang together, or assuredly we shall all hang separately. —BENJAMIN FRANKLIN, attributed (at the signing of the Declaration of Independence)

Something there is that doesn't love a wall. —ROBERT FROST, "Mending Wall"

The Universe

Had I been present at the creation, I would have given some useful hints for the better ordering of the universe. —ALFONSO X, KING OF CASTILE AND LEÓN, attributed

. . . the essential function of the universe, which is a machine for making gods. —HENRI BERGSON, *The Two Sources of Morality and Religion*

A man said to the universe:
"Sir, I exist!"
"However," replied the universe,
"The fact has not created in me
A sense of obligation."
    —STEPHEN CRANE, *War Is Kind*

   —listen: there's a hell
of a good universe next door; let's go.
     —E.E. CUMMINGS, *1 x 1*

Now, my own suspicion is that the universe is not only queerer than we suppose, but queerer than we *can* suppose. —J.B.S. HALDANE, *Possible Worlds and Other Essays*

The universe is not hostile, nor yet is it friendly. It is simply indifferent. —JOHN H. HOLMES, *The Sensible Man's View of Religion*

The universe begins to look more like a great thought than a great machine. —JAMES JEANS, *The Mysterious Universe*

The universe ought to be presumed too vast to have any character. —CHARLES SANDERS PEIRCE, *Collected Papers*

I do not value any view of the universe into which man and the institutions of man enter very largely and absorb much of the attention. Man is but the place where I stand, and the prospect hence is infinite. —HENRY DAVID THOREAU, *Journal*

Upheaval — See CRISIS AND UPHEAVAL

Value

> For what is worth in anything,
> But so much money as 'twill bring.
> —SAMUEL BUTLER (*d* 1680), *Hudibras*

The worth of a thing is known by its want. —THOMAS D'URFEY, *Quixote*

Nothing can have value without being an object of utility. —KARL MARX, *Das Kapital*

What we obtain too cheap, we esteem too lightly: it is dearness only that gives everything its value. —THOMAS PAINE, *The American Crisis*

Everything is worth what its purchaser will pay for it. —PUBLILIUS SYRUS, *Maxims*

The cost of a thing is the amount of what I will call life which is required to be exchanged for it, immediately or in the long run. —HENRY DAVID THOREAU, *Walden*

Midas's Law: Possession diminishes perception of value, immediately. —JOHN UPDIKE, in *New Yorker*

[This aspect of human nature has long been commented upon. Fénelon wrote in *Télémaque*: "Mankind, by the perverse depravity of their nature, esteem that which they have most desired as of no value the moment it is possessed, and torment themselves with fruitless wishes for that which is beyond their reach."]

Vanity — See CONCEIT, EGOTISM, AND VANITY

Variety

Variety is the soul of pleasure. —APHRA BEHN, *The Rover*

It is far more delightful to be fond of the world because it has thousands of aspects and is different everywhere . . . ; for every divergence deserves to be cherished, simply because it widens the bounds of life. Let us be united by everything that divides us! —KAREL ČAPEK, *Letters from Spain*

> Variety's the very spice of life,
> That gives it all its flavor.
> > —WILLIAM COWPER, *The Task*

> Glory be to God for dappled things—
> > For skies of couple-color as a brinded cow;
> > > For rose-moles all in stipple upon trout
> > > that swim.
> > > > —GERARD MANLEY HOPKINS, "Pied
> > > > Beauty"

Letting a hundred flowers blossom and a hundred schools of thought contend is the policy for promoting progress in the arts and sciences and a flourishing socialist culture in our land. —MAO TSE-TUNG, speech (1957)

Vengeance — See REVENGE

Vice and Sin

All sin tends to be addictive, and the terminal point of addiction is what is called damnation. —W.H. AUDEN, *A Certain World*

Be sure your sin will find you out. —BIBLE, *Numbers* 32:23

The vices we scoff at in others laugh at us within ourselves. —THOMAS BROWNE, *Christian Morals*

Half the vices which the world condemns most loudly have seeds of good in them and require moderate use rather than total abstinence. —SAMUEL BUTLER (d 1902), *The Way of All Flesh*

Pleasure's a sin, and sometimes Sin's a pleasure. —LORD BYRON, *Don Juan*

A private sin is not so prejudicial in this world as a public indecency. —MIGUEL DE CERVANTES, *Don Quixote de la Mancha*

Vice is its own reward. —QUENTIN CRISP, *The Naked Civil Servant*

That which we call sin in others is experiment for us. —RALPH WALDO EMERSON, *Essays*

When our vices leave us, we flatter ourselves with the idea that we have left them. —LA ROCHEFOUCAULD, *Maxims*

The world loves a spice of wickedness. —HENRY WADSWORTH LONGFELLOW, *Hyperion*

I prefer an accommmodating vice to an obstinate virtue. —MOLIÈRE, *Amphitryon*

There is no vice so simple but assumes
Some mark of virtue on his outward parts.
    —SHAKESPEARE, *The Merchant of Venice*

The gods are just, and of our pleasant vices
Make instruments to plague us.
    —SHAKESPEARE, *King Lear*

Sin recognized—but that—may keep us
  humble,
But oh, it keeps us nasty.
                    —STEVIE SMITH, "Recognition Not
                                        Enough"

All sins are attempts to fill voids. —SIMONE WEIL,
Gravity and Grace

Victory and Defeat

The defeats and victories of the fellows at the top
aren't always defeats and victories for the fellows at
the bottom. —BERTOLT BRECHT, *Mother Courage*

The tragedy of life is not that man loses but that he
almost wins. —HEYWOOD BROUN, *Pieces of Hate*

I came, I saw, I conquered. (*Veni, vidi, vici.*) —JULIUS
CAESAR, quoted by Suetonius in *Lives of the Caesars*

Victory at all costs, victory in spite of all terror, victory however long and hard the road may be; for without victory there is no survival. —WINSTON CHUR-
CHILL, speech (1940)

As always, victory finds a hundred fathers but defeat
is an orphan. —COUNT GALEAZZO CIANO, *The Ciano
Diaries 1939–1943*

Victory is no longer a truth. It is only a word to
describe who is left alive in the ruins. —LYNDON B.
JOHNSON, speech (1964)

. . . like that boy in Kentucky, who stubbed his toe
while running to see his sweetheart. The boy said he
was too big to cry, and far too badly hurt to laugh.
—ABRAHAM LINCOLN, quoted in *Frank Leslie's Illustrated Newspaper* (1862)

   [Lincoln was describing how he felt after an election in which the Democrats had won. Adlai Ste-

venson quoted this remark to describe his own feelings after losing the 1952 presidential election.]

To the victor belong the spoils of the enemy. —WILLIAM LEARNED MARCY, speech (1832)

Another such victory over the Romans, and we are undone. —PYRRHUS, comment after the costly battle at Asculum, quoted in Plutarch's *Parallel Lives*
[From this came the term "Pyrrhic victory."]

> For when the One Great Scorer comes to mark
>   against your name,
> He writes—not that you won or lost—but how
>   you played the Game.
>   —GRANTLAND RICE, "Alumnus Football"

Sure, winning isn't everything. It's the only thing.
—HENRY ("RED") SANDERS, quoted in *Sports Illustrated*
[This is usually attributed to Vince Lombardi—who may well have said it, though written evidence is lacking.]

Nothing except a battle lost can be half so melancholy as a battle won. —ARTHUR WELLESLEY, DUKE OF WELLINGTON, military dispatch (1815)

Violence and Force

> Keep violence in the mind
> Where it belongs.
>   —BRIAN ALDISS, "Charteris"

All they that take the sword, shall perish with the sword. —BIBLE, *Matthew* 26:52

I say violence is necessary. It is as American as cherry pie. —H. RAP BROWN, press conference (1967)

The use of force alone is but *temporary*. It may subdue for a moment; but it does not remove the necessity of subduing again: and a nation is not governed, which is perpetually to be conquered. —EDMUND BURKE, speech (1775)

It is better to be violent, if there is violence in our hearts, than to put on the cloak of nonviolence to cover impotence. —MOHANDAS K. GANDHI, *Non-Violence in Peace and War*

The world does not grow better by force or by the policeman's club. —WILLIAM J. GAYNOR, *Letters and Speeches*

> Force without judgment falls of its own weight.
> —HORACE, *Odes*

In violence, we forget who we are. —MARY MCCARTHY, *On the Contrary*

> Who overcomes
> By force, hath overcome but half his foe.
> —JOHN MILTON, *Paradise Lost*

It is unfair to blame man too fiercely for being pugnacious; he learned the habit from Nature. —CHRISTOPHER MORLEY, *Inward Ho!*

One kills a man, one is an assassin; one kills millions, one is a conquerer; one kills everybody, one is a god. —JEAN ROSTAND, *Thoughts of a Biologist*

Nothing is ever done in this world until men are prepared to kill one another if it is not done. —GEORGE BERNARD SHAW, *Major Barbara*

Virtue

Virtue is like a rich stone, best plain set. —FRANCIS BACON, *Essays*

Whenever there are great virtues, it's a sure sign something's wrong. —BERTOLT BRECHT, *Mother Courage*

What after all
Is a halo? It's only one more thing to keep clean.
—CHRISTOPHER FRY, *The Lady's Not for Burning*

That virtue which requires to be ever guarded is scarce worth the sentinel. —OLIVER GOLDSMITH, *The Vicar of Wakefield*

Virtue would not go so far if vanity did not keep it company. —LA ROCHEFOUCAULD, *Maxims*

We need greater virtues to sustain good fortune than bad. —LA ROCHEFOUCAULD, *Maxims*

It is a distinction to have many virtues, but a hard lot. —FRIEDRICH NIETZSCHE, *Thus Spake Zarathustra*

When men grow virtuous in their old age, they only make a sacrifice to God of the devil's leavings.
—ALEXANDER POPE, *Thoughts on Various Subjects*

So our virtues
Lie in the interpretation of the time.
—SHAKESPEARE, *Coriolanus*

Always do right. This will gratify some people, and astonish the rest. —MARK TWAIN, speech (1901)

Few men have virtue to withstand the highest bidder.
—GEORGE WASHINGTON, letter (1779)

Vision

Where there is no vision, the people perish. —BIBLE, *Proverbs* 29:18

If I have seen further it is by standing on the shoulders of giants. —ISAAC NEWTON, letter (1675)

[This image had been used earlier by the Roman

poet Lucan and by Bernard of Chartres, and appeared in a proverb in George Herbert's *Jacula Prudentum*: "A dwarf on a giant's shoulders sees farther of the two."]

You see things; and you say, "Why?" But I dream things that never were; and I say, "Why not?" —GEORGE BERNARD SHAW, *Back to Methuselah*

[A favorite quotation of Robert F. Kennedy and sometimes assumed to have originated with him.]

Vision is the art of seeing things invisible. —JONATHAN SWIFT, *Thoughts on Various Subjects*

War

I have never understood this liking for war. It panders to instincts already catered for within the scope of any respectable domestic establishment. —ALAN BENNETT, *Forty Years On*

The way to win an atomic war is to make certain it never starts. —GEN. OMAR BRADLEY, speech (1948)

War is like love, it always finds a way. —BERTOLT BRECHT, *Mother Courage*

Laws are silent in time of war. —CICERO, *Pro Milone*

All great civilizations, in their early stages, are based on success in war. —KENNETH CLARK, *Civilization*

War is nothing but the continuation of politics with the admixture of other means. —KARL VON CLAUSEWITZ, *On War*

War is too serious a matter to leave to soldiers. —GEORGES CLEMENCEAU, quoted by J. Hampden Jackson in *Clemenceau and the Third Republic*

[Sometimes quoted as "War is too important to be

left to the generals." Also attributed to Talleyrand and Briand.]

Either war is obsolete or men are. —R. BUCKMINSTER FULLER, quoted in *New Yorker*

Frankly, I'd like to see the government get out of war altogether and leave the whole field to private industry. —JOSEPH HELLER, *Catch-22*

Older men declare war. But it is youth that must fight and die. And it is youth who must inherit the tribulation, the sorrow, and the triumphs that are the aftermath of war. —HERBERT HOOVER, speech (1944)

The first casualty when war comes is truth. —HIRAM WARREN JOHNSON, attributed

Make no mistake. There is no such thing as a conventional nuclear weapon. —LYNDON B. JOHNSON, speech (1964)

A war regarded as inevitable or even probable, and therefore much prepared for, has a very good chance of eventually being fought. —GEORGE F. KENNAN, *The Cloud of Danger*

Everything, everything in war is barbaric. . . . But the worst barbarity of war is that it forces men collectively to commit acts against which individually they would revolt with their whole being. —ELLEN KEY, *War, Peace and the Future*

The most persistent sound which reverberates through man's history is the beating of war drums. —ARTHUR KOESTLER, *Janus*

It is well that war is so terrible, or we should grow too fond of it. —ROBERT E. LEE, remark made at Fredericksburg, Va. (1862)

It is fatal to enter any war without the will to win it.
—GEN. DOUGLAS MACARTHUR, speech (1952)

We hear war called murder. It is not: it is suicide.
—RAMSAY MACDONALD, quoted in *The Observer*

War will never cease until babies begin to come into the world with larger cerebrums and smaller adrenal glands. —H.L. MENCKEN, *Minority Report: H.L. Mencken's Notebooks*

War hath no fury like a non-combatant. —C.E. MONTAGUE, *Disenchantment*

Ever since the invention of gunpowder . . . I continually tremble lest men should, in the end, uncover some secret which would provide a short way of abolishing mankind, of annihilating peoples and nations in their entirety. —BARON DE MONTESQUIEU, *The Persian Letters*

The quickest way of ending a war is to lose it.
—GEORGE ORWELL, *Shooting an Elephant*

> Diplomats are just as essential to starting a war as Soldiers are for finishing it. You take Diplomacy out of war and the thing would fall flat in a week.
> —WILL ROGERS, *The Autobiography of Will Rogers*

Little girl. . . . Sometime they'll give a war and nobody will come. —CARL SANDBURG, *The People, Yes*

> [Charlotte Keyes wrote an article in *McCall's* in 1966 titled "Suppose They Gave a War and No One Came." This was used as an antiwar slogan during the time of the war in Vietnam.]

War's a profanity, because let's face it, you've got two opposing sides trying to settle their differences by killing as many of each other as they can. —GEN. H. NORMAN SCHWARZKOPF, quoted in *New York Times*

There is many a boy here today who looks on war as all glory, but, boys, it is all hell. —GEN. WILLIAM T. SHERMAN, speech (1880)

> [This appears to be the basis for the quote commonly ascribed to Sherman: "War is hell."]

To fight and conquer in all our battles is not supreme excellence; supreme excellence consists in breaking the enemy's resistance without fighting. —SUN-TZU, *The Art of War*

There is no instance of a country having benefited from prolonged warfare. —SUN-TZU, *The Art of War*

War is fear cloaked in courage. —GEN. WILLIAM C. WESTMORELAND, in *McCall's*

As long as war is regarded as wicked, it will always have its fascination. When it is looked upon as vulgar it will cease to be popular. —OSCAR WILDE, *Intentions*, "Critic as Artist"

War and Peace

The only excuse for war is that we may live in peace unharmed. —CICERO, *De Officiis*

There never was a good war or a bad peace. —BENJAMIN FRANKLIN, letter (1773)

> [Franklin's wording is probably the best known, but similar thoughts have been voiced (even if they have not governed people's actions) at least since Roman times. Cicero, in *Epistolae ad Atticum*, said: "I cease not to advocate peace. It may be unjust, but even so it is better than the justest of . . . wars." And Erasmus, in *Adagia*, wrote in 1500: "The most disadvantageous peace is better than the most just war." See also Tacitus (*Annals*), in this section.]

In peace sons bury fathers, but war violates the order of nature, and fathers bury sons. —HERODOTUS, *Histories*

Certain peace is better and safer than anticipated victory. —LIVY, *Ab Urbe Condita*

> Peace hath her victories
> No less renowned than war.
> —JOHN MILTON, "To the Lord General
> Cromwell"

Peace is not only better than war, but infinitely more arduous. —GEORGE BERNARD SHAW, *Heartbreak House*

A bad peace is even worse than war. —TACITUS, *Annals*

They make a desert and call it peace. —TACITUS, *Agricola*

To be prepared for War is one of the most effectual means of preserving peace. —GEORGE WASHINGTON, speech (first annual address to Congress, 1790)

[The advocacy of preparedness has echoed throughout history, from ancient times to the Strategic Defense Initiative. Vegetius said in the fourth century A.D.(in *De Rei Militari*): "Let him who desires peace prepare for war." And Ronald Reagan, in a speech in 1984, said: "None of the four wars in my lifetime came about because we were too strong. It is weakness . . . that invites adventurous adversaries to make mistaken judgments."]

Weakness — See FAULTS AND WEAKNESSES

Wealth — See also MONEY; RICH AND POOR

Every man thinks God is on his side. The rich and powerful know He is. —JEAN ANOUILH, *The Lark*

Riches are a good handmaid, but the worst mistress.
—FRANCIS BACON, *De Dignitate et Augmentis Scientiarum*

Wealth maketh many friends. —BIBLE, *Proverbs* 19:4

Ye cannot serve God and mammon. —BIBLE, *Matthew* 6:24

It is easier for a camel to go through the eye of a needle, than for a rich man to enter the kingdom of God. —BIBLE, *Matthew* 19:24

The rich are more envied by those who have a little, than by those who have nothing. —CHARLES CALEB COLTON, *Lacon*

In every well-governed state, wealth is a sacred thing; in democracies it is the only sacred thing. —ANATOLE FRANCE, *Penguin Island*

If your Riches are yours, why don't you take them with you to t'other World? —BENJAMIN FRANKLIN, *Poor Richard's Almanac*
   [An idea succinctly expressed in the title of the 1936 play by Moss Hart and George Kaufman, *You Can't Take It With You*.]

He is not fit for riches who is afraid to use them. —THOMAS FULLER, *Gnomologia*

Wealth is not without its advantages, and the case to the contrary, although it has often been made, has never proved widely persuasive. —JOHN KENNETH GALBRAITH, *The Affluent Society*

It is better to live rich than to *die* rich. —SAMUEL JOHNSON, quoted in James Boswell's *The Life of Samuel Johnson*

Men do not desire merely to be *rich*, but to be *richer* than other men. —JOHN STUART MILL, *Essay on Social Freedom*

We may see the small value God has for riches by the people he gives them to. —ALEXANDER POPE, *Thoughts on Various Subjects*

A great fortune is a great slavery. —SENECA, *Ad Polybium de Consolatione*

To suppose, as we all suppose, that we could be rich and not behave as the rich behave, is like supposing that we could drink all day and keep absolutely sober. —LOGAN PEARSALL SMITH, *Afterthoughts*

If all the rich men in the world divided up their money amongst themselves, there wouldn't be enough to go around. —CHRISTINA STEAD, *House of All Nations*

That man is the richest whose pleasures are the cheapest. —HENRY DAVID THOREAU, *Journal*

Weather

A cloudy day, or a little sunshine, have as great an influence on many constitutions as the most real blessings or misfortunes. —JOSEPH ADDISON, *The Spectator*

It ain't a fit night out for man or beast. —W.C. FIELDS, in the film *The Fatal Glass of Beer*

    [This was one of Fields' catchphrases.]

These [messengers] will not be hindered from accomplishing at their best speed the distance which they have to go, either by snow, or rain, or heat, or by the darkness of night. —HERODOTUS, *Histories*

    [An adaptation of this is inscribed on the main post office in New York City: "Neither snow, nor rain, nor heat, nor gloom of night stays these couriers from the swift completion of their appointed rounds."]

The first fall of snow is not only an event, it is a magical event. You go to bed in one kind of world and wake up in another quite different, and if this is not enchantment then where is it to be found? —J.B. PRIESTLEY, *Apes and Angels*

The fog comes
on little cat feet.

It sits looking
over harbor and city
on silent haunches
and then moves on.
—CARL SANDBURG, "Fog"

There is a sumptuous variety about the New England weather that compels the stranger's admiration— and regret. The weather is always doing something there; always attending strictly to business; always getting up new designs and trying them on people to see how they will go. But it gets through more business in spring than in any other season. In the spring I have counted one hundred and thirty-six different kinds of weather inside of twenty-four hours. —MARK TWAIN, speech (1876)

Everybody talks about the weather, but nobody does anything about it. —CHARLES DUDLEY WARNER, attributed

[The statement appeared in an unsigned editorial in the *Hartford Courant,* on which Werner was then an editor. It is often credited to Mark Twain.]

Weight

Outside every fat man there was an even fatter man trying to close in. —KINGSLEY AMIS, *One Fat Englishman*

[See also George Orwell, in this section.]

I see no objection to stoutness—in moderation.
—W.S. Gilbert, *Iolanthe*

A really busy person never knows how much he weighs. —Edgar Watson Howe, *Country Town Sayings*

Fat Is a Feminist Issue. —Susie Orbach, (book title)

I'm fat, but I'm thin inside. Has it ever struck you that there's a thin man inside every fat man, just as they say there's a statue inside every block of stone?
—George Orwell, *Coming up For Air*

> [Cyril Connolly wrote in *The Unquiet Grave*: "Imprisoned in every fat man a thin one is wildly signalling to be let out." See also Kingsley Amis, in this section.]

Wickedness — See EVIL

The Will

> "There's no free will," says the philosopher;
> "To hang is most unjust."
> "There is no free will," assents the officer;
>   "We hang because we must."
>   —Ambrose Bierce, *Collected Works*

He who believes in freedom of the human will has never loved and never hated. —Marie von Ebner-Eschenbach, *Aphorisms*

To deny the freedom of the will is to make morality impossible. —J.A. Froude, *Short Studies*

All theory is against the freedom of the will; all experience for it. —Samuel Johnson, quoted in James Boswell's *The Life of Samuel Johnson*

Where the willingness is great the difficulties cannot be great. —NICCOLÒ MACHIAVELLI, *The Prince*

We have to believe in free will. We've got no choice. —ISAAC BASHEVIS SINGER, in *The Times* (London)

Wind — See WEATHER

Wine — see also DRINKING

> And much as Wine has played the Infidel,
> And robbed me of my Robe of Honor—Well,
> I often wonder what the Vintners buy
> One half so precious as the stuff they sell.
> —EDWARD FITZGERALD, *The Rubáiyát of
> Omar Khayyám*

It has become quite a common proverb that in wine there is truth. (*In vino veritas.*) —PLINY THE ELDER, *Natural History*

A good general rule is to state that the bouquet is better than the taste, and vice versa. —STEPHEN POTTER, *One-Upmanship*

> It's a naive domestic Burgundy without any
> breeding, but I think you'll be amused by
> its presumption.
> —JAMES THURBER, cartoon caption in
> *New Yorker*

Winning — See VICTORY AND DEFEAT

Winter — See SEASONS

Wisdom and Sense

The price of wisdom is above rubies. —BIBLE, *Job* 28:18

[This idea is similarly expressed in Proverbs 8:11: "Wisdom is better than rubies."]

In much wisdom is much grief: and he that increaseth knowledge increaseth sorrow. —BIBLE, *Ecclesiastes* 1:18

> Knowledge and wisdom, far from being one,
>   Have ofttimes no connection. Knowledge
>   dwells
> In heads replete with thoughts of other men;
> Wisdom in minds attentive to their own.
>   —WILLIAM COWPER, *The Task*

Common sense is the best distributed thing in the world, for everyone thinks he is so well-endowed with it that even those who are hardest to satisfy in all other matters are not in the habit of desiring more of it than they already have. —RENÉ DESCARTES, *Discourse on Method*

The art of being wise is the art of knowing what to overlook. —WILLIAM JAMES, *The Principles of Psychology*

It's bad taste to be wise all the time, like being at a perpetual funeral. —D.H. LAWRENCE, "Peace and War"

>   To know
> That which before us lies in daily life,
> Is the prime Wisdom; what is more, is fume,
> Or emptiness, or fond impertinence.
>   —JOHN MILTON, *Paradise Lost*

Be wisely worldly, be not worldly wise. —FRANCIS QUARLES, *Emblems*

It is not wise to be wiser than is necessary.
  —PHILIPPE QUINAULT, *Armide*

Nine-tenths of wisdom is being wise in time.
  —THEODORE ROOSEVELT, speech (1917)

A man is wise with the wisdom of his time only, and ignorant with its ignorance. —HENRY DAVID THOREAU, *Journal*

Common sense is not so common. —VOLTAIRE, *Philosophical Dictionary*

> Wisdom is ofttimes nearer when we stoop
> Than when we soar.
> —WILLIAM WORDSWORTH, *The Excursion*

Wit — See HUMOR AND WIT

Wives — See MARRIAGE

Women — See also MEN AND WOMEN

Women love the lie that saves their pride, but never an unflattering truth. —GERTRUDE ATHERTON, *The Conqueror*

One is not born a woman, one becomes one.
—SIMONE DE BEAUVOIR, *The Second Sex*

Women are never stonger than when they arm themselves with their weaknesses. —MARIE ANNE DU DEFFAND, letter (to Voltaire)

Women never have young minds. They are born three thousand years old. —SHELAGH DELANEY, *A Taste of Honey*

The happiest women, like the happiest nations, have no history. —GEORGE ELIOT, *The Mill on the Floss*

When a woman behaves like a man, why doesn't she behave like a nice man? —EDITH EVANS, quoted in *The Observer*

The great question that has never been answered and which I have not yet been able to answer, despite my thirty years of research into the feminine soul, is "What does a woman want?" —SIGMUND FREUD, quoted in Ernest Jones' *Sigmund Freud: Life and Work*

There is no female mind. The brain is not an organ of sex. As well speak of a female liver. —CHARLOTTE PERKINS GILMAN, *Women and Economics*

The female of the species is more deadly than the male. —RUDYARD KIPLING, "The Female of the Species"

A woman will always sacrifice herself if you give her the opportunity. It is her favorite form of self-indulgence. —W. SOMERSET MAUGHAM, *The Circle*

Women have simple tastes. They can get pleasure out of the conversation of children in arms and men in love. —H.L. MENCKEN, *A Mencken Chrestomathy*

Women would rather be right than reasonable. —OGDEN NASH, "Frailty, Thy Name Is a Misnomer"

God created woman. And indeed, that was the end of boredom—but of other things too! Woman was God's *second* mistake. —FRIEDRICH NIETZSCHE, *The Antichrist*

Whether they yield or refuse, it delights women to have been asked. —OVID, *Ars Amatoria*

> Prince, a precept I'd leave for you,
>   Coined in Eden, existing yet:
> Skirt the parlor, and shun the zoo—
>   Women and elephants never forget.
>   —DOROTHY PARKER, "Ballade of
>   Unfortunate Mammals"

A woman is like a teabag—only in hot water do you realize how strong she is. —NANCY REAGAN, quoted in *The Observer*

Frailty, thy name is woman! —SHAKESPEARE, *Hamlet*

> Age cannot wither her, nor custom stale
> Her infinite variety: other women cloy
> The appetites they feed; but she makes
>   hungry
> Where most she satisfies.
>   —SHAKESPEARE, *Antony and Cleopatra*

Woman's virtue is man's greatest invention. —CORNELIA OTIS SKINNER, attributed

A woman without a man is like a fish without a bicycle. —GLORIA STEINEM, attributed

Women are always eagerly on the lookout for any emotion. —STENDHAL, *On Love*

I know the disposition of women: when you will, they won't; when you won't, they set their hearts upon you of their own inclination. —TERENCE, *Eunuchus*

If the first woman God ever made was strong enough to turn the world upside down all alone, these together ought to be able to turn it back and get it right side up again. —SOJOURNER TRUTH, speech (at Women's Rights Convention, 1851)

If women want any rights more than they's got, why don't they just *take them*, and not be talking about it. —SOJOURNER TRUTH, quoted in Anita King's *Quotations in Black*

Whatever women do they must do twice as well as men to be thought half as good. Luckily, this is not difficult. —CHARLOTTE WHITTON, quoted in *Canada Month*

What is a woman? I assure you, I do not know. . . . I do not believe that anybody can know until she has expressed herself in all the arts and professions open to human skill. —VIRGINIA WOOLF, *Professions for Women*

Wonder — See CURIOSITY

Words — See LANGUAGE; SPEECH AND SPEAKERS

Work

Housekeeping ain't no joke. —LOUISA MAY ALCOTT, *Little Women*

It is necessary to work, if not from inclination, at least from despair. Everything considered, work is less boring than amusing oneself. —CHARLES BAUDELAIRE, *Mon Coeur mis à nu*

Work is the grand cure for all the maladies and miseries that ever beset mankind,—honest work, which you intend getting done. —THOMAS CARLYLE, speech (1866)

I don't like work—no man does—but I like what is in the work—the chance to find yourself. —JOSEPH CONRAD, *Heart of Darkness*

It is better to wear out than to rust out. —RICHARD CUMBERLAND, quoted in George Horne's "Sermon on the Duty of Contending for the Truth"

Man is so made that he can only find relaxation from one kind of labor by taking up another. —ANATOLE FRANCE, *The Crime of Sylvestre Bonnard*

Men, for the sake of getting a living, forget to live. —MARGARET FULLER, *Summer on the Lakes*

When work is a pleasure, life is a joy! When work is a duty, life is slavery. —MAXIM GORKY, *The Lower Depths*

Every calling is great when greatly pursued. —OLIVER WENDELL HOLMES, JR., speech (1885)

I like work: it fascinates me. I can sit and look at it for hours. —JEROME K. JEROME, *Three Men in a Boat*

Work expands so as to fill the time available for its completion. —C. NORTHCOTE PARKINSON, *Parkinson's Law*

In a hierarchy every employee tends to rise to his level of incompetence. —LAURENCE J. PETER, *The Peter Principle*

Work is a necessity for man. Man invented the alarm clock. —PABLO PICASSO, quoted in *New Yorker*

Work and love—these are the basics. Without them there is neurosis. —THEODORE REIK, *Of Love and Lust*

One of the symptoms of approaching nervous breakdown is the belief that one's work is terribly important, and that to take a holiday would bring all kinds of disaster. If I were a medical man, I should prescribe a holiday to any patient who considered his work important. —BERTRAND RUSSELL, *The Conquest of Happiness*

There is perhaps only one human being in a thousand who is passionately interested in his job for the job's sake. The difference is that if that one person in a thousand is a man, we say, simply, that he is passionately keen on his job; if she is a woman, we say she is a freak. —DOROTHY L. SAYERS, in *Unpopular Opinions*

The test of a vocation is the love of the drudgery it involves. —LOGAN PEARSALL SMITH, *Afterthoughts*

Perpetual devotion to what a man calls his business, is only to be sustained by perpetual neglect of many other things. —ROBERT LOUIS STEVENSON, *Virginibus Puerisque*

Work keeps at bay three great evils: boredom, vice, and need. —VOLTAIRE, *Candide*

No race can prosper till it learns that there is as much dignity in tilling a field as in writing a poem. —BOOKER T. WASHINGTON, *Up from Slavery*

The World

This world, after all our science and sciences, is still a miracle; wonderful, inscrutable, *magical* and more, to whosoever will *think* of it. —THOMAS CARLYLE, *On Heroes, Hero-Worship and the Heroic in History*

The eternal mystery of the world is its comprehensibility. —ALBERT EINSTEIN, quoted in Daniel J. Boorstin, *The Discoverers*

This is the way the world ends
Not with a bang but a whimper.
　　　　　—T.S. ELIOT, "The Hollow Men"

Some say the world will end in fire,
Some say in ice.
From what I've tasted of desire
I hold with those who favor fire.
But if it had to perish twice,
I think I know enough of hate
To say that for destruction ice
Is also great
And would suffice.
　　　　　—ROBERT FROST, "Fire and Ice"

453

For every man the world is as fresh as it was at the first day, and as full of untold novelties for him who has the eyes to see them. —THOMAS HENRY HUXLEY, *A Liberal Education*

> The world is so full of a number of things,
> I'm sure we should all be as happy as kings.
> —ROBERT LOUIS STEVENSON,
> "Happy Thought"

God made everything out of the void, but the void shows through. —PAUL VALÉRY, *Mauvaises pensées et autres*

The world is a comedy to those that think; a tragedy to those that feel. —HORACE WALPOLE, letter (to Horace Mann, 1769)

> The world is everything that is the case.
> The world is the totality of facts, not of things.
> —LUDWIG WITTGENSTEIN, *Tractatus Logico-Philosophicus*

> The world is too much with us; late and soon,
> Getting and spending, we lay waste our
>   powers:
> Little we see in Nature that is ours;
> We have given our hearts away, a sordid boon!
> —WILLIAM WORDSWORTH, "The world is
>   too much with us"

Worry — See ANXIETY

Worth — See VALUE

Writing and Writers — See also STYLE

The writer must be universal in sympathy and an outcast by nature; only then can he see clearly. —JULIAN BARNES, *Flaubert's Parrot*

When I am dead, I hope it may be said:
"His sins were scarlet, but his books were
    read."
            —HILAIRE BELLOC, "On His Books"

Beneath the rule of men entirely great,
The pen is mightier than the sword.
            —EDWARD BULWER-LYTTON, *Richelieu*

[The wording may have been new, but the idea was
not. Shakespeare had written in *Hamlet*: "Many
wearing rapiers are afraid of goose-quills." And
Robert Burton had written in *The Anatomy of Melancholy*: "How much more cruel the pen may be
than the sword."]

Literature is the art of writing something that will be
read twice; journalism what will be grasped at once.
—CYRIL CONNOLLY, *Enemies of Promise*

That is one last thing to remember: *writers are
always selling somebody out.* —JOAN DIDION,
Slouching towards Bethlehem

If you would be a reader, read; if a writer, write.
—EPICTETUS, *Discourses*

You don't write because you want to say something;
you write because you've got something to say. —F.
SCOTT FITZGERALD, *The Crack-Up*, ed. Edmund Wilson

No tears in the writer, no tears in the reader. —ROB-
ERT FROST, "The Figure a Poem Makes"

It takes a great deal of history to produce a little literature. —HENRY JAMES, *Life of Nathaniel Hawthorne*

No man but a blockhead ever wrote except for money.
—SAMUEL JOHNSON, quoted in James Boswell's *The
Life of Samuel Johnson*

It is the glory and merit of some men to write well, and of others not to write at all. —LA BRUYÈRE, *Les Caractères*

If you steal from one author, it's plagiarism; if you steal from many, it's research. —WILSON MIZNER, quoted in Alva Johnston's *The Legendary Mizners*

> True ease in writing comes from art, not
>   chance,
> As those move easiest who have learn'd to
>   dance.
> > —ALEXANDER POPE, *An Essay on
> > Criticism*

A confessional passage has probably never been written that didn't stink a little bit of the writer's pride in having given up his pride. —J.D. SALINGER, *Raise High the Roof Beam, Carpenters; and Seymour: an Introduction*

Writing is not a profession but a vocation of unhappiness. —GEORGES SIMENON, quoted in *Paris Review*

Remarks are not literature. —GERTRUDE STEIN, *The Autobiography of Alice B. Toklas*

Writing, when properly managed, (as you may be sure I think mine is) is but a different name for conversation. —LAURENCE STERNE, *Tristram Shandy*

Fiction gives us a second chance that life denies us. —PAUL THEROUX, in *New York Times*

Literature is strewn with the wreckage of men who have minded beyond reason the opinions of others. —VIRGINIA WOOLF, *A Room of One's Own*

I would venture to guess that Anon, who wrote so many poems without signing them, was often a woman. —VIRGINIA WOOLF, *A Room of One's Own*

Wrongdoing — See CRIME; VICE AND SIN

Youth — See also ADOLESCENCE; AGE AND AGING; CHILDREN AND CHILDHOOD

Youth is easily deceived, because it is quick to hope. —ARISTOTLE, *Rhetoric*

Young men are fitter to invent than to judge, fitter for execution than for counsel, and fitter for new projects than for settled business. —FRANCIS BACON, *Essays*

To me it seems that youth is like spring, an over-praised season—delightful if it happens to be a favored one, but in practice very rarely favored and more remarkable, as a general rule, for biting east winds than genial breezes. —SAMUEL BUTLER (d 1902), *The Way of All Flesh*

If youth did not matter so much to itself it would never have the heart to go on. —WILLA CATHER, *Song of the Lark*

Youth is something very new: twenty years ago no one mentioned it. —COCO CHANEL, quoted in Marcel Haedrich's *Coco Chanel, Her Life, Her Secrets*

Young men are apt to think themselves wise enough, as drunken men are apt to think themselves sober enough. —LORD CHESTERFIELD, *Letters to His Son*

It is better to waste one's youth than to do nothing with it at all. —GEORGES COURTELINE, *La Philosophie de Georges Courteline*

Almost everything that is great has been done by youth. —BENJAMIN DISRAELI, *Coningsby*

If youth is the season of hope, it is often so only in the sense that our elders are hopeful about us; for no age is so apt as youth to think its emotions, partings, and resolves are the last of their kind. —GEORGE ELIOT, *Middlemarch*

Alas, that Spring should vanish with the Rose!
That Youth's sweet-scented Manuscript
    should close!
The Nightingale that in the Branches sang,
Ah, whence, and whither flown again, who
    knows!
> —EDWARD FITZGERALD, *The Rubáiyát of
> Omar Khayyám*

Everybody's youth is a dream, a form of chemical madness. —F. SCOTT FITZGERALD, "The Diamond as Big as the Ritz"

Youth's the season made for joys,
    Love is then our duty.
> —JOHN GAY, *The Beggar's Opera*

No young man believes he shall ever die. —WILLIAM HAZLITT, *Literary Remains*

When I was one-and-twenty
    I heard a wise man say,
"Give crowns and pounds and guineas
    But not your heart away;
Give pearls away and rubies
    But keep your fancy free."
But I was one-and-twenty,
    No use to talk to me.
> —A.E. HOUSMAN, "When I was
> one-and-twenty"

Youth is a continual intoxication; it is the fever of reason. —LA ROCHEFOUCAULD, *Maxims*

If youth be a defect, it is one that we outgrow only too soon. —JAMES RUSSELL LOWELL, speech (1886)

It's all that the young can do for the old, to shock them and keep them up to date. —GEORGE BERNARD SHAW, *Fanny's First Play*

Youth is wholly experimental. —ROBERT LOUIS STEVENSON, "Letter to a Young Gentleman . . ."

Youth is not a time of life—it is a state of mind. . . . Youth means a temperamental predominance of courage over timidity, of the appetite for adventure over a life of ease. —SAMUEL ULLMAN, "Youth"

Index of Authors Quoted

461